Rowan
University

The

Domosh
Collection

A Gift

Keith & Shirley Campbell Library
Music Library at Wilson Hall
Frank H. Stewart Room & University Archives

Back Door to Richmond

Back Door to Richmond

The Bermuda Hundred Campaign,
April–June 1864

William Glenn Robertson

DELAWARE
Newark: University of Delaware Press
London and Toronto: Associated University Presses

Associated University Presses
440 Forsgate Drive
Cranbury, NJ 08512

Associated University Presses
25 Sicilian Avenue
London WC1A 2QH, England

Associated University Presses
2133 Royal Windsor Drive
Unit 1
Mississauga, Ontario
Canada L5J 1K5

The paper used in this publication meets the requirements
of the American National Standard for Permanence of Paper
for Printed Library Materials Z39.48-1984.

Library of Congress Cataloging-in-Publication Data

Robertson, William Glenn, 1944–
    Back door to Richmond.

    Bibliography: p.
    Includes index.
    1. Bermuda Hundred Region (Va.)—History, Military.
2. Virginia—History—Civil War, 1861–1865—Campaigns.
I. Title.
E476.57R63   1987   973.7'36   85-41048
ISBN 0-87413-303-3 (alk. paper)

Printed in the United States of America

To the memory of
William Aaron Wright
Private, Barham's Virginia Cavalry Battalion
and
Benjamin Person Robertson
Private, 12th North Carolina Infantry Regiment

Contents

Maps

Preface

Although it is occasionally forgotten, Ulysses S. Grant's great spring offensive of 1864 included a subsidiary operation of major proportions in the James River basin. In this operation a Federal force of over forty thousand men, organized as the Army of the James under Major General Benjamin F. Butler, was to seize and fortify a base, sever Confederate communication lines, distract the attention of Confederate reinforcements, and, if possible, capture Richmond. By the time all this was accomplished, Grant and the Army of the Potomac would have disposed of the Army of Northern Virginia and would be ready to join Butler in administering the *coup de grace* to Confederate forces in Virginia.

Unfortunately, the campaign did not unfold according to the Federal plan. Grant was unable to brush Robert E. Lee's forces aside as quickly as he had anticipated, and when he did arrive, he found that Butler's army had been defeated and forced back from Richmond to its base on a peninsula known as Bermuda Hundred. When the focus of operations shifted to Petersburg, the Army of the James lost its independence and became operationally only a part of Grant's larger command. Had it not been for a chance characterization of Butler's army at Bermuda Hundred as being in "a bottle strongly corked," it is unlikely that the Bermuda Hundred Campaign would be even as well known as it is. Postwar writers, however, seized upon the phrase and have used it ever since to castigate Butler and his army for a seemingly inept campaign.

The present study is an attempt to reassess the Bermuda Hundred Campaign in several respects. First, was it really an abject failure from the Federal point of view? Second, if the campaign failed, where did the fault lie—with Butler, as has been so frequently maintained, or should others, such as Butler's subordinates and even Grant, bear part of the blame? Third, is the "bottle" image that has been perpetuated by writers over the years an apt description of the position held by the Army of the James after its defeat at Drewry's Bluff? Fourth, since every campaign has two sides, what role did the Confederates play in affecting the outcome?

In addition to providing answers to these relatively analytical questions, it is hoped that the present study will provide some inkling for the modern reader of what it was like actually to participate in a field campaign during the American Civil War. Too often, for reasons of space or otherwise, military history becomes merely a description of impersonal units moving mechanically across the landscape

9

according to the dictates of cardboard generals. This type of writing generally omits the human element so obviously important in warfare at all levels, and therefore does a disservice both to participants and later readers alike. Therefore, although it has lengthened the work perceptibly, considerable mention has been made of the experiences of individual soldiers on both sides, as reflected in published personal accounts and contemporary correspondence. In the case of the latter, the original capitalization and punctuation (or lack thereof) have been retained to preserve the flavor of the times.

No study of this length could be completed without the aid of people too numerous to enumerate. The author's heartfelt thanks go out to the courteous and well-trained staffs at the various document repositories cited in the bibliography. Without their help, much time would have been wasted and many gaps in the record left unfilled. In addition, the author wishes to thank the late Dr. Edward Younger, his adviser and major professor at the University of Virginia, for guiding this study in its formative stages as a dissertation. I am grateful to H. M. Sumerall for the fine work he did on the maps for this study. Last, but most certainly not least, the author owes an enormous debt of gratitude to his parents, who patiently provided so much aid and encouragement over so long a period of time.

Back Door
to Richmond

☆ 1 ☆

The Federal Plan of Campaign

On 12 March 1864, Lieutenant General Ulysses S. Grant succeeded Major General Henry W. Halleck as general-in-chief of the armies of the United States. Fresh from a series of victories in the Western Theater, Grant was now responsible for coordinating the Federal efforts in all theaters in order to bring the Civil War to a successful conclusion for the Union. To accomplish this, Grant had to formulate a plan of campaign for the Federal forces in the Eastern Theater, as well as for the western armies with which he was more familiar. Fortunately, he had been giving the problem some thought since the beginning of the year, when the Lincoln administration had requested his views on future military operations in the East.

Writing to Halleck from Nashville, Tennessee, in January 1864, Grant had rejected the customary overland advance toward Richmond in favor of an entirely different course of action. He proposed a drive from Suffolk, a town in southeastern Virginia, to Raleigh, North Carolina, by a force of approximately sixty thousand men. While advancing toward Raleigh, the invading army would ensure the destruction of the important railroad facilities at Weldon, North Carolina, and any track within reach. The breaking of the rail link between Richmond and the port of Wilmington, North Carolina, when coupled with the threat to other lines posed by the army's arrival at Raleigh, would force the Confederates to evacuate Richmond and probably most of Virginia as well.[1]

Grant had continued to favor this plan at least through the middle of February, when he confided it to Major General John Foster, recently commanding on the North Carolina coast. Believing that Grant's plan required modification, Foster presented his own opinions to Halleck on 26 February 1864. The Federal army should not advance directly from Suffolk, which would necessitate three difficult river crossings, but should sail up the James River to the vicinity of Petersburg and then march down the railroad to Weldon. Otherwise, Foster agreed with Grant's ideas, particularly with the size of the Federal column, which should be at least sixty thousand men. A smaller force would not be strong enough to secure Weldon, although it might operate successfully against Petersburg.[2]

After arriving in Washington and conferring with Lincoln, Grant set aside his North Carolina scheme in favor of a more conventional line of advance. The original plan had recognized the importance of the railroads connecting Lee's army and Richmond with the lower South, and especially the port of Wilmington. With the severing of these railroads anywhere below Richmond, Robert E. Lee would be forced to fight a major battle to restore his supply lines, or he would soon find himself without provisions. If the Army of Northern Virginia could be held in front while the railroads were broken in its rear, the choices open to the Confederate commander would be grim. Even if the North Carolina thrust was not the best possible plan, cutting Lee's supply lines south of Richmond merited consideration as part of any future operations.[3]

In March Grant began to formulate the basic principles under which the Federal armies would operate during the coming campaign. The first to be observed was that of concentration. This meant that Federal garrisons scattered throughout areas of only peripheral importance either would be consolidated or transferred to more significant fields of operation. Second, the movements of all Union forces operating against the Confederacy were to be coordinated. Since the Confederate government had elected to defend all of its territory against larger Federal forces, coordinated pressure by Union armies on all sides would force the Confederates either to relinquish important positions or to stretch their limited resources to the breaking point. To implement these principles, Grant proposed simultaneous advances by the primary Federal armies as well as by several smaller commands. This would exert maximum pressure on the Confederacy, already under great strain, and would also protect Federal communication lines without wasting large numbers of troops in garrison roles.

In the spring campaign, there would be two major Federal offensives. One of these would be a drive by Major General William T. Sherman's armies from Chattanooga, Tennessee, toward Atlanta, Georgia. More important because it aimed at Richmond and the Confederacy's most able field commander, an overland advance toward the Confederate capital would be made by Major General George Meade's Army of the Potomac. Meade's advance was to be overland in order to engage Lee outside of Richmond's heavy fortifications while simultaneously covering Washington. Should Lee be forced into the Richmond defenses without having been destroyed, Grant anticipated crossing the James River and besieging the Confederate capital from astride its southern communication lines.

Supplementing the two primary offensives were to be three smaller operations. The first was to be an advance by an army under Major General Nathaniel Banks from New Orleans toward Mobile, Alabama. Second, Major General Franz Sigel would lead another small army into the Shenandoah Valley of Virginia. Finally, forces in the coastal Department of Virginia and North Carolina would advance from Hampton Roads up the south side of the James River toward Richmond. While the operations of Banks and Sigel were important, Grant gave this third column higher priority, considering it to be the left wing of the grand Federal offensive in which the Army of the Potomac represented the center and Sherman's forces the right wing.[4]

Grant was not the first to have considered a southern approach toward Richmond

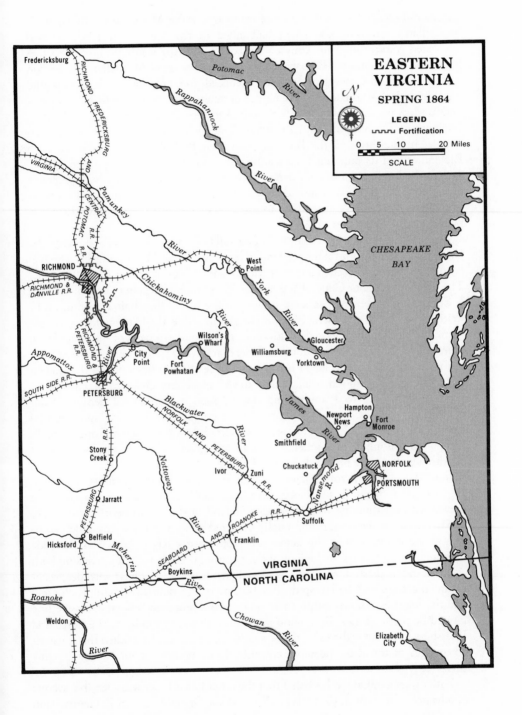

EASTERN
VIRGINIA

SPRING 1864

LEGEND
〰〰 Fortification

0   5   10   20 Miles
SCALE

Fredericksburg

Potomac   River

Rappahannock

RICHMOND FREDERICKSBURG AND POTOMAC R.R.

VIRGINIA

River

CHESAPEAKE
BAY

VIRGINIA CENTRAL R.R.

Pamunkey

River

West
Point

RICHMOND

Chickahominy

River

York   River

Gloucester

RICHMOND &
DANVILLE R.R.

Wilson's
Wharf

Williamsburg

Yorktown

RICHMOND & PETERSBURG R.R.

River

City
Point

Fort
Powhatan

Appomattox

SOUTH SIDE R.R.

PETERSBURG

Blackwater

James   River

Hampton
Newport
News

Fort
Monroe

NORFOLK AND PETERSBURG R.R.

River

Smithfield

PETERSBURG R.R.

Stony
Creek

Nottoway

Ivor   Zuni

Chuckatuck

NORFOLK

Nansemond R.

PORTSMOUTH

Jarratt

River

R.R.

SEABOARD

AND   ROANOKE   R.R.

Suffolk

Hicksford   Belfield

Meherrin

Franklin

VIRGINIA

NORTH CAROLINA

Boykins

River

Roanoke

Weldon

Chowan   River

Elizabeth
City

River

and its railroads as a possible plan of campaign. After Major General George B. McClellan's Peninsula Campaign had failed in the summer of 1862, he had advocated transferring the Army of the Potomac to the south bank of the James River and advancing via Petersburg. Nothing had come of McClellan's suggestion since General-in-Chief Halleck had dismissed the proposal as dangerous and impracticable;[5] yet the idea had remained dormant only until the following November. Within two days of each other, both Brigadier General John Barnard, Chief Engineer of Washington, and Brigadier General John Gibbon, a division commander in the Army of the Potomac, had submitted plans for an advance upon Richmond and its railroads from south of the James. Differing slightly in details, such as the landing point and the necessity of occupying Petersburg, both proposals agreed that the expedition should be waterborne and would require naval cooperation. Like McClellan's suggestion to Halleck four months previously, these two plans had also been rejected.[6]

Less than a month after Barnard's and Gibbon's plans had been shelved, the James River strategy for taking Richmond had been revived by two officers who had become disgusted with the seemingly inept leadership of the Army of the Potomac. The dissidents, Major General William B. Franklin and Brigadier General William F. Smith, had taken their scheme straignt to the top of the chain of command by writing directly to President Lincoln. Larger in scope than its predecessors, the Franklin-Smith plan proposed an advance on the southern bank of the James by an army of 150,000 men, while another Federal army 100,000 strong paralleled it on the northern bank. The larger army would seize the rail lines, while the smaller force invested Richmond itself, unless the Confederates chose to evacuate their capital. According to Franklin and Smith, such a plan would permit a concentration of forces, provide a secure line of communication, and allow Federal troops to approach within twenty miles of their objective without fighting. Lincoln had buried this impractical scheme by promising to refer it to his military advisers.[7]

Although no more proposals for a Federal advance via the James River had been submitted to Washington, Major General Benjamin Butler, commander of the Department of Virginia and North Carolina, had been making studies of such a movement ever since he had assumed command of the department in November 1863. Butler's investigation had finally centered upon a thirty-square-mile peninsula at the confluence of the James and Appomattox Rivers known as Bermuda Hundred. Deep ravines at the foot of the peninsula, along with the rivers on both sides, would facilitate turning the enclosed area into a secure base with deepwater communication back to Hampton Roads. One of the railroads linking Richmond and the lower South lay within three miles of the proposed Federal defensive line formed by these ravines. Richmond itself was only sixteen miles to the north and Petersburg less than eight miles to the south. The more Butler studied the apparent advantages of the site, the more enthusiastic he became about basing an army there.[8]

Butler was not alone in his belief that the lower James River was a feasible avenue of advance. Far away in Columbus, Ohio, Major General Samuel P. Heintzelman

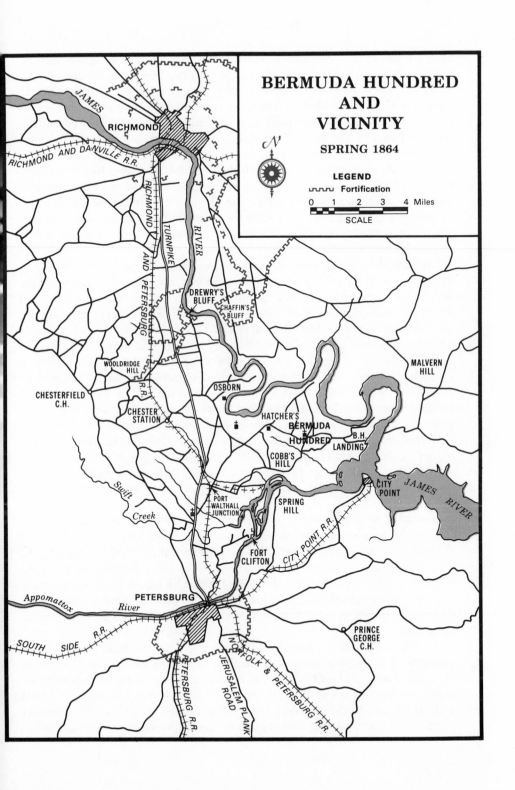

BERMUDA HUNDRED
AND
VICINITY

SPRING 1864

N

LEGEND

〜〜〜 Fortification

0 1 2 3 4 Miles

SCALE

JAMES

RICHMOND

RICHMOND AND DANVILLE R.R.

RICHMOND AND PETERSBURG TURNPIKE

RIVER

DREWRY'S
BLUFF

CHAFFIN'S
BLUFF

WOOLDRIDGE
HILL

OSBORN

MALVERN
HILL

CHESTERFIELD
C.H.

CHESTER
STATION

HATCHER'S

BERMUDA
HUNDRED

B.H.
LANDING

COBB'S
HILL

Swift

CITY
POINT

JAMES RIVER

PORT
WALTHALL
JUNCTION

SPRING
HILL

Creek

CITY POINT R.R.

FORT
CLIFTON

Appomattox

PETERSBURG

River

PRINCE
GEORGE
C.H.

SOUTH SIDE R.R.

PETERSBURG R.R.

JERUSALEM PLANK ROAD

NORFOLK & PETERSBURG R.R.

closely followed the operations of commanders serving in more active districts. Intrigued by newspaper accounts of an unsuccessful raid toward Richmond by some of Butler's troops, Heintzelman drafted a plan of his own and thoughtfully sent it to Butler on 17 February 1864. Heintzelman proposed a waterborne advance up the James River, preceded by a naval feint in the York River, and followed by landings on both banks of the James River slightly above Bermuda Hundred. The force placed ashore on the south bank would quickly destroy the railroads within reach, then cross the river and join the main body in its advance toward Richmond along the north bank. If necessary, the movement could be reversed, with the combined expedition advancing toward the city from the south. Heintzelman also outlined diversionary tactics that would obscure the point of attack. Butler never acknowledged Heintzelman's gratuitous advice, but it may have been instrumental in shaping his own ideas.[9]

Unaware of the earlier proposals for a campaign in the James River valley, Grant began to search for additional troops to augment his offensive columns. Many departments were guilty of hoarding units that were badly needed elsewhere, and one of the chief culprits seemed to be the Department of the South, comprising the states of South Carolina, Georgia, and Florida. The commander of this department was Major General Quincy Adams Gillmore, conqueror of Fort Pulaski and besieger of Charleston. In addition, Gillmore also controlled the X Corps, which consisted of most of the combat troops in the department. His recent operations against Fort Sumter had met with a notable lack of success, for which he blamed certain officers of the United States Navy. Since affairs in his department were at a stalemate, Gillmore was seeking a new locale in which to exercise his talents.[10]

Having decided that some of the combat units in Gillmore's department could operate to better advantage in different surroundings, Grant ordered X Corps veterans absent on furlough to rendezvous in a central northern location. Warned by this preliminary order that something was afoot, on 19 March 1864, Gillmore informed Halleck, now Chief of Staff in Washington, that at least ten thousand men could be removed from the Department of the South without danger. Gillmore asked to be transferred with his troops to a more active area of operations, but Grant had not planned to bring Gillmore north with the X Corps. Consequently, on 26 March Gillmore was told that all surplus troops in the Department of the South should be readied for duty elsewhere, but that his request to accompany them was still under consideration. Unless Grant changed his mind, Gillmore was destined to remain in South Carolina, where success would probably continue to elude him.[11]

As March drew to a close, Grant decided to visit the headquarters of the Department of Virginia and North Carolina to arrange for the expedition from Hampton Roads. Although Grant had never met Benjamin Butler personally, he must have been aware of Butler's turbulent career. It was rumored that Grant wished to remove Butler from department command and place the operations under another officer with greater field experience. Butler's replacement was assumed to be Major General William F. Smith, author of an earlier James River plan and a favorite of Grant's from the Chattanooga Campaign.[12] This speculation acquired substance when Grant called Smith to Washington for a conference on 31 March and then ordered him to report to Butler at Fort Monroe. After meeting with Smith, Grant and his official party, which included staff officers John A. Rawlins and Cyrus Comstock, Mrs. Grant, and Congressman Elihu Washburne, boarded the ship that would carry them to Hampton Roads.[13]

It is probable that Grant had already received Halleck's opinion of Benjamin Franklin Butler.[14] Halleck loathed Butler, and the feeling was vigorously returned. The enmity between the two men apparently sprang from the fact that Halleck was a professional soldier trained in the classical tradition at West Point, a learned translator of foreign military treatises, while Butler was a politician with only a prewar militia commission for martial qualifications. Butler was not the only politician with slight military training to be given high rank in the Union armies, and Halleck railed against all of them, but particularly Butler. Consequently, when Halleck fumed that entrusting troops to "military charlatans" was little short of murder, he obviously had Butler in mind. Butler, on the other hand, complained of "West Pointers" who were either inept, overcautious, or wasted their time translating obscure foreign books.[15]

A prominent criminal lawyer and Democratic politician in Massachusetts before the war, Butler had achieved notoriety in 1860 at the national Democratic Convention where he stoutly supported Jefferson Davis for the presidency of the United States for fifty-seven consecutive ballots. Butler, however, was not a friend of Davis's Confederacy. After Fort Sumter he had taken advantage of his position as a brigadier general in the state militia to lead Massachusetts's first regiments to the relief of defenseless Washington. Quickly occupying Annapolis and Baltimore, he had pushed through to the capital, and some credited him with having saved Washington and Maryland for the Union. Commissioned by Lincoln as the first major general of volunteers, Butler had next been sent to Fort Monroe as commander of what was then known as the Department of Virginia. There some of his troops had lost an insignificant but highly publicized skirmish at Big Bethel. There, too, Butler had issued his famous declaration labeling fugitive slaves as "contraband" of war.[16]

In August of 1861, Butler had been in overall command of the land forces during the successful attack on the Confederate forts at Cape Hatteras. The following year he had served in a similar capacity with the expedition that captured New Orleans. Installed as commander of the Crescent City, Butler had quickly aroused Confederate wrath by his infamous "woman order." While there Butler had also been the subject of rumors that he had greatly increased his fortune through illicit trading with the enemy and even through outright thievery. Relieved from his post in New Orleans by Lincoln after an altercation with the city's foreign consuls, Butler had been without a command until November 1863, when he had returned to Fort Monroe as commander of the Department of Virginia and North Carolina.

There his main tasks had been the supervision of Federal defensive enclaves in coastal North Carolina and Virginia, and the administration of the city of Norfolk.[17]

More important than Butler's previous career was his questionable ability to direct what Grant had come to consider the left wing of his grand offensive. Butler's actual combat experience was nil, since he had never personally led a large column in field operations. Big Bethel had been a mere skirmish fought by subordinates, the action against the Hatteras forts had been primarily a naval show, and New Orleans had required a police commissioner more than a combat commander. In truth, Butler had never really had the opportunity to fight a major battle. His troops had always been immobilized on garrison duty, which had sharpened his administrative skills, but had taught him nothing about maneuvering masses of men on a field of battle.[18]

Rather than trust such an important assignment to an untried officer, Grant had considered the possibility of removing Butler from command of the department. He soon discovered that political considerations had made Butler's position quite secure. As just another Democratic politician, Butler would have lacked importance under a Republican administration, but as a prominent Democrat who supported the war effort, Butler had much greater influence. In the Civil War, political necessities had raised a great many civilians to high military positions, and unless they made especially egregious blunders, political necessities kept them there. Benjamin Franklin Butler of Massachusetts was just such an officer. Lincoln did not want Butler removed unless Grant absolutely required it, and Grant, without personal knowledge of the man, was willing to keep an open mind until after their meeting at Fort Monroe. Nevertheless, in case Butler proved to be incompetent, Grant was bringing along an able subordinate for him. William F. Smith could lead the combat troops if Butler was amenable to remaining behind at department headquarters, and he could stand at Butler's elbow and offer sound professional advice if he was not.[19]

Grant and his party arrived at Fort Monroe at 9:00 A.M. on 1 April. Their first views of Butler probably was something of a shock, for his physical appearance was bizarre. Grant, who did not cut a dashing figure himself, ventured no description, but an officer in the 5th Massachusetts Cavalry who saw Butler in May wrote: "He is by all odds the most shocking and disreputable looking man I ever clapped my eyes on. He had his hat perched sideways on his head and looked more like a New York 'Blood-tub' or a 'plug-ugly' than anything else."[20] Colonel Theodore Lyman, who saw Butler in July, was equally critical:

> He is the strangest sight on a horse you ever saw: it is hard to keep your eyes off him. With his head set immediately on a stout shapeless body, his very squinting eyes, and a set of legs and arms that look as if made for somebody else, and hastily glued to him by mistake, he presents a combination of Victor Emmanuel, Aesop, and Richard III, which is very confusing to the mind.[21]

Butler's personal characteristics were not readily apparent. Grant would be exposed to some of these in joint planning sessions. Butler's extremely quick mind would be immediately demonstrated, and a glance around the post would show his vaunted administrative ability was not to be overestimated. Other facets of Butler's personality that may have been visible were his resourcefulness, his energy, and his adaptability to the realities of changing situations. Not so obvious, perhaps even purposefully concealed, were his habit of cursing profusely, his harsh and unconventional ways of dealing with incompetence or disobedience, and his tendency to reward or punish subordinates in extravagant fashion. Sometimes revealed unconsciously, although perhaps not in the conversations with Grant, was a naiveté which seemed to clash with Butler's public image as a backstage manipulator. Certainly Colonel Comstock of Grant's staff missed this aspect of Butler's character, for he confided to his diary on the first night of the visit: "Butler is sharp, shrewd, able, without conscience or modesty—overbearing. A bad man to have against you in a criminal case."[22]

After an exchange of pleasantries, Grant and Butler proceeded to discuss the role Butler's troops would play in the approaching campaign. Neither a list of the participants nor a detailed record of their conversations during the conference is extant, but a few things are known. Initially, there was some discussion regarding the Federal garrisons in North Carolina, which were being threatened by large Confederate forces. According to Butler, the idea of sending his troops there was raised as one means of cooperating with the Army of the Potomac. William F. Smith argued strongly in favor of such a move, perhaps because it was similar to Grant's initial plan of January.[23] Grant had kept his new plan to himself and a few trusted aides, and Smith was apparently unaware that the North Carolina operation was no longer under serious consideration.[24]

Before the conference, Grant decided to seek out Butler's ideas for the spring campaign before revealing his own. Grant's reticence gave Butler his opportunity to present the results of his study of the lower James River basin. First, Butler listed the advantages offered by an advance upon Richmond from the south: the city's defensive fortifications were less formidable there, and the ground was high and suitable for maneuvering. Moreover, the Bermuda Hundred peninsula would be an excellent base for such a campaign, once a defensive line was constructed across its narrow neck. Next, Butler suggested that City Point, a village located at the juncture of the James and Appomattox Rivers across from Bermuda Hundred, should be seized as a supply terminus. In addition, two defensive positions on the lower James, Fort Powhatan and Wilson's Wharf, would have to be secured to protect the army's line of communications. Butler ended his presentation by suggesting that the Army of the Potomac come to the James and make Bermuda Hundred its base of operations. Grant replied that such a course of action would be emphatically rejected by the authorities in Washington, who feared that the capital might be exposed to a Confederate counterthrust.[25]

Pleased that Butler's formulation differed from his own only in degree, Grant posed a hypothetical question. Since the Army of the Potomac could not uncover Washington by coming to the James River, might not Butler's mobile force, if augmented sufficiently by reinforcements and supported by the navy, seize Bermuda Hundred and threaten Richmond by itself: Butler replied affirmatively. Grant then asked if the Confederates could be surprised. Once more the answer was affirmative. Butler had obviously been expecting such a question, for he instantly produced a list of ruses that could be employed to confuse the Confederates. At no point did he give credit to General Heintzelman in Ohio, who had independently devised a similar plan in February and had graciously shared it with Butler.[26]

Impressed by Butler's efficiency, Grant proceeded to formulate general goals for Butler's troops. Here accounts of the conference diverge slightly but significantly. As Butler remembered his instructions, his first duty after arriving in the Bermuda Hundred-City Point area would be to fortify a base so that it would be safe from all attacks. Once this task was completed, Butler's troops were to threaten the city of Petersburg briefly and then move toward Richmond from the south, breaking that city's rail communications. Meanwhile the Army of the Potomac would drive Lee and his army southward. If all went well, the two Federal armies would unite on the banks of the James just outside of Richmond within ten days of the opening of the campaign. To Butler, Grant's emphasis upon the establishment of a fortified base made that his primary goal. Only after this was accomplished to Butler's satisfaction would he begin offensive operations against Richmond in coordination with the more powerful Army of the Potomac.[27]

In Grant's version of the plan, Butler was to secure a base on the southern bank of the James River as far upstream as possible, just as in Butler's account. For Grant, however, this was not the primary goal. Much more important was an early advance toward Richmond that might succeed in capturing the city, and at least would permanently block the railroads. Such a move would not only reduce Lee's supplies, but it would force the Confederates to retain units around Richmond that otherwise might be used to reinforce the Army of Northern Virginia. Thus, while Butler believed his most important task was to secure a base for future activity, Grant expected Butler to concentrate upon denying Lee vital supplies and reinforcements.[28] Grant later wrote that during the conference he "pointed out the apparent importance of getting possession of Petersburg, and destroying railroad communication as far south as possible." He admitted, however, that he had specified Butler's objective to be Richmond.[29]

After admonishing Butler to be ready to move on the same day as the Army of the Potomac, Grant brought the conference to a close. Both Grant and his chief of staff, John A. Rawlins, had been favorably impressed with Butler, so the question of removing him for reasons of gross incompetence had never arisen. Even if Butler took the field in person, which was his right as department commander, the capable William F. Smith would be there to assist him. Little did Grant know that Smith would eventually display idiosyncrasies that would make him totally unfit for the role of Butler's adviser, and that even then Smith was sulking because he favored a different plan of his own invention.[30]

After leaving Butler, Grant conferred briefly with Acting Rear Admiral Samuel P. Lee, commander of the North Atlantic Blockading Squadron, who would be responsible for furnishing naval support for Butler's army. Grant was restrained in his discussion with Lee, but did let it be known that he was requesting the Navy Department to add several ironclad warships to Lee's fleet. William F. Smith explained the purpose of the vessels by announcing that he would be leading an offensive movement against Richmond from Hampton Roads and would need the navy's cooperation. Beyond that tantalizing bit of information the two generals were unwilling to go. Lee would have to consult Butler at a later time for more details.[31]

Having concluded his official business, Grant sailed with his guests for Norfolk in hopes of visiting the city before departing for Washington that night. A violent storm, however, forced the party to return to Fort Monroe until the weather improved. When dawn of the next morning found the storm unabated, Grant took the opportunity to discuss further the plan of campaign with Butler.[32] So that there should be no mistake about basic principles, Grant drafted a letter of general instructions for Butler's guidance. Butler was informed that he should collect 20,000 men from his own department, combine them with 10,000 more from the Department of the South, and operate with the united force against Richmond from the south bank of the James River. Major General William F. Smith would command the troops from Butler's department and Major General Quincy A. Gillmore would accompany his men from South Carolina. Gillmore was to report with his units around 18 April and Butler was to be ready to begin his advance shortly thereafter.

The final part of the letter was as explicit as Grant thought he could be under the circumstances:

> When you are notified to move take City Point with as much force as possible. Fortify, or rather intrench, at once, and concentrate all your troops for the field there as rapidly as you can. From City Point directions cannot be given at this time for your further movements.
>
> The fact that has already been stated, that is, that Richmond is to be your objective point, and that there is to be co-operation between your force and the Army of the Potomac, must be your guide. This indicates the necessity of your holding close to the south bank of the James River as you advance. Then, should the enemy be forced into his intrenchments in Richmond, the Army of the Potomac would follow, and by means of transports the two armies would become a unit.

In closing, Grant recommended a cavalry raid against the railroad to Weldon as a supplement to Butler's landing. As long as he remained within these guidelines, Butler was free to work out the details on his own.[33]

On 3 April the weather cleared, allowing Grant and his traveling companions to sail for Washington.[34] It would be the middle of June before Grant would see Butler again, but he would have occasion to think of him often before many weeks had passed. Meanwhile, a Confederate intelligence report began to make its way to

Richmond: "It is rumored and believed that Richmond will be attacked from three different points, viz, Suffolk, the Peninsula, and through Gloucester."[35]

NOTES

1. *War of the Rebellion: A Compilation of the Official Records of the Union and Confederate Armies*, 70 vols. in 128 parts (Washington, D.C.: Government Printing Office, 1880–1901), Series 1, 33:394–395. (Cited hereinafter as *O.R.A.*, with no series indicated unless it is other than Series 1.)

2. Ibid., 602–604. For a modern critic, see T. Harry Williams, *Lincoln and his Generals* (New York: Alfred A. Knopf, 1952), 296.

3. The role of the railroads is described in Robert C. Black, III, *The Railroads of the Confederacy* (Chapel Hill: The University of North Carolina Press, 1952), 243; George Edgar Turner, *Victory Rode the Rails* (Indianapolis, Ind.: Bobbs-Merrill Company, 1953), 346; and Angus James Johnston, II, *Virginia Railroads in the Civil War* (Chapel Hill: The University of North Carolina Press, 1961), 195, 198. For R. E. Lee's opinion, see *O.R.A.*, 33:1275.

4. The plan and its underlying principles are described in Ulysses S. Grant, *Personal Memoirs of U. S. Grant* (New York: Charles L. Webster & Company, 1886), 2:127–132, 134, 138–141, 146–147; and in *O.R.A.*, 46, pt. 1, 11–21.

5. *O.R.A.*, 11, pt. 3, 337. See also Williams, *Lincoln and his Generals*, 139.

6. *O.R.A.*, 21:807–808, 812–813.

7. Ibid., 868–870; Williams, *Lincoln and his Generals*, 199; Roy P. Basler, ed., *The Collected Works of Abraham Lincoln*, 9 vols. (New Brunswick, N.J.: Rutgers University Press, 1953), 6:15.

8. Benjamin F. Butler, *Autobiography and Personal Reminiscences of Major-General Benj. F. Butler: Butler's Book* (Boston: A. M. Thayer & Co., 1892), 621–627.

9. Manuscript Journal, Samuel P. Heintzelman Papers, Library of Congress, Washington, D.C.; *O.R.A.*, 51, pt. 1, 1287–1288.

10. *O.R.A.*, 35, pt. 1, 493–494, and pt. 2, 15–16. For Gillmore's differences with the navy, see George H. Gordon, *A War Diary of Events in the War of the Great Rebellion, 1863–1865* (Boston: James R. Osgood and Company, 1882), 243, 245, 246, and J. Cutler Andrews, *The North Reports the Civil War* (Pittsburgh: University of Pittsburgh Press, 1955), 491–492.

11. *O.R.A.*, 35, pt. 2, 20, 23–24, 28–29; Grant, *Personal Memoirs*, 2:128; *O.R.A.*, 33:729, 752–753.

12. Grant, *Personal Memoirs*, 2:132; Butler, *Butler's Book*, 627; Charles Francis Adams, *Studies Military and Diplomatic, 1775–1865* (New York: Macmillan, 1911), 268, 270; George M. Wolfson, "Butler's Relations with Grant and the Army of the James in 1864," *The South Atlantic Quarterly* 10 (October 1911): 389.

13. *O.R.A.*, 33:770, 861; *O.R.A.*, 51, pt. 1, 1153; John A. Rawlins to his wife, 2 April 1864, in James Harrison Wilson Papers, Library of Congress, Washington, D.C.; Cyrus B. Comstock Diary, 31 March 1864, Library of Congress, Washington, D.C.; *O.R.A.*, 35, pt. 2, 31–32.

14. Bruce Catton, *Grant Takes Command* (Boston: Little, Brown, 1969), 147.

15. Williams, *Lincoln and his Generals*, 322; Allan Nevins, *The War for the Union: The Organized War to Victory, 1864–1865* (New York: Charles Scribner's Sons, 1971), 15; Stephen E. Ambrose, *Halleck: Lincoln's Chief of Staff* (Baton Rouge: Louisiana State University Press, 1962), 60, 168, 206–207; George Agassiz, ed., *Meade's Headquarters 1863–1865: Letters of Colonel Theodore Lyman from the Wilderness to Appomattox* (Boston: Atlantic Monthly Press, 1922), 193.

16. In recent years a rash of Butler biographies have appeared, with marked variation in quality. Brief but fair-minded and well-documented are Robert S. Holzman, *Stormy Ben Butler* (New York: Macmillan, 1954), and Hans L. Trefousse, *Ben Butler, the South Called Him Beast!* (New York: Twayne Publishers, 1957). Biased and unreliable is Robert Werlich, *"Beast" Butler* (Washington, 1962). A solid defense of Butler and his accomplishments can be found in Richard S. West, Jr., *Lincoln's Scapegoat General: A Life of Benjamin F. Butler, 1818–1893* (Boston: Houghton Mifflin, 1965). Less thorough and penetrating is Howard P. Nash, Jr., *Stormy Petrel: The Life and Times of General Benjamin F. Butler, 1818–1893* (Rutherford, N. J.: Fairleigh Dickinson University Press, 1969). Perhaps the most judicious analysis of Butler's life and services can be found in Harold B. Raymond, "Ben Butler: A Reappraisal," *Colby Library Quarterly* series 6, no. 11 (September 1964): 445–479. Butler provided his own version of his life story in *Butler's Book*.

For specific material cited in the text, see West, *Lincoln's Scapegoat General*, 45, 82, 243; Raymond, "Ben Butler," 447, 449; Ezra J. Warner, *Generals in Blue: Lives of the Union Commanders* (Baton Rouge: Louisiana State University Press, 1964), 61.

17. Warner, *Generals in Blue*, 61; West, *Lincoln's Scapegoat General*, 138–143, 149–151, 186–204, 219–229, 295–308; Raymond, "Ben Butler," 445, 478. Angered by the insults visited upon his men by the ladies of New Orleans, Butler had decreed that any female guilty of such conduct in the future would be "treated as a woman of the town plying her avocation."

18. West, *Lincoln's Scapegoat General*, 243; Raymond, "Ben Butler," 450.

19. Adam Badeau, *Military History of Ulysses S. Grant, From April 1861, to April 1865*, 3 vols. (New York: D. Appleton and Company, 1885), 2:246–248; Catton, *Grant Takes Command*, 146, 255–256; William F. Smith, "Butler's Attack on Drewry's Bluff," in Robert U. Johnson and Clarence C. Buel, eds., *Battles and Leaders of the Civil War*, 4 vols. (New York: The Century Company, 1884, 1888), 4:206n.

20. Charles P. Bowditch, "War Letters of Charles P. Bowditch," *Massachusetts Historical Society Proceedings* 57 (October 1923–June 1924):476.

21. Agassiz, ed., *Meade's Headquarters*, 192.

22. Williams, *Lincoln and his Generals*, 186; Horace Porter, *Campaigning with Grant* (New York: The Century Company, 1906), 246; Members of the Regiment, *The Story of the Twenty-First Regiment Connecticut Volunteer Infantry, During the Civil War* (Middletown, Conn.: Stewart Printing, 1900), 406–407; Badeau, *Military History*, 2:44, 259; Butler, *Butler's Book*, 644–645; Catton, *Grant Takes Command*, 206; Cyrus B. Comstock Diary, 1 April 1864, LC.

23. Butler, *Butler's Book*, 636. Certain statements by Butler permit the inference that Smith had attended at least part of the session.

24. See John A. Rawlins to his wife, 13 April 1864 in James Harrison Wilson Papers, LC.

25. Grant, *Personal Memoirs*, 2:132–133; Badeau, *Military History*, 2:45–46; Butler, *Butler's Book*, 627–628.

26. Albert D. Richardson, *A Personal History of Ulysses S. Grant* (Hartford, Conn.: American Publishing Company, 1868), 388–389; Butler, *Butler's Book*, 628–629.

27. Butler in later life wrote three versions of what he understood his instructions to have been, all of which substantially agree. The first is a memorandum dated 8 January 1879, located in the Benjamin F. Butler Papers, Library of Congress, Washington, D.C. The second is a letter to W. P. Darby [Derby], dated 26 June 1882, also in the Butler Papers, LC. The final version is the account presented in *Butler's Book*, 629, 631. Butler wrote in the latter work, (638): "General Grant had told me, in conversation, if I could hold the Petersburg and Richmond Railroad cut for ten days, and secure our proposed base at Bermuda and City Point, that by that time he would join me there, or on the James above Richmond, having either whipped Lee's army or forced it into the intrenchments around Richmond, when the combined armies of the Potomac and my command would invest Richmond, the navy holding the James as we approached." The ten-day figure especially loomed large in Butler's thinking.

28. Badeau, *Military History*, 2:33–34, 241–248.

29. *O.R.A.*, 46, pt. 1, 16.

30. Butler, *Butler's Book*, 631; Richardson, *Personal History of U. S. Grant*, 389; John A. Rawlins to his wife, 23 April 1864, in James Harrison Wilson Papers, LC; James Harrison Wilson, *The Life of John A. Rawlins* (New York: The Neale Publishing Company, 1916), 206; Smith, *Battles and Leaders*, 4:206n.

31. *Official Records of the Union and Confederate Navies in the War of the Rebellion*, 30 vols. (Washington, D. C.: Government Printing Office, 1894–1922), Series 1, 9:584. (Cited hereinafter as *O.R.N.*, with no series indicated unless it is other than Series 1.)

32. *O.R.A.*, 33:790; Cyrus B. Comstock Diary, 1 and 2 April 1864, LC; John A. Rawlins to his wife, 2 April 1864, in James Harrison Wilson Papers, LC. According to Smith, *Battles and Leaders*, 4:206, Butler first raised the Bermuda Hundred plan at this second session, but since this is at variance with all other testimony, and it also leaves Grant and Butler nothing to talk about on 1 April, Smith's version is here discounted. Smith admitted he was not present at the 2 April meeting, although he had been invited by Butler and had been informed of the Bermuda Hundred plan on the previous day. Ibid., 206n.

33. *O.R.A.*, 33:794–795.

34. Cyrus B. Comstock Diary, 3 April 1864, LC.

35. *O.R.A.*, 51, pt. 2, 846.

☆ 2 ☆

Federal Preparations
4–30 April 1864

Forty years old in 1864, William Farrah Smith was known throughout the army by the nickname "Baldy," not because he lacked hair, but in order to distinguish him from all the other Smiths in the service. Having graduated from West Point in 1845 near the top of his class, he had chosen the Engineers for his branch of the service and he was so proficient that he had been retained for a time as an instructor on the West Point faculty. An assignment in Florida during the immediate prewar years had further perfected his craft, but it had also cursed him with recurring attacks of malaria, which served to increase his natural tendency toward irascibility. Upon the outbreak of war, Smith had briefly served under Butler at Fort Monroe, then he had departed to organize a volunteer infantry regiment. By late 1862, he had risen to the rank of major general and commanded the VI Corps in the Army of the Potomac. At that point, his open criticism of his superiors had served to halt temporarily his meteoric rise. Smith detested Major General Ambrose Burnside, then commander of the Army of the Potomac, and he joined his close friend, Major General William B. Franklin, in publicly ridiculing Burnside's generalship. Even though Burnside was removed from army command, Smith's carping backfired when the Senate refused to confirm his promotion to major general.[1]

Reduced in rank and deprived of his corps command, Smith appeared to be on the way down just as fast as he had risen. If it had not been for a random assignment to the Federal army at Chattanooga as an engineer, he probably would have ended his career in some obscure staff position. In Tennessee, fate gave him a second chance. By performing brilliantly in opening a secure supply line to the besieged Federal garrison in Chattanooga, Smith came to the attention of U. S. Grant, who was favorably impressed. From then on, Smith attended Grant's strategy sessions, including those in which future movements of the eastern armies were considered. At the time, Grant even considered Smith seriously as a replacement for George Meade, commander of the Army of the Potomac.[2]

Although the War Department seemed willing to accept the abrasive Smith in Meade's place, Grant eventually changed his mind. By 11 March 1864, the general-in-chief had firmly decided to retain Meade. Once more Baldy Smith was without employment, and once more Grant rescued him by assigning him to duty in the Department of Virginia and North Carolina as Butler's unofficial adviser. At the same time, Grant reinitiated Smith's promotion to major general, which had been blocked in the Senate until Grant forced it through. Butler himself knew of Smith's accomplishments and, shortly after taking over his department in late 1863, he had requested Smith's transfer to Fort Monroe. The transfer had not been approved then, but Smith was now to join Butler after all.[3]

Smith's ups and downs had not mellowed his disposition. To his subordinates he was generally gracious, and his habit of serving champagne cocktails at his field headquarters was known far and wide. On the other hand, his superiors usually served to bring out his less appealing qualities. Even James Harrison Wilson, his former student and devoted admirer, recognized this facet of Smith's character, describing him as a "conscientiously contentious man."[4] Besides a propensity toward criticism of his superiors, Smith had another flaw that hindered his usefulness in field command: he was too dilatory in his movements. In the view of one of Grant's staff officers, Smith "was overanxious to prepare for every possible contingency. His skill was great, his judgment cool, but his movements were somewhat too elaborate."[5] Butler would later write that Smith was guilty of the sin of " 'interminable reconnoissances'—waiting and waiting, not going at a thing when he was told, but looking all around to see if he could not do something else than what he was told to do, or do it in a different way from what he was told."[6] This view would be corroborated by observers in the ranks, but the prime evidence substantiating such a charge had not yet unfolded.[7]

Already Baldy Smith had a grievance, but it was still directed more toward Grant than Butler. Smith remained obsessed with the plan of campaign that Grant had submitted to Halleck in January. Two weeks before coming to Fort Monroe, Smith had written confidentially to his young protégé, James H. Wilson, advocating a drive on Weldon, North Carolina, from the coast. Wilson was to "tell Grant" if he agreed that such a scheme was feasible, but Smith feared that Grant's mind had already been swayed by Meade and Halleck.[8] Wilson deeply admired Smith, and he may have spoken to Grant about Smith's note, but he was probably too interested in maintaining his own position to press the matter. Smith, however, was not the type of man to let the subject drop. Although Butler had invited him to attend the conference with Grant on 2 April, Smith had declined in the belief that Grant would confer privately with him later. Much to Smith's surprise, Grant did not meet with him afterward and had given Butler a letter of instructions that seemed to endorse Butler's ideas. In Smith's own words, "After that of course I said nothing."[9]

Although he had told Admiral Lee that he was going to lead an expedition up the James, Smith continued to argue for the North Carolina operation after Grant returned to Washington. Early in April, he wrote another letter to Wilson proposing a drive on Weldon and again asking Wilson discreetly to pass the word along. This time Wilson gave Smith's letter to John A. Rawlins, Grant's chief of staff, who in turn read it to Grant. Rawlins did not like Smith, nor Wilson for that matter, and he took malicious pleasure in exposing their machinations. As Rawlins confided to his wife on 13 April, "This letter showed General Grant just what sort of man he has to deal with in General Smith. Knowing him, he will get along with him better."[10]

On the same day that Rawlins wrote to his wife, the War Department issued Special Order No. 146, part of which officially assigned Smith to duty under Butler.[11] Smith's hopes were now in ruins. Not only had his cherished plan of campaign been rebuffed with crushing finality, but he was formally subordinated to Butler as well and could act only at that officer's pleasure. Forced to implement a plan he opposed, under a commander for whom he had contempt, Smith decided to avoid contact with Butler as much as possible. Years later he wrote: "As I was engaged in organizing and drilling my troops during that month [April], I had little to do with him [Butler] until we landed at Bermuda Hundred."[12]

None of the conflicts brewing among their commanders were evident to the thousands of troops already implementing the first stages of concentration. Those who did venture a precampaign assessment of their generals were divided in their opinions. A private in the 25th Massachusetts Infantry was not sure that Butler was the man for the task at hand:

> The first year of the war Gen. Butler was the busiest and most successful general we had, but since then he has kind o' taken to niggers and trading. As a military governor he is a nonesuch . . . but as a commander of troops in the field, he is not just such a man as I should pick out.[13]

Yet another soldier praised a quality of Butler's that endeared him to many enlisted men:

> It was a proverb in the department that whatever else old "cockeye" lacked in generalship, he was a bountiful provider. When other armies were on their uppers and the cooks' stores ran for weeks on "salt horse," "sow belly" and wormy "hard tack," we had soft bread, fresh meat and often a vegetable ration.[14]

Those men in the ranks who worried about Butler's tactical competence took comfort, as did Grant, in the fact that Baldy Smith was to be the senior corps commander.[15]

During the first half of April, regiments from all parts of Butler's domain began to arrive at a staging area near Yorktown. Down from Point Lookout, Maryland, where they had been serving as prison guards, came the 2nd and 12th New Hampshire Infantry Regiments. Other units came to the Peninsula from the south side of Hampton Roads, where they had garrisoned the fortifications protecting Norfolk and Portsmouth. As each regiment landed at Yorktown, it followed a standard routine. First, the regimental camp was established with great care, which provided some basis for the rumor that the quarters would be used for several months. A ruse to fool Confederate spies, this stratagem was transparent to many veterans, who put no great effort into their "homes." As soon as the camp was finished, the troops began a grueling series of company, battalion, and regimental drills. At frequent intervals, inspections were held to determine how much new clothing and equipment had to be requisitioned. Throughout it all, the men speculated endlessly about their destination, which was rumored to be as far away as Texas.[16]

While his men drilled, Butler wrestled with the administrative problems incident to preparing an army for active campaigning. His first concern was to secure the best subordinate commanders Grant could furnish. This meant asking for experienced men like Brigadier Generals William Brooks, William Hazen, and Thomas Neill, as well as Colonel Hiram Burnham, whose promotion was expected momentarily. Grant approved Butler's requests for Brooks and Burnham, but Hazen and Neill were ordered elsewhere. More easily obtained were the services of Brigadier Generals Gilman Marston and Edward Hincks, already serving in the department.[17] To command his cavalry, Butler wanted Brigadier General James H. Wilson, then heading the Cavalry Bureau in Washington. Since Wilson had never served with Butler, he believed that the request for his transfer had originated with his friend William F. Smith.[18] Grant had already decided to use Wilson in the Army of the Potomac, and offered Butler Colonel August V. Kautz instead. Since Kautz was outranked by the colonels of Butler's cavalry regiments, Grant hastily promoted him to brigadier general.[19]

In addition to personnel matters, there were many other problems to be resolved. Halleck was asked to furnish certain units that had served under Butler before, as well as additional cavalry and artillery. A contingent of the Invalid Corps was sought to provide rear-area security and two regiments of black troops were requested for a similar mission. Shipping had to be collected to move thousands of men and horses and hundreds of tons of munitions and supplies upriver. A thousand new cavalry horses had to be pried loose from Halleck, a task accomplished only after Grant's personal intervention. Recruits had to be brought from camps of instruction in the North and allocated to understrength commands. Of lesser importance to the campaign, but vital to the men involved, were Butler's efforts to alleviate the suffering of three regiments that had lost all their baggage during their transfer to Yorktown. More ominous was a letter from a friend in Norfolk warning Butler that certain members of his staff were talking freely about the plan of campaign.[20]

While Butler's preparations proceeded apace, Acting Rear Admiral Samuel Phillips Lee patiently waited for the generals to detail the services required from the North Atlantic Blockading Squadron. Optimistically, Lee informed Assistant Secretary of the navy Gustavus V. Fox on 4 April: "If you will give the right means for the James River route to Richmond, it can and will be taken. It is now the time to do this big thing. . . . The upper James is the point for naval cooperation, and now is the time."[21] Still, the army's secrecy was inconvenient. Hearing rumors in Washington that the expedition was bound for City Point, Secretary of the Navy Gideon Welles sought confirmation on 7 April from General Halleck. Halleck knew nothing of the movement and a telegram from Grant was required to clarify

Butler's destination. Thus enlightened, Welles gave Lee permission to cooperate with the army as long as it did not weaken the blockade of Wilmington. Further details would have to come from Butler.[22]

In an effort to secure Lee's wholehearted assistance in the big offensive to come, Butler moved quickly to honor a navy request for army aid in searching the creeks and inlets on the south side of Hampton Roads. On 9 April, Confederate naval raiders operating from a secluded cove had mounted a torpedo boat attack on Lee's flagship that had severely damaged it. The army obliged Lee on 12 April by sending a column westward from Portsmouth to Suffolk and by landing other units along the James and Nansemond Rivers between Suffolk and Smithfield. Finding no Confederates east of their defensive positions along the Blackwater River, the Federals soon withdrew to their bases and resumed preparations for the approaching campaign.[23]

Butler's attention were also distracted by developments in North Carolina, which was being stripped of troops to augment the force assembling at Yorktown. The commander of the District of North Carolina, Major General John Peck, believed that a major Confederate threat was developing against the Federal enclaves at New Berne, Plymouth, and Washington. Grant and Butler were not concerned, arguing instead that once the Federal offensives in Virginia had begun, the Confederate pressure in North Carolina would slacken. Both generals favored abandoning the exposed North Carolina garrisons anyway, and on 20 April Butler sought to remove five regiments to Virginia.[24] On the same day a Confederate force under Brigadier General Robert Hoke overran Plymouth and captured the entire garrison. Once the disaster at Plymouth was confirmed, Butler was given permission to evacuate Washington. While some of the troops reinforced the remaining outpost at New Berne, two regiments were brought to Hampton Roads to join the James River expedition.[25]

About the middle of April, Butler's quartermaster received a cryptic order to prepare sufficient transportation for moving several million rations to North Carolina. Assuming that Grant was having second thoughts about the campaign up the James, Butler drafted a letter to the general-in-chief in which he offered to implement whatever plan Grant had decided upon. Carried to Grant's headquarters by William F. Smith, who served as messenger at his own request, the letter elicited an immediate reply.[26] To Butler's relief, and Smith's continued displeasure, Grant dismissed the order for the North Carolina rations as a subordinate's mistake, and he explicitly confirmed the plan adopted at the Fort Monroe conference:

> All the force that can be taken from the coast has been ordered to report to you at Fort Monroe by the 18th instant, or as soon thereafter as possible. What I ask is, that with them, and all you can concentrate from your own command, you seize upon City Point and act from there, looking upon Richmond as your objective point.[27]

Two days later, on 18 April, Grant sent Lieutenant Colonel Frederick Dent to Butler with a final set of instructions. First, Butler was reminded to be ready to move on the same day as the Army of the Potomac. Second:

You also understand that with the forces here I shall aim to fight Lee between here and Richmond, if he will stand. Should Lee, however, fall back into Richmond, I will follow up and make a junction with your army on the James River. Could I be certain that you will be able to invest Richmond on the south side, so as to have your left resting on the James above the city, I would form the junction there. Circumstances may make this course advisable anyhow. I would say, therefore, use every exertion to secure footing as far up the south side of the river as you can, and as soon as possible.

If you hear of our advancing from that direction, or have reason to judge from the action of the enemy that they are looking for danger to that side, attack vigorously, and if you cannot carry the city, at least detain as large a force there as possible.[28]

Nowhere in the two letters did Grant refer to Petersburg as either a primary or a secondary goal. Indeed, Richmond was specifically stated to be Butler's objective. Perhaps Grant thought the Petersburg question had been covered satisfactorily at the Fort Monroe conference. More likely, Grant considered Petersburg's capture to be one of those details best left to Butler's own judgment. According to military critic Theodore Dodge, "It does not appear that Grant at this time paid much heed to the James River plan. He believed that he could demolish Lee on the northern route."[29] If Grant truly wanted Butler to capture Petersburg, he should have made some reference to it in his mid-April letters. Unfortunately, Grant's last opportunity to influence Butler's campaign was allowed to pass without clarification.

With his instructions confirmed, Butler's only concern was meeting Grant's timetable for beginning the expedition. Smith's XVIII Corps at Yorktown would have no difficulty in getting ready, but as April slipped away many of Gillmore's X Corps units had not even arrived in Virginia. This delay, which threatened to upset the entire schedule, had two causes. First, although Halleck had drafted Gillmore's orders on 4 April, they had not been received until 11 April, more than twice the normal transit time.[30] Second, Gillmore's troops were scattered throughout a wide area. A number of regiments in Florida had to travel first to the coast, then to staging areas in South Carolina, and finally to Virginia, where the X Corps would be reorganized at Gloucester Point, across the York River from Yorktown. Although preliminary movement orders were issued to twenty-three X Corps units on 12 April, and several departed the next day, Gillmore believed the transfer could not be completed before 20 April.[31]

On 16 April, two of Gillmore's regiments arrived at Fort Monroe, but others had not even received movement orders by then. Butler meanwhile was preparing wharves at Gloucester Point and stockpiling equipment for X Corps' use. Shortly thereafter, Butler received a letter from Gillmore announcing that the transfer of the X Corps to Virginia was being delayed by problems of concentration. On the evening of 18 April, Brigadier General Israel Vogdes arrived from Hilton Head with two more X Corps units. Vogdes carried a letter explaining that he would command the elements of the X Corps already in Virginia until the arrival of Brigadier General Alfred H. Terry from South Carolina, who would then relieve him. Gillmore planned to remain at Hilton Head until his last regiment was ready to depart. Disappointed, Butler informed Grant that Gillmore probably could not reach Virginia before 30 April.[32]

While Gillmore made explanations and Butler fretted, the men of the X Corps slowly began to move. After a short march to an embarkation point, the troops sailed to Hilton Head where unserviceable gear was discarded and some units were paid. At Hilton Head they boarded other vessels that carried them past Cape Hatteras to Virginia. Some soldiers, recalling their fallen comrades, left the Department of the South with regret, while others were only too happy to be departing. As W. H. Coley of the 7th Connecticut Regiment explained in a letter to his sister, "I never liked the Southern Dept. there is to many Fleas & Misquitoes to trouble a person." Many of the vessels, particularly those carrying artillery batteries, were overcrowded at departure. Life aboard ship was made even more unpleasant by the use of drinking water distilled from the ocean, and by a strict order forbidding the troops to smoke. Until Cape Hatteras was reached, the soldiers' only diversions were singing, dancing, fishing, and shooting at porpoises.[33]

When Cape Hatteras loomed ahead, simple amusements were forgotten. Not all of the transports met rough weather as they rounded the Cape, but some encountered storms that blew them far off course. In almost every unit, large numbers of soldiers became seasick and took to their bunks when not making frequent trips to the rail. The 7th New Hampshire Infantry was particularly amused by "one man who lay in his bunk singing hymns and reading psalms for his own consolation . . . but who, when the storm was ended, at once turned his penitence into profanity and his fear into bravery." A New York soldier noted in his diary that nearly his entire regiment was ill and that he had not been out of his bunk for forty hours. Fortunately, calmer seas were ahead, and as their vessels neared Hampton Roads, the spirits of the men began to improve.[34]

While Gillmore's troops trickled slowly into Hampton Roads, Benjamin Butler's attention was drawn to an entirely new problem. The difficulty stemmed from an agreement between the Lincoln administration and the government of France that permitted the removal of some French-owned tobacco stored in Richmond and Petersburg. Over the vehement objection of Secretary of the Navy Welles, it had been agreed that two French warships would convoy two merchant vessels up the James River to City Point, where the tobacco would be loaded. A time limit of five months had been placed on the operation, with the expiration date set for 23 April 1864. By 11 April, several of the French vessels had arrived at Hampton Roads, and the French commander gave notice of his intention to proceed upriver in two days time. This declaration spawned a flurry of telegrams from both Butler and Admiral Lee to their superiors, asking if the movement should be allowed to proceed in view of its potentially disastrous effect on security.[35]

The question of the French tobacco was eventually referred to Grant, who realized that to halt the movement peremptorily would inform the Confederates that the James River was to be used as an axis of advance. At the same time, to allow the operation to continue would open a conduit for similar information to be passed to Richmond. To Grant, the best course seemed to be a firm adherence to the 23 April deadline on the grounds that any other arrangement would require complete renegotiation of the original agreement. Accordingly, the French chargé d' affaires was requested on 21 April to recall the French ships already ascending the James and hold the others at Hampton Roads until further notice. Just as the Federals had feared, word immediately began to circulate in Richmond that Butler had ordered the French away from City Point. Fortunately for Butler and Grant, the Confederates readily accepted the reason given for demanding the French departure. By 28 April, all of the French vessels had finally cleared the James River and no further difficulties arose from that source.[36]

Near the end of the French tobacco controversy, Butler received a blunt letter from Admiral Lee demanding details of the James River operation so that the navy might know what was required of it. After an exchange of letters and a conference at Fort Monroe, the army's needs were finally clarified. First, Butler wanted the navy to occupy the James River up to a point known as Osborn and the Appomattox River as far as Port Walthall, so as to protect the army's debarkation from Confederate fleet action. Second, Butler requested naval gunfire support until the army was established ashore and safely entrenched. In return, Butler promised to aid in clearing the rivers of obstructions and he offered the services of a small fleet of army gunboats. He also agreed to furnish blockships to seal the channel against a sortie by the Confederate ironclads at Richmond. The deadline for all preparations was set at 30 April.[37]

In response to the army's requests, S. P. Lee informed Butler that his ironclads drew too much water to ascend the James River beyond Trent's Reach, on the northern side of the Bermuda Hundred peninsula, and that only wooden gunboats could ascend the Appomattox. Furthermore, in the James River below City Point there was a natural obstruction known as Harrison's Bar, which could be crossed by the largest vessels only at high tide. Also, the Confederates had probably filled the rivers with torpedoes and other barriers, which would have to be removed before the streams could be navigated safely. Nor, in Lee's opinion, was surprise possible because of the presence of numerous Confederate signal stations along the James. Within these limitations, Lee pledged the "intelligent and hearty co-operation" of the North Atlantic Blockading Squadron, and he readily accepted the assistance of Brigadier General Charles Graham's army gunboats.[38]

Privately, Lee was worried about the Confederate squadron based at Richmond, which included three powerful ironclads, and he sought reinforcements from the Navy Department. He was also concerned about the lack of time in which to prepare his own ships, as well as the difficulty of obtaining qualified pilots to guide his fleet over the treacherous sandbars.[39] When informed by Lee of the army's plans, Secretary of the Navy Welles was even more skeptical:

> Only four days to improvise a navy, and they are to proceed up a river whose channel is not buoyed out. The scheme is not practical, yet it has the sanction of General Grant. It must, however, be a blind, intended to deceive the enemy, and to do this effectually he must first deceive our own people. A somewhat formidable force has been gathered in General Butler's department, and there is no doubt but that General B. himself fully believes he is to make a demonstration up James River. It may be that this is General Grant's intention

also, but if it is, I shall be likely to have my faith in him impaired. Certainly there have been no sufficient preparations for such a demonstration and the call upon the Navy is unreasonable.[40]

Although much of official Washington remained in ignorance of the details of the forthcoming expedition, security continued to be a problem for Butler. After the French were removed from potentially damaging contact with the Confederates, representatives of the Northern press threatened to become another source of leakage. It was not unusual for newspapermen during the Civil War to publish information regarding troop movements and campaign plans that could be of great value to the other side.[41] Nevertheless, the press had to be handled carefully, since scorning a reporter often resulted in unfavorable coverage of the offending commander's activities. Well aware of these realities, Butler attempted to ensure both security and a favorable press by handling cases involving reporters individually.[42] Several reporters were already filing dispatches from Fort Monroe, and the concessions made by some of them in order to retain their favored status are shown in a letter from William Stiner of the *New York Herald* to his managing editor:

> Since I spoke to Genl. Butler on Monday relative to his order regarding Southern papers, I have not seen him, but I learn today that the Editorial in Wednesdays Herald displeases him very much. As General Butler takes *chief command* of operations in this Department, it might be better not to offend him. In fact your promise and that of Mr. [James Gordon] Bennett to me was to the effect that nothing should be said against him.[43]

On 28 April, still another problem came to Butler's attention, when August Kautz, the army's new cavalry commander, sought to modify the cavalry's role in the plan of campaign. Butler had originally decided that the cavalry would leave Portsmouth simultaneously with the main expedition and head directly for the Blackwater River defense line south of Petersburg. A crossing would be forced at the village of Franklin, after which the column would march thirty-five miles farther to Hicksford, and there destroy the Petersburg Railroad bridge over the Meherrin River. While studying Butler's plan, Kautz had learned that the Blackwater line had never been penetrated in strength, and that the depth of the water at Franklin would require the building of a bridge under hostile fire. These factors led him to favor a more northern crossing of the Blackwater, and the substitution of railroad bridges over the Nottoway River and Stony Creek for the Meherrin span. When Kautz presented his proposal to Butler, he feared the worst; to his surprise, Butler readily consented to the change. Relieved, Kautz returned to Portsmouth and resumed his efforts to put his four regiments into fighting trim.[44]

Kautz was later to write that "I always found Genl. Butler thus reasonable and our relations were always of the most agreeable character." Several of Butler's subordinates, however, held a different opinion. Brigadier General Alfred Terry, temporary commander of the X Corps units in Virginia, had already felt the sting of Butler's pen because he had presumed to communicate directly with Chief of Staff Halleck. Terry would soon revert to division command and thus his rebuke was of little consequence, but the question of William F. Smith's relations with Butler was of an entirely different magnitude. Having seen his North Carolina proposal summarily rejected, Smith continued to brood upon his situation, even while preparing his troops for the Bermuda Hundred expedition.[45]

Smith's state of mind is made evident in two letters he wrote during the last week of April. On 26 April, in a letter to Colonel O. E. Babcock of Grant's staff, Smith suggested that a capable staff officer should be attached to Butler to ensure that Grant's purposes were not thwarted. After discussing the idea with Colonel Cyrus Comstock, Babcock indirectly broached the subject with Grant, but the general-in-chief dismissed it out of hand.[46] While waiting for Babcock to reply, Smith sent a personal letter to his old friend, Major General William B. Franklin. After telling Franklin how near he had been to command of the Army of the Potomac, Smith noted that his wife was soon to give birth. Although personal affairs weighed heavily upon Smith's mind, other considerations caused him to tell Franklin:

> I am here in an anomalous position under Butler with a campaign, or movement rather, before us which I dread as being full of unnecessary risks & of the kind that may produce the most terrible disaster. . . . I came near having what I should most have preferred a large column to move on the South Side of the James but that has been reduced to a force that can't do much good & may be swallowed up & is under Butler & is to move in the worst possible way.[47]

Butler's problems with Quincy Gillmore were of an entirely different sort. Although the campaign was to begin at any moment, Gillmore was still in South Carolina. Instead of hastening his departure for Virginia, his primary concern seemed to be the difficulty in getting Senate confirmation of his promotion to major general. If Gillmore's promotion were rejected, Alfred Terry would have to take over the X Corps, since his commission as brigadier general antedated Gillmore's. In a private letter, Gillmore's chief of staff, Brigadier General John Turner, suggested that Butler might wish to take some action in regard to Gillmore's confirmation problems, and he plainly stated that a "pointed note" to Grant was in order. Rather than bother Grant, Butler wrote to his friend Senator Henry Wilson, asking that the matter be tabled indefinitely if confirmation of Gillmore's promotion appeared doubtful.[48]

Much more troublesome than Gillmore's promotion was his continued delay in moving the X Corps to Virginia. Admittedly, his units had been widely dispersed when Halleck's order was received, but that excuse rapidly lost validity as April faded. Although Gillmore had initially hoped to have his command in Virginia by 20 April, at least two of his regiments were still in Florida on 23 April, and a number of others awaited instructions in South Carolina. The last large batch of movement orders for X Corps units was finally issued on 24 April, but Gillmore continued to remain at Hilton Head, dispatching individual units throughout the few remaining days of the month. On 27 April, he told a subordinate that he planned to relinquish command of the Department of the South "in a few days," but he still appeared to be in no hurry to leave South Carolina.[49]

Upon reaching Hampton Roads, Gillmore's units were directed up the York River to the X Corps staging area at Gloucester Point. There the new arrivals were astonished to find thousands of men already preparing for the offensive, their tents not only covering the plains around Gloucester, but whitening the ground across the river at Yorktown as well. There too, the newcomers invariably discovered some of their own comrades. At the time, it was customary to offer a furlough to veterans upon expiration of their three-year enlistments, if they would reenlist for the duration of the war. Many of Gillmore's men had reenlisted and were away on their leave when the X Corps was ordered to Virginia. When their furloughs expired, these men were sent first to Washington, D. C., and then to Gloucester Point. Therefore, the arrival of their parent units from the south usually meant a reunion of sorts between the reenlisted veterans and the men who would soon be leaving the army. If there were none of their own number to receive them, the regiments from the Department of the South were generally welcomed by units from their home states or units with whom they had served before.[50]

Other troops besides Gillmore's also arrived at the staging areas during the last days of April. On 26 April, Brigadier General Charles Heckman received orders to transfer his brigade from its camp near Portsmouth to Yorktown. As the soldiers prepared to move, tension began to grip many of them. Some went into a nearby settlement and "raised the mischief." Others proceeded to get drunk on cheap cider furnished by a willing sutler. More than two hundred men from Heckman's brigade and other commands attacked another sutler's tent with bricks, ostensibly because of the man's outrageous prices. These shenanigans resulted in closer supervision of the men by their officers and larger contingents of camp guards until the units moved out. When at last the tents of the troops were struck and carried away, these vague feelings of misgiving became acute. As Private Edmund Cleveland noted in his diary, after their tents were removed, "the boys have been uneasy and amusing themselves by building fires in the camp."[51]

As April waned, the tempo of activity accelerated in the sprawling tent cities lining both banks of the York River. Knapsacks were stored away and shelter tents were issued. All excess baggage was forbidden, causing both officers and men to winnow their personal effects for superfluous items, which would be packed and sent home. Regimental cooks lost most of their mess gear and regimental adjutants were forced to give up most of their record books and writing desks. All units that had managed to retain their dress coats and hats were required to send them away for storage. Replacing all this impedimenta were more useful items, such as two new pairs of army shoes for each man. At the same time, beef, beans, and potatoes disappeared from the menu and bacon and salt pork were substituted. Increasing amounts of time were occupied with drill, including special sessions for bayonet exercises and evolutions of the skirmish line. The men generally took it all in good part, joking that instead of being called the Army of the James, Butler's command would be more aptly named the "Army of the Games."[52]

The monotony of drills and inspections was relieved in several ways. One diversion was to visit friends or relatives in nearby regiments, or just to stroll through the various camps, gazing at such curiosities as the tame bear that was kept as a pet by a Pennsylvania regiment. If promenading grew tiresome, as it usually did after a time, there were occasional opportunities to tour nearby historic sites. Yorktown was the location of Cornwallis's surrender to Washington during the Revolution, as well as the site of McClellan's siege operations in 1862, and it was something of a tourist attraction.[53] The town itself made a very poor impression on the soldiers who visited it. One of them wrote that "Yorktown is hardly as much today as it was in the day of Cornwallis' surrender, and I don't think there has been a nail driven or an ounce of paint used since." Another, who had been there before, commented that "Yorktown has not improved much. The only improvement I can see is that half its buildings have been burned down."[54]

Perhaps the most common pastime was the writing of countless letters by men of all ranks to their friends in the North.[55] In a letter to his wife, Colonel Joseph Hawley, a brigade commander in the X Corps, expressed both his hopes and fears for the approaching campaign:

> A Waterloo summer, only one more momentous is before us. My hopes are cautious, yet I cannot help feeling that success is certain. . . . I pray God that I may do my duty. There may be days or minutes when we must toss away lives like chaff. I wish I felt less afraid to meet God.[56]

Many enlisted men wrote in an equally serious vein. Although they had no knowledge of the plan of campaign, they were vaguely aware that Richmond was to be their goal. All agreed that they faced a stern challenge and warned their correspondents accordingly.[57] For example, William Coley wrote his sister from Gloucester Point: "Frank[ly] I guess I shall see some hard times in Va. this Spring & Summer. For there has got to be some hard fighting in taking Richmond but I hope to come out all right."[58] Some were pessimistic about the forthcoming campaign. A cavalryman with Kautz confided to his father in New York: "I hope this campaign will end the struggle but have no hopes that it will. It is a crying shame that the resources of the country are wasted as they are."[59] Others took a more optimistic tone. One X Corps soldier boasted that his commanders "are making calculations to move forward this time with no idea of retreating," and one of Baldy Smith's men promised that "if I am lucky enough to live to go into Richmond my next letter may be dated there."[60]

By the end of April it was evident to all that the campaign would soon begin. Regimental officers who preferred staff jobs to field command buttonholed friends who could get them into such positions. Recruits and reenlisted veterans who continued to arrive were quickly directed to their units. Health inspections were conducted and men found to be unfit for strenuous campaigning were sent to hospitals. Final adjustments were made in the composition of brigades and divisions, while officers and men hurried to familiarize themselves with the new units recently brigaded with them. On 29 April, two deserters from the 2nd New Hampshire Regiment were executed, as an object lesson to those harboring similar inclinations.[61]

A Grand Review had been scheduled for 30 April, and the preceding days were filled with smaller brigade and division reviews that served as dress rehearsals. On the morning of the appointed day, several of the regiments were mustered for pay, after which all marched out to the review field. Butler and his staff reviewed Smith's XVIII Corps at Yorktown first, while X Corps units across the river at Gloucester paraded for Brigadier General Alfred Terry, since Gillmore was still in South Carolina. For the first time, the soldiers of the Army of the James were able to view themselves in all their might. As Colonel Hawley told his wife, "It was a splendid sight. The troops had no spare plumage for they are stripped for the fight, but the general appearance was grand."[62]

Having seen Smith's XVIII Corps, Butler took a steamer across the river to Gloucester Point where the X Corps under Terry had just finished its own private review. The presence of the commanding general required another performance, however, and the troops were put through their paces once again.[63] For some of the men, the review provided their first look at Butler, who was eclipsed by the more martial appearance of the officers who accompanied him. An enlisted man in the 10th New Hampshire Regiment noted that "Gen. Butler was dressed very plain wore a hat cocked up on one side with a plume on the other side No epilets but the commonest kind of shoulder straps."[64] Even more direct was a soldier in the 118th New York: "General Butler is not a strikingly graceful equestrian. His short, squat sort of figure looked like a hump on his horse."[65]

After the reviews, the weary and dusty troops were allowed to return to their camps, which many did not reach until sunset. Unknown to them, their time of preparation was almost over, for on 28 April U. S. Grant had written a letter to Butler announcing the date on which the spring campaign was to begin. If all went well, the Army of the James would sail up its namesake river on the night of 4 May 1864.[66]

NOTES

1. Mark Mayo Boatner, III, *The Civil War Dictionary* (New York: David McKay 1959), 775; James Harrison Wilson, *Under the Old Flag* (New York: D. Appleton, 1912), 1:271; Warner, *Generals in Blue*, 462–463; Catton, *Grant Takes Command*, 42; James Harrison Wilson, *Life and Services of William Farrar Smith, Major General, United States Volunteers in the Civil War* (Wilmington, Del.: The John M. Rogers Press, 1904), 31, 58.

2. Grant, *Personal Memoirs*, 2:35; Catton, *Grant Takes Command*, 45–46, 65; Warner, *Generals in Blue*, 463; Boatner, *Civil War Dictionary*, 775; Wilson, *Old Flag*, 1:315–316, 325; Wilson, *Life of Smith*, 82. Wilson was the chief sponsor of Smith for Meade's job. Catton, *Grant Takes Command*, 130. Allan Nevins, in *Organized War to Victory*, 8–9, is not sure that Wilson's testimony is enough firmly to establish this idea as Grant's, but T. Harry Williams, in *Lincoln and his Generals*, 292, readily accepts that it is.

3. Williams, *Lincoln and his Generals*, 292–293; Cyrus B. Comstock Diary, 11 March 1864, LC; Warner, *Generals in Blue*, 463; Grant, *Personal Memoirs*, 2:133; Wilson, *Life of Smith*, 69, 83–84; William Farrar Smith, *From Chattanooga to Petersburg Under Generals Grant and Butler* (Boston: Houghton, Mifflin and Company, 1893), 135.

4. Agassiz, ed., *Meade's Headquarters*, 148–149; Thomas L. Livermore, *Days and Events, 1860–1866* (Boston: Houghton Mifflin 1920), 372; Thomas W. Hyde, *Following the Greek Cross or, Memories of the Sixth Army Corps* (Boston: Houghton, Mifflin and Company, 1897), 117; James H. Wilson to Isaac J. Wistar, 11 May 1903, James Harrison Wilson Papers, Library of Congress.

5. Badeau, *Military History*, 2:358–359.

6. Butler, *Butler's Book*, 687. Smith, on the other hand, believed Butler did not reconnoiter enough. Smith, *From Chattanooga to Petersburg*, 153.

7. William Kreutzer, *Notes and Observations Made During Four Years of Service with the Ninety-Eighth N. Y. Volunteers, in the War of 1861* (Philadelphia: Grant, Faires & Rodgers, 1878), 177; Elbridge J. Copp, *Reminiscences of the War of the Rebellion, 1861–1865* (Nashua, N. H.: The Telegraph Publishing Company, 1911), 392.

8. William F. Smith to James H. Wilson, 16 March 1864, James Harrison Wilson Papers, LC; Wilson, *Old Flag*, 1:271.

9. Smith, *Battles and Leaders*, 4:206n.

10. John A. Rawlins to his wife, 13 April 1864, James Harrison Wilson Papers, LC.

11. *O.R.A.*, 33:861. Wilson, in *Life of Rawlins*, 207, speculated that Rawlins's attitude toward Smith and his plan may have "strengthened Grant's decision to attach Smith to Butler's army."

12. Smith, *From Chattanooga to Petersburg*, 136.

13. D. L. Day, *My Diary of Rambles with the 25th Mass. Volunteer Infantry, with Burnside's Coast Division; 18th Army Corps, and Army of the James* (Milford, Mass.: King & Billings, 1884), 109.

14. James Madison Drake, *The History of the Ninth New Jersey Veteran Vols.* (Elizabeth, N. J.: Journal Printing House, 1889), 345.

15. Alfred P. Rockwell, "The Tenth Army Corps in Virginia, May 1864," *Papers of the Military Historical Society of Massachusetts*, 14 vols. (Boston: The Military Historical Society of Massachusetts, 1912), 9:269.

16. Martin A. Haynes, *History of the Second Regiment New Hampshire Volunteers: its Camps, Marches and Battles* (Manchester, N. H.: Charles F. Livingston, 1865), 162–165; A. W. Bartlett, *History of the Twelfth Regiment New Hampshire Volunteers in the War of the Rebellion* (Concord, N. H.: Ira C. Evans, 1897), 169–170; Otis F. R. Waite, *New Hampshire in the Great Rebellion* (Norwich, Conn. & Concord, N. H.: J. H. Jewett & Company, 1873), 156; Isaac Jones Wistar, *Autobiography of Isaac Jones Wistar, 1827–1905: Half a Century in War and Peace* (Philadelphia: The Wistar Institute of Anatomy and Biology, 1937), 440–443; Martin A. Haynes, *A History of the Second Regiment, New Hampshire Volunteer Infantry, in the War of the Rebellion* (Lakeport, N. H., 1896), 215–216 [hereinafter cited as Haynes, *Second New Hampshire* (2)]; *O.R.A.*, 51, pt. 1, 1158; Edmund J. Cleveland, Jr., ed., "The Campaign of Promise and Disappointment—Diary of Private Edmund J. Cleveland," *Proceedings of the New Jersey Historical Society* 67 no. 3 (July 1949):234; John L. Cunningham, *Three Years with the Adirondack Regiment: 118th New York Volunteers Infantry* (Norwood, Mass.: The Plimpton Press, 1920), 98–100; S. Millet Thompson, *Thirteenth Regiment of New Hampshire Volunteer Infantry in the War of the Rebellion, 1861–1865* (Boston: Houghton, Mifflin and Company, 1888), 250.

17. *O.R.A.*, 33:814, 850, 865, 930–931; *O.R.A.*, 51, pt. 1, 1154; Jessie Ames Marshall, ed., *Private and Official Correspondence of Gen. Benjamin F. Butler During the Period of the Civil War*, 5 vols. (Norwood, Mass.: The Plimpton Press, 1917), 4:24, 43.

18. *O.R.A.*, 33:850, 862; Wilson, *Old Flag*, 1:360, 368.

19. Marshall, ed., *Butler's Correspondence*, 4:68; *O.R.A.*, 33:862, 865, 877, 879, 887, 895.

20. *O.R.A.*, 33:808–809, 824, 861, 876–877, 886, 914–915, 930, 938; Butler, *Butler's Book*, 639; Marshall, ed., *Butler's Correspondence*, 4:69, 90, 110, 120.

21. *O.R.N.*, 9:584.

22. *O.R.A.*, 33:814–815, 821; *O.R.N.*, 9:585, 610, 611.

23. *O.R.A.*, 33:834, 837, 850–851; *O.R.A.*, 51, pt. 1, 1157.

24. *O.R.A.*, 33:280–281, 837–838, 877–878, 895–896, 914, 938–939; Marshall, ed., *Butler's Correspondence*, 4:95; Grant, *Personal Memoirs*, 2:138; *O.R.A.*, 51, pt. 1, 1288.

25. *O.R.A.*, 33:312, 946–947, 966–969, 979, 990–991, 1031; Butler, *Butler's Book*, 636.

26. Marshall, ed., *Butler's Correspondence*, 4:76; Butler, *Butler's Book*, 636–637.

27. *O.R.A.*, 33:885–886.

28. Ibid., 904.

29. Theodore A. Dodge, "General Grant," in Theodore F. Dwight, ed., *Critical Sketches of Some of the Federal and Confederate Commanders* (Boston: Houghton, Mifflin and Company, 1895), 39. Grant's awareness in April of the importance of Petersburg cannot be conclusively demonstrated. Horace Porter of Grant's staff, in *Campaigning with Grant*, 36, wrote that Butler had been told to secure Petersburg, but this may have been based upon Grant's statement that he had pointed out verbally the importance of the city to Butler. The British military historian J. F. C. Fuller, in *The Generalship of Ulysses S. Grant* (New York: Dodd, Mead 1929), 219, admitted that Grant had neglected to emphasize the necessity of taking Petersburg in his written orders to Butler, but he maintained that such was still Grant's purpose. William

F. Smith, on the other hand, in his apologia, *From Chattanooga to Petersburg*, 129, spoke of Grant's "want of foresight . . . in not sooner discovering the importance of Petersburg." Theodore Dodge, in "General Grant," made the most perceptive statement when he wrote that "Grant's orders to Butler were very vague, and he could scarcely have supposed that Butler would look upon Petersburg as a *sine qua non* in his problem, even if the same orders to a more skilled soldier could be twisted into meaning so much."

30. O.R.A., 33:34–35; O.R.A., 35, pt. 2, 50–51, 804. Once they moved north, most of Gillmore's troops arrived at Fort Monroe in three days. Stephen Walkley, *History of the Seventh Connecticut Volunteer Infantry* (Southington, Conn., 1905), 129; James H. Clark, *The Iron Hearted Regiment: Being an Account of the Battles, Marches and Gallant Deeds Performed by the 115th N. Y. Vols.* (Albany, N. Y.: J. Munsell, 1865), 102.

31. O.R.A., 35, pt. 2, 49–51; Daniel Eldredge, *The Third New Hampshire and All About It* (Boston: E. B. Stillings and Company, 1893), 451; Rockwell, "Tenth Army Corps," 268; Clark, *Iron Hearted Regiment*, 102; Walkley, *Seventh Connecticut*, 124; W. A. Croffut and John M. Morris, *The Military and Civil History of Connecticut During the War of 1861–65* (New York: Ledyard Bill, 1868), 537; James M. Nichols, *Perry's Saints or the Fighting Parson's Regiment in the War of the Rebellion* (Boston: D. Lothrop and Company, 1886), 199–200.

32. O.R.A., 33:878, 887, 896, 905; O.R.A., 35, pt. 2, 58, 59; Marshall, ed., *Butler's Correspondence*, 4:86, 110.

33. Eldredge, *Third New Hampshire*, 451–453; Henry F. W. Little, *The Seventh Regiment New Hampshire Volunteers in the War of the Rebellion* (Concord, N. H.: Ira C. Evans, 1896), 236–238; William H. Cooley [Coley] to his sister, 21 April 1864, William Henry Cooley Letters, Southern Historical Collection, University of North Carolina, Chapel Hill, N.C.; Clark, *Iron Hearted Regiment*, 102; Herbert W. Beecher, *History of the First Light Battery Connecticut Volunteers, 1861–1865*, 2 vols. (New York: A. T. de la Mare, 1901), 1:322–324.

34. Beecher, *First Connecticut Light Battery*, 1:324; Little, *Seventh New Hampshire*, 238; Clark, *Iron Hearted Regiment*, 102; William L. Hyde, *History of the One Hundred and Twelfth Regiment N. Y. Volunteers* (Fredonia, N. Y.: W. McKinstry & Co., 1866), 73.

35. O.R.N., 9:606–607, 630; Marshall, ed., *Butler's Correspondence*, 4:56, 62, 63; Gideon Welles, *Diary of Gideon Welles*, 3 vols. (Boston: Houghton Mifflin, 1911), 2:9–10; O.R.A., 33:843. The diplomatic aspects of this controversy have been traced in Daniel B. Carroll, *Henri Mercier and the American Civil War* (Princeton: Princeton University Press, 1971), 329–336.

36. O.R.A., 33:849, 896, 1018; Marshall, ed., *Butler's Correspondence*, 4:65, 116, 117, 125–126; John Beauchamp Jones, *A Rebel War Clerk's Diary at the Confederate States Capital*, 2 vols. (Philadelphia: J. B. Lippincott and Co., 1866), 2:193; Edward Younger, ed., *Inside the Confederate Government: The Diary of Robert Garlick Hill Kean, Head of the Bureau of War* (New York: Oxford University Press, 1957), 146–147; *New York Times*, 2 May 1864.

37. O.R.N., 9:690–694, 697; Marshall, ed., *Butler's Correspondence*, 4:77–78, 131–132, 139. Osborn appears on an 1861 Federal map reproduced in Calvin D. Cowles, ed., *Atlas to Accompany the Official Records of the Union and Confederate Armies* Reprint ed., (New York: Thomas Yoseloff, 1958), plate 16, as well as on two Confederate maps in the J. F. Gilmer Papers, SHC. It was located just upstream of the Howlett property, upon which Confederate Battery Dantzler was later constructed.

38. O.R.N., 9:693; Marshall, ed., *Butler's Correspondence*, 4:139–140; Butler, *Butler's Book*, 638. Devices known as torpedoes during the Civil War would be considered mines in modern terminology.

39. O.R.N., 9:690–691, 703, 705, 709–710, 809.

40. Welles, *Welles Diary*, 2:19.

41. Robert E. Lee was an avid reader of Northern papers, which furnished him many clues to Federal movements and intentions. O.R.A., 33:1268–1269, 1272, 1276, 1331–1332.

42. Marshall, ed., *Butler's Correspondence*, 4:135, 136.

43. William H. Stiner to Frederic Hudson, 21 April 1864, James Gordon Bennett Papers, Library of Congress, Washington, D.C. This policy of accommodation had apparently been adopted by *Herald* employees in all theaters, and at times it brought dividends in terms of preferred treatment. Andrews, *North Reports the Civil War*, 68.

44. O.R.A., 33:930–931, 1013; August V. Kautz, "First Attempts to Capture Petersburg," in *Battles and Leaders of the Civil War*, Ed. Robert U. Johnson and Clarence C. Buel (New York: The Century Company, 1884, 1888), 4:533–534; "Brigadier General A. V. Kautz in the Great Rebellion," August V. Kautz Papers, Library of Congress, Washington, D.C.; Rowland Minturn Hall to his father, 16 April 1864, Julia Ward Stickley Collection, North Carolina Division of Archives and History, Raleigh, N.C.

45. "Kautz in the Great Rebellion," Kautz Papers, LC; Marshall, ed., *Butler's Correspondence*, 4:133.

46. Smith's letter has not been located, but it can be reconstructed from Babcock's reply in O.R.A., 33:1019.

47. William F. Smith to William B. Franklin, 28 April 1864, William B. Franklin Papers, Library of Congress, Washington, D.C.

48. Marshall, ed., *Butler's Correspondence*, 4:108; O.R.A., 33:959.

49. O.R.A., 35, pt. 2, 50–51, 68, 71, 73, 75–77; Isaiah Price, *History of the Ninety-Seventh Regiment, Pennsylvania Infantry, During the War of the Rebellion, 1861–65* (Philadelphia: B. & P. Printers, 1875), 245; Alfred S. Roe, *The Twenty-Fourth Regiment Massachusetts Volunteers, 1861–1866* (Worcester, Mass.: The Blanchard Press, 1907), 273; Eldredge, *Third New Hampshire*, 453; Charles K. Cadwell, *The Old Sixth Regiment, its War Record, 1861–5* (New Haven: Tuttle, Morehouse, & Taylor, 1875), 87.

50. George H. Stowits, *History of the One Hundredth Regiment of New York State Volunteers* (Buffalo, N. Y.: Matthews & Warren, 1870), 236–237; J. A. Mowris, *A History of the One Hundred and Seventeenth Regiment, N. Y. Volunteers* (Hartford, Conn.: Case, Lockwood and Company, 1866), 98–99; Price, *Ninety–Seventh Pennsylvania*, 246–248; Little, *Seventh New Hampshire*, 235–236; O.R.A., 33:940, 946; Marshall, ed., *Butler's Correspondence*, 4:132; Croffut and Morris, *Connecticut During the War*, 537; Roe, *Twenty-Fourth Massachusetts*, 271, 273; Eldredge, *Third New Hampshire*, 453; William E. S. Whitman and Charles H. True, *Maine in the War for the Union: A History of the Part Borne by Maine Troops in the Suppression of the American Rebellion* (Lewiston, Me.: Nelson Dingley Jr. & Co., 1865), 201, 220–221; Harvey Clark, *My Experience with Burnside's Expedition and 18th Army Corps* (Gardner, Mass., 1914), 54.

51. O.R.A., 51, pt. 1, 1160; Drake, *Ninth New Jersey*, 169; Herbert E. Valentine, *Story of Co. F, 23d Massachusetts Volunteers in the War for the Union, 1861–1865* (Boston: W. B. Clarke & Co., 1896), 105; Cleveland, ed., "Campaign of Promise," 235–237.

52. Drake, *Ninth New Jersey*, 169, 343–344; Hermann Everts, *A Complete and Comprehensive History of the Ninth Regiment New Jersey Vols. Infantry* (Newark, N. J.: A. Stephen Holbrook, 1865), 103; Valentine, *Story of Co. F*, 105–106; Day, *Rambles*, 137; W. P. Derby, *Bearing Arms in the Twenty-Seventh Massachusetts Regiment of Volunteer Infantry During the Civil War, 1861–1865* (Boston: Wright & Potter Printing Company, 1883), 245; James A. Emmerton, *A Record of the Twenty-Third Regiment Mass. Vol. Infantry in the War of the Rebellion, 1861–1865* (Boston: William Ware & Co., 1886), 171; Cleveland, ed., "Campaign of Promise," 237–239; Samuel H. Putnam, *The Story of Company A, Twenty-Fifth Regiment, Mass. Vols., in the War of the Rebellion* (Worcester, Mass.: Putnam, Davis and Company, 1886), 261; Stowits, *One Hundredth New York*, 244–245; Copp, *Reminiscences*, 335–336; Bartlett, *Twelfth New Hampshire*, 170; Kreutzer, *Ninety-Eighty New York*, 180; Clark, *Iron Hearted Regiment*, 103; Little, *Seventh New Hampshire*, 240–241; Beecher, *First Connecticut Light Battery*, 1:327–328; Nichols, *Perry's Saints*, 200–203; Eldredge, *Third New Hampshire*, 455; Cadwell, *Old Sixth*, 88; Price, *Ninety-Seventh Pennsylvania*, 249, 412; Cunningham, *Adirondack Regiment*, 99; Thompson, *Thirteenth New Hampshire*, 252–254.

53. B. S. De Forest, *Random Sketches and Wandering Thoughts* (Albany, N. Y.: Avery Herrick, 1866), 144–145; Mowris, *One Hundred and Seventeenth New York*, 99; Beecher, *First Connecticut Light Battery*, 1:327; Putnam, *Story of Company A*, 261–262.

54. Day, *Rambles*, 137; Robert Brady, *The Story of One Regiment: The Eleventh Maine Infantry Volunteers in the War of the Rebellion* (New York: J. J. Little & Co., 1896), 167.

55. Thompson, *Thirteenth New Hampshire*, 252.

56. Joseph R. Hawley to his wife, 25 April 1864, Joseph R. Hawley Papers, Library of Congress, Washington, D.C.

57. Copp, *Reminiscences*, 336; William H. Coley to his parents, 20 April 1864, William H. Cooley [Coley] Letters, SHC; Alfred Otis Chamberlin to his parents, 28 April 1864, Alfred Otis Chamberlin Papers, Duke University, Durham, N.C.

58. William H. Coley to his sister, 21 April 1864, William H. Cooley [Coley] Letters, SHC.

59. Rowland Minturn Hall to his father, 16 April 1864, Julia Ward Stickley Collection, NCDAH.

60. John B. Foote to his sister, 26 April 1864, John B. Foote Papers, Duke University, Durham, N.C.; Josiah Wood to "Rana," 28 April 1864, Josiah Wood Papers, Duke University, Durham, N.C.

61. Price, *Ninety-Seventh Pennsylvania*, 248; Livermore, *Days and Events*, 331–333; Brady, *Eleventh Maine*, 168–169; Mowris, *One Hundred and Seventeenth New York*, 99; Emmerton, *Twenty-Third Massachusetts*, 171; Thompson, *Thirteenth New Hampshire*, 252; Luther S. Dickey, *History of the Eighty-Fifth Regiment Pennsylvania Volunteer Infantry, 1861–1865* (New York: J. C. & W. E. Powers, 1915), 314; Haynes, *Second New Hampshire* (2), 216; Bartlett, *Twelfth New Hampshire*, 170–171.

62. Thompson, *Thirteenth New Hampshire*, 254–255; Everts, *Comprehensive History*, 103; Drake,

Ninth New Jersey, 170; Emmerton, *Twenty-Third Massachusetts,* 172; Clark, *My Experience,* 55; Isaac C. Richardson to _____, 13–31 April 1864, Isaac C. Richardson Letters, SHC; Eldredge, *Third New Hampshire,* 455; Roe, *Twenty-Fourth Massachusetts,* 271–272; Valentine, *Story of Co. F,* 106; Clark, *Iron Hearted Regiment,* 103; Little, *Seventh New Hampshire,* 241; Walkley, *Seventh Connecticut,* 129; Cleveland, ed., "Campaign of Promise," 239; Beecher, *First Connecticut Light Battery,* 1:328–329; Joseph R. Hawley to his wife, 1 May 1864, Hawley Papers, LC.

63. Eldredge, *Third New Hampshire,* 455; Roe, *Twenty-Fourth Massachusetts,* 271–272.

64. Isaac C. Richardson to _____, 13–31 April 1864, Isaac C. Richardson Letters, SHC.

65. Cunningham, *Adirondack Regiment,* 99.

66. Valentine, *Story of Co. F,* 106; Roe, *Twenty-Fourth Massachusetts,* 272; Price, *Ninety-Seventh Pennsylvania,* 249; O.R.A., 33:1009; Grant, *Personal Memoirs,* 2:140.

☆ 3 ☆

Confederate Defensive Arrangements
1–30 April 1864

Massive Federal preparations around Hampton Roads in April did not go un-noticed by the Confederates. The first sign had been Grant's visit to Fort Monroe, reported by Confederate Robert Ould, who had been at the fort arranging a prisoner exchange. Ould's report had been independently confirmed by Con-federate agents, who passed the information by boat to the south bank of the James River, where Signal Corps detachments transmitted it to Richmond.[1] There the reports were distributed to Secretary of War Seddon, General Braxton Bragg, the president's military adviser, President Jefferson Davis, and to the commander of the Army of Northern Virginia, Robert E. Lee.

During the 1860s generals were required to make their own analyses of raw intelligence data, and Robert E. Lee was one of the shrewder practitioners of the art. By 6 April, Lee knew of Grant's recent visit to Butler's command. On 8 April, three days before Quincy Gillmore learned the destination of the X Corps, Lee notified Davis that a transfer of Federal troops from South Carolina to Fort Monroe was "very probable." The following day Lee read in a Northern paper of Baldy Smith's assignment to Butler's command, and concluded "that operations are contemplated from that quarter, which they do not wish to trust to General Butler." On 11 April, the very day that Gillmore received his travel orders from Halleck, Lee informed a neighboring commander of Gillmore's assignment to join Butler and Smith. Consequently he advised Major General George Pickett, com-manding in southern Virginia, to strengthen the defenses of Petersburg as quickly as possible. On 12 April, he wrote to Davis about the movement of Federal ships:

> If they are preparing armed transports and launches for disembarking troops I think they can only be intended for the James River. . . . We should be prepared in that quarter. A landing may be intended at City Point to capture Drewry's Bluff.[2]

Since Lee had no command responsibility beyond the bounds of the Army of Northern Virginia, he commented on affairs below Richmond in an advisory

43

capacity only. South of Lee were several departments, whose commanders reported only to Bragg, Seddon, and Davis. The Confederate capital and its immediate environs constituted the Department of Richmond, under the command of Major General Robert Ransom.[3] Below Ransom's department was the Department of North Carolina, which extended from south of the James River (although its exact boundary with Ransom's command was unclear) to the northern border of South Carolina. Carved from this department was the District of the Cape Fear, which controlled the defenses of the port of Wilmington. Major General George Pickett commanded the Department of North Carolina, while Major General W. H. C. Whiting handled affairs at Wilmington.[4]

The posts occupied by Ransom and Whiting had a virtue not shared by Pickett's Department of North Carolina: they were both small areas that could be easily supervised. George Pickett had to defend the railroad center of Petersburg and the Blackwater River line that blocked a Federal advance from Norfolk, while also containing Federal sorties from New Berne, Plymouth, and Washington, North Carolina. To accomplish these diverse tasks, Pickett could call upon the three North Carolina infantry brigades of Brigadier Generals Matt Ransom, Thomas Clingman, and Robert Hoke, the Virginia infantry brigades of Brigadier General Montgomery Corse and Colonel William R. Terry, several cavalry regiments and artillery batteries, as well as a few miscellaneous units. In late February 1864, the date of the last extant return, Pickett's command had numbered approximately 13,500 officers and men.[5]

A professional soldier, Pickett had risen above a poor class standing at West Point through conspicuous service in the west before the outbreak of the Civil War. After Fort Sumter, Pickett had gone with his native Virginia into the Confederacy, and he had been rewarded in due course with a brigadier general's commission. In the Southern army, he had gained a well-deserved reputation for vanity and flamboyance, and a widespread name as a combat leader. Badly wounded at Gaines's Mill in 1862, he had returned to the army as a major general after his convalescence. His great moment had come on 3 July 1863, at Gettysburg, but the famous charge that bore his name had apparently taken something out of him. In order to rebuild his shattered division, Pickett had been detached from the Army of Northern Virginia, and late in September of 1863 he had been assigned at the age of thirty-nine to command the Department of North Carolina. Although his new post permitted him to enjoy the prerogatives of a garrison commander as well as the companionship of his young wife, it was still a far cry from leading a division in Longstreet's Corps of the Army of Northern Virginia.[6]

Ever since his assignment to the department, Pickett had been concerned about the inadequacy of its defenses. Realizing that the Federals could use the James River to outflank the Blackwater defenses and thrust directly at Petersburg and Richmond, Pickett began to bombard the War Department with requests for reinforcements. When his letters brought no satisfaction, he sought personal meetings with the secretaries of war and the navy. These interviews resulted in vague promises but no action of consequence, which forced Pickett to fall back upon his last hope,

Robert E. Lee. Lee advised Pickett to confer with his fellow department commander to the south, General P. G. T. Beauregard. According to a member of Pickett's staff, a conference was arranged, but again nothing tangible resulted.[7] By April 1864, Pickett had become resigned to defending his large department on a shoestring.

Pickett's hopes for continued Federal inaction in his department began to dim as the month of April passed. On 13 April 1864, Confederate agents on the Peninsula reported that most of the Federal troops at Yorktown had departed for Portsmouth, after giving the impression that the coming campaign would take place in North Carolina. This information was contradicted on the following day by Federal deserters who stated that General Ambrose Burnside was concentrating troops at Williamsburg "for an advance up the Peninsula." From the Blackwater line came news of a Federal probe near the village of Franklin. As the day of 14 April progressed, other Blackwater posts reported sizable Federal forces in motion near Suffolk and Chuckatuck. These Federal troops were said to be the advance elements of Burnside's corps, and their ultimate destination was believed to be Weldon, North Carolina. All of these reports were collected by Pickett, who dutifully forwarded them to Braxton Bragg in Richmond.[8]

What Pickett's scouts and agents reported as Burnside's corps were the various units Butler had sent into the territory west and south of Hampton Roads at the request of Admiral Lee. In actuality Burnside remained the whole time with his corps at Annapolis, Maryland, preparing to join the Army of the Potomac. After a few days the temporary nature of Butler's demonstration became increasingly obvious, although Confederate scouts continued to report to Pickett that Burnside's goal was Weldon.[9] By this time Braxton Bragg had become impatient with the flow of contradictory information from Pickett and he warned the department commander "of the evil resulting from exaggerated or unreliable reports," which were "so contradictory as to render them all useless, if not injurious." This rebuke distressed Pickett, who replied that he was only following Bragg's instructions to keep him informed.[10]

Almost as suddenly as it had begun, the stream of misleading reports regarding Federal intentions was replaced by relatively accurate information, although Confederate analysts were unaware of the change. On 17 April Secretary of War Seddon sent Bragg a letter from a Confederate agent in the North that accurately described Grant's offensive plan in Virginia, including Butler's route and destination. Shortly thereafter, Pickett reported the results of a reconnaissance beyond the Blackwater line that correctly explained the recent flurry of Federal activity.[11] At the same time the Signal Corps emphatically stated that the units participating in Butler's probe were not Burnside's. The Signal Corps also noted that "the plan of landing on the south side of the James River, above the Appomattox, is still freely discussed."[12] Such excellent information, however, was forced to compete for attention with other accounts that stated that Burnside had left Portsmouth on his way to Weldon, and that only five hundred Federals were at Yorktown.[13]

All of these reports weighed heavily upon Pickett's mind, since most of his mobile units were not in position to repel a Federal offensive from Hampton Roads. Three of his brigades, along with supporting units, were concentrating around the Federal garrison at Plymouth, North Carolina. Pickett had planned the expedition, but, because of his lackluster performance during a similar offensive against New Berne in February, he had been relegated to the role of rear-area coordinator. Instead, Brigadier General Robert Hoke had been assigned the field command under the direct control of Braxton Bragg. Even worse, in Pickett's view, was the timing of the Plymouth attack. With Butler's forces in Virginia stirring, the Plymouth affair effectively removed most of Pickett's troops from the area of greatest danger in order to pursue an objective of limited value. [14] Fortunately for Pickett, on 15 April the War Department decided to remove the burden of responsibility from his shoulders by replacing him with General P. G. T. Beauregard.

Only six weeks away from his forty-sixth birthday when he accepted Richmond's call to relieve Pickett, Pierre Gustave Toutant Beauregard was already one of the most famous soldiers in the Confederacy. A volatile Creole from Louisiana, he had parlayed a high class standing at West Point into an assignment to the Engineers, the branch in which he pursued his career. During the war with Mexico he had served on Winfield Scott's staff, winning the praise of his superiors and two brevet promotions, as well as receiving two wounds. The interwar years had seen Beauregard supervising such varied projects as Mississippi River channel improvements and the construction of a new customs house at New Orleans. In early 1861 he had briefly been Superintendent of West Point, but the rush of events had brought a sudden end to that assignment. [15]

Resigning from the U. S. Army, Beauregard had quickly gained an appointment as a brigadier general in the Southern forces and an assignment to duty at Charleston, South Carolina, where the Fort Sumter situation was still unresolved. A victory there in April 1861 had begun Beauregard's rise to fame, and this was followed by another success at First Bull Run. This triumph had in turn brought Beauregard one of the coveted promotions to full general, dating from 21 July 1861. The following year Beauregard had been transferred to the Western Theater under Albert Sidney Johnston, and he had assumed command of the Army of the Mississippi upon Johnston's death at Shiloh. He had then supervised the Confederate retreat into Mississippi, until relieved of army command while recuperating from illness. Reassigned to Charleston as commander of the Department of South Carolina, Georgia, and Florida, Beauregard had conducted a successful defense of the city against Gillmore's X Corps and a powerful Federal fleet. [16]

Beauregard's physical appearance complemented his service record. According to his biographer, T. Harry Williams:

> Nearly all observers noted that he looked French or foreign. He was five feet seven in height and weighed about one hundred and fifty pounds. He had dark hair and eyes and a sallow, olive complexion. His features were marked by a broad brow, high cheekbones, a cropped mustache, and a protruding chin. His eyes fascinated most people; large, melancholy, with drooping lids, they were likened by one man to the eyes of a bloodhound with his fighting instincts

asleep but ready to leap into instant action. In manner he was courteous, grave, sometimes reserved and severe, sometimes abrupt with people who displeased him. His expression was fixed, impassive; associates saw him go for months without smiling.[17]

In 1861 Beauregard's hair had been black, but by 1864 it had turned white, due either to strain or, as others uncharitably said, to the scarcity of imported dye.[18]

Since boyhood Beauregard had taken Napoleon Bonaparte as his ideal. This conscious projection was mirrored in all facets of his life and career, but it was most evident in his strategic thought. Both Napoleon and Baron Henri Jomini, who had enshrined Bonaparte's theories in print, were staunch advocates of the principle of concentration, and Beauregard emulated them by raising this doctrine into the cardinal tenet of his craft. Unfortunately, he usually encountered difficulty in implementing the principle in practice whenever he drew up a detailed plan. In fact Beauregard had become known for the fantastic, grandiose strategic plans that he periodically forwarded to his superiors. All of the plans advocated concentrating the Confederacy's meager resources to deal with particular Federal threats and rejected, by implication, the prevailing strategy of the Davis administration, which was to defend everything. The plans had always been disapproved, to the detriment of Beauregard's reputation within the Confederate government.[19]

Once he gave up the formulation of grand strategy, Beauregard measurably improved as a combat commander. According to his biographer, "He might be theatrical and theoretical before a fight, but when he went in he went in hard."[20] Even so, Beauregard handled troops well only when they remained within his line of sight. Hampered by his inability to visualize conditions and situations beyond his immediate purview, and given less than outstanding help by an often indifferent staff, Beauregard sometimes lost opportunities to turn partial victories into crushing ones. Nor could he improvise quickly when his initial plans ceased to be applicable to the rapidly changing realities of the battlefield.[21] Yet even with these faults Beauregard was a more than adequate general. In the words of T. Harry Williams: "Perhaps a New York reporter who interviewed him after the war had it right. He said that Beauregard was not a first-class military man but a first-rate second-class man."[22]

By accepting assignment to a department adjoining the Confederate capital, Beauregard came in close proximity to two of his most bitter enemies, Jefferson Davis and Braxton Bragg. The feud with Bragg dated from 1861 when Bragg, a North Carolinian, had been given command of all Louisiana forces, an assignment that Beauregard thought should have been his. The split between the two men widened following the battle of Shiloh, when Bragg blamed Beauregard for the Confederate failure, and it became virtually impossible to bridge after Bragg replaced Beauregard as commander of the Army of Tennessee in mid-1862.[23] Jefferson Davis's obvious favoritism toward Bragg increased Beauregard's hostility, since he and Davis also strongly disliked one another. Much of Beauregard's difficulty with Davis apparently sprang from the personalities of the two men. Beauregard's penchant for bombarding the government with poorly formulated plans called forth equally vitriolic missives from the president rejecting the schemes out of hand.[24] In time Davis's attitude came to penetrate even the middle levels of the Confederate government, causing a clerk in the War Department to observe that "all the military and civil functionaries near the government partake of something of a dislike of [Beauregard]."[25]

Upon notifying the War Department that he was willing to relieve Pickett, Beauregard was instructed to proceed to Weldon, North Carolina, where he would receive further instructions. Before his departure he learned that his new command would be enlarged by the addition of Major General W. H. C. Whiting's District of the Cape Fear. Upon his arrival at Weldon on 22 April, Beauregard found no instructions from Richmond awaiting him. In two telegrams to Bragg, he asked for a pocket map of his new domain, a definition of the limits of the department, and an estimate of the forces at his disposal. Bragg replied that a staff officer who could supply the answers to those questions was on the way to Weldon. The next day, 23 April 1864, P. G. T. Beauregard officially assumed command of the Department of North Carolina and Cape Fear, which he immediately renamed the Department of North Carolina and Southern Virginia. The enlarged department consisted of Virginia south of the James and Appomattox Rivers, and North Carolina east of the mountains. Department headquarters would be at Weldon until further notice.[26]

Beauregard's most pressing task was to familiarize himself with the strength and location of the units under his command. George Pickett, now nominally commanding only a district, held Petersburg with only a few men, while another handful guarded the Blackwater defense line. In North Carolina, one small regiment garrisoned Weldon, two held Wilmington, and two hundred men were at Goldsboro. There were three regiments of infantry at Plymouth, and two more guarded prisoners at Tarboro. The bulk of Beauregard's troops were either moving toward Washington, North Carolina, under Robert Hoke (sixteen infantry regiments, one cavalry regiment, and twenty-five artillery pieces) or threatening New Berne (seven infantry regiments, most of a cavalry regiment and another twenty-five guns).[27]

Beauregard had opposed the deployment of valuable troops against the small Federal enclaves in coastal North Carolina even before he came to Weldon, and he continued his opposition after assuming his new command. With the Federals stirring in Hampton Roads and Burnside's corps poised at Annapolis, Beauregard wanted his mobile units deployed so as to be able to counter any Federal offensive. Consequently, on 25 April, he wrote to Bragg regarding the dispersed nature of his units, the probability of a Federal offensive, and the fact that the Confederate drives on Washington and New Berne were behind schedule. Beauregard refrained from directly seeking permission to cancel the expeditions already in progress, but his disapproval of them was obvious.[28]

In the same letter Beauregard proposed dividing his sprawling department into three military districts: the First, under Pickett at Petersburg, extending from the James River to the Roanoke River; the Second, with neither commander nor headquarters specified, extending from the Roanoke River to the Neuse River in

North Carolina; and the Third, under Whiting at Wilmington, covering the area from the Neuse River to Cape Fear. Beauregard estimated that an adequate defense of the department would require a total of 23,000 mobile troops, roughly divided by districts into groups of 10,000 for the First, 8,000 for the Second, and 5,000 for the Third. While the letter was in transit, Beauregard pointedly suggested by telegram that certain units from his old department should join him. These included Henry Wise's Virginia Brigade, and either Alfred Colquitt's Georgia Brigade or Johnson Hagood's South Carolina Brigade.[29]

Coincidentally or not, action accompanied Beauregard's request for reinforcements, although the War Department believed the units would eventually be assigned to the army of Robert E. Lee. Orders were issued for Colquitt's Brigade to entrain for Wilmington, but before it could depart, Hagood's Brigade was substituted. This outfit began to leave Charleston on 28 April, but would not be concentrated at Wilmington until 4 May. Wise's Virginians were ordered northward on 30 April, confirming a rumor already current among the soldiers, but Beauregard was told to send them on to Richmond. A similar directive on the same day ordered Hagood's men, still en route for Wilmington, to continue to Richmond as well. Furthermore, if Hoke was making no progress against New Berne, he was to go north too. What had begun as a movement to give Beauregard additional forces thus became the opposite, with Beauregard's command being stripped so that troops could be concentrated in central Virginia for the defense of Richmond.[30]

Beauregard agreed with the Davis administration that the general direction of Confederate troop movements should be northward, but he wished to retain some of the units to meet the growing Federal threat to his First Military District. As early as 25 April, Beauregard suggested to Bragg that Petersburg was at least an intermediate goal of the coming Federal offensive. "Are we prepared to resist him in that direction? Can the forces of this Dept. be concentrated in time, are questions worthy of immediate consideration by the War Department."[31] From Wilmington this analysis was seconded by Major General W. H. C. Whiting, who offered to take the matter directly to Bragg and expressed a desire to lead some of Beauregard's troops in the field, should an opportunity present itself. In order to be fully prepared for a Federal advance against Petersburg, Beauregard carefully studied maps of the area and dispatched his engineer, Colonel D. B. Harris, to Pickett's headquarters. Harris was to inspect Petersburg's defenses and reconnoiter positions such as Bermuda Hundred and Fort Powhatan.[32]

Reinforcing Beauregard's theory about Petersburg was some excellent intelligence from Confederate scouts. On 25 April a Confederate boatman reported that up to sixty thousand Federal troops were concentrated on the Peninsula in the vicinity of Yorktown and Williamsburg, many having just arrived by sea. Two days later George Pickett informed Beauregard that although Federal security was tight, two of his agents had been able to penetrate Butler's lines and two more would soon follow. Pickett concluded: "The enemy will either advance up the Peninsula or will move by transports down river and up the James." Beauregard believed that the scouts' reports were exaggerated in terms of numbers, but he did not take the Federal threat lightly. Pickett was therefore authorized to address significant reports directly to Richmond, rather than routing them the normal way through Beauregard's head-quarters at Weldon.[33]

On 28 April Pickett sent both Bragg and Beauregard a report that the number of Federal ships anchored off Newport News had increased by two-thirds, to nine gunboats and nineteen transports. This unusual concentration of shipping was soon ascribed to adverse weather conditions, but a very detailed report transmitted by the Signal Corps could not be so easily discounted. This document estimated Federal strength on the Peninsula to be at least thirty thousand men, noted the presence of Negro regiments and units lately in the Norfolk defenses, stated that Baldy Smith was in command, and emphasized the presence of a double-turreted monitor among Admiral Lee's warships.[34] With the Federal lines becoming in-creasingly difficult to penetrate, on 29 April Beauregard ordered Pickett to mount a reconnaissance from the Blackwater line toward Suffolk and Portsmouth in an effort to obtain information regarding Federal intentions. As the expedition departed, Pickett forwarded another estimate placing thirty thousand Federals on the Penin-sula, and an officer on the Blackwater sent word that Federal troops from North Carolina were arriving in Norfolk by canal.[35]

Although imperfect, Beauregard's information was much better than that reach-ing Robert E. Lee, who earlier had been so accurate in estimating Federal inten-tions. Much of Lee's intelligence data came either from the famed leader of irregulars, John S. Mosby, or from scouts belonging to J. E. B. Stuart's cavalry. These sources indicated that although river traffic down the Potomac was heavy, nothing more than a feint was intended on the Peninsula.[36] Relying upon this analysis, Lee wrote Davis on 30 April: "There will no doubt be a strong demonstra-tion made north or south of the James River, which Beauregard will be able to successfully resist." Therefore Lee advocated bringing most of Beauregard's troops north to reinforce the Army of Northern Virginia.[37]

The possibility that most of his meager force might soon find itself operating north of the James River had also occurred to Beauregard, who informed Bragg that he needed maps of that area. He concluded:

> I take this opportunity to remark that should the operations of the coming campaign make it necessary that I should be placed immediately under the orders of that distinguished officer, General R. E. Lee, I would take pleasure in aiding him to crush our enemies and to achieve the independence of our country.

This letter eventually reached Jefferson Davis, whose endorsement read in part: "I did not doubt the readiness of General Beauregard to serve under any general who ranks him. The right of General Lee to command would be derived from his superior rank."[38] Such pettiness only rendered the task facing a badly outnumbered Confederacy even more difficult.

NOTES

1. O.R.A., 51, pt. 2, 846–849.
2. O.R.A., 33:1265, 1267–1269, 1272–1274, 1276.
3. Ransom replaced Major General Arnold Elzey on 25 April. O.R.A., 33:1312.
4. Walter Harrison, Pickett's Men: A Fragment of War History (New York: D. Van Nostrand, 1870), 121; Douglas Southall Freeman, Lee's Lieutenants: A Study in Command 3 vols. (New York: Charles Scribner's Sons, 1944), 3:451–452. Clifford Dowdey, Lee's Last Campaign (Boston: Little, Brown, 1960), 228–231, strongly indicts the department system as a source of Confederate defeat, and blames Davis for the rigidity of the system.
5. O.R.A., 33:1201–1202.
6. Dowdey, Lee's Last Campaign, 231, 233–234; Boatner, Civil War Dictionary, 651–652; Ezra J. Warner, Generals in Gray: Lives of the Confederate Commanders (Baton Rouge: Louisiana State University Press, 1959), 238–239.
7. Harrison, Pickett's Men, 121–122; LaSalle Corbell Pickett, Pickett and his Men, 2nd ed., (Atlanta: The Foote & Davies Company, 1900), 325–326, 338.
8. O.R.A., 51, pt. 2, 858, 861, 862.
9. Ibid., 862–863, 867–868.
10. Ibid., 863–865.
11. Ibid., 864–869.
12. O.R.A., 33:1292–1293.
13. O.R.A., 51, pt. 2, 871. This report came through the Department of Richmond.
14. Pickett, Pickett and his Men, 337, 339; Freeman, Lee's Lieutenants, 3:335.
15. T. Harry Williams, P. G. T. Beauregard: Napoleon in Gray (Baton Rouge: Louisiana State University Press, 1955), 5–47; Warner, Generals in Gray, 22; Boatner, Civil War Dictionary, 54–55.
16. Williams, Beauregard, 47–205; Warner, Generals in Gray, 22–23; Boatner, Civil War Dictionary, 55; Freeman, Lee's Lieutenants, 3:450.
17. Williams, Beauregard, 51.
18. Ibid., 52–53.
19. Ibid., 5, 69, 71, 75, 93–94. See also George A. Bruce, "General Butler's Bermuda Campaign," Papers of the Military Historical Society of Massachusetts 14 vols. (Boston: Military Historical Society of Massachusetts, 1912), 9:332.
20. Williams, Beauregard, 235.
21. Ibid., 33, 93, 95.
22. Ibid., viii.
23. Grady McWhiney, Braxton Bragg and Confederate Defeat. Vol. I: Field Command (New York: Columbia University Press, 1969), 153, 221, 223, 260–261.
24. Williams, Beauregard, 94, 95, 209.
25. Jones, War Clerk, 2:176. See also Williams, Beauregard, vii.
26. Alfred Roman, The Military Operations of General Beauregard in the War Between the States 1861 to 1865 2 vols. (New York: Harper and Brothers, 1883), 2:193–195, 538–541; O.R.A., 33:1283, 1292, 1307–1308; O.R.A., 51, pt. 2, 872; P. G. T. Beauregard, "Drury's Bluff and Petersburg," North American Review 144, no. 3 (March 1887):245; G. T. Beauregard, "The Defense of Drewry's Bluff," in Battles and Leaders of the Civil War, ed. Robert U. Johnson and Clarence C. Buel, 4 vols. (New York: The Century Company, 1884, 1888), 4:195.
27. Beauregard to Pickett, 23 April 1864, Official Telegrams, 22 April–9 June 1864, P.G.T. Beauregard Papers, Library of Congress, Washington, D.C.; Roman, Military Operations, 2:542.
28. Harrison, Pickett's Men, 122–123; Beauregard, "Drury's Bluff," 246; Beauregard, Battles and Leaders, 4:195; Roman, Military Operations, 2:542–543.
29. Roman, Military Operations, 2:196, 543–544; O.R.A., 51, pt. 2, 874, 876.
30. O.R.A., 33:1312, 1314, 1316–1317, 1325–1326, 1328–1330; O.R.A., 35, pt. 2, 454; Johnson Hagood, Memoirs of the War of Secession (Columbia, S.C.: The State Company, 1910), 217; Daniel E. Huger Smith, ed., Mason Smith Family Letters, 1860–1868 (Columbia: University of South Carolina Press, 1950), 91; John A. Cutchins, A Famous Command: The Richmond Light Infantry Blues (Richmond: Garrett & Massie, 1934), 131. The change in plans was the result of a vigorous request for reinforcements from Robert E. Lee. Other departments besides Beauregard's also contributed. A brigade of Alabamians under Archibald Gracie was called from Tennessee on 25 April, as well as Bushrod

Johnson's Tennessee Brigade from Bristol, Virginia, on 30 April, both to go to Richmond. *O.R.A.*, 33:1312, 1316, 1325, 1329, 1330; Lewellyn A. Shaver, *A History of the Sixtieth Alabama Regiment, Gracie's Alabama Brigade* (Montgomery, Ala.: Barrett & Brown, 1867), 44.

31. *O.R.A.*, 51, pt. 2, 876; Beauregard to Bragg, 25 April 1864, Official Telegrams, 22 April–9 June 1864, Beauregard Papers, LC.

32. *O.R.A.*, 33:1314, 1315; Roman, *Military Operations*, 2:195–196, 541.

33. *O.R.A.*, 51, pt. 2, 875–877; Beauregard to Pickett, 28 April 1864, Official Telegrams, 22 April–9 June 1864, Beauregard Papers, LC.

34. Beauregard to Bragg, 28 April 1864, Official Telegrams, 22 April–9 June 1864, Beauregard Papers, LC; *O.R.A.*, 51, pt. 2, 879–880.

35. Beauregard to Pickett, 29 April 1864, Official Telegrams, 22 April–9 June 1864, Beauregard Papers, LC; John Otey to Beauregard, 30 April 1864, Official Telegrams, 22 April–9 June 1864, Beauregard Papers, LC.

36. *O.R.A.*, 51, pt. 2, 878, 880.

37. *O.R.A.*, 33:1331–1332.

38. Ibid., 1326–1328.

☆ 4 ☆

The Federal Landing
1–5 May 1864

The first of May found P. G. T. Beauregard at Kinston, North Carolina, supervising Robert Hoke's offensive against New Berne. Hoke had four of Beauregard's seven brigades with him, leaving only one in Virginia and two more scattered about North Carolina in garrison roles. Although Hoke's victory at Plymouth had brought him promotion to major general at the age of twenty-six, he suggested that Beauregard assume command of the New Berne expedition as senior officer. Since Beauregard harbored deep reservations about the project, he declined the offer, contenting himself with the role of adviser. On 2 May Hoke's troops began their advance and made contact with the Federals that afternoon. Meanwhile, Beauregard departed for Weldon, pausing along the way to notify Bragg that the offensive had begun.[1]

Ironically, at the same time that Beauregard had become resigned to the New Berne operation, Jefferson Davis began to have second thoughts. On 4 May he telegraphed Beauregard to cancel the expedition if immediate success was not assured and to prepare to return the troops to Virginia at a moment's notice. Davis's change of heart was due primarily to messages he had received from Robert E. Lee that asked for the return of units (such as Hoke's and Pickett's) that had previously been a part of his army. Lee had hinted that without these troops he might have to retreat to a position nearer Richmond to make a stand. Unless the New Berne expedition could be successfully concluded at once, Lee believed Hoke's troops and any others that could be spared should be rushed immediately to Richmond under Beauregard's command.[2]

The strength of Lee's request precipitated prompt action. On 3 May Wise's and Colquitt's Brigades finally separated from Samuel Jones's command at Charleston and started on the long rail trip to Richmond.[3] In an effort to expedite the movement of Hagood's Brigade from Wilmington, Beauregard ordered Chase Whiting to use both passenger and freight trains if necessary. To speed the transfer of Hoke's men regardless of the results at New Berne, Beauregard ordered railroad agents to collect trains at Kinston for the rapid movement of Hoke's brigades to Virginia, commencing 6 May. Half of Hoke's artillery and all of his cavalry were to follow by road. Since several of the brigades coming to Virginia belonged to George Pickett's old division, the War Department ordered Pickett to relinquish his command at Petersburg to Brigadier General Thomas Clingman and proceed to Hanover Junction, where his division was to reassemble.[4]

In acknowledging the order to leave Petersburg, on 4 May Pickett forwarded to Bragg the latest reports regarding Federal activity on the Peninsula. These reports placed Butler's strength at fifty thousand men, many recently arrived from the south. In addition, a large concentration of transports was visible near Fort Monroe. Earlier in the day Pickett had reported that the Federals were probing the Blackwater line and that Butler's troops were rebuilding a wharf in the James River some distance above Newport News.[5] Like other reports Pickett had sent to Richmond, these bits of information vanished into the War Department's bureaucracy without any action being taken. Although he did not say so, Pickett probably believed these would be the last intelligence reports he would send from Petersburg to an indifferent government, since he had his departure orders in hand. Should Butler choose to attack, it appeared that the burden would not fall on George Pickett.

Sixty miles south of Pickett at Weldon, P. G. T. Beauregard had convinced himself that the impending Federal offensive would not strike the Department of North Carolina and Southern Virginia. In a telegram on 4 May to Major General Daniel Harvey Hill, who was without assignment and had applied to serve unofficially on his staff, Beauregard lamented: "I would be glad to have you as volunteer aide but see no prospect now, of active operations in this Dept. for me, Burnside having joined his forces with Meade."[6]

While the Confederates tardily began to concentrate troops in Virginia, Benjamin Butler set in motion a diversion originally suggested by General Heintzelman some months before. Baldy Smith was ordered to send a brigade up the York River to occupy the village of West Point. Smith had no confidence in the diversion, sarcastically asking Butler's chief of staff, "Do you think that particular move will fool anyone?" but he grudgingly complied with the order. On the morning of 1 May, Colonel Guy Henry's brigade from the X Corps landed at West Point and occupied some old fortifications just beyond the town. To give the impression that Henry's men were only the advance party for Butler's whole army, engineers began to reconstruct the damaged wharf and foraging parties spread the word that the rest of the Army of the James was due to arrive soon.[7]

Although the campaign had begun for Henry's troops, many units in the Yorktown and Gloucester camps were still collecting excess baggage to be shipped to Norfolk for storage. Others were still welcoming veterans returning from their reenlistment furloughs. Army paymasters continued to make their rounds, visiting regiments they had not seen for months. There were also new activities of a more ominous character. Beginning on 1 May all units were required to have enough cooked rations on hand to last four days. One hundred rounds of ammunition were issued to each soldier, and a final series of inspections was held to see that each man had his full uniform and two pairs of army shoes. Regiments that had left their weapons in the Department of the South were issued rifles. Signal Corps detachments were assigned to the various headquarters and to the army and navy gunboat squadrons.[8]

Late in the afternoon of 2 May the sky over Yorktown and Gloucester became heavily overcast. High winds sprang up and the staging areas were pelted with rain and hail; men sought whatever shelter they could find on the open plain as the thunder and lightning played above them. Loose papers blew along company streets, and as the wind rose, tents of all sizes were ripped from their moorings, enveloping their occupants in shrouds of canvas or leaving them naked before the violence of the elements. Drenched to the skin, men raced to secure tarpaulins protecting commissary stores or regimental records. Others braved the hailstones in order to prevent their shelter tents from blowing away. Artillerymen and teamsters strove to quiet frightened horses and recapture those that had broken free and were milling about the camps. Then, as suddenly as it had begun, the wind abated and the driving rain slackened into a steady drizzle. As the Army of the James crawled out of its makeshift shelters, the soldiers saw flattened tents in every direction, lying in a sea of mud.[9]

Not even such a violent storm could dampen the spirits of the troops. According to an officer in the 98th New York Regiment, "No army ever took the field with higher spirits, greater confidence in its officers, and brighter hopes of success." Even the introspective Colonel Joseph Hawley was infected with the ebullient sense of impending victory sweeping the camps. To his wife on 3 May he wrote: "I have an altogether different feeling from that which used to possess me when I received marching orders in some cases down South. I have not the horrible feeling that we are to be *wasted.*"[10] Only William F. Smith and a few others continued to doubt that the Army of the James was victory-bound.[11] Among the latter was a reporter for the *New York Times.* Henry J. Winser had attached himself closely to Baldy Smith, and perhaps this colored his view of the coming campaign. Winser was not very optimistic about the possible success of the venture, as he told his managing editor on 3 May:

> The expedition is aimed at Richmond and is intended primarily to divert Lee from Grant. It is looked upon, I believe, as of a desperate character—a sort of forlorn hope ready to be used up in the case of bringing Lee down this way. The chances are considered about even against and for its success. Ten days probably will tell the story.[12]

Butler, who knew that Grant was expecting the expedition to depart on the night of 4 May 1864, had no time to speculate on the future. His primary concern was the X Corps, where Quincy Gillmore's absence was beginning to create difficulties. Unlike Baldy Smith, who at least knew the role he had been assigned to play, Gillmore had not yet conferred with Butler either about the plan or his troops' part in it. Nor had the organization of the X Corps been completed at a time when details involving the order of embarkation for the various units required attention. Countless important matters urgently demanded Gillmore's presence and decision, but he was not to be seen. Even Grant became concerned that Gillmore might not arrive in time, and he informed Butler that the Army of the James might have to delay its departure if Gillmore did not appear soon.[13] The suggestion was especially ominous, because Federal intelligence reports indicated that Beauregard was at Petersburg, some of Hoke's troops had reinforced the Blackwater line, and Confederate probes were becoming bolder. If the Confederates were already moving, any delay in Butler's departure might prove fatal to the success of the operation.[14]

At Hilton Head, Gillmore appeared blissfully unaware that there was any reason for haste. It seemed almost as if Gillmore could not bear to leave the department in which he had made his reputation. Or perhaps it was the appeal of departmental command itself that hindered Gillmore's departure, for in Virginia Butler would command the department and Gillmore would only lead an army corps. At last, on 1 May Gillmore officially relinquished command of the Department of the South and, that night, sailed in the transport *Arago* for Virginia. He was preceded by a letter that accurately forecast the time of his departure from South Carolina. Butler transmitted this welcome news to Grant, but both officers knew that Gillmore had dangerously reduced his margin of safety if the expedition were to depart on time.[15]

On 3 May all infantry units were told to be ready to board ship the next morning, while artillerymen began at once to transfer their weapons and teams to barges. The orders were welcomed by the troops, who were becoming impatient to depart. In one of his "final" letters to his sweetheart, Private Josiah Wood expressed the feelings of most of his comrades: "I feel anxious to start I do not like to wate here I had rather do what fighting we have to and have it over with." Units that had not prepared field rations nor distributed ammunition now diligently applied themselves to those vital tasks. In the 3rd New Hampshire Regiment the men received a last shipment of mail from the North and dispatched a heavy load in return. Throughout the day transports continued to arrive in the river, one of them bearing the 112th New York Regiment from South Carolina. Newspaper reporters assigned to the army were told to be on hand by the evening of 4 May "for a start somewhere."[16]

While his troops were completing their preparations, Butler carried a copy of the order of sailing to Admiral Lee. Since Butler did not want the slow-moving ironclads to delay the procession, Lee's warships were requested to follow the transports. Out in front of everything else was to be Brigadier General Charles Graham's flotilla of wooden army gunboats. Graham would be followed by transports bearing a brigade of Negro troops that had been assigned a special mission. This contingent was designated the "first fleet." The "second fleet," which was to depart Newport News around midnight 4–5 May, consisted of the wooden gunboats of the navy, followed by vessels bearing Smith's XVIII Corps and Gillmore's X Corps. Behind the X Corps came the siege train, hospital boats, supply vessels, and Lee's ironclads last of all. In regard to the position of the ironclads, Butler inquired if the navy's wooden gunboats could protect the transports from a sortie by the Confederate fleet until Lee's monitors reached the scene. Lee's reply, as recorded by his fleet captain, was not encouraging: "There was not one chance in ten that the wooden vessels could do so successfully."[17]

The day of departure, 4 May, dawned warm and fair. Almost at once the vast fields of shelter tents began to collapse, as their former occupants split the tents into halves and packed them for traveling. After final roll calls and a last-minute distribution of rations, regimental officers formed their men into column for the march to the river. At the wharves, quartermasters who had previously been concerned only with wagon transportation found themselves straining to bring men and vessels together at the dock at the same time. Everywhere there was noise and confusion and not a little cursing as the most carefully devised plans and timetables began to go awry. A few men who were determined to avoid service took this opportunity to desert their commands. Over at Gloucester Point it was soon discovered that the loading facilities were inadequate and the lines of men waiting to board ships began to lengthen. The frustration in this sector was relieved only by the report that at long last the steamer *Arago*, with Quincy Gillmore aboard, had arrived from Hilton Head.[18]

As each transport received its full complement of men and equipment, it moved out into the stream, found its appointed place in the line of ships clogging the York River, and anchored. Several vessels, in an attempt to confuse any watching Confederate agents, steamed some distance up the York, thereby giving the impression that Henry's brigade at West Point was to be reinforced. Troops embarking early were the envy of their fellows still on shore. Some units had been awakened by their officers as early as 2:30 A.M., but although a few had boarded their transports by 10:00 A.M., most did not embark until the afternoon and at least one unfortunate outfit was still waiting for transportation at midnight. This unit was part of the X Corps, which had been experiencing difficulty all day, due partially to the late arrival of its commander.[19]

As evening approached, Butler lost his patience and began to prod Gillmore to hasten his movements: "Having waited for your army corps from Port Royal I am not a little surprised at waiting for you here. Push everything forward." The X Corps commander replied that because of the "miserable conveniences" furnished him "no greater speed could have been made under the circumstances," but he did urge his subordinates to greater haste. As a result, while Smith's XVIII Corps was arranged in the order in which the units were scheduled to land, X Corps units were loaded without regard to landing order.[20]

To the men on board ship the scene presented by the flotilla of transports crowded with thousands of men was indescribably grand. Vessels of all sizes and descriptions, all flying large national flags, met the eye in all directions. As night fell the ships one by one dropped down the river and anchored near Fort Monroe, seemingly filling Hampton Roads.[21] The soldiers stood entranced, gazing about them and groping for words with which to describe the scene. A young soldier in the 118th New York Regiment recorded what he saw:

> As twilight faded into darkness, lights appeared on the transports and these, rocking and changing, seem like so many loose stars playing over the river to cheer our departure. Playing bands, men cheering and singing; busy tugs coughing through the fleet bearing orders; neighing horses and noise of escaping steam; soldiers shouting from steamer to steamer—but not a responsi-

ble word as to our destination. The scene is inspiring and the mingled sounds exciting.[22]

Although Yorktown and Gloucester Point were the main centers of activity, other elements of the Army of the James were also ready to depart. At Williamsburg, Brigadier General Isaac Wistar's brigade prepared to march to a newly repaired wharf on the James River at Grove Landing, there to board transports and wait for the invasion fleet to arrive. On the other side of the Peninsula at West Point, Colonel Guy Henry's brigade, its diversionary mission completed, waited to embark after nightfall and join the rest of the Army of the James. Across Hampton Roads near Portsmouth, Brigadier General August Kautz issued final orders to his cavalrymen, preparatory to their early morning departure. And at Fort Monroe itself, Benjamin Butler, gathered his staff and Signal Corps detachment and boarded his headquarters ship, the Greyhound.[23]

While the army was embarking at the York River staging areas, Admiral Lee informed his captains of their destination and time of departure. Seven wooden gunboats were to sail at midnight in order to lead the army transports upriver. Lee's five ironclads (four monitors and the former Confederate ram Atlanta) were to get underway three hours later, pick up the wooden vessels that would tow them upstream, and be ready to sail at dawn, which would come around 4:00 A.M. Upon reaching Fort Powhatan, the Atlanta would support the troops landing there, while the rest of the fleet would continue upstream to the treacherous shoal water around Harrison's Bar. This obstruction had to be reached no later than 1:00 P.M. so that the water would be deep enough to allow the heavy ironclads to pass. After negotiating Harrison's Bar, the wooden gunboats were either to sweep the James and Appomattox Rivers for Confederate torpedoes or take station off the various landing points to provide gunfire support for the army. Only after the channel had been swept clear would the monitors proceed beyond Harrison's Bar.[24]

Dawn of 5 May 1864 proved to be spectacular. Just as the sun rose above the horizon a small but violent thunderstorm broke over the assembled mass of ships. After a few turbulent moments punctuated by brilliant flashes of lightning, the storm dissipated, leaving the day to the majesty of a pleasantly warm sun. To Butler's chagrin, it was immediately apparent that his great expeditionary force was already beginning to fall behind its timetable. Butler had hoped to begin moving his units upriver shortly after midnight, but Gillmore's difficulties in loading the X Corps, along with other delays, had cost the Army of the James precious hours. At 4:00 A.M. Butler signaled Lee to send the navy gunboats upstream, while he took steps to hurry the army transports along.[25]

Ever so slowly the huge armada responded to Butler's prodding and by 6:00 A.M. the head of the fleet was in motion.[26] Brigadier General Charles Graham's three army gunboats had sailed earlier and were already some distance upstream. They were followed by the navy's wooden gunboats and the awkward monitors, each of the latter being towed upriver by two small gunboats.[27] Just leaving Hampton Roads and entering the wide mouth of the James River was the motley assortment of vessels bearing the Army of the James. Collected from all over the North, these ships displayed evidence of their diverse origins and peacetime occupations. There were steamships, both oceangoing and coastal, driven by propellers or great thrashing paddlewheels. These towed behind them graceful sailing vessels or ungainly barges, the latter laden with heavy items such as artillery and planking for temporary wharves.[28] But the greatest cargo of all was men.[29]

William F. Smith's XVIII Corps was leading the way with 16,978 infantrymen and 1,012 artillerymen organized in the three divisions of Brigadier Generals William Brooks, Godfrey Weitzel, and Edward Hincks. Brooks and Weitzel were graduates of West Point and previously had held divisional commands. Hincks, commander of the all-black Third Division, had been a Massachusetts politician, but in the war he had served valiantly at the regimental level and in various administrative assignments.[30] Following Smith's command was Quincy Gillmore's X Corps with 16,812 infantrymen and 1,114 artillerymen, also in three divisions under Brigadier Generals Alfred Terry, John Turner, and Adelbert Ames. Although Gillmore possessed a considerable reputation, his previous assignments had generally required the technical skills of a military engineer, rather than the maneuvering ability of a field commander. Of his divisional officers, Ames and Turner were West Pointers, but only Terry had held divisional command before, Turner having just transferred from the position of Gillmore's chief of staff.[31]

On board their transports the soldiers gazed in awe at the spectacle presented by the fleet. As the vast armada glided majestically upriver without an enemy in view, most of the troops adopted a festive spirit seldom associated with war. Soon the regimental bands began to play such tunes as "Hail Columbia," "Yankee Doodle," and "The Girl I Left Behind Me." As if on an outing on the Hudson or some other Northern stream, the soldiers leaned on the railings, gazing at the passing scenery, or promenaded on the decks of their transports. Their commander continually steamed among them aboard the *Greyhound,* shouting to the transport captains to "Give her all the steam you can," or just waving his cap while he roared, "Forward!" As he came abreast of each ship, Butler's infectious enthusiasm was caught by the troops and many of them spontaneously broke into cheers.[32]

For those soldiers interested in sightseeing, the trip offered many new vistas. First to come into view was the site of the battle between the *U.S.S. Monitor* and the *C.S.S. Virginia,* readily identifiable by the wrecks of the *Virginia's* victims. Farther upstream the vine-covered ruins of the old church at Jamestown appeared to starboard. Periodically, large plantations were visible, surrounded by verdant pastures and fields of cotton and corn. Here and there civilians were observed curiously peering from windows or yards at the passing convoy. On other occasions, groups of slaves carrying bundles came down to the river bank and gestured as if begging to be taken along. Often Colonel R. M. West's 1st and 2nd U. S. Colored Cavalry Regiments could be seen through the trees on the north bank of the James, moving parallel with the fleet.[33]

Rebel earthworks of undetermined age were seen occasionally throughout the trip, but as the ships continued upstream, the long mounds of yellow earth seemed to take on a new freshness. At first only the men with keen eyesight caught glimpses of Confederate scouts along the bank, but as the hours passed and the river narrowed, the presence of Confederate signal stations became obvious to all. On board the transport *Nellie Penz*, in one of the leading divisions of the fleet, the soldiers of the 9th New Jersey Regiment were formed into companies, inspected, and ordered to load their weapons. Signal traffic between the various corps, division, and brigade headquarters aboard the transports also began to increase in intensity.[34]

The majority of the Army of the James was still enjoying its spring cruise when the leading units hit the beach. From the beginning it had been obvious that certain points along the river would have to be permanently garrisoned to protect the water communication route back to Hampton Roads. The first of these positions was a place marked on Federal maps as Wilson's Wharf, a bluff on the north bank of the James that commanded the channel for some distance above and below. Assigned to seize this key position was a portion of the First Brigade of Brigadier General Edward Hincks's Third Division of the XVIII Corps.[35] Butler had long believed that blacks would make good soldiers, and against the opinions of many of his officers and men, he had formed an entire division of two brigades from Negro regiments.[36] One of these brigades, commanded by Brigadier General Edward Wild, had been chosen to secure the supply line of the Army of the James and thus had the honor of leading the invasion force. Scrambling ashore without opposition, the black troops began to entrench at Wilson's Wharf, while the rest of the armada steamed by.[37]

A few miles above Wilson's Wharf was another commanding bluff of equal importance to the Federals, known to both sides as Fort Powhatan, because it was the site of an old Confederate fortification. Fort Powhatan had been intermittently occupied by the Confederates in previous years, but currently it was ungarrisoned. There the remainder of Wild's brigade was landed, once more without resistance. The rest of the fleet anxiously waited downstream while Fort Powhatan was secured. Once underway again, the men on the transports found an American flag floating above the works and a signal detachment communicating with the ships as they passed. Left behind to provide naval protection were the U.S.S. *Atlanta* and two gunboats.[38]

In midafternoon the fleet reached Harrison's Bar, which proved to be no obstacle. City Point lay only a few miles ahead and was visible in the distance. As the advance elements approached, a large Confederate flag was seen flying defiantly on the bluff and a white steamer lay close to shore. The unit assigned to seize City Point was Hincks's Second Brigade, commanded by Colonel Samuel Duncan. As the transports bearing Duncan's men neared the village, they came upon several of Admiral Lee's warships halted just out of range. When Hincks asked the cause of the delay, he was told that Lee was preparing to transfer his flag from the wooden gunboat *Malvern* to an ironclad before risking an engagement. Aware that Graham's army gunboats were already lying off City Point and appalled at such timidity on the part of the navy, Hincks ordered the captain of his transport to push ahead to the village. His decision was partially influenced by a glance downstream, which showed Butler's *Greyhound* pounding hard toward the same objective. Thus the race to be first at City Point was on.[39]

Winning the contest, Hincks's transport nosed up to the ruined wharf alongside the white steamer, which proved to be the flag-of-truce boat *New York* delivering a load of exchanged Confederate prisoners. Without pause, the first troops ashore raced up the bluff toward a Confederate signal detachment frantically transmitting news of the Federal arrival to another station nearer Petersburg. A Confederate officer protested in vain that the Federals were violating a flag-of-truce, as the handful of Confederate signalmen and guards were quickly subdued, except for two or three who managed to escape. The Confederate flag was unceremoniously lowered and replaced by a Federal one, and a Federal signal detachment began to use the Confederate signal platform to communicate with the ships in the river. The time was shortly after 4:00 P.M.[40]

Edward Hincks's black troops now commenced unloading in earnest, while detachments pushed into the village. According to a staff officer who accompanied them, City Point consisted only of "a few shabby houses ranged along two or three short lanes or streets; and the spacious grounds and dilapidated house of one Dr. Eppes."[41] A once-active river port in the cotton and tobacco trade, City Point was connected to Petersburg by rail. After a brief reconnaissance down the track discovered no Confederates, Duncan's regiments returned to the bluff to consolidate their position. Hincks's staff appropriated the shell-damaged Eppes mansion with its magnificent view of both rivers and its excellent rose garden for the general's headquarters, and his quartermaster set to work repairing the damaged wharf. The landing had not cost a single combat casualty, although the unloading operations that followed resulted in one death and two injuries.[42]

While Hincks's men were occupying City Point, the rest of the armada continued a mile and a half upriver to Bermuda Hundred Landing. As Graham's army gunboats chased a Confederate steamer upstream and Lee's navy gunboats began the hazardous task of dragging the river for torpedoes, the soldiers of Baldy Smith's XVIII Corps began to land. The process was hindered by shallow water that prevented the close approach of the transports to the beach. Consequently, ships' boats had to be utilized to get the first contingents on shore. First to land was the 23rd Massachusetts Regiment, Heckman's First Brigade, Second Division.[43] The rest of Heckman's regiments followed immediately, pausing only long enough to establish their organization before fanning out into the countryside. As they prepared to disembark, the captain of the vessel bearing the 9th New Jersey Regiment passed among the infantrymen, shaking the hands of all he could reach. Once ashore, the 9th New Jersey was temporarily assigned to construct a makeshift dock from old canal boats and scrap lumber brought along by the fleet.[44]

Heckman's troops had begun to splash ashore between 5:00 and 6:00 P.M.. With sunset due a few minutes before 7:00 P.M. and the end of twilight less than an hour later, Butler's army would soon be landing in the dark.[45] As night fell, the transports queued up in long lines awaiting their turns to disgorge their cargoes across the still rudimentary wharves, their lights once again illuminating the dark river as they swung at anchor. All through the night units continued to disembark, form into line, and stumble forward in the darkness to temporary bivouac areas. There the troops lay down to rest, after protecting themselves against being trampled by the men and horses who followed them. Some soldiers, unable to sleep, commenced a search for food and water.[46]

At 9:00 P.M., as the landing process was just becoming organized, Butler dispatched a message to Grant and Stanton reporting his progress. Grant must have been pleased to read the sentences "No opposition thus far. Apparently a complete surprise."[47] Other than a few Confederate signalmen caught fishing in the river and a horseman or two in the distance, the Confederates had not put in an appearance at Bermuda Hundred. Could it be that the whole campaign was to be so easy? Where indeed was the enemy?[48]

NOTES

1. O.R.A., 51, pt. 2, 880, 886; Beauregard to Whiting, 1 May 1864, Official Telegrams, 22 April–9 June 1864, Beauregard Papers, LC; Roman, Military Operations, 2:197, 542, 544, 546; O.R.A., 36, pt. 2, 941–942; Thomas S. Kenan, Sketch of the Forty–Third Regiment North Carolina Troops (Infantry) (Raleigh, N. C., 1895), 13.

2. O.R.A., 51, pt. 2, 888–889; Roman, Military Operations, 2:547; O.R.A., 36, pt. 2, 943; Clifford Dowdey and Louis H. Manarin, eds., The Wartime Papers of R. E. Lee (Boston: Little, Brown, 1961), 719.

3. O.R.A., 35, pt. 2, 460–461; O.R.A., 36, pt. 2, 946.

4. Beauregard to Whiting (two telegrams), 4 May 1864, Beauregard to Pickett, 7:30 P.M., 4 May 1864, all in Official Telegrams, 22 April–9 June 1864, Beauregard Papers, LC; Beauregard to railroad agents, 4 May 1864, Letter Book, April–May 1864, Beauregard Papers, LC; Roman, Military Operations, 2:547; O.R.A., 36, pt. 2, 950.

5. O.R.A., 36, pt. 2, 951; O.R.A., 51, pt. 2, 889, 931. The telegram concerning the Blackwater line is misdated 14 May. The wharf referred to was at Grove Landing, which figured in Butler's plans as a secondary embarkation point.

6. Beauregard to Hill, 4 May 1864, Official Telegrams, 22 April–9 June 1864, Beauregard Papers, LC; Hal Bridges, Lee's Maverick General (New York: McGraw-Hill 1961), 262.

7. O.R.A., 33:1019, 1021, 1030–1031; O.R.A., 36, pt. 2, 327, 349; O.R.N., 9:706–707, 710–711; Mowris, One Hundred and Seventeenth New York, 100–102.

8. Little, Seventh New Hampshire, 241; Edlredge, Third New Hampshire, 459; Kreutzer, Ninety-Eighth New York, 178; Charles M. Clark, The History of the Thirty-Ninth Regiment Illinois Volunteer Veteran Infantry (Yates Phalanx) in the War of the Rebellion, 1861–1865 (Chicago, 1889), 174–175; Roe, Twenty-Fourth Massachusetts, 273–274; Price, Ninety-Seventh Pennsylvania, 249; Drake, Ninth New Jersey, 170; Thompson, Thirteenth New Hampshire, 255; O.R.A., 36, pt. 2, 21.

9. Eldredge, Third New Hampshire, 459; Cleveland, ed., "Campaign of Promise," 240; Price, Ninety-Seventh Pennsylvania, 249; Roe, Twenty-Fourth Massachusetts, 274; Valentine, Story of Co. F, 106–107; Stowits, One Hundredth New York, 245; Beecher, First Connecticut Light Battery, 1:329–330.

10. Kreutzer, Ninety-Eighth New York, 181; Joseph R. Hawley to his wife, 3 May 1864, Hawley Papers, LC.

11. Writing to the author of an XVIII Corps regimental history in 1883, Smith said: "I was opposed to the campaign on the James River from its inception. Only one person ever knew of it. I did my duty as an honest soldier to carry out the plan, and when it failed, I told Gen'l Butler what I thought should be done." Quoted in Derby, Bearing Arms, 288. Smith expressed a similar opinion in his own From Chattanooga to Petersburg, 17–18.

12. Henry Jacob Winser to John Swinton, 3 May 1864, John Swinton Papers, Southern Historical Collection, University of North Carolina, Chapel Hill, N.C. Smith had been known to cultivate newsmen before, most recently at Chattanooga. Andrews, North Reports the Civil War, 489.

13. Butler, *Butler's Book*, 639; O.R.A., 36, pt. 2, 326, 327, 345.

14. O.R.A., 51, pt. 1, 1289; O.R.A., 36, pt. 2, 349; Marshall, ed., *Butler's Correspondence*, 4:153; "Kautz in the Great Rebellion," Kautz Papers, LC.

15. O.R.A., 35, pt. 2, 79; Gordon, *War Diary*, 292; Benjamin Butler to U. S. Grant, 2 May 1864, General Correspondence, 1864, Benjamin Butler Papers, LC.

16. Little, *Seventh New Hampshire*, 241; Brady, *Eleventh Maine*, 174; Drake, *Ninth New Jersey*, 197; Cleveland, ed., "Campaign of Promise," 240; Eldredge, *Third New Hampshire*, 460; Beecher, *First Connecticut Light Battery*, 1:330; Roe, *Twenty-fourth Massachusetts*, 274; Josiah Wood to "Rana," 2 May 1864, Josiah Wood Papers, DU; Walter S. Clemence Diary, 3 May 1864, North Carolina Collection, University of North Carolina, Chapel Hill, N.C.; Hyde, *One Hundred and Twelfth New York*, 73; Henry Jacob Winser to John Swinton, 3 May 1864, John Swinton Papers, SHC.

17. O.R.N., 9:721–722.

18. Thompson, *Thirteenth New Hampshire*, 256; De Forest, *Random Sketches*, 145; Livermore, *Days and Events*, 333–334; Walter S. Clemence Memoranda, 4 May 1864, NCC; Cleveland, ed., "Campaign of Promise;" 308; Little, *Seventh New Hampshire*, 241; Kreutzer, *Ninety-Eighth New York*, 182–183; Price, *Ninety-Seventh Pennsylvania*, 249; Cunningham, *Adirondack Regiment*, 100–101; Drake, *Ninth New Jersey*, 197–198; Eldredge, *Third New Hampshire*, 460; Roe, *Twenty-fourth Massachusetts*, 276; Clark, *My Experience*, 56; Jerome Tourtellotte, *A History of Company K of the Seventh Connecticut Volunteer Infantry in the Civil War* (n. p., 1910), 212; O.R.A., 36, pt. 2, 391–392; Beecher, *First Connecticut Light Battery*, 1:330; Clark, *Thirty-Ninth Illinois*, 175.

19. Thompson, *Thirteenth New Hampshire*, 256; Cleveland, ed., "Campaign of Promise," 308; Cunningham, *Adirondack Regiment*, 100–101; Roe, *Twenty-fourth Massachusetts*, 276; Little, *Seventh New Hampshire*, 241; Clark, *My Experience*, 56; Clark, *Iron Hearted Regiment*, 103.

20. O.R.A., 36, pt. 2, 392–393.

21. De Forest, *Random Sketches*, 145–146; Everts, *Comprehensive History*, 103; Foster, *New Jersey and the Rebellion*, 707; Livermore, *Days and Events*, 334; J. Waldo Denny, *Wearing the Blue in the Twenty-fifth Mass. Volunteer Infantry, with Burnside's Coast Division, 18th Army Corps, and Army of the James* (Worcester, Mass.: Putnam & Davis, 1879), 267.

22. Cunningham, *Adirondack Regiment*, 101.

23. O.R.A., 35, pt. 2, 21, 376–368, 394; Bartlett, *Twelfth New Hampshire*, 171–172; Mowris, *One Hundred and Seventeenth New York*, 102.

24. O.R.N., 9:723–726.

25. Beecher, *First Connecticut Light Battery*, 1:331; O.R.A., 36, pt. 2, 432; Marshall, ed., *Butler's Correspondence*, 4:163.

26. Drake, *Ninth New Jersey*, 171; Thompson, *Thirteenth New Hampshire*, 256.

27. *New York Times*, 8 May 1864; Thompson, *Thirteenth New Hampshire*, 256; Kreutzer, *Ninety-Eighth New York*, 183. This reversal of the ironclads' position in the fleet had been necessitated by the delay in starting the transports.

28. Thompson, *Thirteenth New Hampshire*, 256; Haynes, *Second New Hampshire*, 166; Beecher, *First Connecticut Light Battery*, 1:331; Smith, *Battles and Leaders*, 4:207.

29. All told, the infantry and artillery components of the Army of the James numbered 35,916 officers and enlisted men. Completing the army were 2,901 cavalrymen massed at Portsmouth under Brigadier General August Kautz, and 1,800 black cavalrymen who would parallel the invasion fleet on the Peninsula. When and if the cavalry detachments joined the main body, Benjamin Butler would command a field army of some 40,617 officers and enlisted men of all arms. Andrew A. Humphreys, *The Virginia Campaign of '64 and '65: The Army of the Potomac and the Army of the James* (New York: Charles Scribner's Sons, 1883), 137. Allan Nevins's statement in *Organized War to Victory*, 13–14, that the strength of the Army of the James was 53,000 men is incorrect. Nevins apparently used the figure given for all the troops in the Department of Virginia and North Carolina on 30 April 1864, found in O.R.A., 33:1053.

30. Humphreys, *Virginia Campaign*, 137; Warner, *Generals in Blue*, 47, 229–230, 548–549; Boatner, *Civil War Dictionary*, 89, 402–403, 899–900.

31. Humphreys, *Virginia Campaign*, 137; Warner, *Generals in Blue*, 5–6, 497–498, 512–513; Boatner, *Civil War Dictionary*, 11–12, 831, 853–854. Concerning Gillmore, a battery commander wrote: "He had had little experience in command in the field, and his ability there was yet to be shown. At any rate he was not known as an enterprising general or prompt to take advantage of opportunities. He was not specially popular with those who had served under him in South Carolina." Rockwell, "Tenth Army Corps," 269. Similar opinions can be found in Kreutzer, *Ninety-Eighth New York*, 177; Joseph R. Hawley

to Mr. Faxon, 25 April 1864, Hawley Papers, LC; John Chipman Gray, *War Letters 1862–1865 of John Chipman Gray and John Codman Ropes* (Boston: Houghton Mifflin, 1927), 275, 278.

32. Thompson, *Thirteenth New Hampshire*, 256; Kreutzer, *Ninety-Eighth New York*, 183; *New York Times*, 8 May 1864; Cunningham, *Adirondack Regiment*, 102; Bruce, "General Butler's Bermuda Campaign," 311.

33. Beecher, *First Connecticut Light Battery*, 1:332; Roe, *Twenty-fourth Massachusetts*, 276–277; Clark, *My Experience*, 56; Haynes, *Second New Hampshire*, 167; Cunningham, *Adirondack Regiment*, 101–102; Price, *Ninety-Seventh Pennsylvania*, 249–250; Emmerton, *Twenty-Third Massachusetts*, 172–173; Cadwell, *Old Sixth*, 88–89; Putnam, *Story of Company A*, 263; Walter S. Clemence Memoranda, 5 May 1864, NCC; Thompson, *Thirteenth New Hampshire*, 256; Kreutzer, *Ninety-Eighth New York*, 183; O.R.A., 36, pt. 2, 327.

34. Foster, *New Jersey and the Rebellion*, 707; Valentine, *Story of Co. F*, 107; Everts, *Comprehensive History*, 104; Cleveland, ed., "Campaign of Promise," 308; Walter S. Clemence Memoranda, 5 May 1864, NCC; Cunningham, *Adirondack Regiment*, 102; Drake, *Ninth New Jersey*, 171–198; J. Willard Brown, *The Signal Corps, U. S. A. in the War of the Rebellion* (Boston: B. Wilkins & Co., 1896), 427–428; O.R.A., 36, pt. 2, 21, 22, 26.

35. The units involved were the 1st and 22nd Regiments of U. S. Colored Troops and two sections of Battery B, 2nd U. S. Colored Artillery Regiment. O.R.A., 36, pt. 2, 165.

36. Raymond, "Ben Butler," 465–467.

37. Memorandum of order of movement up James River, General Correspondence, 1864, Benjamin Butler Papers, LC; O.R.A., 36, pt. 2, 165; Livermore, *Days and Events*, 334.

38. Butler, *Butler's Book*, 670; O.R.A., 36, pt. 2, 21, 165; Livermore, *Days and Events*, 334; Cunningham, *Adirondack Regiment*, 102; Brown, *Signal Corps*, 427; O.R.N., 9:728–729. The landing force was composed of the 10th and 37th U. S. Colored Troops and two sections of Battery M, 3rd New York Artillery.

39. O.R.A., 36, pt. 2, 165, 432; O.R.N., 10:15; Livermore, *Days and Events*, 334–336; *New York Times*, 8 May 1864.

40. Livermore, *Days and Events*, 335–336; *New York Times*, 8 May 1864; O.R.A., 36, pt. 2, 21–22, 432; Brown, *Signal Corps*, 219, 427; Joseph J. Scroggs Diary, 5 May 1864, Civil War Times Illustrated Collection of Civil War Papers, United States Army Military History Institute, Carlisle Barracks, Pennsylvania.

41. Livermore, *Days and Events*, 336.

42. Foster, *New Jersey and the Rebellion*, 708; Livermore, *Days and Events*, 333, 337–338; *New York Times*, 8 May 1864.

43. *New York Times*, 8 May 1864 and 10 May 1864; O.R.N., 9:729; Copp, *Reminiscences*, 348; Alfred Otis Chamberlin to his parents, 11 May 1864, Alfred Otis Chamberlin Papers, DU; Valentine, *Story of Co. F*, 107–108; Emmerton, *Twenty-Third Massachusetts*, 173.

44. Derby, *Bearing Arms*, 246, 252; Clark, *My Experience*, 56; Putnam, *Story of Company A*, 263–264; Samuel H. Putnam, Regimental Record—Co. A, 25th Mass. Vols., Duke University, Durham, N.C.; Walter S. Clemence Diary, 5 May 1864, NCC; Everts, *Comprehensive History*, 104; Drake, *Ninth New Jersey*, 171–172; Foster, *New Jersey and the Rebellion*, 237–238, 708; Cleveland, ed., "Campaign of Promise," 309; Cunningham, *Adirondack Regiment*, 102; Bartlett, *Twelfth New Hampshire*, 172.

45. Valentine, *Story of Co. F*, 107–108; Samuel H. Putnam, Regimental Record—Co. A, 25th Mass. Vols., DU; Drake, *Ninth New Jersey*, 172; Cleveland, ed., "Campaign of Promise," 309. The time of sunset is computed from the article on "Sunrise, Sunset, and Daylight" in Boatner, *Civil War Dictionary*, 819–821. Sunset on 5 May 1864 occurred around 6:50 P.M. and the end of evening nautical twilight approximately an hour later.

46. Bartlett, *Twelfth New Hampshire*, 172; Cunningham, *Adirondack Regiment*, 102–103; Haynes, *Second New Hampshire*, 167; Thompson, *Thirteenth New Hampshire*, 257; Price, *Ninety-Seventh Pennsylvania*, 251; Kreutzer, *Ninety-Eighth New York*, 184; De Forest, *Random Sketches*, 215; Beecher, *First Connecticut Light Battery*, 1:332–333; Clark, *Thirty-Ninth Illinois*, 177; Clark, *My Experience*, 56. According to Butler, some 10,000 men, with artillery, had been landed by 8:00 P.M., but this probably includes Hincks's forces at City Point and below. Butler, *Butler's Book*, 640. In Columbus, Ohio, old General Heintzelman, upon hearing of the landing, wrote in his journal: "From the details of the movement he evidently received my letter of some two months ago, or there are some remarkable coincidences." Manuscript Journal, 9 May 1864, Samuel P. Heintzelman Papers, LC.

47. O.R.A., 36, pt. 2, 430; Marshall, ed., *Butler's Correspondence*, 4:165.

48. Emmerton, *Twenty-Third Massachusetts*, 173; Drake, *Ninth New Jersey*, 171–172; O.R.A., 36, pt. 2, 34.

☆ 5 ☆

Confederate Reaction and Federal Consolidation 5–6 May 1864

P. G. T. Beauregard spent the morning of 5 May 1864 at Weldon engaged in routine administrative tasks. First, he divided his department into the three military districts he had proposed earlier. Next he attempted to expedite the movement of troops through his territory according to the demands of the War Department. Yet all the while in the back of Beauregard's mind was a nagging concern that a Federal offensive against his department still might be imminent. Pickett had reported earlier that the Federals had reconstructed an obscure wharf on the James River and Beauregard thought the move significant enough to inform Braxton Bragg. At the same time he suggested that the troops on the Blackwater line should be kept in place to cover Petersburg. At 11:30 A.M. Beauregard again rejected Harvey Hill's offer to serve on his staff because there seemed little possibility of action. This time, however, Beauregard added, "Should prospects change, will telegraph you again."[1]

Shortly after the note to Hill left Beauregard's office, the telegraph began to clatter with an incoming message. George Pickett at Petersburg reported that his scouts had just sighted a Federal fleet of undetermined size ascending the James River.[2] Without waiting for further details, Beauregard began to devise his response. At noon he sent a telegram to Hoke recalling the New Berne expeditionary force to Weldon. A message to Chase Whiting authorized the use of all available trains to move Hagood's Brigade northward. To Pickett, Beauregard wired: "Should it become necessary, call directly on War Department for assistance until your troops reach you."[3]

Just before 12:30 P.M. another urgent message arrived from Pickett: "Please send up some troops at once. Where are my brigades, Corse's and Kemper's?"[4] In reply, Beauregard gave Pickett permission to halt Johnson Hagood's South Carolinians whenever they arrived in Petersburg. He also ordered Pickett to "Remain in command of your present district until further orders, and assume command of all troops that may arrive therein." Subsequent telegrams informed Pickett that Corse's and Kemper's Brigades had been ordered to Virginia from North Carolina, and advised the district commander to concentrate his forces around Petersburg. Braxton Bragg was also informed of Pickett's requests for aid.[5]

The next telegram from Pickett placed the Federal vanguard above Fort Powhatan and in sight of City Point. At 12:35 P.M. Beauregard passed this news along to Bragg, noting that he had authorized Pickett to halt Hagood in Petersburg.[6] As the progress of Butler's invasion fleet up the James became clear from Pickett's continuing reports, Beauregard cast around for spare units that could be rushed to Petersburg. A regiment at Kinston was ordered north, and three of Brigadier General James Martin's North Carolina regiments were directed to Weldon. The quartermaster at Weldon was told to expedite the movement of troops from Kinston to Petersburg. A new telegram was addressed to Harvey Hill: "Come on. Will be glad to see you."[7]

As the afternoon of 5 May wore on in peaceful Weldon, Beauregard realized that he was too far from Petersburg to direct events. He had already given Pickett permission to communicate directly with the War Department, and this grant of authority was repeated in an afternoon telegram. The same message stated that Beauregard was awaiting instructions from Bragg. When the instructions arrived, they showed that Bragg, although much nearer Petersburg, was more out of touch with Pickett's situation than Beauregard. Bragg's telegram ordered Beauregard to forbid Pickett to halt Hagood's Brigade, which was to continue its journey to Richmond. This incredible news Beauregard dutifully transmitted to Pickett at 4:30 P.M. With Hagood beyond his control, Pickett would have to make a stand with the units already at hand.[8]

In Petersburg, Pickett was undergoing a severe test. The first news of the Federal advance had been telegraphed to him from Ivor Station that morning[9] and confirmation had come almost immediately from a staff officer who was at Ivor inspecting the Blackwater defenses. A glance at the forces available to Pickett confirmed the gravity of the situation. In Petersburg itself there was only one regiment, the 31st North Carolina Infantry of Thomas Clingman's Brigade.[10] The rest of Clingman's troops were either scattered along the Blackwater line or in reserve behind it. As for cavalry, there was none in Petersburg; they too were guarding the Blackwater. Pickett was more fortunate in his supply of artillery, since the Washington Artillery Battalion of New Orleans, which had wintered in Petersburg, was still in town. There was also a poorly armed force of local reserves and second-class militia, which could be made available at short notice.[11] Beyond this there was nothing with which to face Butler's thousands. In Douglas Freeman's expressive phrase, "A defenseless region awaited the invader as if it had been a rich mansion with its door unlocked and unguarded."[12]

Having concluded that the Federal movement was not a feint, Pickett ordered the 31st North Carolina into the defensive works east of town on the road to City Point. It was joined there by the Washington Artillery, which managed to get thirteen guns into line by impressing civilian teams met on the streets. The town alarm was rung to alert the city reserves and militia, while riders hastened into adjoining counties to call out additional local defense companies. By the end of the day, some five or six hundred of these patriotic, but woefully ill-prepared citizens had responded. Still, Pickett desperately needed horsemen to distract the attention of the Federals and thereby concel the weakness of his infantry force. He therefore ordered Major John Scott, who was without a command, to lead a provisional force of thirty mounted civilians toward City Point as a cavalry screen. With the departure of Scott's men, Pickett had deployed the last of his immediately available forces. Altogether they could not have numbered much more than 1,400 troops of all descriptions.[13]

The only other units under Pickett's direct control were on the Blackwater line, over forty miles away by rail. Shortly after noon, General Clingman at Ivor Station received a telegram from Pickett ordering Clingman and one of his remaining regiments to return at once to Petersburg. A train was sent for the unit, but it did not arrive at Ivor until nearly 6:00 P.M. Clingman selected the 51st North Carolina Infantry for the trip and the men began to cook rations and draw ammunition in preparation for the movement. At least one soldier, Isham Pitman, found time to scrawl a few lines to his wife:

> I in haste rite you a shorte note to let you her that we are ordered to Richmon as the Yankes are advancing ther I hav no other news only my feete has bearly got well and it is go again and perhaps no more to return . . . May God have mercy on you as I go & spear me to return safe is the Prare of one that Loves you I have got to Draw Ration have no moe time to rite I will rite as soon as I can a gain if Life is speared[14]

Having deployed his meager forces and recalled part of Clingman's Brigade, Pickett could only wait and hope. He had kept both Beauregard in Weldon and Adjutant General Samuel Cooper in Richmond informed of the progress of Butler's fleet. Beauregard had replied to Pickett's urgent calls for help with advice and assurances that aid from North Carolina was on the way. He had even tried to get Pickett the authority to utilize Hagood's South Carolina Brigade, due in Petersburg at any moment, until Bragg had vetoed the idea. By contrast, Cooper refused even to acknowledge Pickett's transmissions. As the number of Federal transports counted by his signalmen mounted to fifty-nine, Pickett's impatience at the silence from Richmond began to show. In his sixth telegram to Cooper, he demanded: "I have telegraphed you five times this morning and received no answer. Please answer this." But this message also went unacknowledged.[15]

Throughout the afternoon of 5 May Pickett continued to transmit reports of the Federal advance. The fleet was above Fort Powhatan, it was off Berkeley Plantation, it was passing Swynyard Landing—and with every report it was growing in size.[16] By 3:00 P.M. Pickett could wait no longer. With Federal gunboats lying off City Point and Petersburg virtually defenseless, he telegraphed Cooper that he was sending a courier to Richmond by special train in the hope of eliciting some response. Pickett's mood was rapidly becoming one of desperation and the memories of his earlier warnings found their way into the message: "Why have not my suggestions and entreaties been carried out about the iron-clads and torpedoes? You had better, if possible, either send troops or have trains ready to re-enforce this point, or from here to Richmond should the enemy land at Bermuda Hundred." As before, the only answer from Richmond was silence.[17]

A little after 4:00 P.M., the signal station nearest to City Point reported men in blue uniforms on the signal platform in the village. Pickett rightly concluded that City Point had fallen and so informed Richmond, pleading: "Troops are arriving from the South. Can't I detain them? Answer at once." There was no answer from the War Department. A copy of Pickett's telegram was routed to Beauregard at Weldon and he in turn passed it on to Bragg at 6:15 P.M. At the end of this telegram and in a similar message thirty minutes later, Beauregard again requested the authority to stop Hagood's Brigade in Petersburg when it reached that point.[18]

By nightfall Pickett had learned the Federal destination, which he reported in another plaintive telegram to Adjutant General Cooper:

> Have you received any telegrams from me to-day? I have sent a great many and received no answers. Have you any guards or any force between this city and Richmond? The enemy have landed at Bermuda Hundred. Unless you guard the railroad they will cut off communication. Reply at once.[19]

Although he had correctly diagnosed the situation and was truly in danger of being cut off from Richmond, the frantic Pickett received only a 9:30 P.M. message from Beauregard: "Have no troops to send. . . . Do the best you can, with what you have."[20] This was small consolation to an officer who had virtually nothing with which to oppose an army of thousands, and who by all rights should not even have been in Petersburg, since he had his relief orders in his pocket. Most probably, Pickett "with all his heart, wished he had taken an earlier train to Hanover Junction."[21]

In Weldon, Beauregard had more options than Pickett. With a major attack occurring in one of his districts, Beauregard could either remain in Weldon and handle affairs at arms-length or go to Petersburg to direct the Confederate response in person. The harried Pickett no doubt expected Beauregard to come north at once, but shortly after 10:00 P.M. his hopes were dashed when Beauregard wired: "Am unfortunately too unwell to go to Petersburg tonight: but will do so tomorrow evening or next day." In his stead Beauregard dispatched Major General D. H. Hill to Petersburg to confer with Pickett about the situation there. But Hill was only a volunteer aide-de-camp; the burden of responsibility still lay with Pickett alone.[22]

Although the War Department inexcusably gave Pickett no guidance on 5 May, it was aware of the Federal landings. Major General Robert Ransom's Department of Richmond, which controlled the north side of the James River and the fortifications at Drewry's Bluff, had been receiving reports of Butler's progress throughout the day. In addition, the Confederate Navy Department had its own personnel on the river and they too sent in sighting information. Gradually the news began to permeate the bureaucracy from Jefferson Davis down to War Department clerks.[23] That night Davis informed Robert E. Lee of the Federal landings and the Confederate troop dispositions in the Department of Richmond. Little mention was made of Pickett and Beauregard.[24]

Compared with Pickett's meager forces, Robert Ransom was flush with troops. In addition to the Richmond garrison, he could deploy Eppa Hunton's and Seth Barton's Virginia Brigades of Pickett's old division, as well as Archibald Gracie's Alabama Brigade recently transferred from Tennessee. Also present, having arrived the previous night from western Virginia, was Brigadier General Bushrod Johnson's Tennessee Brigade. Johnson's Brigade had relieved Hunton's during 5 May so that the Virginians could depart for Hanover Junction, but after only one hour in their new camp, the Tennesseans were ordered across the James River to Drewry's Bluff. The commander of the tiny contingent of Confederate Marines holding Fort Darling, keystone of the Drewry's Bluff defenses, had already been instructed to inform Johnson on his arrival "to watch out for the railroad."[25]

Having taken these precautions, Ransom and his superiors sat back to await events. No thought was given to dispatching any aid to Pickett in Petersburg. This lapse, coupled with Bragg's refusal to allow Pickett to commandeer reinforcements from the troops arriving by rail from the south, guaranteed Pickett's inability to hold his ground if pressed. Unknowingly, the Federals had landed almost directly in the gap betwen two Confederate departments that had an unclear common boundary. Without a quick clarification of responsibilities and the guiding hand of an overall coordinator, the Confederate departmental system might contribute to an impending debacle of considerable magnitude.[26]

As the cumbersome Confederate bureaucracy slowly responded to the Federal threat, Benjamin Butler was planning his next move at Bermuda Hundred. During the night of 5–6 May, while his troops were still streaming ashore, Butler held a conference with his two corps commanders. At the meeting Butler announced he had received information from a spy that Richmond was almost devoid of troops. He proposed to take advantage of this unexpected opportunity by advancing upon the Confederate capital without waiting for the entire army to be landed. By this time there were already ten thousand men ashore who could be utilized as the striking force. Richmond was little more than sixteen miles away and the night was fair and not especially dark. Such a bold push through unknown territory at night toward the most important of Confederate positions would be a gamble, but the results might be equally spectacular.

According to Butler's later testimony, both Baldy Smith and Quincy Gillmore vigorously opposed the scheme. Fearing that he could not obtain satisfactory results from the reluctant corps commanders, Butler next asked his good friend from New Orleans days, Brigadier General Godfrey Weitzel, if he would lead such an expedition. Weitzel also demurred, on the grounds that the advance was exceedingly risky, that failure after opposition by the corps commanders might injure Butler's reputation, and that Smith and Gillmore would probably take steps to hinder an early start. Briefly Butler considered leading the advance himself, but with the landing not yet completed and his cavalry not yet heard from, he decided that the place of the army commander was at headquarters. Consequently, with the night almost spent, Butler sadly shelved the idea of an immediate advance on Richmond.[27]

Dawn of 6 May found the river shrouded in mist, but the sun soon burned it away, bringing the invasion fleet once more into view. Regiments had been coming ashore all night and the flow continued over the makeshift wharves throughout the morning. The latecomers were mostly X Corps units, and their commander had already begun to make excuses for their tardiness. Just as he had complained about the inadequate embarkation facilities at Gloucester Point, Gillmore now explained his troops' delay in terms of the miserable unloading facilities at Bermuda Hundred Landing. For those units already on shore, dawn brought the call to rise. Men stretched, shook out their blankets, boiled water for coffee, and surveyed their new surroundings. Some found the time to take a brief swim in the waters of the James, and members of one regiment amused themselves by chasing and capturing a young rabbit. Most of the troops, however, had time only to drink their coffee and bolt a few mouthfuls of hardtack before their officers called them into line.[28]

The first brigade to land, Brigadier General Charles Heckman's, was also the first to hit the road. Preceded by a skirmish line, Heckman's regiments led the rest of the Army of the James west from the landing site. Two miles inland, at Enon Church, a crossroads was reached. According to plan, the XVIII Corps took the left hand road, which ran in a southerly direction, while the X Corps continued westward. At first the men marched easily, admiring the magnificent stands of pine and oak lining the roads as well as the well-tended fields and occasional houses. Morale was high, since the men were glad to be off the transports and advancing so near to Richmond without opposition. But soon even the warbling of the birds and the ever-changing vistas could not distract the soldiers from the oppressive heat of the sun.[29]

Gradually at first, but more rapidly as the miles lengthened, the roadside came to be littered with discarded clothing and accoutrements of all descriptions. Because some men farther back in the column picked up various items and carried them forward for a time before also discarding them, the piles of unwanted equipment slowly moved forward. Nevertheless, the result was the same. An artilleryman who followed the infantry reported that "We literally walked on discarded blankets," and a Pennsylvanian estimated that something like twenty thousand pairs of new army shoes had been thrown away. A Maine soldier, appalled at the waste, calculated that a third army corps could have been clothed with the castoff material of the XVIII and X Corps. The valuable material was not allowed to remain discarded, however, because the marching soldiers were followed closely by local citizens who collected those items useful to the Confederacy.[30]

Without regard to the trail it was leaving behind, the Army of the James continued its march. The only sign of opposition was a lone horseman who remained just out of rifle range of the advancing XVIII Corps and on occasion insolently beckoned the Federals on. Otherwise there was no one to contest the army's progress, as the vacant houses and a deserted Confederate camp attested. At 8:30 A.M. Baldy Smith's vanguard reached a high plateau overlooking a great bend in the Appomattox River. There a large outcropping of limestone in the face of the bluff gave the area its name of Point of Rocks. There too was the large Cobb plantation, which greatly impressed the Federals with its "Northern air of neatness and repair." From the plateau Graham's gunboats could be seen puffing slowly up the Appomattox River. In the middle distance lay a Confederate earthwork and beyond that the spires of Petersburg's churches stood out clearly against the sky. Because of its commanding position, Cobb's Hill had been the site of a Confederate signal station, and the makeshift platform atop an outbuilding was soon occupied by signalmen in blue. Since Butler had selected the plateau's western edge as the southern anchor of his defensive line, Smith's leading elements were permitted to halt at Cobb's and wait for the rest of the XVIII Corps to arrive.[31]

Soon engineers were staking out the locations of fortifications and quartermasters were laying out campsites. The Cobb mansion was found to sit upon the position designated for a large fort, so the house was razed by men of the 2nd New Hampshire Infantry and the bricks from the chimney used to close a well. The outbuilding with the signal platform was allowed temporarily to remain and nearby the chief surgeon of the XVIII Corps established his hospital. Around noon the heavy work of fortifying the position began, and in a short time large mounds of dirt could be seen stretching northward in the direction of the X Corps sector. As the troops worked, Butler and Smith toured the lines, accompanied by the cheers of the men.[32]

Upon reaching the Enon Church crossroads, Gillmore's soldiers continued straight ahead, pausing only to form a skirmish line as a precaution. Unlike Smith's regiments, the units from the Department of the South were unaccustomed to strenuous marching with full field kit and the heat of the day affected them even more adversely. Their path also was littered with valuable items of clothing and equipment. In front, Confederate resistance was nonexistent. Shortly before 10:00 A.M. Gillmore's leading units reached the house of the Hatcher family, which was not far from the designated halting point. From Hatcher's the skirmishers proceeded gingerly until they approached a building in the forest known as Ware Bottom Church. A picket line was established near the church and, less than a mile in rear, Gillmore's men began to construct their half of Butler's defensive line. The work progressed slowly because many of the X Corps regiments, late in landing or imbued with the deliberateness of their commander, did not arrive at their designated positions until nearly sunset.[33]

In a 2:30 P.M. message to Grant, Butler reported proudly that all his units were ashore and "that we have taken the positions which were indicated to the commanding general at our last conference and are carrying out that plan."[34] There was some justification for Butler's elation. The river line had been secured, City Point had been seized, and a large Federal army had landed without incident less than twenty miles from Richmond. Protective entrenchments were slowly rising in front of all positions and a signal network had been established linking all occupied points. All this had been done in less than twenty-four hours, although it had been facilitated by the lack of Confederate opposition.[35]

With the first part of the plan accomplished, a decision regarding the next step had to be made. The absence of Confederate troops, along with the favorable reports of spies and escaped slaves,[36] pointed toward an immediate advance, but the incomplete state of the defensive line called for delay. Construction of protective fortifications seemed particularly important, because Grant's army was not yet within cooperating distance. The immediate advance on Richmond that Butler had so vigorously championed the night before did not look so appealing in the bright afternoon sun. Perhaps the Confederates were only biding their time. If so, prudence dictated a cautious probe westward to discover their positions.

In midafternoon Butler decided to send a brigade of the XVIII Corps toward the Richmond and Petersburg Railroad, two-and-a-half miles away. At the suggestion of Smith, Butler directed Gillmore to assist the demonstration by sending forward a detachment to protect Smith's right flank. Smith selected Brigadier General Charles Heckman's brigade for the probe, and Heckman's troops departed at 4:00 P.M. Gillmore, however, refused to order any of his men forward, probably because many of his units had not yet completed their march from the landing. Butler and Smith were informed of Gillmore's decision in a terse message from X Corps headquarters: "The project of striking the railroad to-night with a detachment from this command has been abandoned for what I deem good and sufficient reasons." As a substitute, other XVIII Corps units supported Heckman's advance by maneuvering beyond the Federal works.[37]

Unwilling to await the results of the XVIII Corps' maneuvers, Butler resolved to make a reconnaissance of his own on the X Corps front. Gathering his staff and a few mounted orderlies, he made his way through the X Corps camps toward the Federal picket line near Ware Bottom Church. Recognizing their commanding officer, the troops turned out to salute Butler with cheers and renditions of "Hail to the Chief" from regimental bands. Without pausing to acknowledge the greetings, Butler and his retinue continued forward to the picket line, then rode beyond it to the bank of a creek a short distance ahead. Suddenly, amidst a burst of gunfire, a group of Confederate horsemen dashed from concealment toward the startled Federals. In a mad race for the Federal lines, Butler and most of his party escaped safely, to the renewed cheers of the troops. However, the experience had a sobering effect on all concerned, and it was not destined to be repeated.[38]

On the river, where Admiral Lee's warships were carrying out their assigned tasks in support of the army, another event of the day instilled caution in the Federals. Upstream from Bermuda Hundred Landing three wooden gunboats were gingerly searching for Confederate torpedoes, when suddenly the U.S.S. Commodore Jones was blown apart by a tremendous explosion. Although several members of the Confederate Submarine Battery Service wee subsequently captured and forced to reveal the location of other torpedoes, sixty-nine crewmen of the Commodore Jones paid for the information with their lives. The loss of the Commodore Jones gave dramatic support to Admiral Lee's earlier decision not to risk his ironclads higher up the James. Butler might fume, but the cautious Lee would now require every foot of the river to be swept clean before moving farther upstream. Like the army, the navy had decided that the pace of the advance toward Richmond should be slowed.[39]

NOTES

1. *O.R.A.*, 51, pt. 2, 891–892; Beauregard to Whiting, 5 May 1864, Beauregard to Pickett, 5 May 1864, Beauregard to Sanford, 5 May 1864, Beauregard to Major F. Molloy, 5 May 1864, Beauregard to Bragg, 5 May 1864, Beauregard to Hill, 11:30 A.M., 5 May 1864, all in Official Telegrams, 22 April–9 June 1864, Beauregard Papers, LC; Roman, *Military Operations*, 2:547, 548.

2. This telegram has not been found, although there is a slight possibility that it is the Pickett to Cooper telegram reporting four ships, found in *O.R.A.*, 36, pt. 2, 955. More likely, it is the one alluded to in Pickett to Cooper and Beauregard, *O.R.A.*, 36, pt. 2, 964, which is misdated 6 May. The time of its arrival can be inferred from the contents of Beauregard's telegram to Hill at 11:30 A.M. and those to Hoke and Pickett at noon.

3. Beauregard to Hoke, noon, 5 May 1864, Beauregard to Whiting, 5 May 1864, Beauregard to Pickett, noon, 5 May 1864, all in Official Telegrams, 22 April–9 June 1864, Beauregard Papers, LC; Roman, *Military Operations*, 2:547–548.

4. Quoted in Beauregard to Bragg, 12:30 P.M., 5 May 1864, Official Telegrams, 22 April–9 June 1864, Beauregard Papers, LC.

5. Beauregard to Pickett, 12:30 P.M., 5 May 1864, and Beauregard to Pickett, untimed, 5 May 1864 (two telegrams), Beauregard to Bragg, 12:30 P.M., 5 May 1864, all in Official Telegrams, 22 April–9 June 1864, Beauregard Papers, LC; Roman, *Military Operations*, 2:548, 549.

6. *O.R.A.*, 36, pt. 2, 955; Beauregard to Bragg, 12:35 P.M., 5 May 1864, Official Telegrams, 22 April–9 June 1864, Beauregard Papers, LC. There are slight punctuation differences between the two versions, with the Library of Congress copy making more sense.

7. John M. Otey to Colonel Crawley, 5 May 1864, Beauregard to Hill, 5 May 1864, both in Official Telegrams, 22 April–9 June 1864, Beauregard Papers, LC; Beauregard to Martin, 5 May 1864, Beauregard to Weldon Quartermaster, 5 May 1864, both in Letter Book, April–May 1864, Beauregard Papers, LC.

8. Beauregard to Pickett, untimed, 5 May 1864, Beauregard to Pickett, 4:30 P.M., 5 May 1864, both in Official Telegrams, 22 April–9 June 1864, Beauregard Papers, LC; Roman, *Military Operations*, 2:548, 549.

9. *O.R.A.*, 36, pt. 2, 964. This message is definitely misdated. A 6 May date for a sighting report from the lower James River of the kind described therein makes no sense whatever. However, the notation on the message "Received Richmond, 3.35 A.M.," if correct, may explain why Pickett received no answer from the War Department on 5 May. Apparently, for some unknown reason, Pickett's telegrams to Richmond were not reaching that city until many hours later, in this case not until the next day.

10. Harrison, *Pickett's Men*, 124; Memorandum of Movements, Co. F, 31st N.C., Wilson G. Lamb Papers, North Carolina Division of Archives and History, Raleigh, N.C. The 31st North Carolina Infantry had an aggregate present on 28 March 1864 of 583 officers and men, but an effective total of only 527. Field return of Clingman's Brigade, 28 March 1864, Thomas L. Clingman Military Papers, Southern Historical Collection, University of North Carolina, Chapel Hill, N.C.

11. Harrison, *Pickett's Men*, 124; *O.R.A.*, 51, pt. 2, 896; William Miller Owen, *In Camp and Battle with the Washington Artillery of New Orleans* (Boston: Ticknor and Company, 1885), 308–310; Fletcher H. Archer, "The Defense of Petersburg on the 9th of June, 1864," in George S. Bernard, ed., *War Talks of Confederate Veterans* (Petersburg: Fenn and Owen, 1892), 114; Bessie Callender, "Personal Recollections of the Civil War," unpublished typescript in Visitor Center, Petersburg National Military Park, Petersburg, Virginia.

12. Freeman, *Lee's Lieutenants*, 3:457.

13. Harrison, *Pickett's Men*, 124; Memorandum of Movements, Co. F, 31st N.C., Wilson G. Lamb Papers, NCDAH; *O.R.A.*, 51, pt. 1, 222, 225, 227–228, 231; Owen, *Washington Artillery*, 310–311; Archer, "Defense of Petersburg," in Bernard, ed., *War Talks*, 114; Callender, "Personal Recollections," 6–7; John Scott, "A Ruse of War," in *The Annals of the War Written by Leading Participants North and South* (Philadelphia: The Times Publishing Company, 1879), 381–382. The 31st North Carolina

contributed an effective total of 527 men, the reserves and militia an estimated 500 by the end of the day, the artillery, including the Washington Artillery and two other batteries, 402 (O.R.A., 33:1201), and Scott's cavalry 31, making Pickett's total effective force 1,460 men.

14. William H. S. Burgwyn Diary, 4 [5] May and 7 [8] May 1864, North Carolina Division of Archives and History, Raleigh, N.C.; Walter Clark, ed., Histories of the Several Regiments and Battalions from North Carolina in the Great War 1861–65, 5 vols. (Goldsboro, N.C.: Nash Brothers, 1901), 3:210–211; Isham Pitman to his wife, 5 May 1864, in Confederate Papers—Miscellaneous, Southern Historical Collection, University of North Carolina, Chapel Hill, N.C.

15. O.R.A., 36, pt. 2, 956, 957.

16. Ibid., 956; O.R.A., 51, pt. 2, 892. One of these telegrams is marked "Received 8.30 A.M.," presumably 6 May. If correct, this is another example of Pickett's messages to Richmond having been somehow delayed for many hours, and this may help to explain Cooper's silence.

17. O.R.A., 36, pt. 2, 957. This message from Pickett at least reached Richmond, as noted in the endorsement: "This was sent to General Bragg and returned in the morning of the 6th instant marked in pencil 'seen,' as will appear on the second fold. Riely."

18. O.R.A., 36, pt. 2, 956, 957; O.R.A., 51, pt. 2, 891; Beauregard to Bragg, telegrams of 6:15 P.M. and 6:45 P.M., 5 May 1864, Official Telegrams, 22 April–9 June 1864, Beauregard Papers, LC; Roman, Military Operations, 2:549.

19. O.R.A., 36, pt. 2, 958.

20. Beauregard to Pickett, 9:30 P.M., 5 May 1864, Official Telegrams, 22 April–9 June 1864, Beauregard Papers, LC.

21. Dowdey, Lee's Last Campaign, 233.

22. Beauregard to Bragg, 10:00 P.M., 5 May 1864, Official Telegrams, 22 April–9 June, 1864, Beauregard Papers, LC; O.R.A., 51, pt. 2, 891; Special Orders No. 3, Department of North Carolina and Southern Virginia, in General D. H. Hill Papers, Virginia State Library, Richmond, Va.; O.R.A., 36, pt. 2, 960. Beauregard's message was addressed to Bragg but the Petersburg operator was to furnish Pickett a copy.

23. O.R.A., 51, pt. 2, 892–893; O.R.N., 10:11; Jones, War Clerk, 2:198.

24. Dunbar Rowland, ed., Jefferson Davis, Constitutionalist: His Letters, Papers and Speeches, 10 vols. (Jackson: Mississippi Department of Archives and History, 1923), 6:247–248; O.R.A., 51, pt. 2, 887 (misdated 4 May here).

25. Jefferson Davis, The Rise and Fall of the Confederate Government, 2 vols. (New York: D. Appleton and Company, 1881), 2:510–511; O.R.A., 33, 1299; Rowland, ed., Davis Papers, 6:247; O.R.A., 36, pt. 2, 246, 958; Bushrod R. Johnson Diary, 5 May 1864, Johnson Papers, National Archives, Washington, D.C.

26. For discussion of the jurisdiction problem, see Freeman, Lee's Lieutenants, 3:451, and Dowdey, Lee's Last Campaign, 228–232.

27. Memorandum, 8 January 1879, Benjamin Butler Papers, LC; Butler to W. P. Darby [Derby], 26 June 1882, Benjamin Butler Papers, LC; Butler, Butler's Book, 640–642; T. A. Bland, Life of Benjamin F. Butler (Boston: Lee & Shepard, 1879), 149–150. All of these accounts appear to be based upon the Memorandum of 8 January 1879, which may have been produced to aid in the preparation of Bland's biography. After the publication of Bland's Life, Quincy Gillmore categorically denied the truth of the Bland-Butler version in a letter to the New York Times: "I never opposed or had opportunity or occasion to oppose any movement or expedition in the direction of Richmond, either on 5 May or any other time, and the command of the expedition was never offered to me, directly or indirectly." New York Times, 3 July 1879. Baldy Smith also disputed the Bland-Butler account. In a letter to W. P. Derby on 7 February 1883, Smith commented: "With reference to Gen'l Butler's assertion of the position taken by Gen'l Gillmore and myself as to his march upon Richmond, we have both denied it in the public prints. The denial was unanswered." Quoted in Derby, Bearing Arms, 288. Also appearing in Derby's regimental history was Butler's version of the incident as related in the letter to Derby cited in this note. Derby, Bearing Arms, 285. The claims of Gillmore and Smith notwithstanding, the Bland-Butler account has been accepted as true by Bruce Catton in Never Call Retreat (Garden City: Doubleday 1965), 346–347, and Allan Nevins in Organized War to Victory, 47.

28. Cunningham, Adirondack Regiment, 103, O.R.A., 36, pt. 2, 472–473; Roe, Twenty-Fourth Massachusetts, 277; De Forest, Random Sketches, 147; Walter S. Clemence Memoranda, 6 May 1864, NCC.

29. Day, Rambles, 138; Drake, Ninth New Jersey, 172–173; Cleveland, ed., "Campaign of Promise," 309; Clark, My Experience, 56–57; Beecher, First Connecticut Light Battery, 1:333, 338; Putnam, Story of Company A, 264; Haynes, Second New Hampshire, 167.

30. Copp, *Reminiscences*, 355; Stowits, *One Hundredth New York*, 246; Cunningham, *Adirondack Regiment*, 104; Brady, *Eleventh Maine*, 175–176; Eldredge, *Third New Hampshire*, 461; Beecher, *First Connecticut Light Battery*, 1:338; Price, *Ninety-Seventh Pennsylvania*, 251; Clark, *Iron Hearted Regiment*, 104.

31. Emmerton, *Twenty-Third Massachusetts*, 174; Drake, *Ninth New Jersey*, 172–173; Bartlett, *Twelfth New Hampshire*, 172–173; Cleveland, ed., "Campaign of Promise," 309; O.R.A., 36, pt. 2, 22, 474; Kreutzer, *Ninety-Eighth New York*, 185; Cunningham, *Adirondack Regiment*, 104; Day, *Rambles*, 138; Thompson, *Thirteenth New Hampshire*, 257; Putnam, *Story of Company A*, 264; Brown, *Signal Corps*, 427.

32. Copp, *Reminiscences*, 360; Bartlett, *Twelfth New Hampshire*, 173; Haynes, *Second New Hampshire*, 167–168; Kreutzer, *Ninety-Eight New York*, 184–185; Derby, *Bearing Arms*, 252; Thompson, *Thirteenth New Hampshire*, 257; Cunningham, *Adirondack Regiment*, 105; Cleveland, ed., "Campaign of Promise," 310.

33. Little, *Seventh New Hampshire*, 242; Clark, *Thirty-Ninth Illinois*, 177–178, 310–311; Walkley, *Seventh Connecticut*, 130; Stowits, *One Hundredth New York*, 246; Clark, *Iron Hearted Regiment*, 104; Cadwell, *Old Sixth*, 89; O.R.A., 36, pt. 2, 474; Price, *Ninety-Seventh Pennsylvania*, 252–253; Dickey, *Eighty-Fifth Pennsylvania*, 321; Eldredge, *Third New Hampshire*, 461–462; Tourtellotte, *History of Company K*, 168; Roe, *Twenty-Fourth Massachusetts*, 277–278.

34. O.R.A., 36, pt. 2, 471.

35. Ibid., 31–32.

36. *New York Times*, 10 May 1864.

37. Butler, *Butler's Book*, 642–643; O.R.A., 36, pt. 2, 153–154, 475, 518; Thompson, *Thirteenth New Hampshire*, 157–158; Bartlett, *Twelfth New Hampshire*, 172.

38. Little, *Seventh New Hampshire*, 242; Walkley, *Seventh Connecticut*, 131; Clark, *Thirty-Ninth Illinois*, 308–310; Beecher, *First Connecticut Light Battery*, 1:340–341.

39. O.R.N., 10:3–5, 9–16, 46; O.R.A., 36, pt. 2, 22; Brown, *Signal Corps*, 427; William B. Avery, "Gunboat Service on the James River," *Personal Narratives of Events in the War of the Rebellion, Being Papers Read Before the Rhode Island Soldiers and Sailors Historical Society*, Third Series, no. 3 (Providence, R.I.: The Society, 1884), 17.

☆ 6 ☆

The Battles of Port Walthall Junction
6–7 May 1864

At 5:00 A.M. on 6 May, P. G. T. Beauregard wired Adjutant General Cooper: "Am I authorized to control to best advantage, as I may think proper, all troops now in this Dept. or arriving?" This authority was crucial, because the only unit that could reach Petersburg from the south in time to reinforce Pickett was Hagood's Brigade, in transit from Wilmington. Unless Beauregard received permission to retain Hagood, George Pickett's only source of aid would be Richmond, since Beauregard's own troops were still scattered from New Berne to the Blackwater line. Cooper's answer, transmitted through Pickett, was vague: "Please urge forward by rail the troops ordered from the south to Petersburg, which is much threatened." This was not the broad grant of authority that Beauregard sought, but it did imply that Hagood's men could be used at Petersburg. Now everything depended upon the dilapidated Southern railroad system.[1]

Sensing the tone of desperation in Pickett's reports, Beauregard attempted to encourage his subordinate. At 7:00 A.M. Pickett was informed that Harvey Hill was on his way to Petersburg with Beauregard's personal instructions. Three hours later Beauregard wired the district commander that several hundred of Hagood's men had just passed through Weldon, with more to follow. Yet Pickett doubted that he could wait for Hagood's arrival and he suggested that he might have to burn the Appomattox River bridges at Petersburg. Around 10:30 A.M. Beauregard counseled Pickett not to destroy the railroad bridge before such a drastic step became absolutely necessary. Thirty minutes later Pickett was authorized to communicate directly with Braxton Bragg. As a final gesture, Colonel D. B. Harris, already in Petersburg, was instructed at noon to join Hill in advising Pickett. At the same time Beauregard told Harris that his illness precluded his own presence at Petersburg until noon of the next day, or possibly even later.[2]

The best way for Beauregard to aid Pickett was to expedite the flow of troops northward. From Wilmington, Chase Whiting reported that all of Hagood's Brigade had passed that point and 1,100 of Henry Wise's Virginians were ready to depart, but that the remainder of Wise's Brigade would not arrive at Wilmington until the next day. Whiting also asked Beauregard, "Can you save Petersburg?" To a large extent the answer depended upon how soon Robert Hoke could bring his four brigades back from New Berne. To that end, Beauregard on 6 May repeatedly urged Hoke to hurry northward. Instead of marching his men to Weldon, Hoke was to move toward Kinston, where rail transportation would await him. He was also to send his cavalry commander, Brigadier General James Dearing, north to command the various cavalry regiments in Pickett's district.[3] Having prodded Hoke, Beauregard ordered army quartermasters throughout North Carolina to collect troop trains at Kinston. To protect the trains against a possible Federal cavalry raid north of Weldon, Beauregard ordered a South Carolina infantry unit known as the Holcombe Legion to Weldon. Half of the Legion joined the Weldon garrison and the remaining five companies were scattered along the Petersburg Railroad as far north as Stony Creek.[4]

By midafternoon Beauregard had done all he could to meet the crisis. To a request for troops from D. H. Hill at Petersburg, Beauregard replied that more of Hagood's men had passed Weldon, with the remainder due there by 4:00 P.M. Also, half of Wise's Brigade was scheduled to reach Weldon that night.[5] Shortly thereafter the telegraph at Beauregard's headquarters tapped out a message signed by Jefferson Davis himself: "Through General Bragg and otherwise you are no doubt well informed of events in this direction. I hope you will be able at Petersburg to direct operations both before and behind you, so as to meet necessities." Somewhat bemused by the president's solicitous tone, Beauregard at 3:30 P.M. wired that he was still too ill to travel but hoped to leave for Petersburg the next morning.[6]

As the day progressed, George Pickett's situation continued to deteriorate. A train bearing three hundred of Hagood's South Carolinians had arrived during the night, but, lacking the authority to halt it, Pickett had to allow it to disappear up the track toward Richmond.[7] Throughout the morning he watched helplessly as the Army of the James ponderously advanced from Bermuda Hundred Landing. By midmorning his signalmen reported the abandonment of the signal station at Cobb's Hill and the presence of Federal troops within three miles of the Richmond and Petersburg Railroad. All of this disturbing news was relayed to Adjutant General Cooper, but silence remained Cooper's only reply. Finally Pickett gave up on Cooper and, relying upon Beauregard's authorization, he began to address his telegrams directly to Braxton Bragg:

> Do you intend holding the railroad between this place and Richmond? I sent General Cooper eight or ten telegrams on yesterday, but received no reply. The enemy will try to cut the railroad to-day, advancing from Bermuda Hundred, I think.[8]

In his reply Bragg ordered Pickett to concentrate Hagood's arriving units five miles beyond Petersburg at Port Walthall Junction.[9] There the Richmond and Petersburg Railroad was joined from the east by a branch line that terminated at Port Walthall on the Appomattox River south of Cobb's Hill. If the Federals were going to operate against the railroad, Port Walthall Junction was a logical place for them to strike. Thus the deployment of Hagood's men to the junction would almost assure their service against Butler. The arrival of these fresh troops was eagerly anticipated, for Pickett was well aware of his inability to defend Petersburg with the force at hand. During the day more militia companies appeared from surrounding counties to swell the ranks of Petersburg's defenders, but many of these men seemed not to take their role seriously.[10]

As the Federals cautiously advanced from Bermuda Hundred, Pickett realized that his little force might have to fight on two fronts. Not only was he threatened by the Federals at Cobb's Hill, but Hincks's black regiments at City Point also might choose to advance at any moment. Facing Hincks was the 31st North Carolina Infantry, supported by the local defense companies and the Washington Artillery Battalion. In front of these troops, Major Scott's makeshift cavalry screen of armed civilians patrolled. The Federal advance from Bermuda Hundred precluded rein-forcing these weak units and indeed required that some sort of force be scraped together to guard the city's northern approaches. To meet the new threat Pickett deployed the 51st North Carolina Infantry and a battery of the Washington Artillery two miles beyond the city near an earthwork known as Fort Clifton, on the north bank of the Appomattox River. To give the impression that this handful of defenders was hourly being reinforced, Pickett shuttled railroad locomotives in and out of town, to the accompaniment of much whistling and the noisy cheers of cooperating citizens. He also spent several hours riding along the lines encouraging the troops.[11]

Although some of the local militiamen adopted a holiday air, many citizens of Petersburg and Richmond grew anxious over the fate of their cities. In Petersburg, Mrs. Pickett opened her home to townspeople who were frightened and needed reassurance, and numbers of them came. Wives of the militiamen began to worry about their husbands, especially after a trickle of refugees from the vicinity of City Point began to appear on the streets. In Richmond the militia was also mobilized, but the populace seemed less concerned because of their greater distance from the landing site and their larger garrison. Local diarists who remarked upon the Federal presence recorded that the city remained calm. On the other hand, a Federal officer held captive in Libby Prison found "great excitement in the city."[12]

While Pickett fretted and Richmond's citizens hoped for the best, Major General Robert Ransom was taking steps of his own to counter the Federal threat. Ransom's most important position was the complex of defenses radiating from Fort Darling at Drewry's Bluff. Stretching southwestward from the fort for approximately three miles were two lines of entrenchments that barred the direct route to Richmond from Petersburg and Bermuda Hundred. The normal garrison at Drewry's Bluff consisted of approximately 450 Marines and artillerymen, but this was now clearly inadequate.[13] At 3:00 A.M. the small Tennessee brigade of Brigadier General Bushrod Johnson, numbering only 1,168 men, crossed the James River to Drewry's Bluff and filed into the fortifications. Two hours later, Johnson's men were joined by the first contingent of Hagood's Brigade, which Pickett had forwarded against his better judgment.[14]

Upon his arrival at Drewry's Bluff, Johnson rode out to explore the surrounding territory. During his absence Ransom ordered Hagood's men to move by train seven miles south to Port Walthall Junction. Since no train was available, Lieutenant Colonel A. T. Dargan and his three hundred men of the 21st South Carolina Infantry started toward the junction on foot. At 11:00 A.M., shortly after Johnson returned, he received a peremptory order from Ransom to march his entire command to the junction and defend the railroad at all costs. Until Ransom's order, Johnson had had no idea that the railroad was in danger, but he at once put his brigade in motion and marched to within two miles of the junction. There a courier joined him with a dispatch from the commander at Drewry's Bluff. Major F. W. Smith reported that the Federals were advancing near Ware Bottom Church and he suggested that Johnson return to Fort Darling. Since Ware Bottom Church was almost due east of the brigade's position, Johnson decided to remain where he was. Meanwhile, his place at Drewry's Bluff was taken by Brigadier General Archibald Gracie's Alabama Brigade, which arrived from Richmond by steamer.[15]

Just before 3:30 P.M. a second train carrying three hundred more of Hagood's men rolled into Petersburg. This detachment, three companies each of the 21st and 25th South Carolina Regiments, was dispatched northward to Port Walthall Junction by Pickett, as required by Bragg's instructions of the morning.[16] Its departure was greatly regretted because of disturbing reports from the Blackwater line that Federal cavalry were assaulting the river defenses. Thus when signalmen reported a Federal advance from the vicinity of Cobb's Hill late in the afternoon, Pickett could only hope for a miracle.[17]

Ever since Butler's landing at Bermuda Hundred, Confederate efforts had been directed toward finding enough troops to seal off the peninsula before the Army of the James could strike the Richmond and Petersburg Railroad. By 4:00 P.M. Confederate units were slowly concentrating on both the northern and southern shoulders of the Federal penetration. On the northern flank, Johnson's Brigade faced the bulk of the Federal X Corps, while Gracie's Brigade was steaming down the James River to reinforce Drewry's Bluff. To the south Pickett had only one regiment and a battery covering the XVIII Corps' approach routes to Petersburg, while another regiment supported by artillery and militia watched Hincks at City Point. Directly in the middle of the gap at Port Walthall Junction stood the three hundred men of the 21st South Carolina Infantry. Somewhere on the railroad between the junction and Petersburg was a train carrying another three hundred South Carolinians, while far below Petersburg were other units on trains, the rest of Hagood's men as well as Wise's and Colquitt's Brigades. Marching toward trains waiting at Kinston, North Carolina, were the four brigades under Hoke.[18] Still, until the decrepit Southern railroads delivered their cargoes to the point of conflict, the little band of Hagood's men at Port Walthall Junction had to shoulder the burden alone.

At exactly 4:00 P.M. Brigadier General Charles Heckman ordered his brigade to leave its bivouac at Cobb's Hill. The brigade, consisting of the 23rd, 25th, and 27th Massachusetts Infantry Regiments and the 9th New Jersey Infantry, numbered 2,700 officers and men, most of them veterans, although they had not been under fire for nearly a year. Joining them was one section (two guns) of Battery L, 4th U. S. Artillery. Heckman himself was a small, thin officer, noted for a nervous manner and a pugnacious disposition. On this day his orders were simple: advance to the railroad and develop the Confederate strength and dispositions, but under no circumstances bring on a general engagement.[19]

Once beyond the Federal pickets, Heckman's brigade pushed cautiously forward, preceded by a skirmish line. The road from Cobb's Hill meandered first through a ravine, then past an old mill, and finally emerged on another plateau crowned by a large open area known variously as the Barnes farm, Dr. Walthall's, or the Mary Dunn plantation. Beyond the ravine Confederate pickets were discovered, but they retired readily before the Federal advance. Reaching the eastern edge of the plateau, the leading units saw the Dunn plantation stretching before them, "a parallelogram of cleared fields, undulating, but so nearly level that many points commanded a view of the whole." To the south was a dense forest, and to the north was the wooded bed of Ashton Creek. At the far end of the fields a row of bushes and a fence masked the Richmond and Petersburg Railroad. Splitting the plantation was the roadbed of the abandoned Port Walthall branch line.[20]

Unknown to the Federals, the junction at that moment was defended solely by Lieutenant Colonel Dargan's 300 South Carolinians, who had arrived from Drewry's Bluff between 3:30 and 4:00 P.M. Just as Dargan prepared to resist the advance of Heckman's 2,700 men, the train bearing the remainder of the 21st South Carolina and three companies of the 25th South Carolina arrived from Petersburg. With them was Colonel Robert Graham, who assumed overall command of his own 21st South Carolina under Dargan and the battalion of the 25th South Carolina under Major John Glover. Hastily forming his 600 men into line, Graham led them 300 yards east of the railroad to a sunken country road that served as a natural entrenchment. Posting Glover's battalion on the left with his flank resting on Ashton Creek, and Dargan's regiment on the right with his open flank resting in the woods, Graham sent out skirmishers and awaited the Federal attack.[21]

Heckman noted Graham's arrival, but he could not determine the size of the Confederate force without closer inspection. In the center of the field he deployed the 25th and 27th Massachusetts Regiments, with the latter slightly in advance on the right. The 23rd Massachusetts was placed on their left in the edge of the woods lining the long field, while the 9th New Jersey was kept in column to guard against a Confederate flank attack from the north. The artillerymen unlimbered their two guns on the left of the 27th Massachusetts and opened fire upon the half-hidden Confederates. Satisfied with the alignment of his brigade, Heckman ordered the advance to continue. The time was just after 5:00 P.M. and the late afternoon sun shone directly into the eyes of the Federal infantrymen.[22]

The Confederate skirmishers retreated before the Federals until a slight depression in the field was reached. There the Federal skirmishers fired a volley, which was answered by Graham's entire command in the sunken road. Skirmishers on both sides scrambled for cover as the firing became general. After a few minutes

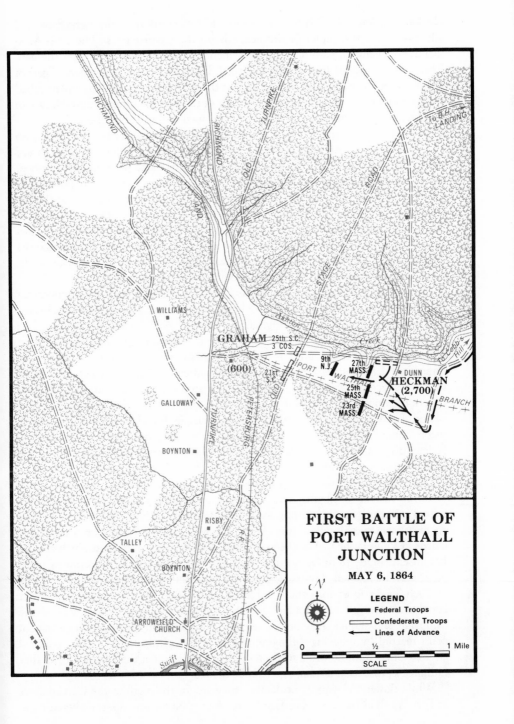

**FIRST BATTLE OF
PORT WALTHALL
JUNCTION**

MAY 6, 1864

LEGEND

▬ Federal Troops
▭ Confederate Troops
← Lines of Advance

0   ½   1 Mile

SCALE

Heckman ordered the 9th New Jersey to leave its position on the right flank and advance across the center of the field toward the Confederates. The 25th Massachusetts opened a path and the Jerseymen followed Heckman through the gap. Receiving a sharp fire from the sunken road, Heckman ordered a charge and part of the 9th swept forward in a ragged rush. At the same instant, thirteen bullets felled the general's horse and another struck him in the hand. Without pause Heckman mounted a horse offered by an aide and continued to direct the action.[23]

In the meantime the 9th New Jersey had reached the swale, but it could go no farther. Seeing its difficulty, Heckman directed it to retire, which was done in less than perfect order. This left the 27th Massachusetts once more in the advance, supported by the 25th Massachusetts. Although he was actually in no danger, Heckman believed that he was facing at least two Confederate brigades and that he would have difficulty in reaching the railroad.[24] These conclusions, coupled with the lateness of the hour, dictated a withdrawal. Heckman ordered the 27th Massachusetts to cover the retreat by executing a series of maneuvers that distracted the Confederates. The scarcity of stretchers compelled the Federals to leave their eight dead behind, although all of the sixty wounded were retrieved.[25]

Even before Heckman's return, Baldy Smith had concluded that the movement had been a failure. Smith, however, believed that success could have been achieved had Gillmore participated as originally requested. At 8:30 P.M. he suggested to Butler that a larger force be sent toward the railroad on the following day. Both corps should contribute units to the column, so as not to endanger the army's unfinished defense line.[26] Several hours later, after the details of Heckman's affair had been received, Smith again proposed to strike the railroad at Port Walthall Junction. Since Heckman and two of Smith's staff officers who had been present agreed that at least one veteran Confederate brigade defended the junction, Smith recommended that the expedition consist of one brigade from each of the five Federal divisions. He added that part of the troops should make a diversion at the Dunn plantation, while the remainder struck the railroad nearer to Richmond.[27]

Butler agreed to consider Smith's suggestions, but on one matter he had already made up his mind. Quincy Gillmore's failure to cooperate with Smith and his refusal to furnish an explanation for his conduct were only the latest in a series of aggravations stretching back into April. Gillmore had been slow in moving the X Corps to Virginia, he had not been available for planning conferences, he had been late in embarking from Gloucester Point and late in debarking at Bermuda Hundred. Now he had failed to participate in a movement that might have severed one of Richmond's most important rail links. With these facts before him, Butler concluded that Gillmore would only hinder the successful prosecution of the campaign and should therefore be removed. Rather than precipitate a distasteful court-martial by relieving Gillmore, Butler characteristically adopted a political course. Once again he wrote to Senator Henry Wilson, but this time he asked that Gillmore's promotion to major general be denied.[28]

While Butler and Smith considered strategies for the morrow, the Confederates at Port Walthall Junction gave thanks for their good fortune. Outnumbered more than four to one, Colonel Graham's six hundred infantrymen had repulsed a veteran Federal brigade supported by artillery, thereby saving the railroad at a cost of only two killed and thirty-three wounded.[29] Soon after the Federals withdrew, Confederate reinforcements began to arrive. From Richmond came an artillery battery, Captain J. D. Hankins's Surry Light Artillery.[30] Johnson's Brigade also appeared, and it occupied a position behind the railroad embankment to the right rear of Graham's South Carolinians. From Petersburg came the remainder of the 25th South Carolina Infantry and the 27th South Carolina, both of Hagood's Brigade. Hagood arrived with them and reported to Johnson for orders. By late evening the Confederate force at the Junction comprised the two brigades Heckman imagined he had been facing that afternoon. The breach in the Confederate defenses was not sealed, but by midnight of 6 May the situation had markedly improved for the Confederates.[31]

Not everyone was aware of the improvement. George Pickett, who had seen all his potential reinforcements continue northward, was for some reason still being excluded from the flow of information. Long after the railroad had been successfully defended, he still did not know what forces, if any, were stationed beyond Port Walthall Junction. Unknown to Pickett, the only troops capable of countering attacks upon the railroad were being guided by Robert Ransom's Department of Richmond. While Hagood's and Johnson's soldiers bivouacked at Port Walthall Junction, Gracie's Brigade occupied the Drewry's Bluff fortifications. If the Federals were to attack Drewry's Bluff on the next day, Johnson's force would support Gracie. None of this was communicated to Pickett, who suffered through another sleepless night, fearing for the safety of Petersburg and the railroad.[32]

While Pickett tossed and turned during the early morning hours of 7 May, Benjamin Butler decided to adopt Baldy Smith's suggestion for a new attack on the railroad. The objectives of the movement were, first, to make the Confederates believe that Butler's ultimate goal was Petersburg, and, second, to destroy as much of the railroad as possible.[33] Butler ordered Quincy Gillmore to assign three of his brigades temporarily to Smith for the expedition, and Gillmore reluctantly selected the brigades of Colonels Harris Plaisted, William Barton, and Jeremiah Drake. These units, together with Brigadier General Hiram Burnham's brigade from the XVIII Corps, were placed under the control of Brigadier General William Brooks. Charles Heckman's brigade was to cooperate with Brooks by returning to the Dunn plantation for a reenactment of the previous day's probe. Counting Heckman's troops, nineteen infantry regiments totaling over 8,000 men were involved. Brooks also received an artillery battery and the only available cavalry regiment, the First New York Mounted Rifles.[34]

Seventy miles to the south, P. G. T. Beauregard resumed his efforts to speed reinforcements to Virginia. At 7:30 A.M. he telegraphed Pickett that he was too ill to leave Weldon, but that troops would be forwarded as they became available. Beauregard feared that the Federal cavalry force that had crossed the Blackwater River was heading for the Petersburg Railroad. If Pickett was to receive reinforcements in time to stabilize the situation around Petersburg, that railroad had to be kept open at all costs. Unfortunately the cavalry regiments needed to defend the railroad were not immediately available. Although the 7th Confederate Cavalry and the 62nd Georgia Cavalry on the Blackwater could be recalled quickly, the rest of Beauregard's mounted units were still in North Carolina. Consequently, Beauregard ordered Robert Hoke to rush his cavalry northward, and to send Brigadier General James Dearing in command.[35]

Below Weldon reinforcements were rolling toward Virginia as fast as the worn-out railroads could carry them. Wise's Brigade was nearest at hand, with part of it being expected to reach Weldon sometime during the day.[36] Farther south, Hoke's four brigades were still tramping the dusty roads leading to Kinston. First to arrive in Kinston was Colonel William Lewis's North Carolina Brigade, which entered the town at 1:00 P.M. and boarded the cars at sunset. Following close behind Lewis were the North Carolina regiments of Brigadier General Matt Ransom, brother of Robert Ransom.[37] Far to the north in Virginia, August Kautz's troopers that very afternoon sent the Stony Creek bridge on the Petersburg Railroad crashing down in flames. The race between the horses of iron and those of flesh and blood seemed to have been won by the latter.[38]

Little more could be done by the Confederates facing the Army of the James until Beauregard's troops reached Virginia. At Petersburg, Pickett shifted another artillery battery north of the Appomattox, but his little band of men could not long delay a determined Federal advance. In Richmond, guards removed the Federal officers held in Libby Prison and placed them aboard trains for evacuation south via Danville. Within the government bureaucracy, Secretary of the Navy Mallory and Secretary of War Seddon quarreled over responsibility for the James River obstructions, which prevented Commodore J. K. Mitchell's ironclads from attacking the Federal invasion fleet. On land, Brigadier General Seth Barton's Virginia Brigade moved into the Drewry's Bluff defenses, joining Gracie's Brigade already there. As senior officer, Barton deployed both brigades in the outer defense line, which he found to be badly located. His request to withdraw to the intermediate fortifications brought no response, so Barton remained where he was.[39]

Midway between Barton's two brigades at Drewry's Bluff and Pickett's half-brigade at Petersburg was Bushrod Johnson's force at Port Walthall Junction. Born in Ohio and raised as a Quaker, Johnson was a West Point graduate who had spent much of his adult life in Tennessee. A tall man with course features that were seldom animated with strong emotion, he had commanded a brigade of Tennesseans in the western theater since July 1862. Originally organized in five regiments, but now consolidated into three because of losses, Johnson's Brigade had arrived in eastern Virginia only two days earlier.[40] With the Tennesseans at Port Walthall Junction were the 21st, 25th, and 27th South Carolina Regiments of Hagood's Brigade, augmented by Hankins's Battery and a provisional battery manned by convalescents and furloughed men from Petersburg. Due to the earlier date of his commission, Johnson commanded the united force, although Hagood's three regiments comprised 1,500 of the 2,668-man infantry contingent.[41] Also present, though serving as an unranked mounted scout, was Brigadier General Roger Pryor, who had come from Petersburg in search of action. More welcome still was Major General D. H. Hill, one of the Confederacy's most tenacious fighters. Hill had ridden out from Pickett's headquarters early in the morning to survey conditions at the junction. Upon finding Johnson, a friend from Chickamauga days, he consented to remain.[42]

Johnson's troop deployment reflected the order in which the various units had arrived at Port Walthall Junction on 6 May. Hagood's Brigade held its old position along the railroad, with its right resting just north of the junction itself and its left ending at the intersection of the Richmond turnpike and the railroad. Johnson's Brigade prolonged Hagood's line to the south, still paralleling the tracks. The artillery was spaced at intervals behind the infantry on higher ground. When scouts reported no enemy nearer than Ware Bottom Church, three miles away, Johnson hesitantly decided to probe forward to discover the Federal intentions. At 10:00 A.M. Hagood led his regiments out from behind the railroad and started down the Old Stage Road, which slanted in a northeasterly direction from the junction. Skirmishers preceded the column, while D. H. Hill accompanied the advance guard. They had hardly traveled a mile when they suddenly met an approaching squadron of Federal cavalry. Shots rang out and the second battle for the railroad was joined.[43]

The cavalry proved to be eight companies of Colonel Benjamin Onderdonk's First New York Mounted Rifles, which had been assigned by Brooks to lead the expedition. Pausing only for a moment, the Mounted Rifles swept down the road in an impromptu charge that disintegrated under the fire of the Confederate infantrymen. Having shown that an enemy force was blocking the road, the horsemen fell back upon their own infantry. Although they were subjected to much derision by the footsoldiers, the cavalrymen had done their job. After the Mounted Rifles retired, Brooks directed Brigadier General Hiram Burnham to develop the Confederate position further with his brigade. Burnham ordered his leading regiment, the 8th Connecticut, to form a skirmish line and advance along the west side of the road, supported by the 13th New Hampshire. His remaining regiments, the 10th New Hampshire and 118th New York, also deployed west of the road.[44]

While Burnham's men changed from column into line, Johnson Hagood positioned the 27th South Carolina east of the road and three companies of the 25th South Carolina to the west. Soon the firing grew in intensity, particularly on the Confederate left. Fearful of being outflanked, Bushrod Johnson ordered Hagood to withdraw to his original position behind the railroad. As Hagood's men safely completed their retreat, a second Federal force was observed approaching from the vicinity of the Dunn plantation. This proved to be Heckman's brigade, which had been ordered to distract Confederate attention from Brooks's main force. To meet this new threat Johnson sent two of his Tennessee regiments and two of Hankins's guns into the woods south of the road along which Heckman was advancing. As the artillery opened fire, the Federals deployed in line-of-battle and slowly edged forward toward the railroad. To prevent his small detachment from being overwhelmed, Johnson recalled it to the main line, but not before a Federal battery had exploded the ammunition chest of one of Hankins's advanced pieces. Otherwise, the Tennesseans safely rejoined their comrades behind the railroad.[45]

While Heckman attracted Johnson's attention, Brooks's main force slowly deployed far to Heckman's right front. Since Burnham's brigade, which had opened the action, was gradually moving westward away from the Old Stage Road, Brooks called up Colonel Jeremiah Drake's brigade from its position in the rear of the Federal column. At noon Brooks ordered the brigade to advance in support of Burnham, and Drake's four Indiana, Maine, and New York regiments soon came into line on Burnham's left. Drake also deployed two artillery pieces of Battery L, 4th U. S. Artillery, which had accompanied the infantry. The guns opened fire on the Confederates behind the railroad embankment, catching them in a crossfire with Heckman's pieces.[46]

As Heckman, Drake, and Burnham skirmished with the Confederates, Brooks ordered Colonel Harris Plaisted and his brigade to leave the Old Stage Road and detour through the woods toward the Richmond turnpike and the railroad. According to a scouting party of Onderdonk's Mounted Rifles, the distance to the railroad was short and the woods thick, but passable. Deploying his three regiments into separate columns, Plaisted struck out through the underbrush. On the right the 100th New York Infantry entered a convenient ravine and soon reached the turnpike out of sight of the Confederates. Pushing ahead, the New Yorkers easily gained the railroad. Plaisted then ordered the 24th Massachusetts and the 10th Connecticut to detour behind the 100th New York and strike the tracks on its right. As they marched they heard volleys of musketry nearby, which signified that the Confederates had discovered the flanking column.[47]

Upon returning from his abortive morning advance, Johnson Hagood had placed two regiments behind the railroad and another in reserve on the turnpike. Around 2:30 P.M. he saw the Federals appear on his left flank down the tracks and he called the 21st South Carolina forward into line. As the regiment tried to take position on Hagood's left, it received several accurate volleys from the 100th New York and other Federal regiments. Suddenly the men of the 21st South Carolina broke and ran for the rear. To prevent the unit's collapse from spreading to other regiments, Hagood, his staff, and D. H. Hill rushed to halt the rout. After much shouting and cursing, the officers succeeded in rallying the regiment on its colors. Hagood then ordered the men of the 21st to lie down while he aligned his remaining units with them, so as to present a solid front to the triumphant Federals. In addition he called to Bushrod Johnson for support. Fearing an advance by Heckman, Johnson declined to transfer any of his infantry to the left, but he did send two artillery pieces, These guns, however, soon ran out of ammunition and were retired from the field.[48]

Hagood's men faced not only Plaisted's troops but also part of the last available Federal brigade, Colonel William Barton's. Brooks ordered Barton to advance to the railroad on Plaisted's left, while maintaining contact with Burnham's right. Pushing slowly through the tangled underbrush, Barton found the terrain so difficult that his brigade lost contact with its skirmish line. After striking the

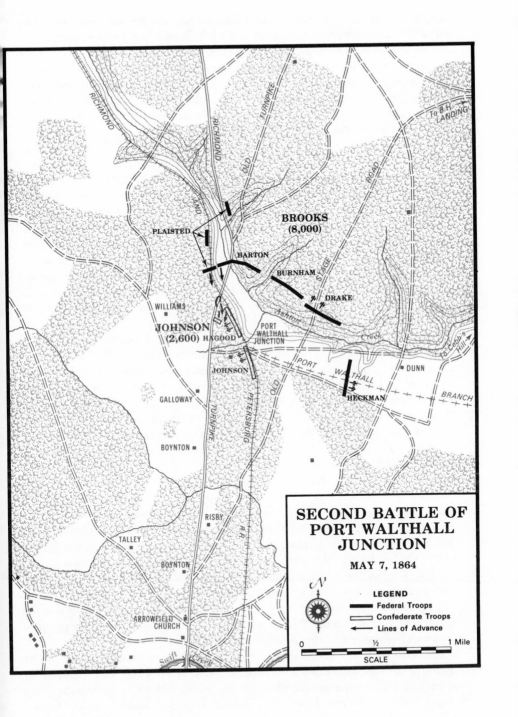

SECOND BATTLE OF
PORT WALTHALL
JUNCTION

MAY 7, 1864

LEGEND
━━━ Federal Troops
▭ Confederate Troops
← Lines of Advance

0   ½   1 Mile
SCALE

turnpike, he tried to continue toward the railroad, but he was forced to detour because of the rough ground. Veering to the left, Barton found himself on the edge of a natural amphitheater. Below him lay a meadow broken by a small stream, while the Confederates held the railroad on the opposite ridge. In the face of Confederate fire, Barton maneuvered his right regiments down through the meadow and up the far slope, until one of them, the 48th New York, connected with the 100th New York of Plaisted's brigade. Together, these two regiments occupied the railroad and traded volleys with Hagood's South Carolinians.[49]

When it was found that the two New York regiments masked each other's fire, Colonel George Dandy of the 100th New York sent several companies back down the railroad to aid in wrecking the track. This task originally had been entrusted to the pioneers of the 24th Massachusetts, but the Bay Staters were finding railroad wrecking to be a highly specialized occupation. Arriving on the track at 3:00 P.M., the men of the 24th carried no special tools and were further hampered by the hard-packed roadbed. As a result, when the unit withdrew, only about one hundred feet of track had been uprooted. Fortunately for the Federals, the detachment of the 100th New York succeeded in destroying a small trestle, while other men cut the telegraph lines paralleling the tracks. Otherwise, the railroad was untouched. Even more disheartening was the presence along the track of extra rails and ties, stockpiled by the Confederates for just such an emergency.[50]

The wrecking crews had been at work only a short time when Colonel Plaisted received an order to withdraw from the railroad. According to Plaisted the order came directly from General Brooks, but Brooks categorically denied this in the report he filed after the battle. No matter who gave the order to retreat, Plaisted proceeded to execute it, calling in his pioneers and withdrawing his whole brigade by the same route it had used to advance. This retrograde movement in turn exposed the right flank of Barton's brigade. To extricate Barton, Brooks called for two of Plaisted's regiments to deploy behind Barton's men as supports, and with this aid Barton's brigade gradually disengaged.[51]

On Barton's left, Burnham's brigade continued to stand firm on the ridge overlooking Ashton Creek. Beyond Burnham, Drake's four regiments also waited, interested in the proceedings to their right, but uninvolved, while the Federal artillery continued to lob shells at the Confederates across the valley.[52] Some distance to Drake's left, Heckman's brigade was equally quiescent. When Brooks had begun his drive to the railroad, he had sent word to Heckman to advance in earnest, but Heckman believed the Confederates facing him were too strong for such a maneuver. He therefore directed the 9th New Jersey to occupy the swale it had reached the previous day, then ordered the men to lie down. There they lay throughout the afternoon, baking in the glare of the sun and suffering more casualties from sunstroke than from enemy bullets.[53]

Although he denied having ordered Plaisted's withdrawal, Brooks decided shortly thereafter to take his entire force back to Bermuda Hundred. According to his report, he ordered the retreat when he discovered that all of his brigades were engaged and he "had no force left to destroy the road." Federal casualty figures, however, refute the argument that Brooks lacked sufficient troops to accomplish his mission. Only Barton's brigade had been closely engaged, and it had suffered the heaviest loss, 196 men killed, wounded, and missing. In Plaisted's brigade, the 100th New York alone had been in action and it had lost twenty-seven men. Plaisted had held the 10th Connecticut in reserve and had used half of the 24th Massachusetts as a flank guard, leaving only half of the latter regiment to destroy the railroad. Only one of Burnham's four regiments had taken part, the 8th Connecticut, which lost seventy-two men. The rest of Burnham's casualties totaled only eleven. On Burnham's left, Drake's four regiments together had suffered only ten casualties. At the Dunn plantation, Heckman had lost only sixteen men from hostile fire, but nearly one hundred from sunstroke.[54]

In sum, Brooks had brought nineteen infantry regiments to the scene, but only six had been fully engaged. His total casualties from enemy fire amounted to 24 killed, 268 wounded, and 53 missing. In exchange for this sacrifice, Brooks had been able to place upon the railroad only half a regiment. The results amounted to one hundred feet of track ruined, one small trestle burned, and several telegraph lines broken. In addition, as Brooks began to retreat, some of Plaisted's men discovered and wrecked a large steam sawmill that allegedly had been working for the Confederate government.[55]

Post-battle reactions by the opposing sides are revealing. As the Federals broke off contact and withdrew around sunset, men in the ranks began to grumble. A junior officer in the 13th New Hampshire Infantry called the Federal performance "dawdling damphoolishness" and "Possibly the nearest answer ever made to the question: 'How to fight without winning?' 'How to advance without going ahead?'" Soon an even more pointed query began to make the rounds: "How long will it take to get to Richmond if you advance two miles every day and come back to your starting point every night."[56] Meanwhile, among the Confederates there were few complaints.[57] With only six infantry regiments, numbering a little over 2,600 men, the Confederates had protected the railroad from all but minimal damage by a Federal force at least three times as large. The price of this success had not been cheap and, like the Federal losses, the casualties had not been evenly distributed. Johnson's Brigade had lost only 7 of its 1,168 men, while Hagood's Brigade had lost a total of 177 of its 1,500 soldiers.[58]

During the day, as the action at Port Walthall Junction waxed and waned, George Pickett at Petersburg began to feel trapped. The last message from Beauregard had come through at noon, and a few hours later, the telegraph line to the south had inexplicably gone dead. To discover the source of the trouble, a locomotive was dispatched toward Stony Creek. Meanwhile, the direct line to Richmond ceased to function, because of the Federal efforts at Port Walthall Junction. Telegraphing Richmond via a more westerly line, Pickett explained the situation to Bragg and asked that more units be sent from Richmond to the junction. A little later, after the scouting train returned from Stony Creek, Pickett informed Bragg that Federal horsemen had already burned one railroad bridge south of Petersburg and were on the way to another. Efforts to reach Beauregard had been unsuccessful, although Pickett was attempting to bridge the gap in the telegraph line by courier. He begged Bragg, "Can't you communicate with General Beauregard?"[59]

In a 5:00 P.M. message to Bushrod Johnson, Pickett suggested a retreat to Swift Creek, three-and-a-half miles north of Petersburg, if Johnson could not hold Port Walthall Junction. By the time this message reached the junction, the situation there was much improved. With the appearance of the 11th South Carolina Regiment and the 7th South Carolina Battalion of Hagood's Brigade, plus a battery of the Washington Artillery, Johnson commanded 3,500 men of all arms. Although Port Walthall Junction temporarily seemed secure, Pickett feared a Federal advance toward Petersburg from City Point and at 7:00 P.M. he again suggested that Johnson retire to Swift Creek. As the hours passed with no evidence that Johnson was obeying his suggestions, Pickett finally issued a direct order to retreat, which reached Johnson at 10:00 P.M. This was reported to Bragg, who had informed Pickett that he could not reach Beauregard. Acknowledging Bragg's telegram, Pickett suggested petulantly, "Beauregard ought to force his way up." Unknown to Pickett and Bragg, Beauregard was preparing to come north that very night, but the break in the Petersburg Railroad forced him to select a circuitous route via Greensboro, North Carolina.[60]

Although his nominal superior was Robert Ransom, Bushrod Johnson decided to obey Pickett's order to withdraw southward from Port Walthall Junction. He may have been influenced by the possibility that the Federals remained between him and Ransom.[61] Before 11:00 P.M. Johnson put his artillery in motion and followed with the infantry at midnight. At Swift Creek the guns were placed in a line of works 200 yards south of the stream and the infantry took position in support. By 3:00 A.M. 8 May, all Confederate troops except a handful of pickets were safely across Swift Creek. With Johnson's retreat, Confederate forces no longer barred access to Richmond's direct communication links with the south. Barton's and Gracie's Brigades at Drewry's Bluff, and Hagood's, Johnson's, and Clingman's Brigades near Petersburg were on the shoulders of the Federal penetration, but the vital center was wide open to exploitation.[62]

Fortunately for the Confederates, neither Benjamin Butler nor his corps commanders were in any great rush to take advantage of their opportunity. Butler's attitude is evident from a brief report he sent to Secretary of War Stanton at 1:00 P.M., just as Brooks's engagement was beginning. Informing Stanton of the probes against the railroad, Butler noted that he was "intrenching for fear of accident to the Army of the Potomac." Butler clearly realized that his position on the edge of the Confederacy's most important communication zone could be exceedingly dangerous if the Confederates concentrated a sizable force against him. Should Grant be defeated in northern Virginia or fail to hold Lee's undivided attention, Confederate units might converge from north and south to squeeze the isolated Army of the James between them. Stanton had reported during the morning that Grant's army was engaged near Chancellorsville but that the results were not yet known. In case the battle went against the Federals, Butler asked Stanton for ten thousand reinforcements.[63]

While Butler worried more about his difficulties than his opportunities, neither of his chief subordinates appeared anxious for an immediate advance in strength. Smith did not seem greatly concerned about Brooks's failure to damage the railroad significantly, and he planned no more than a cavalry scout on the morrow. Having been relieved of offensive responsibilities by the transfer of three of his brigades to Brooks, Gillmore spent the day drawing up contingency plans for the defense of his sector of the works. As a result of this defensive emphasis at the highest levels, the Army of the James slowly began to lose the elan that had characterized it upon landing, which was the very quality needed to complete its mission.[64]

Throughout the day, while Brooks's five brigades maneuvered at Port Walthall Junction, the rest of the Army of the James labored to improve its new home. Behind a screen of pickets, the remaining regiments of the X and XVIII Corps raised the mounds of earth that would provide their security against Confederate attack. Men not detailed to the fatigue parties or the picket line spent the day surveying their new surroundings or foraging for fresh food and water. At Bermuda Hundred Landing, several artillery batteries came ashore, while detachments of veterans arriving from furlough were diverted to serve as stevedores unloading supplies. Sometime during the day Butler moved his headquarters from the landing to Cobb's Hill. Afloat, Admiral Lee lost another gunboat when the *U.S.S. Shawsheen* was surprised by a Confederate artillery detachment and destroyed with heavy casualties. Once more the danger of relaxing one's guard had been demonstrated to the Federals.[65]

NOTES

1. Beauregard to Cooper, 5:00 A.M., 6 May 1864, Official Telegrams, 22 April–9 June 1864, Beauregard Papers, LC: O.R.A., 36, pt. 2, 963–964.

2. Beauregard to Pickett, 6 May 1864 (four telegrams), and Beauregard to D. B. Harris, 6 May 1864, all in Official Telegrams, 22 April–9 June 1864, Beauregard Papers, LC; Roman, *Military Operations*, 2:550.

3. O.R.A., 36, pt. 2, 964; O.R.A., 51, pt. 2, 897; Beauregard to Hoke, 6 May 1864 (four telegrams), Official Telegrams, 22 April–9 June 1864, Beauregard Papers, LC; Roman, *Military Operations*, 2:550.

4. Beauregard to Lieutenant Colonel Lewis, Major Willis, Captain Granger, Captain Drewry, all 6 May 1864, Official Telegrams, 22 April–9 June 1864, Beauregard Papers, LC; Beauregard to Colonel J. W. Hinton, 6 May 1864 (two messages), Letter Book, April–May 1864, Beauregard Papers, LC. The Legion's cavalry component had been detached in March to form the 7th South Carolina Cavalry. O.R.A, 33:1232.

5. Hill to Beauregard, 2:00 P.M., 6 May 1864, P. G. T. Beauregard Papers, North Carolina Division of Archives and History, Raleigh, N.C.; Beauregard to Hill, 3:00 P.M., 6 May 1864, Official Telegrams, 22 April–9 June 1864, Beauregard Papers, LC.

6. O.R.A., 51, pt. 2, 894; Beauregard to Davis, 3:30 P.M., 6 May 1864, Official Telegrams, 22 April–9 June 1864, Beauregard Papers, LC; Roman, *Military Operations*, 2:550; Williams, *Beauregard*, 211. T. Harry Williams tends to find Beauregard's illness a little too coincidental and speculates: "Was he trying to avoid command responsibility? Or was he reluctant to come closer to Richmond and Davis?"

7. O.R.A., 36, pt. 2, 239. D. S. Freeman estimated this contingent of Hagood's men passed through Petersburg at approximately 3:00 A.M. Freeman, *Lee's Lieutenants*, 3:457. However, a member of the unit placed its arrival at Petersburg on the afternoon of the previous day. Henry Kershaw DuBose, *The History of Company B, Twenty-First Regiment (Infantry), South Carolina Volunteers* (Columbia, S. C.: The R. L. Bryan Company, 1909), 45–47.

8. O.R.A., 36, pt. 2, 965; O.R.A., 51, pt. 2, 895.

9. O.R.A., 51, pt. 2, 895. Bragg's message is not extant, but it can be inferred from Pickett's telegram to Bragg of 3:30 P.M.

10. Owen, Washington Artillery, 311.

11. Ibid.; Scott, Annals of the War, 382–383; O.R.A., 51, pt. 1, 222, 225, 228; William H. S. Burgwyn Diary, 5 [6] May 1864, NCDAH; Pickett, Pickett and His Men, 344; George E. Pickett, The Heart of a Soldier as Revealed in the Intimate Letters of Genl. George E. Pickett, C. S. A. (New York: Seth Moyle, 1913), 123–125; Edgar Warfield, A Confederate Soldier's Memoirs (Richmond: Masonic Home Press, 1936), 168.

12. Pickett, Pickett and His men, 343–344; Callender "Personal Recollections," 6–9; Judith W. McGuire, Diary of a Southern Refugee, During the War, 3rd ed. (Richmond: J. W. Randolph & English, 1889), 262; Jones, War Clerk, 2:199–200; George W. Grant Diary, 6 May 1864, George W. Grant papers, Duke University, Durham, N.C.

13. Humphreys, Virginia Campaign, 141; O.R.A., 33:1299; O.R.A., 36, pt. 2, 988.

14. O.R.A., 36, pt. 2, 239; Bushrod R. Johnson Diary, 6 May 1864, Johnson Papers, NA. See also Freeman, Lee's Lieutenants, 3:460–461.

15. O.R.A., 36, pt. 2, 239; Shaver, Sixtieth Alabama, 45–46; Bushrod R. Johnson Diary, 6 and 7 May 1864, Johnson Papers, NA.

16. Pickett somehow thought a Colonel Mercer was in charge. O.R.A., 51, pt. 2, 895. The fortuitous dispatch of Hagood's Brigade, of which this was a part, to Port Walthall Junction turned out to be a decision of such consequence that several officers later took credit for it. Mrs. Pickett and Walter Harrison said George Pickett did it on his own responsibility, although his telegrams belie this. Pickett, Pickett and His Men, 342; Harrison, Pickett's Men, 125. Beauregard also claimed responsibility for the order, writing that he persuaded the War Department to modify the original order to send Hagood's men to Richmond. Beauregard, "Drewry's Bluff", 247; Beauregard, Battles and Leaders, 4:196; Roman, Military Operations, 2:197–198. No message directly requesting such a change in Hagood's orders is extant in Beauregard's official telegram books in the Library of Congress, however. Jefferson Davis credited Robert Ransom with the decision in Davis, Rise and Fall, 2:508, and according to Bushrod Johnson's report, Lieutenant Colonel Dargan's men moved to Port Walthall Junction on the orders of Ransom. However, Ransom may have been acting on orders from Braxton Bragg. Pickett himself forwarded Graham's contingent to Port Walthall Junction on Bragg's orders. It therefore appears that the much-maligned Bragg should receive the credit for throwing a blocking force, albeit a small one, in the path of the Federal advance.

17. O.R.A., 51, pt. 2, 895–897.

18. Two of Hoke's brigades, Lewis's and Ransom's, received the order to move to Kinston on the morning of 6 May and marched shortly thereafter, but Terry's Brigade did not start until dark, and part of it did not move until dawn of 7 May. At least one regiment of Ransom's Brigade, the 49th North Carolina, also delayed its start until 7 May. John Paris Diary, 6 May 1864, and William Beavans Diary, 6 May 1864, both in Southern Historical Collection, University of North Carolina, Chapel Hill, N.C. Lawson Harrill, Reminiscences, 1861–1865 (Statesville, N. C.: Brady, 1910), 21; Clark, ed., North Carolina Regiments, 3:349–350; Henry A. Chambers Diary, 6 May 1864, North Carolina Division of Archives and History, Raleigh, N.C. David Emmons Johnston, The Story of a Confederate Boy in the Civil War (Portland, Ore.: Glass and Prudhomme, 1914), 244; Edward Baker Loving Diary, 6 May 1864, Virginia State Library.

19. O.R.A., 36, pt. 2, 146, 153–154; Emmerton, Twenty-Third Massachusetts, 174; Putnam, Story of Company A, 265; Derby, Bearing Arms, 252; Clark, My Experience, 57; Cleveland, ed., "Campaign of Promise," 310; Walter S. Clemence Memoranda, 6 May 1864, NCC; Drake, Ninth new Jersey, 173, 175. The description of Heckman is in Kreutzer, Ninety-Eighth New York, 185.

20. Putnam, Story of Company A, 265; Denny, Wearing the Blue, 270–271; Derby, Bearing Arms, 252–253; O.R.A., 36, pt. 2, 154, 156; Day, Rambles, 138; Cleveland, ed., "Campaign of Promise," 310; Drake, Ninth New Jersey, 174–175; Cowles, ed., O. R. Atlas, plate 77, 3. The quotation is from Emmerton, Twenty-Third Massachusetts, 175.

21. O.R.A., 36, pt. 2, 251, 255–256; DuBose, History of Company B, 48; Hagood, Memoirs, 219–221; William Valmore Izlar, A Sketch of the War Record of the Edisto Rifles, 1861–1865 (Columbia, S. C.: The State Company, 1914), 44; F. S. Dibble, "South Carolina Command in Virginia," Confederate Veteran 23 (October 1915):458.

22. O.R.A., 36, pt. 2, 154, 156–157, 255; Denny, Wearing the Blue, 271; Emmerton, Twenty-Third Massachusetts, 175; Putnam, Story of Company A, 266; Valentine, Story of Co. F, 108; Derby, Bearing

Arms, 253–254; Cleveland, ed., "Campaign of Promise," 310–311; Walter S. Clemence Memoranda, 6 May 1864, NCC; Everts, *Comprehensive History*, 104.

23. Valentine, *Story of Co. F*, 108–109; Denny, *Wearing the Blue*, 271–273; Drake, *Ninth New Jersey*, 175–176, 198–199; O.R.A., 36, pt. 2, 154, 156–157; Derby, *Bearing Arms*, 253–254; Putnam, *Story of Company A*, 266; Cleveland, ed., "Campaign of Promise," 310–312; Emmerton, *Twenty-Third Massachusetts*, 175; Alfred Otis Chamberlin to his parents, 11 May 1864, Alfred Otis Chamberlin Papers, DU.

24. Drake, *Ninth New Jersey*, 175–176, 199; Cleveland, ed., "Campaign of Promise," 311; Derby, *Bearing Arms*, 254; O.R.A., 36, pt. 2, 154. In later years Heckman denied he had been so badly fooled about the size of the Confederate force opposing him. See his comments in Derby, *Bearing Arms*, 246.

25. O.R.A., 36, pt. 2, 154, 157; Drake, *Ninth New Jersey*, 175–176, 199; Derby, *Bearing Arms*, 246–247, 254–255, 511; Samuel H. Putnam, Regimental Record—Co. A, 25th Mass. Vols., DU; Everts, *Comprehensive History*, 104–105.

26. O.R.A., 36, pt. 2, 475. Unaware of the presence of Johnson's Brigade, Smith assumed that Gillmore would have been able to catch Graham's troops in flank, while Heckman fixed them in front. Later writers have also taken this view. See Rockwell, "Tenth Army Corps," 275. To say that Gillmore's detachment would have encountered Confederates, however, does not absolve the X Corps' commander of the failure to make an advance when requested to do so by Butler. Although Gillmore might not have reached the railroad, he could at least have discovered Johnson's presence and possibly even have put Johnson's small force out of action.

27. O.R.A., 36, pt. 2, 475, 521.

28. Butler, *Butler's Book*, 644; O.R.A., 36, pt. 2, 518.

29. O.R.A., 36, pt. 2, 239–240, 251, 255–256, 521; Drake, *Ninth New Jersey*, 198; Izlar, *Edisto Rifles*, 46. The figures are Graham's. Slightly smaller totals can be found in O.R.A., 36, pt. 2, 253, and Hagood, *Memoirs*, 221.

30. Benjamin Washington Jones, *Under the Stars and Bars: A History of the Surry Light Artillery* (Richmond: Everett Waddey Co., 1909), 167–168. Pickett also claimed that he had sent forward a battery of artillery. O.R.A., 51, pt. 2, 895.

31. O.R.A., 36, pt. 2, 239–240, 251–252; Hagood, *Memoirs*, 221. Hagood's Brigade still lacked one regiment and one battalion yet to arrive. The reasons for the regiment's delay are explained in Anne King Gregorie, ed., "Diary of Captain Joseph Julius Wescoat, 1863–1865," *South Carolina Historical Magazine* 59 (April 1958):84.

32. O.R.A., 51, pt. 2, 897; O.R.A., 36, pt. 2, 965, 966; Pickett, *Pickett and His Men*, 344.

33. O.R.A., 36, pt. 2, 521–522; Butler to W. P. Darby [Derby], 26 June 1882, Butler Papers, LC.

34. O.R.A., 36, pt. 2, 34, 124, 154, 519–521; Bruce, "General Butler's Bermuda Compaign," 318–319. Heckman was not direcly under Brooks's control.

35. Beauregard to Pickett, 7:30 A.M., 7 May 1864, Beauregard to Hoke, 7 May 1864, Beauregard to Dearing, care of Hoke, 7 May 1864, all in Official Telegrams, 22 April–9 June 1864, Beauregard Papers, LC. For the progress of one of Hoke's units see Clark, ed., *North Carolina Regiments*, 2:778–779.

36. Beauregard to Pickett, 10:15 A.M., 7 May 1864, and Beauregard to Cooper, 10:30 A.M., 7 May 1864, Official Telegrams, 22 April–9 June 1864, Beauregard Papers, LC.

37. John Paris Diary, 7 May 1864; SHC; Cary Whitaker Diary, 7 May 1864, Southern Historical Collection, University of North Carolina, Chapel Hill, N.C.; William Beavans Diary, 7 May 1864 SHC; Harrill, *Reminiscences*, 21; Clark, ed., *North Carolina Regiments*, 3:349–350; Henry A. Chambers Diary, 7 and 8 May 1864, NCDAH.

38. O.R.A., 36, pt. 2, 172.

39. Owen, *Washington Artillery*, 311; Pickett, *Heart of a Soldier*, 123; Callender, "Personal Recollections," 8; George W. Grant Diary, 7 May 1864, DU; O.R.N., 10:625–626; O.R.A., 36, pt. 2, 971, 973.

40. Charles M. Cummings, *Yankee Quaker Confederate General: The Curious Career of Bushrod Rust Johnson* (Rutherford, N. J.: Fairleigh Dickinson University Press, 1971), 38–282; O.R.A., 36, pt. 2, 239, 246.

41. O.R.A., 36, pt. 2, 251–252; Jones, *Surry Light Artillery*, 167–168; O.R.A., 51, pt. 1, 222; Warner, *Generals in Gray*, 121, 157.

42. Mrs. Roger A. Pryor, *Reminiscences of Peace and War* (New York: Macmillan, 1904), 288; O.R.A., 36, pt. 2, 240; Hagood, *Memoirs*, 221–223.

43. O.R.A., 36, pt. 2, 240, 251; Hagood, *Memoirs*, 223–224; Jones, *Surry Light Artillery*, 168.

44. O.R.A., 36, pt. 2, 73, 107, 124, 132–133, 136, 138, 170; Kreutzer, *Ninety-Eighth New York*, 178; Cunningham, *Adirondack Regiment*, 105–106; Thompson, *Thirteenth New Hampshire*, 259.

45. O.R.A., 36, pt. 2, 154–155, 240, 245–246, 251; Hagood, Memoirs, 223; Drake, Ninth New Jersey, 178, 199; Day, Rambles, 139; Putnam, Story of Company A, 267–268; Samuel H. Putnam, Regimental Record—Co. A, 25th Mass. Vols., DU; Walter S. Clemence Memoranda, 7 May 1864, NCC; Cleveland, ed., "Campaign of Promise," 313; Everts, Comprehensive History, 105; Jones, Surry Light Artillery, 168–169.

46. O.R.A., 36, pt. 2, 107–108, 124, 133.

47. O.R.A., 36, pt. 2, 74–75, 84–85, 87, 101, 124; Stowits, One Hundredth New York, 246–247.

48. O.R.A., 36, pt. 2, 74, 87, 240–241, 251–252; Hagood, Memoirs, 223–227; Stowits, One Hundredth New York, 247–248; O.R.A., 51, pt. 1, 222, 225. Three of the 21st South Carolina's ten companies had been detached earlier and were not involved in the rout. DuBose, History of Company B, 51, 54.

49. O.R.A., 36, pt. 2, 74, 87, 101–102; Nichols, Perry's Saints, 205–208; Clark, Iron Hearted Regiment, 105–106; Abraham J. Palmer, The History of the Forty-Eighth Regiment New York State Volunteers, in the War for the Union. 1861–1865 (New York: Charles T. Dillingham, 1885), 145.

50. O.R.A., 36, pt. 2, 74, 84–85, 87; Stowits, One Hundredth New York, 247–248. The estimate of one hundred feet was made by the colonel of the 24th Massachusetts, who directed the work. For other estimates, see O.R.A., 36, pt. 2, 74, 84, 124.

51. Hagood, Memoirs, 225; O.R.A., 36, pt. 2, 74–75, 124–125, 251–252; Nichols, Perry's Saints, 208–210; Clark, Iron Hearted Regiment, 106–109.

52. O.R.A., 36, pt. 2, 108, 111, 124, 133, 136–138; Thompson, Thirteenth New Hampshire, 259–260; Cunningham, Adirondack Regiment, 106.

53. O.R.A., 36, pt. 2, 155; Cleveland, ed., "Campaign of Promise," 313–314; Drake, Ninth New Jersey, 176–179, 346–349; Derby, Bearing Arms, 256; Day, Rambles, 140; Clark, My Experience, 57; Putnam, Story of Company A, 267; Emmerton, Twenty-Third Massachusetts, 177; Samuel H. Putnam, Regimental Record—Co. A, 25th Mass. Vols, DU; Josiah Wood to "Rana," 8 May 1864, Josiah Wood Papers, DU; Walter S. Clemence Memoranda, 7 May 1864, NCC.

54. O.R.A., 36, pt. 2, 74–75, 84–85, 102, 108, 124–125, 133, 136–138, 155; Derby, Bearing Arms, 256.

55. O.R.A., 36, pt. 2, 75, 85, 118, 125, 155, 171, 241; Hagood, Memoirs, 227.

56. Thompson, Thirteenth New Hampshire, 259, 260; Bruce, "General Butler's Bermuda Campaign," 321.

57. Hagood was apparently miffed at Johnson's unwillingness to support him during the crisis on the left and by the corresponding disparity in casualties between the two brigades. Therefore he credited Harvey Hill with having engineered the victory. Hagood, Memoirs, 223, 224, 226. Beauregard, on the other hand, praised Johnson highly for his role in the action. Roman, Military Operations, 2:198.

58. O.R.A., 36, pt. 2, 241, 245, 252, 253; Hagood, Memoirs, 225–226; Dibble, "South Carolina Command," 458–459; Izlar, Edisto Rifles, 46–48. Hankins's Battery lost five men wounded. Jones, Surry Light Artillery, 170.

59. O.R.A., 51, pt. 2, 899.

60. O.R.A., 36, pt. 2, 242, 252; O.R.A., 51, pt. 1, 222, 226, pt. 2, 899–900; Jones, Surry Light Artillery, 171; Hagood, Memoirs, 226; Beauregard to Bragg, 6:00 P.M., 7 May 1864, Official Telegrams, 22 April–9 June 1864, Beauregard Papers, LC.

61. O.R.A., 36, pt. 2, 972; O.R.A., 51, pt. 2, 901.

62. O.R.A., 36, pt. 2, 242, 252; O.R.A., 51, pt. 1, 222, 226; Hagood, Memoirs, 227–228; Izlar, Edisto Rifles, 49; Jones, Surry Light Artillery, 171, 174; Bushrod R. Johnson Diary, 7 May 1864, Johnson Papers, NA.

63. O.R.A., 36, pt. 2, 471, 517; Butler, Butler's Book, 643–644. U. S. Grant, who at 3:00 P.M. 7 May learned of Butler's successful landing, was also concerned that Lee might detach troops to crush Butler. One of the reasons he gave for ordering the Army of the Potomac to move toward Spotsylvania Court House was to forestall this possibility. Grant, Personal Memoirs, 2:208, 211; Badeau, Military History, 2:133; Porter, Campaigning with Grant, 78.

64. O.R.A., 36, pt. 2, 518–519, 523.

65. Price, Ninety-Seventh Pennsylvania, 253–254; Brady, Eleventh Maine, 176–177; Dickey, Eighty-Fifth Pennsylvania, 321; Little, Seventh New Hampshire, 243, 259; Cadwell, Old Sixth, 89–90; Clark, Thirty-Ninth Illinois, 178; Bartlett, Twelfth New Hampshire, 174; Beecher, First Connecticut Light Battery, 1:343; Eldredge, Third New Hampshire, 462; Thompson, Thirteenth New Hampshire, 278; O.R.A., 36, pt. 2, 32, 95, 147, 265, 268, 520; O.R.N. 10:27–31.

☆ 7 ☆
Kautz's First Raid
5–10 May 1864

Just after sunrise on 5 May, the day that the Army of the James sailed toward Bermuda Hundred, Brigadier General August Kautz led his small cavalry division out of its camps near Portsmouth. With their horses prancing to the music of a regimental band, Kautz's 1,750 men rode beyond the defensive fortifications and headed due west. In the advance was Colonel Samuel Spear's Second Brigade, consisting initially of eleven companies of the 11th Pennsylvania Cavalry. Following Spear was Colonel Simon Mix's First Brigade, consisting of the 3rd New York Cavalry and six companies of the 1st District of Columbia Cavalry. Although small in size, the latter unit was an especially potent fighting force, because it was armed with the Henry repeating rifle. Rounding out Kautz's command was a section of the 8th New York Battery.[1]

At the outpost of Bowers Hill, Spear's Second Brigade added eight companies of the 5th Pennsylvania Cavalry, and upon reaching the village of Suffolk the column was joined by the remaining four companies of the 5th Pennsylvania. These additions brought Kautz's strength to approximately 2,500 officers and men.[2] Just beyond Suffolk, Kautz halted the division to await the return of scouts sent to gather information on the Blackwater River defenses. Kautz had no intention of forcing his way across the lower Blackwater, but he wished to give that impression to any Confederates watching the column. Therefore, when he resumed the march, he guided the division toward the lower Blackwater fords. The day was nearly spent when Spear's troopers reined in their mounts at a crossroads known locally as Andrews Corners. The Pennsylvanians were already eating supper when the First Brigade arrived around 9:00 P.M.[3]

The halt at Andrews Corners allowed the men and animals to rest after their thirty-five-mile march, and it also strengthened the impression that Kautz's objective was a crossing of the lower Blackwater. At midnight the column resumed its march, this time in a northeasterly direction. Still led by the 11th Pennsylvania Cavalry, Kautz's troopers passed through the village of Windsor and on toward Isle of Wight Court House as dawn was breaking on 6 May. From the Court House the column again turned west, as if heading for Broadwater Bridge. Halting around

95

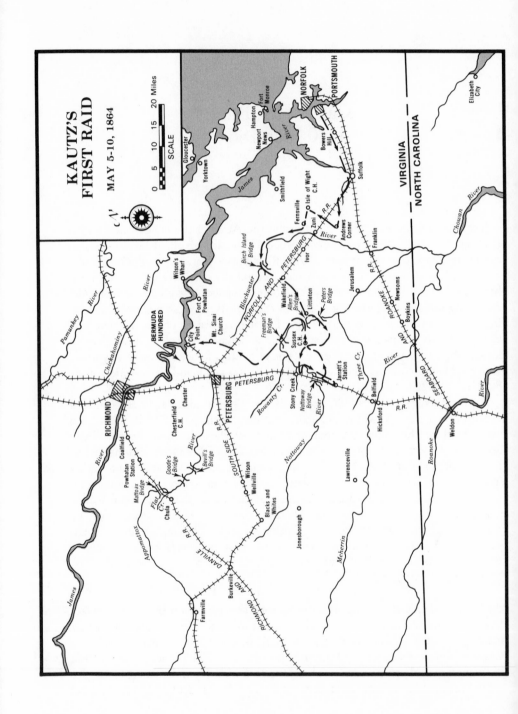

KAUTZ'S
FIRST RAID

MAY 5-10, 1864

SCALE

0   5   10   15   20 Miles

midday at Fernsville near the bridge, the troopers again rested their horses, while detachments probed toward the stream. Satisfied that his feints continued to baffle the Confederates, at 2:00 P.M. Kautz proceeded north from Fernsville on a road paralleling the river. After nearly ten miles, he ordered the column to turn southwest toward his intended crossing point at Birch Island Bridge.[4]

Reaching the bridge in late afternoon, Kautz found two of its three spans already damaged by a Confederate detachment busily at work on the third. A flanking movement by Company A of the 11th Pennsylvania Cavalry soon forced the Confederates to retreat into the surrounding forest. With the bridge in their hands, Kautz's men rapidly replaced enough flooring to allow the entire column to cross the river. Because of the damaged condition of the spans, it was after dark when the last horseman reached the west bank. By that time Kautz's leading regiment was already far along on the road to Wakefield, a station on the Norfolk and Petersburg Railroad. With the river and its defenses behind them, Kautz and his 2,500 troopers were free to rampage all the way to their objective, the Petersburg Railroad.[5]

Arriving in Wakefield at 6:30 P.M., some of Spear's men burned the railroad station, several pieces of rolling stock, and a small amount of government supplies, while others amused themselves by tearing down the telegraph line to Petersburg and uprooting a short section of the track. Exhausted from their fifty-mile march and their destructive activities, Kautz's men rested briefly before departing Wakefield at 2:00 A.M. on 7 May. The 3rd New York Cavalry of Mix's First Brigade led the way toward the hamlet of Littleton ten miles away. Their advance was so rapid that, in Littleton, the troopers surprised a Confederate commissary detachment transporting several wagonloads of rations to Petersburg. The captured wagons contained hams, corn, and hardtack, all of which were appropriated by Kautz's men, whose own rations had already been expended.[6]

After pausing briefly to distribute the booty, the Federals rode southwest from Littleton toward a crossing of the Nottoway River at Peter's Bridge. As the column progressed along the dusty country roads, some of the horses began to fail. Eventually the number of broken-down animals approached forty, leaving their riders afoot. To replace the lost mounts, detachments scoured the countryside, seizing any civilian horses they could find. Their justification was the iron law of necessity, as well as Kautz's order to "live off the country." When enough animals had been found, the troopers continued their march unmolested through the verdant Virginia countryside. After Peter's Bridge, there was only one more river crossing between the Federal cavalry and the Petersburg Railroad.[7]

As Kautz triumphantly rode deeper into the Confederate rear, both Pickett and Beauregard watched his progress with dismay. Distracted by Brooks's five brigades at Port Walthall Junction, Pickett could only report Kautz's location periodically to Richmond and Weldon. Besides, there were no spare horsemen available to counter the Federal column. Pickett's cavalry units on the Blackwater were so scattered that no more than 150 men could be collected immediately, but this handful was ordered west to shadow the Federals. Because Pickett believed throughout much of

7 May that Kautz's goal was Petersburg itself, he rearranged his artillery defenses to cover the roads leading south from the city. Beyond that he could do nothing.[8]

Unlike Pickett, Beauregard at least had limited means with which to counter the threat posed by Kautz's cavalry. The railroad could be broken most easily at three major bridges: the Meherrin River bridge at the twin villages of Hicksford and Belfield, the Nottoway River bridge at Nottoway Station, and the Stony Creek bridge. All were guarded by detachments of the Holcombe Legion, no more than five companies in total. Realizing that the bridge garrisons were hopelessly inadequate, Beauregard cast about for reinforcements. The only units near at hand were several regiments of Wise's Virginia Brigade that were in transit from South Carolina to Richmond. Without asking anyone's permission, Beauregard decided to utilize Wise's men. Colonel J. W. Hinton, commanding at Weldon, was directed to send the first four hundred arrivals to the Meherrin River bridge at Hicksford. Hinton was also instructed to distribute the remaining five companies of the Holcombe Legion along the railroad.[9]

Some of Wise's men who had already passed Weldon received orders at Belfield to detrain and defend various positions along the way. Colonel Powhatan Page of the 26th Virginia Infantry was told to hold four hundred of his men at Hicksford, while sending two hundred more to guard the Nottoway bridge. In like manner Colonel William Tabb was ordered to move his 59th Virginia Infantry to Stony Creek for the defense of the bridge there. Until Tabb's men could arrive, Major M. G. Ziegler, commanding sixty men of the Holcombe Legion at Stony Creek, was instructed to defend the bridge at all costs. To ensure communication with the various bridges, Beauregard asked the superintendent of the Weldon telegraph office to set up instruments at Hicksford and Nottoway Station. In case the Confederates were unable to halt the Federal cavalry, Beauregard ordered officials of the Petersburg Railroad to prepare stockpiles of spare bridge timbers.[10]

Having bolstered the defenses along the railroad, Beauregard turned his attention to the now useless Blackwater line. His first messages were directed to Colonel Joel Griffin, whose 62nd Georgia Cavalry was picketing the Blackwater defenses.[11] Shortly thereafter, Beauregard received a telegram from a Major Harding, who was commanding at Franklin instead of Griffin. Harding was concerned about two heavy guns guarding the river at Franklin that seemed in danger of capture.[12] Since Harding was the only officer on the Blackwater line in telegraphic communication with Weldon, Beauregard began to funnel orders both to Griffin's cavalry and to Colonel James Radcliffe's 61st North Carolina Infantry through the major. Griffin was directed to withdraw to Hicksford for the defense of the Meherrin River bridge, while Radcliffe's infantry was to move toward Petersburg. Harding himself was told to retreat along the railroad to Newsom's Station, twelve miles west of Franklin, leaving pickets on the Blackwater.[13]

After reports placed Kautz near Littleton, Beauregard came to believe that Hicksford was the Federal goal. In a new series of telegrams to Major Harding, Beauregard directed him to deploy his command along the line of Three Creek, a small stream between Hicksford and the Nottoway River. Harding's Blackwater pickets were to retreat to the Nottoway and destroy all highway bridges over that stream for some distance south of Littleton. Several times Harding was warned not to destroy any railroad bridges between Weldon and Petersburg. Late in the afternoon, a final telegram from Weldon ordered both Harding and Colonel Radcliffe's 61st North Carolina to withdraw to Hicksford to make a stand, since Beauregard had finally learned where Kautz was. Stony Creek had just telegraphed that Federal cavalry had appeared there in strength.[14]

After crossing the Nottoway River at Peter's Bridge, Kautz's division continued westward past Sussex Court House and by 3:00 P.M. reached Bolling's Bridge on the same stream. Brushing aside a few Confederates trying to wreck the bridge, the cavalrymen found themselves only a short distance from the 100-foot railroad bridge over Stony Creek. While Major Ziegler and his detachment watched from behind a shed at the south end of the bridge, Colonel Mix deployed most of the 3rd New York Cavalry for action. The artillery accompanying the Federal column soon opened fire, supported by a dismounted battalion of skirmishers. This activity distracted the Confederates, while two companies of the 3rd New York crossed the creek farther to the right in an attempt to outflank Ziegler's position. Realizing that further resistance would be both costly and futile, Major Ziegler elected to surrender his small command along with the bridge. A few Confederates made a successful dash for freedom, but Ziegler and fifty-four others emerged from their positions around the shed smiling at their captors. Fought by the 3rd New York alone, the entire action had lasted but a few minutes.[15]

As soon as Kautz arrived, the destruction of the railroad began in earnest. All railroad facilities, including the station, two wood-storage racks, two water tanks, three freight cars filled with lumber, and a large pile of spare bridging material were consigned to the flames. Besides burning the trestle over Stony Creek, the troopers broke a culvert and destroyed a turntable. They also discovered large quantities of corn and bacon, enough to feed Kautz's entire command. After completing the destruction of railroad property, three of Kautz's regiments bivouacked amid the ruins for the night. Meanwhile, their commander contemplated his next move. From prisoners and civilians, Kautz had learned that four hours earlier three trainloads of troops had passed Stony Creek on their way to Petersburg. At least five more trainloads were due at any time. With the railroad clogged with moving troops, Kautz knew he would have to hurry to accomplish any more damage. Having surmised this earlier, he had detached Colonel Spear and the 11th Pennsylvania Cavalry while they were near Bolling's Bridge, sending them south toward Nottoway Bridge.[16]

Spear moved rapidly, but he was too late; the garrison at Nottoway Bridge had been reinforced. Beauregard's telegram to Colonel Tabb of the 59th Virginia Infantry had reached him at Hicksford. Following orders, Tabb had set out toward Stony Creek, but he had gotten only as far as Nottoway Bridge by sunset. There Tabb had learned of the Federal attack at Stony Creek and the surrender of the garrison. Almost at once, Spear's troopers appeared across the river and began to deploy. After surveying the situation, the usually impetuous Spear decided against an assault in the fading light and ordered his men to withdraw after nightfall. Returning to Stony Creek, the 11th Pennsylvania camped near the rest of Kautz's division around 9:00 P.M. [17]

Since Spear reported a strong garrison at Nottoway Bridge, Kautz decided to use almost his entire force to attain its destruction. He devised a plan whereby Spear's Second Brigade would march at 3:00 A.M., 8 May, and approach Nottoway Bridge from the south, while Mix's First Brigade would advance down the railroad from Stony Creek. In the meantime Kautz would take two companies of the 1st District of Columbia and reconnoiter northward from Stony Creek toward the railroad bridge over Rowanty Creek. Believing Nottoway Bridge to be within his grasp, Kautz began his reconnaissance. Reaching the vicinity of Rowanty Bridge, he found its garrison adequate to successfully protect the structure, so he retraced his steps to Stony Creek. There, to his great disgust, he found Colonel Mix and his First Brigade still in camp. Realizing that it was too late to put the original plan into operation, Kautz ordered Mix to recross Bolling's Bridge and follow Spear toward Nottoway Bridge. [18]

While Kautz struggled to salvage his offensive against Nottoway Bridge, in Weldon, Beauregard was trying to discover what had happened on the previous day at Stony Creek. Eventually Colonel Page at Hicksford confirmed the destruction of the Stony Creek bridge. Unaware of the serious situation developing around Nottoway Bridge, Beauregard ordered Colonel Tabb to prepare a temporary span over Stony Creek for the passage of infantry. In another series of telegrams he gathered spare bridging materials and construction personnel to be sent to the damaged area. In order to reopen the direct telegraph line to Petersburg, Beauregard authorized the removal of enough wire from the Weldon-Franklin line to replace that destroyed or hidden by the Federals. Later in the day he ordered Pickett to send trains from Petersburg to Stony Creek, where they would be met by troops arriving from the south. Pickett was also informed that Beauregard was at last preparing to leave for Petersburg, perhaps that same day. [19]

As he worked to minimize the damage already done, Beauregard learned that a Federal force was assaulting Jarratt's Station, located between Nottoway Bridge and Hicksford. Soon word arrived that the Federals had been repulsed and were retreating northward. In case the affair at Jarratt's presaged an assault upon Hicksford, Beauregard asked Colonel Page if he had been joined by units from the Blackwater. He also gave Page the authority to halt any troops that might appear. This order was useful, for at last some of Robert Hoke's brigades from New Berne were puffing through Weldon. By way of final instructions to Page, Beauregard prepared an elaborate plan for the defense of the railroad, based upon the Holcombe Legion and Radcliffe's 61st North Carolina. When and if Radcliffe appeared, Colonel Page would finally be allowed to contiinue his interrupted journey to Petersburg. [20]

Having marshaled his defensive forces and arranged repairs for the damaged rail and telegraph lines, Beuaregard considered the situation on the afternoon on 8 May to be reasonably well in hand. As a precaution, Colonel Hinton at Weldon was ordered to remove all boats from the north bank of the Roanoke River, but this did not indicate that Beauregard believed his headquarters to be in imminent danger. In fact, the news that the Federals had been repulsed at Jarratt's Station apparently led Beauregard to believe that the worst was over. In telegrams to Bragg at Richmond and Whiting at Wilmington, he viewed the situation positively. Late in the afternoon, he informed Bragg that, while he had planned to leave for Petersburg that very afternoon, the Federal activity had forced him to delay his departure until the following morning. Unknown to Beauregard, affairs on the railroad north of Weldon were deteriorating rapidly. The initial reports from Jarratt's Station had been true, but later information would show Beauregard's optimism to be premature.[21]

The only reason that fighting took place around Jarratt's Station on 8 May was that Samuel Spear, like Simon Mix, had disobeyed Kautz's orders. Rather than act as the southern half of Kautz's envelopment of Nottoway Bridge, Spear ordered his troopers to bypass the bridge and head for Jarratt's Station several miles south. Reaching the village at daylight, Spear had the 11th Pennsylvania Cavalry dismount and he sent it toward the Confederate positions around the station. Jarratt's was defended by another detachment of the Holcombe Legion, which vigorously repulsed two Federal charges. Rather than lose more troopers for no tangible reward, Spear broke off the action and ordered his men to withdraw northward along the railroad, destroying it as they went. As a consolation, Spear promised that Jarratt's would be asssaulted again when the 5th Pennsylvania arrived.[22]

Reinforced by the 5th Pennsylvania, Spear ordered the attack upon Jarratt's Station renewed. He deployed a dismounted battalion on each side of the railroad and sent them forward, supported by the fire of four light howitzers. As they neared the outskirts of the village, the troopers broke into a run and with this momentum crushed the Confederate defenses. Considerable numbers of the Holcombe Legion were able to escape, but at least thirty-seven were taken prisoner. Federal losses were slight: two dead and eight wounded. Once in possession of the village, the Pennsylvanians set fire to all railroad structures, several public buildings, and large amounts of Confederate government supplies. Either by accident or design, the fires spread to several private dwellings also.[23]

While Spear was engaged at Jarratt's Station, Colonel Tabb at Nottoway Bridge was intrigued by what appeared to be a Federal wagon train passing across his front. Tabb's force at Nottoway Bridge included his own 59th Virginia, two companies of Page's 26th Virginia, and another company of the ubiquitous Holcombe Legion, some 600 men in all. With such a relatively large force, Tabb believed he could afford to be bold. Accordingly, he set out with 200 men to capture the wagon train, after deploying the rest of his command south of the river along the railroad facing east. Although his troops advanced quickly, Tabb was unable to cut off the Federals, who disappeared in the direction of Jarratt's. After learning from a Federal straggler that Kautz was preparing a major attack upon Nottoway Bridge, Tabb decided to return to the span. He arrived just in time to break up a Federal attack against the troops he had left behind.[24]

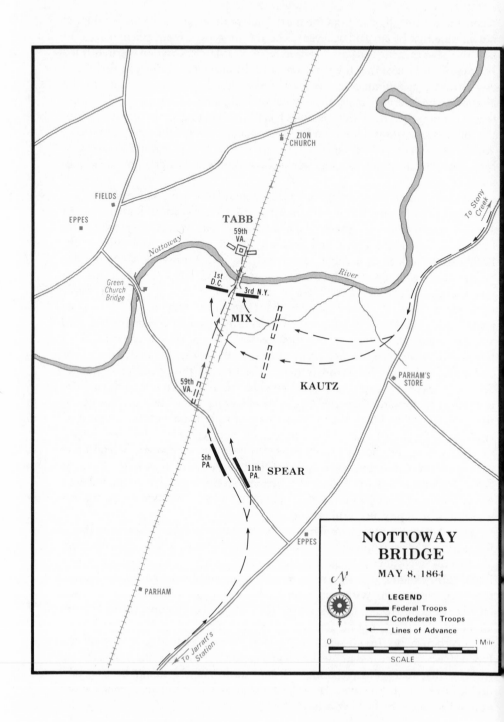

ZION
CHURCH

FIELDS

EPPES

TABB

59th
VA.

Nottoway

Green
Church
Bridge

1st
D.C.

3rd N.Y.

River

To Stony
Creek

MIX

59th
VA.

KAUTZ

PARHAM'S
STORE

5th
PA.

11th
PA.   SPEAR

EPPES

PARHAM

To Jarratt's
Station

NOTTOWAY
BRIDGE

MAY 8, 1864

N

LEGEND
▬▬ Federal Troops
▭▭ Confederate Troops
◄── Lines of Advance

0   1 Mile

SCALE

Ordering Spear to join him, Kautz began to press against Tabb's position south of Nottoway Bridge with Mix's First Brigade. Tabb was only able to resist the Federal pressure briefly. Upon the arrival of Spear's two regiments, he was forced to yield first on the right and then all along the line. With his defensive position crumbling, Tabb ordered a fighting retreat across the bridge toward an old earthwork 300 yards north of the river. As the Confederates raced through the covered wooden span, the bolder Federals were right at their heels. With both sides inextricably mixed, Confederate defenders on the north bank were unable to keep the Federals away from the bridge. Some of the cavalrymen followed the retreating Confederates so closely that they managed to get all the way across the span, while others set fire to the south end of the structure. A few of the defenders tried to extinguish the flames, but by the time they had worked their way to the river through the hail of Federal bullets, the fire was out of control. Within twenty minutes the flaming 210-foot bridge crashed roaring and hissing into the Nottoway River. The second break in Beauregard's railroad had been made.[25]

Seeing the bridge fall, Kautz withdrew his men out of range and an uneasy quiet settled over the field. The entire fight had lasted hardly more than an hour, but casualties had been relatively heavy on both sides. Colonel Tabb had lost three men killed, twenty-two wounded, and twenty missing; the Federals had lost nearly as many. Five cavalrymen had been captured by the Confederates when their impetuous charge carried them across the bridge before its collapse. Upon learning of their misfortune, Kautz sent forward a flag-of-truce requesting an exchange of prisoners. The Confederates readily assented and the swap was made, each side receiving an officer and four men.[26]

While his troopers rested on the battlefield, Kautz pondered the situation. Should he spend more time and ammunition in an effort to outflank Tabb in his redoubt, or should he leave well enough alone? Capturing the Confederates would be easy, because Tabb's force was stationary and was outnumbered at least four to one, but it would not be without cost. More than balancing the gains to be derived from the capture of Tabb's command were other considerations: Kautz already was burdened by approximately 130 prisoners and 30 of his own wounded, other Confederate units might arrive at any moment, ammunition supplies were running low, and finally, the raid's objective had been attained with the destruction of the two bridges. The correct conclusion seemed inescapable, so Kautz "reluctantly left him [Colonel Tabb] to guard where the bridge had been."[27]

Around 5:00 P.M. Kautz and his division headed eastward toward a rendezvous with the Army of the James at City Point. By nightfall both brigades had reached the vicinity of Sussex Court House, where most of the column halted for several hours while two companies of the 11th Pennsylvania seized Allen's Bridge over the Nottoway River. At 3:00 A.M. on 9 May, Kautz's weary troopers resumed their march. Both horses and men were showing the strain of almost continuous movement, and many were without rations. In addition, the column was encumbered by its Confederate prisoners and several hundred slaves who took the opportunity to escape from bondage. Nevertheless, the possibility that an avenging Confederate force might be pounding hard on their trail spurred the exhausted Federals onward.

Beyond Allen's Bridge, Kautz's troopers moved toward the Jerusalem Plank Road. Upon reaching it, they rode northward until they were within nine miles of Petersburg. In no condition to force their way into what they believed to be a heavily fortified town, the Federals swung to the east. Crossing the Norfolk and Petersburg Railroad, they paused long enough to wreck a small bridge, then continued toward City Point. At nightfall the Federals bivouacked at Mount Sinai Church, less than ten miles from their destination. Near noon on the following day, 10 May, Kautz's division walked wearily but proudly into Edward Hincks's lines at City Point. The great cavalry raid, which Grant and Butler had considered so important to the success of the campaign, was over.[29]

In Kautz's wake, the Confederate authorities were left to survey the damage. The railroad between Weldon and Petersburg had been severed in three places: at the Stony Creek bridge, at Nottoway Bridge, and at a point between Nottoway Bridge and Jarratt's Station, a total gap of ten miles. All of the damage, including the bridges, could be repaired. What could not be replaced so easily was the time lost in transporting troops to Bermuda Hundred to confront Butler and supplies to the Army of Northern Virginia facing Grant. Realizing their predicament, both Beauregard and Pickett did all they could to reduce delays. Beauregard, at last on his way to Petersburg via Greensboro, had already stockpiled spare bridge timbers and collected work crews, while Pickett sent trains to Stony Creek to meet the troops coming from the south. Taken together, these countermeasures lessened the effects of Kautz's raid, even though it was impossible to erase them altogether.[29]

The first Confederate unit to experience the full effects of the broken transportation system, other than the part of Wise's Brigade detached to fight Kautz, was Colonel William G. Lewis's North Carolina Brigade. Lewis's men arrived at Jarratt's Station in the late afternoon of 8 May, near the time Kautz's troopers were departing from Nottoway Bridge. The infantrymen at once detrained and advanced up the tracks, but they could not catch the Federals. Returning to Jarratt's, the Confederates viewed the destruction and listened to the inhabitants' tales of Federal thievery. On the morning of 9 May, Lewis's Brigade started for Petersburg on foot, leaving its heavy baggage under guard at Jarratt's until the railroad could be repaired.[30] The men crossed the Nottoway River on the ruins of the wrecked span and continued marching to Stony Creek, which they forded. Awaiting them on the other side were the trains sent from Petersburg by Pickett. At least one soldier boarded the cars with some trepidation: "I was uneasy all the time as I knew how easy it would be for the enemy to throw the train off the track and attack and throw us in confusion and probably kill a good many."[31]

As Lewis's experience showed, the Confederates encountered considerable difficulty in crossing the ten mile gap in the railroad made by Kautz's raid, but they got across nonetheless. Furthermore, the damage would be mended rapidly. One of Lewis's men, left at Jarratt's Station with his unit's baggage, wrote a friend on 10 May that "The road will soon be repaired again," and a War Department official noted on 20 May that one of the bridges had been rebuilt in two days.[32] Even if these estimates proved overly optimistic, the railroad between Weldon and Petersburg would soon be restored to normal operating condition and the Federal cavalry's work would be undone. It remained to be seen whether the precious time purchased by the blood and sweat of Kautz's hardriding troopers would be used to advantage by Benjamin Butler and his lethargic Army of the James.[33]

NOTES

1. O.R.A., 36, pt. 2, 175, 176, 179, 181, 184, 188, 431; *History of the Eleventh Pennsylvania Volunteer Cavalry, Together with a Complete Roster of the Regiment and Regimental Officers* (Philadelphia: Franklin Printing Co., 1902), 108; Samuel H. Merrill, *The Campaigns of the First Maine and First District of Columbia Cavalry* (Portland, Me.: Baily & Noyes, 1866), 233, 235; Edward Wall, "Raids in Southeastern Virginia Fifty Years Ago," *Proceedings of the New Jersey Historical Society* New Series, 3, no. 2, 65.

2. O.R.A., 36, pt. 2, 175, 176, 179, 184.

3. Wall, "Raids," 66; *Eleventh Pennsyvlania Cavalry,* 108; O.R.A., 36, pt. 2, 171, 176, 179, 184, 188.

4. O.R.A., 36, pt. 2, 171, 176, 179, 181, 184, 188; Wall, "Raids," 66–67; *Eleventh Pennsylvania Cavalry,* 108; "Kautz in the Great Rebellion," Kautz Papers, LC.

5. Wall, "Raids," 68–69; O.R.A., 36, pt. 2, 171–172, 176, 179, 184, 188–189, *Eleventh Pennsylvania Cavalry,* 108; "Kautz in the Great Rebellion," Kautz Papers, LC.

6. O.R.A., 36, pt. 2, 172, 176, 179, 184, 189; *Eleventh Pennsylvania Cavalry,* 109; "Kautz in the Great Rebellion," Kautz Papers, LC; Wall, "Raids," 70.

7. O.R.A., 36, pt. 2, 172; "Kautz in the Great Rebellion," Kautz Papers, LC; *Eleventh Pennsylvania Cavalry,* 109; Wall, "Raids," 71–72; James Marion Tucker, "Kautz Raiding Around Petersburg," *Glimpses of the Nation's Struggle,* 6 vols. (St. Paul, Minn.: Review Publishing Co., 1903), 5:125–126.

8. O.R.A., 36, pt. 2, 972; O.R.A., 51, pt. 2, 898, 900.

9. O.R.A., 36, pt. 2, 972; Beauregard to Colonel J. W. Hinton, 7 May 1864 (two letters), Letter Book, April–May 1864, Beauregard Papers, LC.

10. Beauregard to Colonel P. R. Page, 7 May 1864 (two telegrams), Beauregard to Colonel W. B. Tabb, 7 May 1864, Captain John Otey to Commanding Officer, Stony Creek, 7 May 1864, and Beauregard to Superintendent, Petersburg Railroad, 7 May 1864, all in Official Telegrams, 22 April–9 June 1864, Beauregard Papers, LC; Beauregard to Telegraph Superintendent, Weldon, 7 May 1864, Letter Book, April–May 1864, Beauregard Papers, LC; O.R.A., 51, pt. 2, 901.

11. Beauregard to Colonel J. R. Griffin, Franklin, 7 May 1864 (two telegrams), Official Telegrams, 22 April –9 June 1864, Beauregard Papers, LC.

12. Harding's telegram to Beauregard is not extant but the gist of its message can be inferred from a telegram from Beauregard to Harding, 7 May 1864, Official Telegrams, 22 April–9 June 1864, Beauregard Papers, LC. Harding's unit cannot be identified with certainty, but it probably was a detachment of Radcliffe's 61st North Carolina Infantry.

13. Beauregard to Major Harding, Franklin, 7 May 1864 (three telegrams), Official Telegrams, 22 April–9 June 1864, Beauregard Papers, LC.

14. Beauregard to Major Harding, Franklin, 7 May 1864 (four telegrams), and Beauregard to Colonel J. D. Ratcliffe [Radcliffe], c/o Major Harding, 7 May 1864, all in Official Telegrams, 22 April–9 June 1864, Beauregard Papers, LC.

15. O.R.A., 36, pt. 2, 172, 176, 179, 181–182, 262; Wall, "Raids," 73–74; *Eleventh Pennsylvania Cavalry,* 109; "Kautz in the Great Rebellion," Kautz Papers, LC; Tucker, *Glimpses,* 5:129–130.

16. O.R.A., 36, pt. 2, 172, 176, 179, 184–185; "Kautz in the Great Rebellion," Kautz Papers, LC; Wall, "Raids," 74.

17. O.R.A., 36, pt. 2, 172, 185, 189, 262; *Eleventh Pennsylvania Cavalry,* 109.

18. O.R.A., 36, pt. 2, 172, 189; "Kautz in the Great Rebellion," Kautz Papers, LC.

19. Beauregard to Colonel P. R. Page, 8 May 1864 (four telegrams), Beauregard to Pickett, 8 May 1864 (three telegrams), Beauregard to Colonel L. S. [S. L.] Fremont, Wilmington, 8 May 1864, all in Official Telegrams, 22 April–9 June 1864, Beauregard Papers, LC; Beauregard to Superintendent, Telegraph Office, Weldon, 8 May 1864, Letter Book, April–May 1864, Beauregard Papers, LC.

20. Beauregard to Bragg, 8 May 1864, and Beauregard to Colonel P. R. Page, 8 May 1864 (two telegrams), Official Telegrams, 22 April–9 June 1864, Beauregard Papers, LC; Roman, *Military Operations,* 2:553; Beauregard to Colonel P. R. Page, 8 May 1864, Letter Book, April–May 1864, Beauregard Papers, LC.

21. Beauregard to Colonel J. W. Hinton, 8 May 1864, Letter Book, April–May 1864, Beauregard Papers, LC; Beauregard to Bragg, 8 May 1864, and Beauregard to Whiting, 8 May 1864, Official Telegrams, 22 April–9 June 1864, Beauregard Papers, LC; O.R.A., 51, pt. 2, 903; Roman, *Military Operations*, 2:553.

22. "Kautz in the Great Rebellion," Kautz Papers, LC; O.R.A., 36, pt. 2, 185, 189; *Eleventh Pennsylvania Cavalry*, 109.

23. O.R.A., 36, pt. 2, 185, 187–188, 189; *Eleventh Pennsylvania Cavalry*, 109–110; Henry A. Chambers Diary, 9 May 1864, NCDAH; H. W. Barrow to Christian T. Pfohl, 10 May 1864, Christian T. Pfohl Papers, Southern Historical Collection, University of North Carolina, Chapel Hill, N.C.; Cary Whitaker Diary, 9 May 1864, SHC. Each of the Pennsylvania regiments carried two mountain howitzers with them on raids.

24. O.R.A., 36, pt. 2, 262–263.

25. O.R.A., 36, pt. 2, 172–173, 176–177, 179, 182, 185, 188, 189, 263; "Kautz in the Great Rebellion," Kautz Papers, LC; Merrill, *First District of Columbia*, 236–237; *Eleventh Pennsylvania Cavalry*, 110; Wall, "Raids," 75–76; Tucker, *Glimpses*, 5:131–133; Barton H. Wise, *The Life of Henry A. Wise of Virginia, 1806–1876* (New York: The Macmillan Co., 1899, 336.

26. O.R.A., 36, pt. 2, 172–173, 177, 179, 182, 188, 189, 263, 264; "Kautz in the Great Rebellion," Kautz Papers, LC; Merrill, *First District of Columbia*, 236; *Eleventh Pennsylvania Cavalry*, 110; Wall, "Raids," 76.

27. O.R.A., 36, pt. 2, 173; "Kautz in the Great Rebellion," Kautz Papers, LC. Because of Kautz's decision to depart, some Confederates considered Nottoway Bridge a Southern victory. William Lancaster to his wife, 13 May 1864, William Lancaster Letters, Virginia State Library, Richmond, Va.

28. O.R.A., 36, pt. 2, 173, 177, 179, 182, 185, 189–190; "Kautz in the Great Rebellion," Kautz Papers, LC; *Eleventh Pennsylvania Cavalry*, 111; Wall, "Raids," 78–81; Tucker, *Glimpses*, 5:133–135. Casualties in Kautz's command on this particular raid cannot be determined with accuracy because they are embedded in a summary covering this and other raids in May 1864.

29. O.R.A., 51, pt. 2, 906. The ten-mile figure in the text represents the distance between the most distant breaks at Stony Creek and Jarratt's Station. Most of the track in between, with the vital exception of Nottoway Bridge, remained intact. For the effect of Lee's army, see Johnston, *Virginia Railroads*, 200.

30. Cary Whitaker Diary, 8 May 1864, SHC; William Beavans Diary, 8 May 1864, SHC; H. W. Barrow to Christian T. Pfohl, 10 May 1864, Christian T. Pfohl Papers, SHC.

31. Cary Whitaker Diary, 9 May 1864, SHC. For a similar account by a member of Ransom's Brigade, see Henry A. Chambers Diary, 9 May 1864, NCDAH.

32. H. W. Barrow to Christian T. Pfohl, 10 May 1864, Christian T. Pfohl Papers, SHC; Younger, ed., *Kean Diary*, 150.

33. Depending upon their time of arrival at the lower end of the gap (possibly at night) and the availability of trains at the upper end, Confederate infantry units moving north might be delayed from twelve to eighteen hours negotiating the damaged section of the railroad. Regimental baggage and other supplies would be held up considerably longer. Bruce, "General Butler's Bermuda Campaign," 315, estimates the Confederates were delayed for two or three days, but this seems not to have been the case.

☆ 8 ☆

Butler's Demonstration toward Petersburg
8–9 May 1864

Except for those units opposing Kautz, 8 May brought a welcome respite for Confederate forces in Beauregard's department. In Petersburg, Colonel D. B. Harris supervised the construction of a new defense line along the southern bank of Swift Creek. Anchored on the left by earthworks covering Brander's Bridge, the line extended past the turnpike and railroad bridges to the vicinity of Fort Clifton on the Appomattox River. A detachment from Hagood's Brigade guarded Brander's Bridge, while most of Hagood's 2,300 men took up positions covering the turnpike bridge. To provide early warning of a Federal approach, Hagood sent one regiment and a section of artillery across the creek to the ridge beyond. On Hagood's right, Colonel Hector McKethan's 51st North Carolina Infantry of Clingman's Brigade defended the Richmond and Petersburg Railroad bridge. Beyond McKethan, Bushrod Johnson posted his old brigade, led by Colonel John Fulton. Fulton's line ended one-half mile short of Fort Clifton, where a small detachment of his men manned the heavy cannons blocking the Appomattox River. Supporting the infantry were eighteen guns from four artillery batteries. Altogether, Johnson and Pickett could muster less than 5,000 men to oppose the Federals.[1]

While Pickett's units occupied defensive positions on the southern flank of the Federal penetration, Robert Ransom's troops were stationary on the northern flank. Ransom still retained Barton's and Gracie's Brigades near Drewry's Bluff, with Barton as senior officer present. Keeping his infantry close at hand, Barton sent out a reconnaissance party to determine Butler's intentions. After probing the Federal positions all day, Colonel William Shingler's 7th South Carolina Cavalry finally gained a glimpse of the camps of the Army of the James, and also found that Port Walthall Junction was deserted. Barton sent these reports to Richmond. In reply, Ransom ordered him not to disturb the Federals as long as they remained inactive.[2]

In Richmond the atmosphere of anxiety seemed to be dissipating. The alarm bells pealed occasionally and the city militia was still under arms, but gradually the citizens were adjusting to the presence of the Army of the James. Mrs. Judith McGuire was surprised at the equanimity with which most residents accepted the situation: "It is strange how little apprehension seems to be felt in the city. Our trust is first in God, and, under Him, in our brave men."[3] The diary of War Department clerk J. B. Jones also reflected the prevailing mood:

> There has been no fighting below, between this and Petersburg, and we breathe freer, for Beauregard, we know, has made the best use of time. . . .
> A few days more will tell the story of this combined and most formidable attempt to take Richmond; and if it be the old song of failure, we may look for a speedy termination of the war. So mote it be![4]

Even more optimistic was Jefferson Davis, who was already beginning to think in terms of offensive operations against the lethargic Federals. In a note to Bragg proposing a "prompt and earnest attack," Davis pointedly suggested giving Robert Hoke command of the operation if Beauregard's health continued to be a problem.[5]

Although he spent most of 8 May organizing the ultimately futile defense of the Petersburg Railroad, Beauregard also issued another series of orders regarding the movement of troops toward Petersburg.[6] Rolling northward as fast as the dilapidated railroads could carry them were six brigades, two more than the number Pickett and Ransom together were fielding against Butler. Half of Henry Wise's Virginia Brigade was already north of Weldon, although it had been halted to protect the railroad, and one regiment was fighting for its life at Nottoway Bridge. Wise himself and another regiment would reach Weldon after nightfall.[7] Four of the expected brigades belonged to Hoke's New Berne expeditionary force. Lewis's Brigade passed through Weldon during the morning of 8 May and continued northward to Jarratt's Station. Behind Lewis, Matt Ransom's North Carolina Brigade was scattered along the railroad from Kinston and had not yet entrained. In addition to Hoke's units, there was one more Confederate brigade on its way north. Colquitt's Georgia Brigade had been ordered forward by rail from Charleston on 3 May, but on 8 May it was still below Wilmington.[8]

At Bermuda Hundred the Army of the James seemed willing to grant Beauregard time to concentrate his units. 8 May was a Sunday, and in many respects the Federal camps gave the appearance of a holiday in any peacetime garrison. Many soldiers lounged around their bivouac areas, relaxing after three days in the field. Men in one regiment braved the dangers of poisonous snakes and Confederate sharpshooters to take a refreshing "skin bath" in the Appomattox. Several units conducted brief worship services, while in other regiments soldiers spent the day improving their camps, writing letters, updating diaries, and engaging in further rounds of speculation about the course of the campaign. According to a reporter for the *New York Times*, morale was high, but a Maine soldier remarked: "Things do not seem to be in a very prosperous condition when two corps, numbering 40,000 men, are obliged to act on the defensive so early in the campaign."[9]

Throughout the day there were reminders that the Army of the James was still in enemy country. Federal gunboats were active, shelling the southern bank of the Appomattox River, and at times Confederate scouts could be seen across the stream from Cobb's Hill. Moreover, there was still work of a military nature to be done. Large numbers of men were assigned to fatigue duty on the rising fortifications. In addition, the army's front had to be shielded by a line of pickets, who spent the day fending off Confederate cavalry scouts. Back at the landing, supplies continued to come ashore, along with an artillery battery that had been tardy in arriving. Across the James River, Colonel Robert West's two Negro cavalry regiments finally appeared.[10]

During the day Butler sent Secretary of War Stanton a captured Confederate dispatch providing details of the struggle between Lee and Grant in the Wilderness. The Federals had long feared that Lee might somehow detach large forces that would unite with Beauregard's units and crush the exposed Army of the James. This possibility caused Grant to write Halleck on 8 May: "My efforts will be to form a junction with General Butler as early as possible, and be prepared to meet any enemy interposing." At the same time Grant dispatched Philip Sheridan's Cavalry Corps on a raid behind Lee's army. At the end of the raid, Sheridan was to continue southward to the James River across from Bermuda Hundred, resupply his men from Butler's depots, and then return to the Army of the Potomac.[11]

As Grant and Sheridan moved slowly toward him, Butler eagerly awaited word of their approach. He believed that coordination of the movements of the two armies was essential in order to preserve the Army of the James from a massive Confederate counterattack. In sharp contrast to his mood on the night of 5 May when he had advocated an immediate advance upon Richmond, Butler now decided upon a more conservative course of action. Since the reports from Grant indicated only that a great battle was taking place in the Wilderness, Butler resolved to postpone his final advance on Richmond until the Army of the Potomac was nearer. Instead of aggressively seeking the enemy, Butler chose to give his troops a day of rest, while at the same time strengthening the fortifications that sheltered his base.[12]

The decision to wait for Grant did not preclude all offensive operations by the Army of the James. In an effort to further damage the railroad, Butler ordered both corps to advance westward at dawn on 9 May and destroy as much of the track as they could reach. His directive to Gillmore especially emphasized the offensive: "The enemy are in our front with scarcely 5,000 men, and it is a disgrace that we are cooped up here." Preparatory orders issued by both corps were similar. Each man was to carry sixty rounds of ammunition, a full canteen, and at least one day's rations. In addition, Gillmore cautioned the X Corps against the twin vices of marauding and straggling, since "The Tenth Corps is now brought in direct competition with another, and must not be allowed to suffer in any respect by the comparison." Offshore, Admiral Lee ordered the *U.S.S. Shokokon* and *U.S.S. General Putnam* in the Appomattox River to assist the army.[13]

The proposed advance was not to be a half-hearted effort; almost the entire Army of the James would be on the move. Of the twelve brigades within the entrenchments, only Plaisted's, Drake's, and Barton's units, which had fought at Port Walthall Junction, would be left behind. Nevertheless, the goals of even this mighty thrust were limited. Without news from Grant, Butler was unwilling to advance upon Richmond in earnest. Nor did he intend to assault Petersburg, as that would draw him away from the Confederate capital and possibly delay his cooperation with the Army of the Potomac. Instead, Butler sought only to demonstrate against the Confederates around Petersburg, while occupying the railroad long enough to thoroughly wreck it, a modest goal indeed for so large a force.[14]

According to the plan, Smith's divisions were to take the direct road to Port Walthall Junction, striking the railroad and any Confederates that might be foolhardy enough to linger there. Screened by a detachment from the 1st New York Mounted Rifles, Smith's corps was led by Marston's and Burnham's brigades of Brooks's division. Brooks was followed by Wistar's and Heckman's brigades of Weitzel's division. The only other available brigade in the XVIII Corps, the Third Brigade of Brooks's division, was assigned a special role. Temporarily under the direction of Brigadier General John Martindale, it was ordered to guard the left flank of the main column by marching to Port Walthall Junction via the Dunn plantation.[15]

While the XVIII Corps advanced on Port Walthall Junction, Gillmore's X Corps was to push due west, striking the Richmond turnpike first, then the railroad at or near Chester Station. Leading Gillmore's corps was Brigadier General Adelbert Ames's Third Division, but only Colonel Richard White's brigade was making the trip. Following Ames was Brigadier General John Turner's Second Division, consisting temporarily of Colonel Samuel Alford's brigade only. In rear of Turner was Brigadier General Alfred Terry's First Division with the brigades of Colonels Joshua Howell and Joseph Hawley. The lack of cavalry at Bermuda Hundred prevented Gillmore's front from being screened by mounted troops, although Butler promised to make Colonel Robert West's Negro cavalrymen available after a few hours rest.[16]

Brooks's division of the XVIII Corps left its camps promptly at 5:00 A.M., and while pushing toward Port Walthall Junction met no Confederate opposition. Nevertheless, Brooks advanced cautiously, taking approximately four hours to move three miles. Near the junction, Marston's and Burnham's men were halted and deployed in line of battle. The Federals found themselves standing in the midst of the battlefield of 7 May. Scattered about were the bloated, blackened bodies of Federal soldiers, many lying just as they had fallen two days earlier. Most of the dead had been stripped of all usable articles of clothing and equipment. Even more horrifying was the discovery of a Federal corpse pinned to the ground by a bayonet through the mouth and throat, evidently while the man was still alive. Enraged by what they saw, many soldiers swore vengeance against the perpetrators, who were thought to be Tennesseans. Sickened by the sights and smells of the junction, Brooks's men delayed only long enough to do minor damage to the railroad before heading south toward Petersburg.[17]

By this time Godfrey Weitzel's Second Division had also reached the battlefield, exposing Heckman's and Wistar's soldiers to the same grisly scenes that had appalled Brooks's men. Several recruits in Heckman's brigade were unnerved by the appearance of the bodies, many of which had been burned in a brush fire. Yet, miraculously, some victims still clung to life. While passing over the site, the 27th Massachusetts discovered a badly wounded survivor of the 48th New York, and the 9th New Jersey picked up an equally ravaged member of the 115th New York.

Despite their wounds, these men of Barton's brigade had hidden from Confederate searchers for two days. Now in the hands of friends, they were rushed back to Bermuda Hundred for medical treatment.[18]

While the XVIII Corps maneuvered around Port Walthall Junction, Gillmore's X Corps advanced toward Chester Station. At 8:00 A.M. White's brigade reached the railroad just south of the village. Unlike the troops near the junction two days before, White's men came prepared to inflict major damage. Well-equipped engineer companies accompanied the infantry and directed the proceedings. After detachments had established a protective screen, several hundred men took up positions along a section of track. The rails at one end of the section were loosened and the entire track assembly was progressively turned upside down into the ditch, in the manner of a plow turning a furrow. The long line of men then proceeded to another section, while a second group of soldiers loosened the ties, stacked them in piles on the rails, and set them on fire, thereby destroying the ties and warping the iron. Meanwhile, another detachment attacked the telegraph line paralleling the railroad, systematically destroying both poles and wire.[19]

Around 10:00 A.M., Alford's brigade reached the railroad at Chester Station, where it burned the depot and destroyed more track. Since no cavalry was available, Alford's rear was covered by Terry's division, but Terry's force was dwindling as he detached flank guards along the way. Not far beyond the Federal picket line, at Ware Bottom Church, two regiments of Howell's brigade and a section of artillery were left to watch a road leading northward. Approximately one mile farther, at the junction of the Chester Station road and the Richmond turnpike, another of Howell's regiments and two more guns were deposited, leaving Howell to proceed toward the railroad with only a single regiment. Behind Howell came the last X Corps brigade, Hawley's, which left camp at 7:00 A.M. and did not reach Chester Station until noon.[20]

Around midmorning, Smith concluded that the Confederate force facing him near Port Walthall Junction could be trapped if Gillmore made a great left wheel southward from Chester Station. In reality, the only Confederates near Smith were a few scouts watching his progress, but Smith apparently believed that they were the same units that had stood so firmly at the junction ever since 6 May. If they could be destroyed, all immediate opposition to the Army of the James might be eliminated. Therefore Smith advised Butler to order Gillmore to turn the X Corps southward. Butler listened attentively to Smith's suggestion and at once gave his approval. At 10:15 A.M. Gillmore began to implement the revised plan. Unfortunately, by that time the handful of Confederates who might have been caught in such a ponderous trap had retreated.[21]

During their brief stay near Port Walthall Junction the men of Brooks's and Weitzel's divisions buried the dead, uprooted some track, and knocked down the telegraph line that the Confederates had reestablished the previous day. When the orders to move arrived, Brooks's division shielded itself with a skirmish line from Marston's brigade and headed in a southwesterly direction along the Old Stage Road toward the railroad and the turnpike. As Burnham's brigade passed the junction, the men were delighted to see the army commander riding nearby. Butler acknowledged their greetings but requested that cheers be omitted due to the nearness of the enemy. Silently the men pushed forward into the woods. "For miles around, the country was covered with primitive, tangled southern forests. Front, rear and flank, all was wood." By then it was almost noon and the temperature was approaching 102° in the shade. [22]

Just as his brigades crossed the railroad, Brooks finally met the elusive Confederates. A line of skirmishers could be seen in the trees on the far side of Timsbury Creek and an exploding shell signaled the presence of artillery. In response, Brooks deployed Burnham on the left and Marston on the right, with the railroad tracks as his axis. In Weitzel's division, marching parallel with Brooks on the turnpike, Heckman's brigade formed line of battle astride the turnpike and was joined on its right by Wistar's brigade. Smith's XVIII Corps now faced due south, with Brooks's division on the left and Weitzel's division on the right. Far to the east, near the swamps around the mouth of Swift Creek, was Martindale's brigade. When all was ready, the long lines of blue-clad men resumed their advance through the dense underbrush in the oppressive afternoon heat. Soon heat prostration began to take a larger toll than the random Confederate bullets that whizzed overhead, clipping the foliage. [23]

By midafternoon the Federals were in sight of their objective, the road and rail bridges over Swift Creek. East of the railroad Burnham entered a large field that stretched all the way to the creek. In the middle of the field was the abandoned Shippen house. On Burnham's right, Marston's brigade occupied the thick belt of woods between railroad and turnpike. Heckman's brigade straddled the turnpike just north of a small frame building known as Arrowfield Church. Prolonging Heckman's line in the woods west of the pike was Wistar's brigade. Facing Heckman was Confederate infantry deployed in line of battle, while across Swift Creek several guns periodically sent shells whistling toward the Federal line. Unsure of their next move, both Brooks and Weitzel halted their troops. [24]

On the south bank of Swift Creek, Bushrod Johnson was under orders to refrain from starting a general engagement. Thus he took no action when the Army of the James confronted his only units north of the creek, the 11th South Carolina Infantry and part of the 25th South Carolina, which occupied a slight rise south of Arrowfield Church. Unaware of what was happening at Swift Creek and believing that the Federals were advancing on Drewry's Bluff, Braxton Bragg at 11:10 A.M. wired Pickett to "Push forward all the troops as fast as they arrive to recover the position lost and reopen the road telegraph to this point." Pickett relayed Bragg's message to Johnson and directed him to "move forward at once and see what the enemy are doing." This order reached Johnson at 2:00 P.M. Although he realized it was patently absurd for him to leave his strong defensive position, he ordered Hagood to cross the creek with his brigade and advance toward the Federals. [25]

At 3:45 P.M., while Hagood was moving his troops to the turnpike bridge, Johnson received a message from Pickett delaying the advance until reinforcements arrived. This order was soon followed by one canceling the attack entirely. Since it was too late to recall all of Hagood's men, the attack was modified into a reconnaissance in force.[26] As the 21st South Carolina began to cross the turnpike bridge under Federal artillery fire, Colonel D. B. Harris dashed up to Hagood with the new orders for a reconnaissance. Like everyone else on the field, Hagood knew that the Federals were present in strength; a reconnaissance could only cause needless casualties. Just as Hagood and Harris were speaking, the crackle of musketry beyond the creek signaled that Colonel F. H. Gantt's 11th South Carolina was becoming heavily engaged. With no time to lose, Hagood rushed the 21st South Carolina across the fire-swept bridge and up the hill on the right of the turnpike. Concluding from the activity around him that a general advance was beginning, Colonel Gantt decided that a charge was in order and sent his men forward.[27]

Awaiting Hagood's South Carolinians were the Massachusetts and New Jersey regiments of Heckman's brigade, the same troops who had met Hagood's men on 6 May at Port Walthall Junction. East of the turnpike with its flank extending into a thicket of young pines was the 25th Massachusetts, supported in rear by the 23rd Massachusetts; west of the road was the 27th Massachusetts, supported by the 9th New Jersey. As the South Carolinians approached, yelling wildly, the colonels of Heckman's front regiments ordered their men to cease firing individually and wait for the command to fire by volley. On came the 11th, 21st, and part of the 25th South Carolina, until they were within fifty yards of the Federals. Then, "Fire," and a thunderous volley crashed into the first line of charging Confederates. According to a young soldier in the front rank of the 25th Massachusetts, "that line of grey melted away like snow." The charge had been so headlong that several Confederates ran into the Federal lines and were taken prisoner. The others milled about aimlessly while their surviving officers labored in vain to organize a new assault. All the while the sweating Federals poured volley after volley into the confused mass.[28]

To close the action Heckman ordered his rear regiments to charge. Anticipating this, Hagood had already ordered a withdrawal and the remnants of his command rushed pell-mell down the slope to the bridge and the safety of the far side of the creek. Their retreat was covered by the 25th South Carolina, which held the bridge and checked pursuit. Left behind were the dead and most of the wounded. Hagood's abortive reconnaissance cost his brigade a total of 9 officers and 128 men killed, wounded, and missing.[29] Surprisingly, Federal losses were equally heavy. Heckman's brigade suffered 13 men killed and 100 wounded, while Wistar's brigade on Heckman's right lost a total of 26 men.[30]

As Hagood's troops streamed across Swift Creek, Godfrey Weitzel ordered his two brigades to occupy the hill that the South Carolinians had so recently vacated. There they were bombarded by the guns of the Surry Light Artillery positioned south of the creek. To counter the Confederate fire, Weitzel deployed a section of Battery D, 4th U.S. Artillery on the turnpike, but the gunners met such a storm of shot and shell that they were soon compelled to withdraw. By then it was late afternoon and Weitzel, who had been given discretionary authority over the advance, decided not to assault the Confederate positions behind Swift Creek. Instead he ordered his units to hold the ground gained and replenish their ammuni-

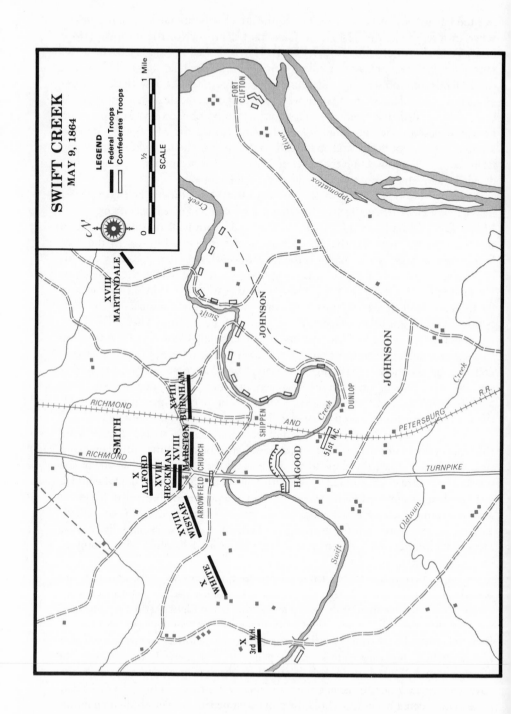

SWIFT CREEK
MAY 9, 1864

LEGEND

Federal Troops
Confederate Troops

SCALE

0   ½   1 Mile

tion.[31] Behind Weitzel's tired men elements of Gillmore's X Corps deployed in support. White's brigade of Ames's division formed on Wistar's right, and Alford's brigade of Turner's division remained in blocking positions around Chester Station, while Hawley's brigade waited near Port Walthall Junction. Upon orders from Terry, one of Hawley's regiments was detached and sent to watch Brander's Bridge.[32]

As the evening shadows lengthened, the men of the XVIII and X Corps made themselves as comfortable and secure as possible, seeking food if they had exhausted their rations or constructing impromptu entrenchments with tin cups and bayonets. Their line stretched from Brander's Bridge on the Federal right, past Arrowfield Church, across the turnpike and the railroad, all the way to Burnham's brigade at the Shippen farm. Units near the railroad took the opportunity to wreck the track behind their positions. On the battlefield the wounded of both sides were brought to the church where a temporary hospital had been established. Nearby, burial details methodically dug graves for the Confederate dead, who lay where they had fallen. In the 9th New Jersey Infantry a soldier, apparently overcome by the events of the day, put his gun muzzle in his mouth and committed suicide.[33]

While the opposing forces skirmished around Swift Creek, other units were also in action. Martindale's brigade spent the afternoon near the mouth of Swift Creek engaging the Tennesseans in Fort Clifton at long range. Also moving against Fort Clifton were several of Charles Graham's army gunboats, supported by one of Admiral Lee's vessels, the *U.S.S. General Putnam*. Their efforts proved as fruitless as Martindale's cannonade, because the elevation of the fort and the narrowness of the river gave the Confederate gunners the advantage. In midafternoon, after the *Brewster* had been destroyed and the *Chamberlin* grounded on a sandbar, Graham and the navy decided to withdraw from Fort Clifton.[34]

The retreat by the gunboats had a marked effect on the final Federal offensive venture of the day, an advance by 1,800 of Edward Hincks's men from City Point. Hincks pushed along the south bank of the Appomattox with no difficulty, except for a slight case of mistaken identity between his cavalry and a landing party from the gunboats, until he too had come within range of Fort Clifton. Since the fort was across the river from Hincks's force and could not be neutralized by the gunboats, Hincks decided to seek a more inland route to Petersburg. Unfortunately for the Federals, every attempt to discover such a covered passage was blocked by Major John Scott's civilian troopers. Eventually Hincks admitted defeat and returned to City Point.[35]

With Hincks's retreat the last Federal offensive of the day sputtered and died. Butler had succeeded in his limited goals of demonstrating against Petersburg and destroying a considerable amount of railroad track. In addition, the three brigades left behind at Bermuda Hundred had continued to improve the defensive fortifications, using what were euphemistically known as "Gillmore's rifles" (picks and shovels).[36] Satisfied with the day's accomplishments, Butler reported to Secretary of War Stanton:

> We have landed here, intrenched ourselves, destroyed many miles of railroad, and got a position which, with proper supplies, we can hold out against the

whole of Lee's army. . . . Beauregard, with a large portion of his command, was left south by the cutting of the railroads by Kautz. That portion which reached Petersburg under Hill I have whipped to-day. . . . General Grant will not be troubled with any further re-enforcements to Lee from Beauregard's force.[37]

South of Swift Creek, the Confederates also had cause to rejoice. Aside from the afternoon confusion that had led to the sacrifice of part of Hagood's Brigade, George Pickett had successfully defended Petersburg against two corps advancing from the north, a combined land and water thrust against Fort Clifton, and a probe south of the Appomattox from City Point. All this had been accomplished by only two-and-one-half infantry brigades, a few hundred artillerymen, and some poorly armed civilians. From North Carolina the news was equally good. Beauregard had left Weldon by train early in the morning and a succession of telegrams announced his progress via Raleigh, Greensboro, and Danville. Even more exhilarating to the haggard defenders of Petersburg was the arrival at nightfall of Lewis's Brigade, which had just negotiated the gap in the railroad around Stony Creek and Nottoway Bridge. Lewis's men were met with jubilation by the Petersburg residents, who thronged the streets to welcome them. With the appearance of these relatively fresh regiments and the promise of more to come, Pickett's time of trial was almost over.[38]

NOTES

1. O.R.A., 36, pt. 2, 242–243, 250, 975; Hagood, Memoirs, 228.

2. O.R.A., 36, pt. 2, 975–977; O.R.A., 51, pt. 2, 901–902.

3. McGuire, Southern Refugee, 264.

4. Jones, War Clerk, 2:202.

5. O.R.A., 51, pt. 2, 902.

6. Beauregard to Major Willis (Quartermaster, Kinston), 8 May 1864, Beauregard to Hoke (two telegrams), 8 May 1864, Official Telegrams, 22 April–9 June 1864, also Beauregard to Colonel J. W. Hinton, Weldon (three letters), 8 May 1864, Beauregard to Hoke, 8 May 1864, and Beauregard to Dearing, 8 May 1864, Letter Book, April–May 1864, all in Beauregard Papers, LC.

7. O.R.A., 51, pt. 2, 903, 904; Cutchins, Richmond Light Infantry Blues, 132; John Paris Diary, 8 May 1864, SHC.

8. For Lewis, see Cary Whitaker Diary, 8 May 1864, SHC; William Beavans Diary, 8 May 1864, SHC; H. W. Barrow to Christian T. Pfohl, 10 May 1864, Christian T. Pfohl Papers, SHC. For Ransom, see Harrill, Reminiscences, 21; Clark, ed., North Carolina Regiments, 3:350; Henry A. Chambers Diary, 8 May 1864, NCDAH; Edward Phifer to his mother, 29 May 1864, Phifer Family Papers, Southern Historical Collection, University of North Carolina, Chapel Hill, N.C.; John Washington Calton to his sister, undated but 8 May 1864, John Washington Calton Letters, North Carolina Division of Archives and History, Raleigh, N.C. For Terry and Corse, see Charles T. Loehr, War History of the Old First Virginia Infantry Regiment, Army of Northern Virginia (Richmond, Va.: Wm. Ellis Jones, 1884), 45; O.R.A., 51, pt. 2, 904. For Colquitt, see O.R.A., 36, pt. 2, 946, and O.R.A., 51, pt. 2, 904.

9. Thompson, Thirteenth New Hampshire, 262; Nichols, Perry's Saints, 210; Drake, Ninth New Jersey, 179, 199; Walter S. Clemence Memoranda, 8 May 1864, NCC; Cunningham, Adirondack Regiment, 107; Derby, Bearing Arms, 258; H. Clay Trumbull, War Memories of an Army Chaplain (New York: Charles Scribner's Sons, 1898), 32–33; Cleveland, ed., "Campaign of Promise," 314; Valentine, Story of Co. F, 110; De Forest, Random Sketches, 218; Kreutzer, Ninety-Eighth New York, 185; New York Times, 11 May 1864; Brady, Eleventh Maine, 177.

10. O.R.N., 10:46, 94; Walter S. Clemence Diary, 8 May 1864, NCC; Clark, My Experience, 57;

Emmerton, *Twenty-Third Massachusetts*, 177; Valentine, *Story of Co. F*, 110; Cunningham, *Adirondack Regiment*, 107; Roe, *Twenty-fourth Massachusetts*, 279; Bartlett, *Twelfth New Hampshire*, 174; Dickey, *Eighty-fifth Pennsylvania*, 321–322; Eldredge, *Third New Hampshire*, 462; Price, *Ninety-Seventh Pennsylvania*, 254; Beecher, *First Connecticut Light Battery*, 1:347; O.R.A., 36, pt. 2, 146; *New York Times*, 11 May 1864.

11. O.R.A., 36, pt. 2, 526, 552, 561; Grant, *Personal Memoirs*, 2:153–154. J. F. C. Fuller, in *Generalship of Grant*, 242, notes that Sheridan would tend to relieve any Confederate pressure building against the Army of the James.

12. Memorandum, 8 January 1879, Butler Papers, LC; Butler to W. P. Darby [Derby], 26 June 1882, Butler Papers, LC; Butler, *Butler's Book*, 645. Butler's decision to keep the Army of the James inactive on 8 May has been strongly criticized by some writers, particularly Rockwell, "Tenth Army Corps," 276, and Wolfson, "Butler's Relations," 381.

13. Butler to W. P. Darby [Derby], 26 June 1882, Butler Papers, LC; O.R.A., 36, pt. 2, 34, 556–559; Valentine, *Story of Co. F*, 110; Cunningham, *Adirondack Regiment*, 107; Thompson, *Thirteenth New Hampshire*, 262; Bartlett, *Twelfth New Hampshire*, 174; Eldredge, *Third New Hampshire*, 462; Beecher, *First Connecticut Light Battery*, 1:347; De Forest, *Random Sketches*, 217; O.R.N., 10:33.

14. O.R.A., 36, pt. 2, 75, 77; Butler to W. P. Darby [Derby], 26 June 1882, Butler Papers, LC.

15. O.R.A., 36, pt. 2, 106, 126, 138, 148, 170; De Forest, *Random Sketches*, 147–148; Cunningham, *Adirondack Regiment*, 107; Thompson, *Thirteenth New Hampshire*, 263; O.R.A., 51, pt. 1, 1259.

16. O.R.A., 51, pt. 1, 1231–1232; O.R.A., 36, pt. 2, 588, 589.

17. O.R.A., 36, pt. 2, 126, 133, 138; Cunningham, *Adirondack Regiment*, 107; Thompson, *Thirteenth New Hampshire*, 263, 268–269.

18. Drake, *Ninth New Jersey*, 349–350; Valentine, *Story of Co. F*, 110; Cleveland, ed., "Campaign of Promise," 315–316; Derby, *Bearing Arms*, 258.

19. O.R.A., 36, pt. 2, 96, 106, 107, 556, 589, 592; Price, *Ninety-Seventh Pennsylvania*, 254–255.

20. O.R.A., 36, pt. 2, 45, 47, 50, 58, 69, 96, 97, 588, 589; Mowris, *One Hundred and Seventeenth New York*, 104; O.R.A., 51, pt. 1, 1232; Dickey, *Eigty-Fifth Pennsylvania*, 314–315, 322; Brady, *Eleventh Maine*, 177–178; Little, *Seventh New Hampshire*, 243–244; Tourtellotte, *History of Company K*, 168. Upon reaching the railroad, Howell was ordered to return to Ware Bottom Church with his last unit.

21. O.R.A., 36, pt. 2, 589, 593. Bruce, "General Butler's Bermuda Campaign," 323, is especially critical of Smith for this decision.

22. Cunningham, *Adirondack Regiment*, 107; Thompson, *Thirteenth New Hampshire*, 263; Valentine, *Story of Co. F*, 110; Drake, *Ninth New Jersey*, 199; Cleveland, ed., "Campaign of Promise," 315; Bartlett, *Twelfth New Hampshire*, 422; Samuel H. Putnam, Regimental Record—Co. A, 25th Mass. Vols., DU; O.R.A., 36, pt. 2, 126. The description of the countryside is in Kreutzer, *Ninety-Eighth New York*, 186.

23. O.R.A., 36, pt. 2, 99, 126, 133, 138, 148–149, 155; Cunningham *Adirondack Regiment*, 107; Thompson, *Thirteenth New Hampshire*, 263–265, 269; Derby, *Bearing Arms*, 247–248, 260; Drake, *Ninth New Jersey*, 179, 199, 204; Cleveland, ed., "Campaign of Promise," 315–317; Bartlett, *Twelfth New Hampshire*, 174–175; Haynes, *Second New Hampshire* (2), 221; O.R.A., 51, pt. 1, 1259–1260.

24. O.R.A., 36, pt. 2, 126, 133, 138; Thompson, *Thirteenth New Hampshire*, 264, 268, 270; Derby, *Bearing Arms*, 247–248, 259; Drake, *Ninth New Jersey*, 204, 350–351; Valentine, *Story of Co. F*, 110; Samuel H. Putnam, Regimental Record—Co. A, 25th Mass. Vols., DU; Bartlett, *Twelfth New Hampshire*, 176; O.R.A., 36, pt. 2, 126, 149.

25. O.R.A., 36, pt. 2, 243, 978; Hagood, *Memoirs*, 228–229; Izlar, *Edisto Rifles*, 50. See also O.R.A., 36, pt. 2, 977, 981, 982; O.R.A., 51, pt. 2, 907.

26. O.R.A., 36, pt. 2, 243–244, 979. Judging from his return messages to Bragg, Pickett was especially distracted by Kautz's activities on the railroad south of Petersburg. O.R.A., 51, pt. 2, 906–907. Obviously George Pickett was nearing his breaking point. It is quite possible that his decision to cancel the attack was made at the insistence of D. H. Hill.

27. O.R.A., 36, pt. 2, 252; Hagood, *Memoirs*, 228–230; DuBose, *History of Company B*, 55–56.

28. Drake, *Ninth New Jersey*, 179–180; Cleveland, ed., "Campaign of Promise," 316; Valentine, *Story of Co. F*, 110; Clark, *My Experience*, 58; Derby, *Bearing Arms*, 248:259, 260; Emmerton, *Twenty-Third Massachusetts*, 178; Denny, *Wearing the Blue*, 277–278; O.R.A., 36, pt. 2, 155; Putnam, *Story of Company A*, 269–270. The quotation is from Samuel H. Putnam, Regimental Record—Co. A, 25th Mass. Vols., DU.

29. Cleveland, ed., "Campaign of Promise," 317; Emmerton, *Twenty-Third Massachusetts*, 178; Valentine, *Story of Co. F*, 111; Derby, *Bearing Arms*, 260–261; Hagood, *Memoirs*, 229–230; Jones, *Surry*

Light Artillery, 174; Izlar, *Edisto Rifles,* 50–51; Dibble, "South Carolina Command," 459; O.R.A., 36, pt. 2, 244.

30. O.R.A., 36, pt. 2, 150, 156; Putnam, *Story of Company A,* 273; John Y. Foster, *New Jersey and the Rebellion: A History of the Services of the Troops and People of New Jersey in Aid of the Union Cause* (Newark: Martin R. Dennis & Co., 1868), 239; Emmerton, *Twenty-Third Massachusetts,* 179; Derby, *Bearing Arms,* 262; Croffut and Morris, *Connecticut During the War,* 541; Bartlett, *Twelfth New Hampshire,* 746; Haynes, *Second New Hampshire* (2), 222.

31. O.R.A., 36, pt. 2, 149, 155–156; Derby, *Bearing Arms,* 261; Cleveland, ed., "Campaign of Promise," 315, 317; Haynes, *Second New Hampshire* (2), 222; Walter S. Clemence Memoranda, 9 May 1864, NCC; Jones, *Surry Light Artillery,* 175.

32. O.R.A., 36, pt. 2, 50, 57–59, 69, 97, 106, 107, 149; Waite, *New Hampshire in the Great Rebellion,* 202, 240; Price, *Ninety-Seventh Pennsylvania,* 255–256; Mowris, *One Hundred and Seventeenth New York,* 104; O.R.A., 51, pt. 1, 1232; Walkley, *Seventh Connecticut,* 132; Little, *Seventh New Hampshire,* 244; Copp, *Reminiscences,* 365–366; Eldredge, *Third New Hampshire,* 462–463.

33. Derby, *Bearing Arms,* 261, 511–512; Valentine, *Story of Co. F,* 111; Cleveland, ed., "Campaign of Promise," 317–318; O.R.A., 36, pt. 2, 137; De Forest, *Random Sketches,* 148; Emmerton, *Twenty-Third Massachusetts,* 178–179; Putnam, *Story of Company A,* 272–274.

34. O.R.A., 36, pt. 2, 28, 146, 147, 243; O.R.A., 51, pt. 1, 1259–1260, pt. 2, 906; O.R.N. 10:46, 94; *New York Times,* 12 May 1864.

35. O.R.A., 36, pt. 2, 22–23, 28–29, 165–166, 594; Livermore, *Days and Events,* 338–342; Scott, *Annals of the War,* 383; William H. S. Burgwyn Diary, 7 [9] May 1864, NCDAH; Solon A. Carter to his wife, 11 May 1864, Solon A. Carter Papers, United States Army Military History Institute, Carlisle Barracks, Pa.; Joseph J. Scroggs Diary, 9 May 1864, *Civil War Times Illustrated* Collection of Civil War Papers, United States Army Military History Institute, Carlisle Barracks, Pa.

36. For varying estimates of the amount of track damaged and the effectiveness of the destruction, see Cadwell, *Old Sixth,* 90; Beecher, *First Connecticut Light Battery,* 1:350–351; Hagood, *Memoirs,* 231; Jones, *Surry Light Artillery,* 176–177. For work on the fortifications, see O.R.A., 36, pt. 2, 75–77, 109; Nichols, *Perry's Saints,* 210; Roe, *Twenty-Fourth Massachusetts,* 279; Stowits, *One Hundredth New York,* 252.

37. O.R.A., 36, pt. 2, 11.

38. O.R.A., 51, pt. 2, 903, 906; Beauregard to Bragg and Pickett from Danville, 10:25 P.M., 9 May 1864, Official Telegrams, 22 April–9 June 1864, Beauregard Papers, LC; William H. S. Burgwyn Diary, 7 [9] May 1864, NCDAH; Clark, ed., *North Carolina Regiments,* 3:275; Cary Whitaker Diary, 9 May 1864, SHC; William Beavans Diary, 9 May 1864, SHC; John Paris Diary, 9 May 1864, SHC. By the end of 9 May, Ransom's Brigade was resting at Stony Creek, Terry's Brigade was on the railroad below Weldon, and Corse's was preparing to board the cars at Kinston. The 3rd North Carolina Cavalry, marching overland, was north of Tarboro, North Carolina. Edward Phifer to his mother, 29 May 1864, Phifer Family Papers, SHC; Loehr, *First Virginia,* 45; George Wise, *History of the Seventeenth Virginia Infantry, C.S.A.* (Baltimore: Kelly, Piet & Company, 1870), 174; Henry Machen Patrick to his wife, 19 May 1864, Henry Machen Patrick Letters, North Carolina Division of Archives and History, Raleigh, N.C.

☆ 9 ☆

The Battle of Chester Station
9–10 May 1864

During the late afternoon of 9 May, Benjamin Butler met with Gillmore and Smith to discuss the plan of operations for the next day. Having heard nothing from Grant, Butler decided to threaten Petersburg a while longer, and he may even have believed that the city could be taken. At the very least, a determined assault by both corps in the morning would breach the Confederate defenses at Swift Creek and carry all the way to the Appomattox River. That would permit the destruction of the Swift Creek railroad bridge and bring the much larger bridge over the Appomattox within range of Federal guns. The chances for success would be considerably enhanced by having Edward Hincks repeat his earlier demonstration from City Point. If the timing was right, the Confederates might be so attracted to affairs at Swift Creek that Hincks could walk into Petersburg unopposed.[1]

After sending a message to Hincks setting the time for his advance, Butler asked Smith and Gillmore for additional comments. When none were forthcoming, he departed with his escort for Cobb's Hill. Immediately after Butler's departure Gillmore proposed to Smith an alternate plan of operations. Gillmore's proposal called for the Army of the James to withdraw from Swift Creek that very night and return to the Bermuda Hundred base, destroying the railroad on the way. A pontoon bridge would then be constructed over the Appomattox near Cobb's Hill and most of the Army of the James would cross to the south bank of the river. From there the Federals could operate against all transportation lines entering Petersburg as well as the city itself. In Gillmore's opinion, such a scheme would cost fewer casualties than Butler's plan and would guarantee destruction of the communication lines below Petersburg, which Butler's plan could not.[2]

Smith agreed that Gillmore's plan was preferable to Butler's, especially since he believed that Kautz's cavalry would continue to operate south of Petersburg. According to Smith, both Brigadier General Godfrey Weitzel and Colonel Arthur Dutton, a member of Smith's staff, also saw merit in Gillmore's proposal. As a result, Smith and Gillmore decided to submit the new plan to Butler at once. At 7:00 P.M. Gillmore drafted an explanation of the proposal, signed it jointly with Smith, and dispatched it by Brigadier General Charles Devens to Butler's headquarters. Although respectful in tone, the letter disregarded the fact that Butler had sought comments from his corps commanders only a half hour previously, but had received none.[3]

Arriving at his headquarters, Butler began to read a pile of dispatches that had arrived during his absence. Immediately his attention was drawn to several telegrams from Secretary Stanton bearing news from Grant. The first telegram, sent at 10:00 A.M., read:

> Advices from the front give reason to believe that General Grant's operations will prove a great success and complete victory. On Saturday night the enemy had been driven at all points, and Hancock was pushing forward rapidly to Spotsylvania Court-House, where heavy firing was heard yesterday. It was reported yesterday by a deserter that the enemy's only hope was in heavy reenforcements from Beauregard.

The second message followed at 3:20 P.M.:

> A bearer of dispatches from General Meade has just reached here by way of Fredericksburg; states that on Friday night Lee's army fell back, and yesterday were in full retreat for Richmond, Grant pursuing with his army. Hancock passed Spotsylvania Court-House before daylight yesterday morning.

At 4:00 P.M. the final telegram was dispatched:

> A dispatch from General Grant has just been received. He is on the march with his whole army to form a junction with you, but had not determined his route. Another dispatch from him is being translated.[4]

Ever since April, one of Butler's guidelines had been that the Army of the James and the Army of the Potomac would coordinate their movements in the ultimate drive upon Richmond. Before the arrival of these telegrams containing the first positive news of Grant's progress, Butler had been unwilling to move against Richmond alone, preferring instead to make demonstrations and secure his base. Now at last Butler was informed by the Secretary of War that Lee was in hasty retreat toward Richmond and Grant was following close behind. If Stanton's information were true, the Army of the James could not afford to spend more time dallying around Petersburg, but should prepare to advance toward Richmond in order to meet Grant. Adapting to the changed situation, Butler at 9:30 P.M. informed Hincks that good news from Grant necessitated the cancellation of the advance on Petersburg.[5]

About the same time that Butler was writing Hincks, the Gillmore-Smith proposal arrived. Incensed that his subordinates would pretend to accept his initial plan, only to reject it immediately upon his departure, Butler composed a caustic response addressed to the corps commanders jointly:

> While I regret an infirmity of purpose which did not permit you to state to me, when I was personally present, the suggestion which you make in your

written note, but left me to go to my headquarters under the impression that another and far different purpose was advised by you, I shall [not] yield to the written suggestions which imply a change of plan made within thirty minutes after I left you. Military affairs cannot be carried on, in my judgment, with this sort of vacillation.[6]

Butler concluded the message with his revised orders for the next day. The Army of the James would withdraw from Swift Creek in order to begin preparations for a "subsequent early demonstration up the James from the right of our position."[6]

Although he was not yet aware of it, Butler would soon receive a slight reinforcement for the coming advance. His plea for aid had at last reached Grant, who had told Halleck: "If matters are still favorable with Butler send him all the reenforcements you can." With no faith whatsoever in Butler and much personal animosity toward him, Halleck released only the 1,800-man 1st Connecticut Heavy Artillery Regiment from the Washington defenses for Butler's use. Trained to handle siege artillery, this large regiment would be sent to join the Army of the James as infantry, although Butler was prohibited from using it in field operations. Other than the 1st Connecticut, Halleck sent Butler nothing until 12 May when the 5th Massachusetts Colored Cavalry, a green outfit 1,200 strong, was ordered to join the Army of the James.[7]

While the generals devised new strategies, the men in the ranks remained vigilant. On the left of the Federal line at Swift Creek the pickets of Brooks's division became involved in a series of small but vicious skirmishes with the Tennesseans across the stream. During lulls in the picket fighting, the Federals heard train whistles within the Confederate lines and correctly assumed that this signified the arrival of reinforcements. Around Arrowfield Church the men of Weitzel's division also spent a sleepless night. Kept awake by the skirmishing on their left, the soldiers were forced to listen helplessly to the shrieks and moans of Confederate wounded lying outside the Federal lines near the creek. Throughout the division, men ate cold rations because they were too close to the Confederate positions to be permitted the luxury of fires. Two miles northward at Port Walthall Junction, Hawley's brigade and two sections of the 1st Connecticut Light Battery camped on the deserted battlefield among the unburied Confederate corpses. Even farther north, Howell's brigade continued to guard the Federal rear against a Confederate advance from Drewry's Bluff. Like the troops at Swift Creek, Hawley's and Howell's men waited nervously for the night to pass.[8]

Between 8:00 and 9:00 A.M. Butler informed Quincy Gillmore that X Corps units would relieve Weitzel's division of the XVIII Corps on the turnpike and eventually form the army's rear guard. Although Gillmore favored having the X Corps lead the withdrawal, the original orders stood: White's brigade of Ames's division would relieve Wistar's brigade on the Federal right, and Alford's brigade of Turner's division would replace Heckman's regiments around Arrowfield Church. Baldy Smith had been requesting the relief of his units for many hours, but Gillmore had refused to accommodate him until Butler's order. Before 11:00 A.M. Alford's fresh troops replaced Heckman's weary soldiers, who gladly fell back a short distance to rest and make coffee. At the same time White replaced Wistar. On the Federal left Brooks's division had to disengage on its own. During the day Marston's and Burnham's brigades gradually withdrew, destroying the railroad as they went, until by 4:00 P.M. they were out of range. North of them Martindale's brigade finally came out of the Swift Creek bottomlands and began to destroy the railroad near Port Walthall Junction.[9]

On the turnpike the withdrawal was accelerated by the arrival of dispatches that indicated that X Corps elements north of Port Walthall Junction were under heavy attack. Shortly after 11:00 A.M. Adelbert Ames informed Butler that he was moving with White's brigade toward Alfred Terry's threatened units. White's regiments started up the turnpike at double-quick time through the shimmering heat waves of another excessively hot day. At noon Godfrey Weitzel ordered Wistar's brigade to hurry northward behind White. Weitzel followed with Heckman's brigade, but at a more leisurely pace. Moving north at the same time was the 3rd New Hampshire Infantry, detached from Hawley's brigade on the previous day. Behind the departing troops Colonel Samuel Alford calmly deployed his pickets half a mile from the creek as a rear guard for the Army of the James. Quincy Gillmore remained nearby throughout the early afternoon, supervising the recovery of all stragglers and wounded men. Screened by Alford, Brooks's division returned to Bermuda Hundred via the Dunn plantation, while Weitzel and Ames raced northward to reinforce Terry.[10]

Although unaware of Butler's decision to withdraw, the defenders of Petersburg felt a sense of renewed confidence on the morning of 10 May. Just before 9:00 A.M., P. G. T. Beauregard stepped down from his special train and assumed the powers of command previously held by Pickett and Bushrod Johnson.[11] At the same time, the number of available troops began to increase dramatically. Pickett had made his epic defense of Petersburg and its railroads with only Johnson's, Hagood's, and part of Clingman's Brigades. By contrast, before the day was over Beauregard would have seven brigades in the immediate vicinity. Lewis's Brigade had already arrived. Early on 10 May half of Wise's Brigade reached the city, with the rest close behind. About mid-morning Matt Ransom's Brigade rolled into town, while at the same time Terry's Brigade traversed the Stony Creek gap. Corse's Brigade was still on the railroad around Weldon, but it was at last moving rapidly forward.[12]

Upon the arrival of Robert Hoke at 1:30 P.M., Beauregard asked Braxton Bragg to clarify the meaning of one of Bragg's telegrams of the previous night. Although the telegram is not extant, Bragg had apparently directed Hoke to move north against the Federals with "his whole force." Since communication with Richmond was possible only by an indirect route, Beauregard and Hoke realized it would be hours before they could hear from Bragg. Therefore Beauregard continued to develop his own plans with little reference to Richmond.[13] First, he arranged for large stocks of food and ammunition to be sent from Weldon and directed James Dearing to assemble his cavalry on the railroad to protect the movement. To relieve the shortage of horsemen at Petersburg, Beauregard halted a detachment of the 5th South Carolina Cavalry that was passing through the city with a group of remounts.

To ensure that his authority remained untrammeled within his own department, he rebuked Colonel J. W. Hinton, commanding at Weldon, for having communicated directly with Bragg.[14]

While Beauregard organized the Confederate rear, Bushrod Johnson at Swift Creek sought to discover the intentions of the Army of the James. The day began commonly enough with Federal soldiers slipping down to the creek to fill canteens, and at 7:00 A.M. a Federal battery resumed its futile efforts to destroy the railroad bridge by shellfire. Yet, two hours later, a battery of the Washington Artillery opened on the Federals and drew no reply. After similar cannonades at noon and 1:30 P.M. elicited no response, Johnson sent his skirmishers forward. They discovered a Federal picket line, but no large units nearby. Shortly after 2:00 P.M., in an effort to recover his wounded and bury his dead, Johnson Hagood obtained permission from his superiors to send a flag-of-truce into the Federal lines. Upon reaching the pickets of Alford's brigade, Hagood's emissaries discovered that almost the entire Army of the James had retired from the field. Although their petition was quickly rejected, the Confederates were detained within the Federal lines by Quincy Gillmore's order until the Federal withdrawal was completed at 4:00 P.M. By that time the Confederates had already guessed that Butler's army was retreating from Swift Creek. Yet, as Johnson noted in his report, they seemed to be retreating "without any manifest cause."[15]

Although the Federal withdrawal was due to the messages Butler had received from Stanton, it was executed in haste because of the situation developing north of Port Walthall Junction. When the X Corps advanced toward Chester Station on 9 May, Colonel Joshua Howell and three of his regiments had established a blocking position near Ware Bottom Church. Located only a mile from the Federal entrenchments, Howell was relatively safe, although he was continuously in contact with Confederate skirmishers. Much more exposed was Colonel Alvin Voris's 67th Ohio Infantry, which Howell had posted at the juncture of the Richmond turnpike and the road from Bermuda Hundred to Chester Station. Voris's only support was one section of the 1st Connecticut Light Battery. If threatened, his nearest sources of aid were Howell's force a mile to his right and Hawley's brigade (under Colonel Joseph Abbott since Hawley was ill) three miles to the south at Port Walthall Junction. In late afternoon on 9 May, the black cavalrymen screening Voris had been routed, and he had been obliged to fall back a short distance to avoid being flanked. As darkness approached in the dense woods around the crossroads, Voris had sensed Confederate forces closing in on him and he had called to Quincy Gillmore for relief. Gillmore had ordered two regiments and another section of artillery from the Bermuda Hundred entrenchments to join Voris, but the courier did not reach the designated units until after 2:00 A.M. on 10 May.[16]

The Confederate pressure against Howell's brigade was directed by Major General Robert Ransom, who had ridden down to Drewry's Bluff on the afternoon of 9 May. Unaware of Butler's turn toward Petersburg, Ransom had concluded that the Federals' preoccupation with the railroad left them open to counterattack, if their units could be precisely located. Finding that Seth Barton and Archibald Gracie had probed the Federal positions around Ware Bottom Church too gently to learn anything, Ransom had ordered each of them to repeat the process with a regiment early the next morning. After dark Jefferson Davis had visited Ransom at his headquarters, and the president of the Confederacy had personally approved the plan.[17]

At 5:15 A.M. on 10 May, the Confederate advance began. Gracie's regiment stretched from the bank of the James River to the Richmond turnpike, while Barton deployed the 14th Virginia Infantry from the turnpike westward to the railroad. Since the railroad and turnpike diverged slightly, by the time Barton's regiment had crossed Proctor's Creek, its right no longer touched the railroad. At that point both Gracie and Barton received orders from Ransom to halt and await the arrival of their brigades. Soon the remainder of the two brigades appeared, accompanied by Ransom, who proceeded to berate Barton because his skirmish line did not reach the railroad. Given no time to explain, Barton quickly ordered two companies to fill the gap. He then stumbled into an altercation with the irascible Ransom over whether they were in place or not. Still more harsh words passed between the two generals during the deployment of Barton's remaining regiments. Eventually all was ready to Ransom's satisfaction and the troops started forward through the woods.

With Gracie's troops deployed on his left and Barton's men advancing in front, Ransom sought the enemy. Almost at once he discovered that part of Gracie's skirmish line overlapped Barton's. Barton was already aware of the problem and was attempting to correct it, but it furnished yet another pretext for Ransom to take offense at the hapless officer's actions. After the skirmish line was rearranged, the brigades resumed their advance into the dense forest. Soon bullets fired by Federal skirmishers began to slap their way through the foliage. As the Federal pickets slowly withdrew, the right wing of Barton's Brigade bent forward until it crossed the Chester Station road. Gradually the action began to center on two clearings in the forest, the turnpike crossroads on the Confederate left and the Winfree farm opposite the Confederate center and right. Barton's Brigade had stumbled upon the small blocking force of Colonel Voris.[18]

By the time Barton's Virginians had made contact with his skirmishers, Voris had been joined by the reinforcements Gillmore had sent during the night. Moving at 3:00 A.M., the 13th Indiana and 169th New York Infantry and two guns of the 4th New Jersey Light Battery had arrived at dawn. Voris had arranged his three regiments in a long crescent-shaped skirmish line covering Winfree's farm and the crossroads, with the 13th Indiana on the left, the 67th Ohio in the center, and the 169th New York on the right. The section of Connecticut artillery remained at Winfree's and the New Jersey section was posted just north of the crossroads on the turnpike, each section being supported by detachments of infantry. Four companies of the 13th Indiana were retained at the crossroads as a reserve and some Negro cavalry guarded the flanks.[19]

Once in contact with the Federal pickets, Barton's men vigorously pushed forward through the forest. Soon the Confederates were near enough for the Federal

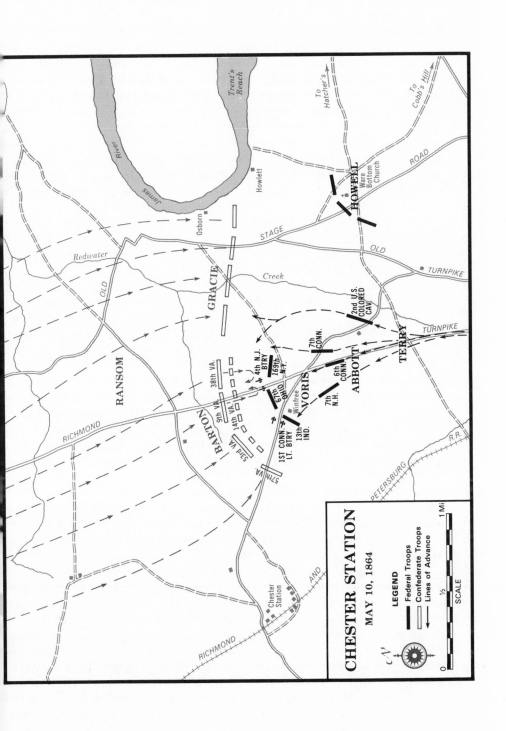

CHESTER STATION

MAY 10, 1864

LEGEND

Federal Troops
Confederate Troops
Lines of Advance

SCALE

0   ½   1 Mi

artillerymen to begin firing antipersonnel rounds over their own infantry at the advancing gray ranks. Slowly but surely the thin Federal line was pressed back, reducing the size of the defensive perimeter. The dense woods and rough terrain, however, made it difficult for Barton to press his advantage. His men had lost contact with Gracie's Alabamians, and Barton himself was having trouble with a skittish horse, but still he maintained the pressure. About 11:00 A.M. the 38th and 9th Virginia began a concerted drive along the turnpike that penetrated to the two guns of the 4th New Jersey Battery. Several companies of the 169th New York Infantry supporting the artillery panicked and fled to the rear, taking one of the gun limbers with them. With charging Confederates pouring around their right flank and driving straight down the pike, the gun crews retreated with their only movable gun. The other gun was left to Barton's Virginians as a prize of war.[20]

The Confederate charge had not been without cost. The colonel of the 38th Virginia had been mortally wounded and his men had lost their organization during their rush through the trees. Moreover, they were beginning to encounter small-arms fire from the right side of Voris's line and an artillery bombardment from Colonel Howell's position at Ware Bottom Church. These difficulties caused the left wing of Barton's Brigade to end its advance near the abandoned gun, as the troops milled about in confusion. By this time the woods had caught fire from an exploding artillery shell and the tinder-dry pine forest filled rapidly with crackling flames and choking, curling smoke.[21]

On the right the remainder of Barton's Brigade continued down the Chester Station road toward the Winfree house. To check them, the gunners of the 1st Connecticut Light Battery began to fire canister. As his ammunition supply dwindled and the Confederates drove in from three sides, Lieutenant George Metcalf feared for the safety of his section. Suddenly, up the road came the reinforcements for which Voris had been calling frantically. Reining in their horses behind the beleaguered gunners were Brigadier General Alfred Terry and Colonel Joseph Abbott, who had marched Hawley's three regiments toward the sound of the firing. Careening along behind the officers were the other four Connecticut guns. With the cannoneers clinging to handrails to avoid falling under the flashing hooves and thundering wheels, the battery whirled into the Winfree lane in a cloud of dust. At the command "Action front," they took position by Metcalf's exhausted section, which was allowed to go to the rear.[22]

Taking charge of the action, Terry ordered the 7th New Hampshire Infantry to support the artillery at Winfree's, then he turned his attention to the serious situation on the turnpike. There he deployed the 7th Connecticut east of the road and the 6th Connecticut to the west, then sent both regiments forward. In the face of this new force, Barton's weary men gave ground, allowing the 7th Connecticut to regain the abandoned cannon on the turnpike. At the other end of the Federal line, the Confederates made repeated advances against the troops around Winfree's. Threatened on three sides, the 7th New Hampshire Infantry fell back a short distance, but it was eventually able to resume its former position. In the Federal center, part of the 6th Connecticut became confused in the forest and retired precipitately, forcing Terry to fill the gap with his last reserves, a company of engineers and the provost guard. On the right, the 7th Connecticut also had a few bad moments in the burning woods when it believed it was being outflanked from the direction of Ware Bottom Church. This final Confederate threat was met by the dismounted troopers of the 2nd U. S. Colored Cavalry, supported by the mountain howitzers of the 1st New York Mounted Rifles and Battery D, 1st U.S. Artillery, all of which had just reached the field.[23]

As fresh units extended the Federal line eastward, Barton's Brigade found its own flank threatened. When he received no reply to a message reporting that his left was turned, Barton went personally to Ransom with the same information. Upon seeing Barton, Ransom exploded into another tirade about the worthlessness of Barton's Brigade and its commander. Ransom believed he had seen Barton riding "aimlessly" over the field during the action and was positive he had witnessed many of Barton's men fleeing through the trees east of the pike. Barton hotly denied the charges, but Ransom curtly sent him back to his men, smarting under the day's latest rebuke. To protect Barton's flank, Ransom ordered Archibald Gracie to extend his regiments westward to connect with Barton's men near the turnpike. Gracie's troops had done little all day except skirmish around Ware Bottom Church, and they joined Barton without incident. Believing that nothing further could be accomplished with Barton's men, Ransom decided to break off the action.[24]

Ransom's decision to withdraw proved wise, because Federal reinforcements from Swift Creek were beginning to arrive. White's brigade of Ames's division was the first to appear, although its ranks were depleted by numbers of sunstruck men who had dropped by the roadside. Following White was Wistar's brigade, which had also suffered severely from the 100° heat. Although Wistar's soldiers were thrown forward as skirmishers into the burning woods, White's men were allowed to rest by the road. By the time the last Federal regiment reached the field, both sides had united under a flag-of-truce to rescue the casualties who lay in the path of the forest fire raging around the crossroads. Unfortunately the rescuers were unable to save all the wounded from the flames. At 4:20 P.M., while the work of mercy continued, Gillmore ordered Terry to fall back slowly toward Bermuda Hundred. Terry complied by extending his right toward Colonel Howell at Ware Bottom Church while withdrawing his left slightly down the turnpike. Shortly after 5:00 P.M. Howell's brigade departed for the fortifications, and Terry's units followed close behind.[25]

Out of 3,400 troops engaged at one time or another, Terry had lost 280 men killed, wounded, and missing. In exchange, he had taken more than forty prisoners.[26] Terry believed that he had been outnumbered by the Confederates, but in reality this had not been the case. Barton's Brigade numbered only 1,945 men on 10 May, and many of these had been left behind that morning because of Ransom's haste to depart. Barton's casualties amounted to a total of 249 men. Gracie's Brigade on Barton's left contained 2,197 men on 10 May but these troops had not been seriously engaged. Only during the early phases of the action were Barton's Virginians numerically stronger than Voris's regiments, and after the arrival of

Terry's reinforcements, Barton had been contending against superior numbers. Because of the heavily wooded terrain, however, neither side had been able to determine the true strength of the other.[27]

In Richmond, Jefferson Davis and his advisers spent the day anxiously awaiting the outcome of Ransom's fight near Chester Station. As the hours passed, a new threat to Richmond materialized with the approach of Major General Philip Sheridan's Cavalry Corps, which was raiding southward from the Army of the Potomac. With the capital menaced from two directions, Davis concluded that only a prompt offensive by the Confederate forces at Petersburg could alleviate the situation. At 3:30 P.M. Bragg telegraphed Beauregard that Ransom had advanced and found the Federals too strong for him: "Let us know when you will be ready [to attack], that Ransom may co-operate. Every hour is now very important." Bragg's next telegram was even more explicit: "We are seriously threatened here from above. You should make a heavy demonstration and change to attack, if practicable, at an early hour in the morning."[28]

In Petersburg, Beauregard was not to be hurried by telegrams from Richmond. During the afternoon Terry's Brigade arrived, giving the department commander seven brigades at Petersburg. With Corse's and Colquitt's Brigades due shortly, and James Martin's North Carolina Brigade en route from that state, Beauregard soon had ten brigades to deploy against Butler.[29] He organized the troops into two divisions under Pickett and Hoke, and attached a battalion of artillery to each division. Wise's Brigade and the remaining artillery garrisoned Petersburg, where Henry Wise relieved Pickett as commander of the First Military District. At 7:15 P.M. Beauregard informed Bragg that he would be ready to take the offensive by the following night.[30] Even as he wrote, Pickett, who had been laboring under extreme pressure since 5 May, finally collapsed under the strain and took to his quarters. The man who had saved Petersburg for the Confederacy was not destined to be among the leaders of the Confederate counterattack.[31]

NOTES

1. O.R.A., 36, pt. 2, 35, 590, 593, 624; Butler, Butler's Book, 645; "Kautz in the Great Rebellion," Kautz Papers, LC. In William F. Smith's postwar accounts of the day's events, there is no mention of the conference with Butler, although Smith's later consultations with Gillmore are prominently featured. Smith, Battles and Leaders, 4:208; Smith, From Chattanooga to Petersburg, 117–118.

2. Butler, Butler's Book, 645; O.R.A., 36, pt. 2, 35, 36, 593, 624; "Kautz in the Great Rebellion," Kautz Papers. LC.

3. O.R.A., 36, pt. 2, 35, 36, 590, 624; Smith, Battles and Leaders, 4:208; Smith, From Chattanooga to Petersburg, 117–118.

4. All three messages are in O.R.A., 36, pt. 2, 587. The 10:00 A.M. message is listed as having been received at 11:55 P.M. If this is correct, Butler had not received this dispatch when he made his decision to alter the plan of operations for the next day. Its arrival therefore only confirmed the news in the two following telegrams (sent later but somehow received earlier) that were instrumental in changing Butler's mind. According to Butler, Butler's Book, 645–646, the 3:20 P.M. message was the first one to be received.

5. O.R.A., 36, pt. 2, 35, 593–594; Butler, Butler's Book, 646–647.

6. O.R.A., 36, pt. 2, 35. Smith's and Gillmore's replies are in O.R.A., 36, pt. 2, 36, 624. In later years Smith asserted that Butler's vanity had caused the army commander to reject his suggestions out of

hand (Smith, *From Chattanooga to Petersburg,* 119), yet Butler had been quite willing to follow Smith's advice prior to the evening of 9 May, the most recent example having taken place that very morning.

7. O.R.A., 36, pt. 2, 561, 586, 688; John C. Taylor, *History of the First Connecticut Artillery and of the Siege Trains of the Armies Operating Against Richmond, 1862–1865* (Hartford, Conn.: Press of the Case, Lockwood & Brainard Company, 1893), 51; Frederick H. Dyer, *A Compendium of the War of the Rebellion,* 3 vols. New ed. (New York: Thomas Yoseloff, 1959), 3:1240. During the same period in which the Army of the James received 3,000 troops, the Army of the Potomac was augmented by 24,700 men. O.R.A., 36, pt. 2, 696–697.

8. O.R.A., 36, pt. 2, 45, 66, 126, 134, 138–139, 156, 591; De Forest, *Random Sketches,* 241; Cunningham, *Adirondack Regiment,* 107; Waite, *New Hampshire in the Great Rebellion,* 202, 435; Kreutzer, *Ninety-Eighth New York,* 186–188; Thompson, *Thirteenth New Hampshire,* 265–266; Drake, *Ninth New Jersey,* 180, 350; Denny, *Wearing the Blue,* 281; Derby, *Bearing Arms,* 261–262; Emmerton, *Twenty-Third Massachusetts,* 179–180; Cleveland, ed., "Campaign of Promise," 319; Copp, *Reminiscences,* 366–369; O.R.A., 51, pt. 1, 1238–1239; Beecher, *First Connecticut Light Battery,* 1:349–350.

9. O.R.A., 36, pt. 2, 96, 97, 134, 149, 156, 618, 619, 623–624; Drake, *Ninth New Jersey,* 181; Derby, *Bearing Arms,* 263; De Forest, *Random Sketches,* 148; Thompson, *Thirteenth New Hampshire,* 268–273; O.R.A., 51, pt. 1, 1260.

10. O.R.A., 36, pt. 2, 66, 96, 97, 149, 156, 621–623; Bartlett, *Twelfth New Hampshire,* 177; Drake, *Ninth New Jersey,* 181; Eldredge, *Third New Hampshire,* 463; Waite, *New Hampshire in the Great Rebellion,* 202–203; Copp, *Reminiscences,* 369; O.R.A., 51, pt. 1, 1260; Wistar, *Autobiography,* 449–450.

11. Beauregard to Bragg, 10 May 1864 (two telegrams), Official Telegrams, 22 April–9 June 1864, Beauregard Papers, LC; O.R.A., 51, pt. 2, 915, 919; Pickett, *Pickett and his Men,* 345; Roman, *Military Operations,* 2:554; Bushrod R. Johnson Diary, 10 May 1864, Johnson Papers, NA.

12. One of Lewis's five regiments, the 6th North Carolina, had remained in North Carolina. Richard W. Iobst, *The Bloody Sixth: The Sixth North Carolina Regiment, Confederate States of America* (Durham, N.C.: Christian Printing Company, 1965), 201. For Wise, see O.R.A., 36, pt. 2, 985; Cutchins, *Richmond Light Infantry Blues,* 133; William Lancaster to his wife, 13 May 1864, William Lancaster Letters, VSL; Bushrod R. Johnson Diary, 10 May 1864, Johnson Papers, NA. For Ransom, see Clark, ed., *North Carolina Regiments,* 2:284, 619, 3:135, 350; Harrill, *Reminiscences,* 21; Henry Chambers Diary, 10 May 1864, NCDAH; Edward Phifer to his mother, 29 May 1864, Phifer Family Papers, SHC. For Terry, see Loehr, *First Virginia,* 45; Johnston, *Confederate Boy,* 245; Edwin Baker Loving Diary, 10 May 1864, VSL. For Corse, see Wise, *Seventeenth Virginia,* 174; George C. Cabell, "Account of the Skirmish at Swift Creek," *Southern Historical Society Papers* 16 (1888):223; Arthur Herbert, "The Seventeenth Virginia Infantry at Flat Creek and Drewry's Bluff," *Southern Historical Society Papers* 12 (1884):290.

13. Beauregard to Bragg, 1:30 P.M., 10 May 1864, Official Telegrams, 22 April–9 June 1864, Beauregard Papers, LC; O.R.A., 51, pt. 2, 915. The lost message was probably similar to Bragg's telegram to Pickett dated 11:00 A.M., 9 May 1864. O.R.A., 36, pt. 2, 978.

14. Beauregard to Major Willis (Quartermaster, Weldon), Beauregard to Dearing, Beauregard to Bragg, Beauregard to Hinton, all 10 May 1864, Official Telegrams, 22 April–9 June 1864, Beauregard Papers, LC; Beauregard to Major _____, 10 May 1864, Letter Book, April–May 1864, Beauregard Papers, LC; O.R.A., 51, pt. 2, 919 (misdated 11 May).

15. Beauregard to Bragg, 1:30 P.M., 10 May 1864, Official Telegrams, 22 April–9 June 1864, Beauregard Papers, LC; Cleveland, ed., "Campaign of Promise," 318; O.R.A., 36, pt. 2, 96, 146, 244, 618; O.R.A., 51, pt. 1, 226; Hagood, *Memoirs,* 230–231; Bushrod R. Johnson Diary, 10 May 1864, Johnson Papers, NA.

16. O.R.A., 36, pt. 2, 45–46, 80, 91–93, 104; Brady, *Eleventh Maine,* 178; O.R.A., 51, pt. 1, 1224, 1232, 1240; Beecher, *First Connecticut Light Battery,* 1:351–352; Foster, *New Jersey and the Rebellion,* 708.

17. O.R.A., 51, pt. 2, 908; O.R.A., 36, pt. 2, 223, 230, 977, 980, 981.

18. O.R.A., 36, pt. 2, 214–215, 220, 223–224, 230–232, 984; O.R.A., 51, pt. 1, 221.

19. O.R.A., 36, pt. 2, 104–105, 109–110; O.R.A., 51, pt. 1, 1224, 1240; Beecher, *First Connecticut Light Battery,* 1:356; Foster, *New Jersey and the Rebellion,* 708–709.

20. O.R.A., 36, pt. 2, 105, 216, 232–233, 235; Beecher, *First Connecticut Light Battery,* 1:356–357; George K. Griggs, "Memoranda of Thirty-Eighth Virginia Infantry, From Diary of Colonel George K. Griggs," *Southern Historical Society Papers* 14 (1886):254; O.R.A., 51, pt. 1, 1240; Foster, *New Jersey and the Rebellion,* 709.

21. O.R.A., 36, pt. 2, 92–93, 216, 220, 224, 232–233, 236; Griggs, "Memoranda," 254; Mrs. M. C. Carmichael to her son, 12 May 1864, M. C. Carmichael Letters, Virginia State Library, Richmond, Va.; Beecher, *First Connecticut Light Battery,* 1:373–374, 378.

22. O.R.A., 36, pt. 2, 91, 92, 216; Beecher, *First Connecticut Light Battery*, 1:361–367, 370, 374; O.R.A., 51, pt. 1, 1233.

23. O.R.A., 36, pt. 2, 58–59, 61–62, 69–71, 91, 105, 110–111; O.R.A., 51, pt. 1, 1232–1233, 1239; Little, *Seventh New Hampshire*, 244–247; Waite, *New Hampshire in the Great Rebellion*, 359; Martin Emmons to his brother, 11 May 1864, C. E. Southworth Papers, Duke University, Durham, N.C.; Tourtellotte, *History of Company K*, 127, 168; Beecher, *First Connecticut Light Battery*, 1:364, 367–379; Cadwell, *Old Sixth*, 90; Croffut and Morris, *Connecticut During the War*, 539; Joseph Hawley to his wife, 12 May 1864, Hawley Papers, LC.

24. O.R.A., 36, pt. 2, 216–217, 220–221, 224, 232–234; O.R.A., 51, pt. 1, 221; Shaver, *Sixtieth Alabama*, 46–47. Ransom's charges against Barton appear to have been unfounded.

25. O.R.A., 36, pt. 2, 47, 49, 106, 107, 620; Price, *Ninety-Seventh Pennsylvania*, 257–258; Bartlett, *Twelfth New Hampshire*, 177–178; Beecher, *First Connecticut Light Battery*, 1:373–374, 378; Eldredge, *Third New Hampshire*, 463; Waite, *New Hampshire in the Great Rebellion*, 203; Copp, *Reminiscences*, 370; Nichols, *Perry's Saints*, 210; Clark, *Iron Hearted Regiment*, 110–111; O.R.A., 51, pt. 1, 1233–1234; Brady, *Eleventh Maine*, 178; Dickey, *Eighty-Fifth Pennsylvania*, 315, 322.

26. O.R.A., 51, pt. 1, 1225, 1234, 1240; O.R.A., 36, pt. 2, 105, 110, 111; Beecher, *First Connecticut Light Battery*, 1:378–383; Foster, *New Jersey and the Rebellion*, 709; Little, *Seventh New Hampshire*, 108.

27. O.R.A., 51, pt. 1, 221, 1234; O.R.A., 36, pt. 2, 218, 234, 236, 988; Record Book of Co. I, 53rd Virginia Infantry, R. D. Ferguson Papers, Southern Historical Collection, University of North Carolina, Chapel Hill, N.C.; Henry M. Talley to his mother, 21 May 1864, Henry C. Brown Papers, North Carolina Division of Archives and History, Raleigh, N.C.

28. Jones, *War Clerk*, 2:204; O.R.A., 36, pt. 2, 986; O.R.A., 51, pt. 2, 916; Roman, *Military Operations*, 2:554.

29. Loehr, *First Virginia*, 45; Johnston, *Confederate Boy*, 245–246; Edwin Baker Loving Diary, 10 May 1864, VSL; Wise, *Seventeenth Virginia*, 174; Cabell, "Swift Creek," 223; Herbert, "Seventeenth Virginia," 290; Beauregard to Wise, and Beauregard to Colquitt, both 11 May 1864, Letter Book, April–May 1864, Beauregard Papers, LC.

30. O.R.A., 36, pt. 2, 987; Beauregard to Bragg, 7:15 P.M., 10 May 1864, Official Telegrams, 22 April–9 June 1864, Beauregard papers, LC; O.R.A., 51, pt. 2, 915; Roman, *Military Operations*, 2:199.

31. O.R.A., 51, pt. 2, 920; Roman, *Military Operations*, 2:555.

Major General Benjamin F. Butler
(Photograph courtesy of the U.S. Army Military History Institute, Carlisle Barracks, Pa.)

Major General Quincy A. Gillmore

Major General William F. Smith

Brigadier General August V. Kautz

Butler's Principal Subordinates
(All photographs courtesy of the U.S. Army Military History Institute, Carlisle Barracks, Pa.)

Brigadier General Alfred H. Terry   Brigadier General John W. Turner

Brigadier General Adelbert Ames

Division Commanders, X Corps
(All photographs courtesy of the U.S. Army Military History Institute, Carlisle Barracks, Pa.)

Brigadier General William T. H. Brooks

Brigadier General Godfrey Weitzel

Brigadier General Edward W. Hincks

Division Commanders, XVIII Corps

General P. G. T. Beauregard
(Photograph courtesy of the U.S. Army Military History Institute, Carlisle Barracks, Pa.)

Major General Robert Ransom, Jr.

Major General Robert F. Hoke

Brigadier General Alfred H. Colquitt

Beauregard's Division Commanders
(Ransom and Colquitt photographs courtesy of the Valentine Museum, Richmond, Va
Hoke photograph courtesy of the U.S. Army Military History Institute, Carlisle Barracks
Pa.)

Major General George E. Pickett
(Photograph courtesy of the U.S. Army Military History Institute, Carlisle Barracks, Pa.)

Major General W. H. C. Whiting
(Photograph courtesy of the Valentine Museum, Richmond, Va.)

Brigadier General Charles A. Heckman

Brigadier General Bushrod R. Johnson

Opponents at Port Walthall Junction
(Both photographs courtesy of the U.S. Army Military History Institute, Carlisle Barracks, Pa.)

☆ 10 ☆

The Advance on Drewry's Bluff
11–14 May 1864

Wednesday, 11 May, dawned fair but hot, and the temperature again climbed toward the high nineties. Fatigued from their brief expedition beyond the entrenchments, the men of the Army of the James anticipated a day of relative calm. Except for the usual picket and fatigue duty, there was little to do. A few regiments took the opportunity to move their camps to more advantageous locations, but by and large the day was given over to individual pursuits. Some soldiers passed the time by washing their clothes, while others caught up on their correspondence. In some units the arrival of mail from the outside world enlivened dull campsites as few other occurrences could. For want of something better to do, soldiers in the 9th New Jersey Infantry lustily promoted a fight between two of their own number.[1]

Benjamin Butler's reasons for keeping the army in camp on 11 May were twofold. First, Kautz's exhausted cavalry regiments needed time to catch their breath before departing on another raid. Second, although the fortifications were already strong, Butler wanted "to put the lines in the best possible order to be held with a small force," and that would also require extra time.[2] Thus 11 May was both a day of rest and a day of preparation for the offensive that would begin on the following morning. Unfortunately, this precluded the occupation of the transportation corridor between Petersburg and Richmond, which remained free of Federals for more than twenty-four hours. There is no evidence that either Butler, Smith, or Gillmore were unduly concerned that the Confederates might turn this situation to their own advantage. In fact, Butler told his wife: "We shall demonstrate toward Richmond tomorrow. *I have now done all I agreed to do with Grant.*"[3]

Meanwhile, the Confederates were finally acting to neutralize the Army of the James. Just before 3:00 A.M. on 11 May, P. G. T. Beauregard received a telegram from Braxton Bragg. Although no longer extant, this message apparently required an immediate forward movement by Beauregard's mobile forces under Hoke. Bragg and Secretary of War Seddon had concluded that Hoke should advance due north toward a junction with Robert Ransom's forces concentrated around Drewry's Bluff. If Butler's troops remained on the turnpike blocking Hoke's way, the young North Carolinian was to clear his front of the enemy and to join Ransom at all costs.

Bragg and Seddon believed that Hoke's and Ransom's combined forces would protect Richmond from both the Army of the James and Sheridan's cavalry raiders. Because the movement was of such importance, Beauregard was advised to send Hoke northward as soon as possible.[4]

Although Beauregard did not want Hoke to depart just yet, he acknowledged Bragg's telegram and promised to issue the necessary orders. Still hoping to retain control of events, he suggested: "Would it not be better to complete the organization given in cypher now repeated, and then make a crushing attack on enemy? Please answer." Hearing nothing from Bragg that would permit him to modify the original plan, Beauregard issued the orders for Hoke's advance. Hoke's own division consisted of the brigades of Lewis, Hagood, and Johnson. Since Pickett was ill, Matt Ransom took his place as the other division commander. Ransom also had three brigades, his own, Terry's, and Corse's, part of which had finally reached Petersburg.[5] Each division was to take along four artillery batteries and a company of cavalry. Hoke was to be joined later in the day by Clingman's Brigade, as soon as it could be relieved around Petersburg by some of Henry Wise's regiments. Colquitt's Brigade, which had just arrived from Charleston, was to be held at Petersburg as a reserve. Still in transit were the three regiments of Martin's Brigade.[6]

At 7:00 A.M. Beauregard wired Bragg that the offensive movement so ardently desired by the War Department had finally begun. Believing that Hoke's troops were on the way (although soldiers' diaries indicate it would be three hours yet before Hoke finally got started), Beauregard turned to other matters. Anticipating his own departure from Petersburg, he wired his old friend Chase Whiting to come to Virginia, if Wilmington was relatively secure. Additional telegrams went to the quartermaster at Weldon, a favorite of Beauregard's, and to James Dearing at Hicksford. Both of these men were also to come to Petersburg, Dearing with his cavalry brigade.[7]

At 10:00 A.M., Hoke's command took to the road. Progress was slow because both cavalry and infantry skirmishers had to precede the column in case the Federals were still blocking the way in force. When no Federals were discovered, Confederate officers allowed their men to move in column of fours on the turnpike. The artillery was spaced along the column at intervals and the few baggage and ordnance wagons available followed their individual brigades. Because it was assumed that the Federals were somewhere off to the east, an outer line of cavalry skirmishers and an inner line of infantry pickets paralleled the column on the right flank. In this way Hoke spent the rest of the day marching leisurely across the Federal front. Two or three miles away the men of the Army of the James whiled away the hours washing clothes, writing letters, and generally relaxing.[8]

Before Hoke's departure Beauregard had ordered him to make a "forced reconnaissance" toward Bermuda Hundred on his way to Drewry's Bluff. If the Federals were "re-embarking," Hoke was to turn the reconnaissance into an attack, while Beauregard would cooperate by threatening Hincks at City Point. Both Robert Ransom and Bragg were informed of the change in plans, and Beauregard offered to rescind his order if the War Department disapproved. Around noon Beauregard received a stern reply from Secretary of War Seddon:

Division of your forces is earnestly objected to. It is decidedly preferred that you carry out the instructions given last night, and endeavor to unite all forces.

Surprised at the tone of Seddon's message, Beauregard countermanded his order to Hoke concerning the "forced reconnaissance" and at 12:45 P.M. he informed Seddon of the change.[9]

On its way to Richmond, Beauregard's telegram crossed another of Seddon's. Written at 1:00 P.M., Seddon's wire showed that he was beginning to lose his composure:

This city is in hot danger. It should be defended with all our resources to the sacrifice of minor considerations. You are relied on to use every effort to unite all your forces at the earliest practicable time with the troops in our defenses, and then together either fight the enemy in the field or defend the intrenchments.[10]

Beauregard received Seddon's second telegram around 2:00 P.M. and before he could reply, a message arrived from Bragg approving Hoke's "forced reconnaissance."[11] For Beauregard this was the last straw. First, he had been forced to begin an offensive movement before he was fully ready. Now the secretary of war and the president's military adviser were issuing contradictory directives regarding Hoke's movement, and Seddon seemed to be questioning Beauregard's judgment. In a fit of pique, Beauregard replied to the secretary of war at 2:00 P.M.:

To come here, I relinquished the sick leave I had obtained while in Charleston to recruit my shattered health. I am ready and willing to serve the cause to the utter sacrifice of that health, but if my course be not approved by the War Department I wish to be relieved at once.[12]

At 3:00 P.M., still smarting from Seddon's telegrams, Beauregard wired Bragg: "Please read two telegrams of to-day from Secretary of War and my answer. I must insist on receiving orders only from one source, and that from the general commanding." Shortly thereafter, Beauregard received a soothing telegram from Seddon that expressed dismay at his threat to resign his command. Beauregard was not to be mollified so easily, as a 5:15 P.M. telegram to Davis showed. In that message Beauregard reported the day's events, including Seddon's interference, and informed Davis that he would not leave Petersburg until his last two brigades arrived from Weldon. He closed: "Please inform me if my course is approved by you."[13]

The reason for the uproar in Richmond was not so much Butler's army as Sheridan's cavalry, which had penetrated to within twenty miles of the capital. At Drewry's Bluff, Robert Ransom spent 11 May debating whether he should remain south of the James River facing Butler or return to Richmond to meet the Federal cavalry. During his expedition toward Chester Station with Barton's and Gracie's Brigades, Ransom had ordered his last remaining infantry unit, Eppa Hunton's Virginia Brigade, to Drewry's Bluff. With Sheridan rapidly nearing Richmond, the government wanted Hunton's Brigade returned to the capital, and early on 11 May

Ransom complied. When he learned that Hoke was marching to join him with six brigades, Ransom decided to await the arrival of the troops from the south. While waiting, he requested the return of Hunton to Drewry's Bluff, but to no avail. He also found time to relieve Seth Barton from duty for his alleged misconduct at Chester Station.[14]

At 5:00 P.M., as a violent thunderstorm built up on the western horizon, Hoke met Robert Ransom at Drewry's Bluff. Although Hoke's men were still scattered along the turnpike for several miles, Bragg was informed that the junction desired by the War Department had finally been made. Hoke's 11,000 muskets, however, were woefully short of ammunition and several of the brigades had no wagon train with them. Fortunately these deficiencies could be filled easily in Richmond. More ominous was a report by Hoke that Federal troops had crossed his rear during the march. This meant that the troops still at Petersburg might find it difficult to follow the direct route taken by Hoke. Besides, Beauregard himself might be prevented from coming northward to assume command in person. Even so, there were at last enough troops around Drewry's Bluff to release infantry units to aid the hard pressed Confederate cavalry falling back before Sheridan's victorious troopers. During the night, as the storm clouds began to release their rain, Gracie's Alabamians set off for Richmond.[15]

At 7:00 P.M., having heard that Hoke had joined Ransom, Beauregard sought to learn the results of the on-again, off-again "forced reconnaissance." Forty-five minutes later, he drafted a temperate letter to Seddon explaining the general situation in his department. To both Hoke and Seddon, Beauregard stated that he planned to leave for Drewry's Bluff on the morrow, after the arrival of the last units of Colquitt's and Martin's Brigades. Beauregard hoped that Whiting might reach Petersburg before his departure, but that was doubtful. Still, given the propensity of the Federals to dawdle in their movements, there might be time for Whiting to appear after all.[16]

As Hoke's weary soldiers bivouacked in the woods around Proctor's Creek, the Army of the James began to stir. Joining the infantry in preparing for the forthcoming advance were Kautz's cavalrymen, who had arrived at Bermuda Hundred from City Point during the day. Just before dark a tremendous electrical storm burst overhead, drenching infantry and cavalry alike. The sharp lightning struck several trees near the unfortunate soldiers, many of whom were forced to stand in line in the rain in case the Confederates took advantage of the storm to attack. Gradually the downpour eased to a soft but persistent drizzle that continued throughout the night. As the rain fell on the camps of the Army of the James and the temporary bivouacs of Hoke's Confederates, the opposing pickets remained vigilant. Behind the Confederate pickets Hoke's men tried to sleep beside the road on the damp ground, but behind the Federal sentinels the Army of the James was once more coming to life.[17]

At 9:30 P.M. Butler issued his orders for the next day's advance. Smith was to take his own XVIII Corps plus one of Gillmore's divisions and move northward along the turnpike. As he advanced, Smith would attempt to outflank the Confederates facing him, either surrounding them or forcing them within their fortifications. Meanwhile, Gillmore would protect Smith's rear against possible Confederate attacks emanating from Petersburg, then form the remainder of his troops on the turnpike as a general reserve. To complete the plan, Kautz's cavalry would raid toward the Richmond and Danville Railroad, while Hincks established a new fortified position on the Appomattox River across from Butler's headquarters.[18]

Sometime around 4:00 A.M. on 12 May, the Army of the James lurched into motion. Unknown to the men in the ranks, the Confederate capital was not the objective for which they were striving, except in a very general way. As Butler later explained to Secretary of War Stanton, the advance of the Army of the James was not a serious attempt to capture Richmond. Rather, it was a massive demonstration that would spring Kautz free for another raid and prevent Beauregard from sending units northward to reinforce Lee's army. Of course, should an opportunity for more than a demonstration present itself, there could be a change in plans. Until then, the great forward movement so long anticipated by the soldiers remained a demonstration to the generals.[19]

To alleviate the lack of harmony that had surfaced earlier between his corps commanders, Butler planned to take the field himself, thereby eliminating the bickering between Smith and Gillmore. Because he trusted Smith's professional judgment but doubted Gillmore's ability to lead troops in the field without close supervision, Butler assigned to the XVIII Corps the task of making the demonstration toward Richmond, while Gillmore would guard the army's rear and maintain a mobile reserve. Because the XVIII Corps had only two divisions at Bermuda Hundred, Smith received Brigadier General John Turner's division of Gillmore's X Corps as a reinforcement.[20]

Smith's leading division, Weitzel's, stepped off promptly at daybreak. After marching northward within the Federal lines until he reached the X Corps front, Weitzel turned his column westward toward the turnpike. Almost at once Confederate skirmishers barred the way, forcing Weitzel to deploy his units into line before cautiously resuming the advance. The rain that had begun the previous evening continued to pelt down upon Weitzel's men, most of whom lacked overcoats or ponchos. Waiting for Weitzel to clear the road was Turner's division of the X Corps, which was to serve as the hinge upon which the XVIII Corps pivoted as it changed front from west to north. As soon as Weitzel had passed, Turner deployed his men around the Howlett mansion just beyond the Federal picket line, facing them northward to conform to Weitzel's eventual direction of march. Bringing up the rear was Brooks's division, which followed Weitzel's troops down a road already churned into a muddy paste by thousands of marching feet. With so many units ahead of them, it was 7:00 A.M. before Brooks's soldiers left their camps.[21]

By 9:00 A.M. Weitzel had reached the turnpike and was ready to turn toward Drewry's Bluff and Richmond. Deploying Heckman's brigade on the left and Wistar's brigade on the right, he sent his division forward. At the same time Baldy Smith ordered Turner to advance on Weitzel's right flank. In a long blue line extending approximately a mile and a half, the Army of the James plunged into the dripping forest. Meanwhile, the rain continued to pour down in torrents upon the men. Drenched to the skin, the Federals clawed their way through the dense underbrush, and soon passed through Terry's old battlefield of 10 May, where half-burned corpses still lay unburied in the charred woods. In front, Confederate skirmishers obstinately contested every foot of ground.[22]

Along the turnpike the Federals found unmistakable evidence that large numbers of troops had recently passed that way, many leaving their bare footprints in the mud. Unknown to Weitzel's men, the last of the footprints had been made just a few hours before. Although Robert Hoke had reached Drewry's Bluff on the afternoon of the previous day, many of his troops had halted along the turnpike wherever night had caught them. Several units had camped near the 10 May battlefield, which was just two miles beyond the entrenched line of the X Corps. The Confederates had resumed their march earlier that the Federals, moving between 3:00 and 4:00 A.M. This initial lead had widened because the XVIII Corps had to travel nearly two miles before it left the Federal lines. As a result, several miles separated the opposing armies as both marched northward through the rain.[23]

Driving the Confederate skirmishers before him through a series of ravines filled with dense underbrush, Weitzel soon reached the spot where an insignificant branch of Redwater Creek crossed the turnpike. There the Confederate skirmishers disputing his passage were reinforced by artillery that opened fire on the Federal line, bringing it up short. Precious minutes passed as Weitzel sent for his own artillery and examined the terrain. It was already late morning and the Federal column had advanced less than a mile in a northerly direction. Soon the Confederate guns beyond Redwater Creek withdrew, leaving the way open for the Federals to cross the stream.

It now became apparent to Baldy Smith that he would have to bring more troops into line. On the right flank the James River bent sharply eastward, forcing Turner either to leave a gap between his division and the river or between it and Weitzel. To maintain an unbroken front, Smith ordered Weitzel to sidestep to the right of the turnpike and detached one regiment from Marston's brigade of Brooks's division to serve as the connecting link between Turner and Weitzel. To extend his line westward, Smith deployed two brigades of Brooks's division on Weitzel's left. Brooks's remaining brigade, Marston's, followed Weitzel as a second line.[24]

From left to right, Smith's troops were arrayed as follows: On the far left was Sanders's brigade, composed of only two regiments, since two had been left behind as camp guard. Next was Burnham's brigade, together with Sanders's, comprising Brooks's division. Meeting Burnham's men at the turnpike and extending the line to the right were Heckman's and Wistar's brigades, both of Weitzel's division. To the right of Wistar's brigade was the 98th New York Infantry, which formed the connection with Barton's brigade of Turner's division. On the far right was Turner's other brigade, Alford's. Three miles behind the XVIII Corps, Ames's division of the X Corps occupied a blocking position near Port Walthall Junction and Alfred Terry was preparing to take two of his brigades out to the turnpike as a general reserve.[25]

After a difficult advance of about a mile through the wet, tangled forest, the Federals reached a high ridge overlooking the marshy bed of Proctor's Creek. Across the valley the skirmishers of Corse's Brigade and a section of the Washington Artillery deployed for action along the turnpike. Resting half a mile behind them at a local landmark called the Half-Way House were several more of Robert Hoke's brigades. Hearing the increased firing during the middle of the afternoon, Ransom's and Terry's Brigades prepared to assist Corse, while Clingman's Brigade continued its march toward the Drewry's Bluff fortifications already reached by Hagood's, Johnson's, and Lewis's men. Meanwhile, the rain increased to a heavy downpour. As the last of the baggage wagons passed the Half-Way House, Ransom and Terry expected to be ordered back to Proctor's Creek to dispute the Federal crossing, but no order came because the Army of the James had halted.[26]

Faced by a naturally strong defensive position that appeared to be occupied in force, Baldy Smith paused to consider the alternatives. His line was long and exceedingly thin, and the only available corps reserve was the remainder of Marston's brigade. Before proceeding farther, Smith decided to make a personal reconnaissance. This took time, and at the end of his investigation Smith concluded only that he needed more men. His right was in no danger, but the Confederate position there was strong. If the Federals wanted to cross Proctor's Creek, they would have to extend their left in an effort to outflank their opponents. Smith first sought to have Kautz's cavalry turn the Confederate flank, but Kautz and his men had already departed on their raid. Smith then asked for part of the X Corps. Butler obliged by ordering Gillmore to move to Smith's aid with as many troops as he could spare.[27]

During the afternoon Gillmore had advanced to the turnpike with Hawley's and Plaisted's brigades of Terry's division. Oddly, it had not been anticipated that these troops would be needed for strenuous duty, and many of them had left camp without full loads of ammunition and rations. Now they were called upon to join Smith at the front with no time for additional preparation. With them went two regiments of White's brigade of Ames's division.[28] This left Ames with only a brigade and a half to guard the army's rear and wreck more of the Richmond and Petersburg Railroad. Marching with difficulty along the muddy turnpike, which had been churned into mush by the passage of the XVIII Corps, Gillmore's troops by late afternoon had reached the Perdue farm just beyond Redwater Creek, where they bivouacked.[29]

Gillmore arrived too late for an attack to be mounted, so Smith withdrew his men behind the ridge crest to wait for dawn. There the troops tried to shield themselves from the incessant rain. Some cut branches to form makeshift shelters, while others huddled close to large trees. In many places along the line the miserable soldiers were refused permission to build fires, which would be visible to the enemy across the creek. Not only did this prevent the men from warming themselves, but it also kept them from boiling water for coffee. As the troops lay on the wet ground patiently enduring their lot in silence, the regimental pioneers searched the woods in the rear for casualties of the day's skirmishing. In front, the pickets crept forward to positions near the creek and there suffered their own private torment as the rain continued.[30]

For the Confederate forces 12 May was a day of much activity. In Petersburg, Beauregard finally received approval from Jefferson Davis for his course of action on the previous day.[31] During the morning he instructed Hoke to follow the wishes of the War Department, promising to join him as soon as the last troops arrived from the south.[32] Around noon Beauregard was forced to deploy several regiments at Swift Creek to meet a cavalry probe sent from Port Walthall Junction by Ames. The Federals were not interested in action and soon disappeared, leaving Beauregard free to return to his preparations for departure from Petersburg. Alfred Colquitt's Georgia regiments were relieved by Martin's North Carolina Brigade, which was to join Wise's Brigade as Petersburg's garrison, so that Colquitt could march with Beauregard. Two regiments of Corse's Brigade that had not been present when their parent unit departed were also attached to Colquitt.[33]

Although the war had temporarily bypassed Petersburg, Richmond was threatened on 12 May by Sheridan's cavalry, which had mortally wounded J. E. B. Stuart on the previous day and remained between the outer and intermediate lines of the capital's defenses. Temporary resident Judith McGuire reported that the city was calm, but War Department clerk J. B. Jones hoarded provisions in response to a rumor that the government was preparing to evacuate the capital. Before dawn Robert Ransom had been ordered to return to Richmond from Drewry's Bluff with two brigades. Gracie's Alabamians marched during the night, passing through the suburb of Manchester at dawn, and Barton's Brigade moved northward by boat later in the morning. These troops then spent the day skirmishing in the rain with Sheridan's troopers under the watchful eyes of Jefferson Davis.[34]

At Drewry's Bluff, Robert Hoke was left in command during Ransom's absence, and he spent most of the day bringing his troops up from the Half-Way House and deploying them within the fortifications. During the afternoon he was told to send two more brigades to the capital, and he complied by dispatching Lewis's Brigade by water and marching Terry's Brigade overland. Later, as word of Kautz's movements reached him, Hoke became concerned that the Federals were planning to trap his five brigades between their infantry on the south and their cavalry on the west. Undaunted, he told Bragg, "I shall fight them if met from all sides." Although his suggestions for concentrating his own and Ransom's brigades for decisive action against Butler were disregarded, Hoke continued throughout the rainy night to transmit warnings of the Federal army's progress.[35]

Just before 1:00 A.M. on 13 May, Beauregard received an urgent request from Bragg to send troops to guard the Richmond and Danville Railroad bridges against Kautz's cavalry. The only units available at Petersburg were the 17th and 30th Virginia Regiments of Corse's Brigade and these headed westward by freight train at 6:00 A.M. Having done all he could to save the bridges, Beauregard resumed his preparations to leave for Drewry's Bluff. Late in the morning a train arrived from Weldon bearing Major General Chase Whiting. Unwell, and accompanied by only one aide, Whiting expected a brief conference with Beauregard and a speedy return to Wilmington. Instead, Beauregard asked Whiting to assume temporary command of the department during his absence in the field. After briefing Whiting for less than an hour, Beauregard gathered his staff and rode out of Petersburg at noon. He was escorted by the 3rd North Carolina Cavalry and the three available regiments of Colquitt's Brigade. In order to avoid the Federals blocking the turnpike, the column took a circuitous route via Chesterfield Court House.[36]

Beauregard's choice of an indirect route was fortuitous, because Butler had decided to send the X Corps westward in an effort to outflank the Confederates. Gillmore's force consisted of eleven regiments from Plaisted's, Hawley's, White's, and Marston's brigades, along with an artillery battery and a detachment of the 1st New York Mounted Rifles. A little before 6:30 A.M., the column headed westward on the Chester Station road, while the rain that had plagued the previous day's march continued to fall. Leading the way, Colonel Harris Plaisted's brigade passed through Chester Station at 8:30 A.M. and was followed by Gillmore and the other units. Left behind at Chester Station were Colonel Richard White's two regiments, which were to wait for the flanking column to get into position, then make a diversionary attack along the railroad. Following a road that gradually circled northward, the Federals routed a small Confederate cavalry detachment at a road junction only one mile from Chesterfield Court House. Told by his guides that the Court House road led directly to the end of the Confederate line, Gillmore turned the column eastward after leaving two of Plaisted's regiments behind to protect his rear. According to slaves living in the vicinity, a Confederate fort was not far ahead.[37]

As Gillmore's troops neared the rear of the Confederate defenses, Smith's XVIII Corps was also advancing, but much more slowly. During a dawn reconnaissance Smith had found a hill that commanded the Confederate position beyond Proctor's Creek. After having spent several hours gaining the hill, he sent his skirmishers across the stream. They met no resistance, for the Confederates had departed quietly during the night. Chagrined that his morning's work had been in vain, Smith at 9:00 A.M. ordered his three divisions to resume the general advance. Beyond Proctor's Creek the Federals entered a thick band of woods. Hearing nothing from Gillmore and worried about his left flank, Smith decided to transfer Turner's division from the right end of the line to the left. Turner began the movement in late morning, but it was noon before he could get his brigades through the rough terrain to the turnpike. Meanwhile, the divisions of Brooks and Weitzel probed slowly forward. By noon their skirmishers had pushed beyond the Half-Way House on the turnpike and were engaging Confederates near the substantial Friend house.[38]

Throughout the early afternoon the XVIII Corps gradually pressed forward in the rain against stiffening opposition. Upon reaching the edge of the forest, the Federals found themselves facing a clearing seven hundred years wide, bordered on the north by a line of fortifications. When Smith learned that Confederate works were visible in his front, he crept forward to the edge of the trees and studied the defenses carefully. Almost a mile of earthworks could be seen, all of standard construction, with a ditch in front and many embrasures for artillery. Smith advised Butler, waiting in the rear, "that if the line was held in force by the enemy, it could not be carried by assault, and that I should not attempt it unless I received orders to do so." Butler, who still relied upon Smith's professional judgment because of his own relative inexperience, accepted the recommendation. As a result, skirmishing continued along the front of the XVIII Corps, but the advance ceased.[39]

While Smith's men inched forward on both sides of the turnpike, Gillmore's leading elements reached the swampy valley of Crooked Branch, a tributary of Proctor's Creek. Just beyond was a steep hill that anchored the end of the Confederate defenses. The works generally faced eastward toward the railroad, except for a few yards on the hill that looked southward. None of the trenches fronted to the west, the direction from which the Federals were approaching. Because Plaisted had only one regiment present, Gillmore called Hawley's brigade to the front. Hawley deployed the 7th Connecticut and 7th New Hampshire Regiments along the road and sent the 3rd New Hampshire to the extreme left where a log bridge crossed the branch. Behind Hawley, artillerymen of the 5th New Jersey Battery unlimbered their guns, while Plaisted called up his rear-guard regiments in support. The time was 4:00 P.M.[40]

When he discovered that the swamp along the road was impassable, Gillmore ordered Hawley to make the main assault with the 3rd New Hampshire on the left. Hawley had just begun to shift his units when the 3rd New Hampshire crossed the branch and began to climb the steep grade through the dense underbrush. Reaching the edge of the woods near the crest of the hill, the regiment's commander, Lieutenant Colonel Josiah Plimpton, found himself facing more than a thousand startled Confederates of Matt Ransom's Brigade. Hastily forming his regiment into line of battle, Plimpton drove the Confederates either beyond their works or into a house and outbuildings on the Federal left. Recovering quickly, Ransom's men dug in on the forward slope of their trenches and poured a heavy fire into the New Hampshire troops. Realizing that the Federal regiment was temporarily alone and outnumbered, the Confederates soon began to filter around Plimpton's left flank. Unable to hold his position against the resurgent Confederates, Plimpton ordered the 3rd New Hampshire to withdraw to the edge of the woods, but the soldiers could not be rallied there. Down the hill ran the Federals, in an order described by one participant as "go as you please," until they splashed hurriedly across Crooked Branch to the far bank.[41]

While Hawley's remaining regiments held the line, supported by Plaisted's brigade, the Federal commanders conferred about what to do next. During the conference word arrived that White's men advancing along the railroad had gained possession of the hill, the Confederates having retired eastward. Gillmore then ordered Hawley's and Plaisted's brigades to occupy the vacant position. From there they could see and hear trains bringing Confederate supplies and reinforcements from Richmond. Behind them the heart-rending task of collecting the wounded and the dead had already begun. The victory had been costly, particularly for the 3rd New Hampshire, which had suffered 140 casualties. Confederate losses had also been heavy, especially in the 49th North Carolina, and Matt Ransom himself had suffered a disabling wound in the arm.[42]

Because news of Gillmore's success arrived too late for Butler and Smith to make a corresponding advance along the turnpike, the Army of the James prepared to spend another wet evening in proximity to the enemy. Just before dark Baldy Smith rode among his bedraggled men, raising their spirits with news of a great victory won by Grant near Spotsylvania Court House. On the turnpike, pickets of the XVIII Corps dug in around Charles Friend's outbuildings. Far to the left, Gillmore's weary troops bivouacked on the ground they had captured during the afternoon, which proved to be Wooldridge's Hill. Wet and cold from the evening chill, yet allowed no fires, Hawley's and Plaisted's men huddled together for warmth and wistfully watched the twinkling lights of Confederate campfires in the distance. Around them, the search for casualties continued, while in Wooldridge's house a captured Confederate surgeon operated on friend and foe alike. Behind the barn a burial party dug a common grave for the slain.[43]

Inside the Confederate works all was quiet. With his right flank turned, Hoke had prudently decided to withdraw to an intermediate line of defenses. He had battled Butler's army all day with only four-and-a-half brigades: Hagood's, Johnson's, Clingman's, Ransom's, and half of Corse's. Of these, Ransom's Brigade had been roughly handled at Wooldridge's Hill and had needed help from Corse to secure its safe retreat. Lewis's, Terry's, Gracie's, and Barton's Brigades were still absent at Richmond. Somewhere near Chesterfield Court House, Beauregard was marching to join Hoke with most of Colquitt's Brigade, but there was no way of predicting when he would arrive. During the night Hoke repeatedly wired Bragg, seeking both news of Beauregard and reinforcements to man the works. Receiving no satisfactory reply, Hoke resigned himself to facing a heavy attack the next morning.[44]

While the opposing armies bivouacked south of Drewry's Bluff, Beauregard continued to ride through the stormy night around the Federal left flank. Finally at 3:00 A.M. on 14 May, the department commander reined in his mount at the Drewry mansion near Fort Darling and hastened inside out of the rain. Wasting no time, he conferred immediately with Colonel D. B. Harris and Colonel Walter Stevens, engineer of the Richmond defenses, who was spending the night at Drewry's Bluff. During the briefing Beauregard learned of the gains made by the Federals on the previous day and of Hoke's retreat to the intermediate line of defenses. Colonel Stevens then noted that Robert Ransom had a mobile force of approximately 5,000 men in the Department of Richmond. Turning to matters further afield, he described Lee's position at Spotsylvania Court House. To enable Beauregard to comprehend the situation at a glance, Stevens produced a map showing the relative positions of all the important combatants: Lee, Grant, Sheridan, Butler, Hoke, and Robert Ransom.[45]

As the briefing continued, Beauregard began to envision a grand strategic plan that would change the course of the war in Virginia and possibly end the conflict in a manner acceptable to the Confederacy. Because all of the Confederate forces were centrally located between the Federal armies to the north and south, Beauregard believed the Confederacy should use its interior lines to concentrate first against one Federal army, then against the other, defeating them in detail. Specifically, Beauregard proposed that the Army of Northern Virginia withdraw into Richmond's defenses after detaching 15,000 men to join Beauregard. If need be, 5,000 of this number could come from Ransom's department. Reinforced by Lee's men, Beauregard would attack Butler in front, while Whiting assaulted him in rear with Wise's and Martin's Brigades. Attacked from both sides and cut off from his base, Butler would be destroyed within two or three days after the arrival of Lee's troops. Beauregard would then move northward with 25,000 men to join Lee.

Based on the principles of interior lines, concentration, and defeat in detail, Beauregard's proposal promised a radical solution to the dilemma facing the Confederate War Department. Could Beauregard's theoretical musings, however, be translated into reality? If the Confederate government approved such a bold course of action, could the overworked transportation network move the troops within the allotted time? In Beauregard's view, such questions could be answered later. Rather than waste precious time by drawing up a formal proposal, he dispatched Colonel Stevens to Richmond with instructions to present the plan verbally to Jefferson Davis. Stevens rode away as the dawn of 14 May broke, cool and rainy for the third straight day. Beauregard had been at the Drewry mansion less than two hours and already his latest plan to win the war was on its way to Richmond. [46]

As Colonel Stevens began his ride, there was a stir of activity within the Army of the James. At 4:30 A.M. Baldy Smith sent his skirmishers toward the fortifications that earlier had appeared so formidable. In the dim half-light of a chilly dawn the soldiers cautiously made their way forward. Unknown to the pickets of either side, the forbidding works behind the Confederate sentinels had been empty for several hours. Gradually the Federals gained ground, from tree to tree, from stump to stump, from fence to outbuilding, firing occasionally as they moved. In this way Brook's division passed Charles Friend's brick house on the turnpike and by 8:00 A.M. had driven the Confederate skirmishers within the works. On the flanks Weitzel and Turner brought their divisions forward to extend the Federal line both east and west. Beyond Weitzel, Colonel George Cole's 2nd U. S. Colored Cavalry patrolled the mile-long gap between Weitzel and the river. [47]

A little after 8:00 A.M. skirmishers from the 13th New Hampshire Infantry of Burnham's brigade rushed the Confederate fortifications west of the turnpike, scattering the Confederate pickets to either side. This initial penetration was progressively widened until, by 9:00 A.M., Smith's XVIII Corps had seized the entire line of abandoned works facing them. In the distance a second line could be seen at the far edge of a wide plateau, covered with stumps, brush, and a cluster of abandoned barracks. More formidable than the works just taken, the new line consisted of a series of heavy redoubts on rising ground, connected by a curtain of low parapets and a ditch. To the west the line extended beyond the railroad before turning north. Its eastern anchor was a large work on a high hill a few yards east of the turnpike. From this redoubt, known to the Confederates as Fort Stevens, lines ran both northward to the inner complex around Fort Darling, and southward to the outer line that had just been captured by the Federals.[48]

Rising from their fireless bivouacs on Wooldridge's Hill, Quincy Gillmore's men soon saw Turner's and Brooks's divisions advancing. On Gillmore's orders Terry's division crossed Proctor's Creek, extended its line eastward to meet Turner and then began its own advance. White's, Plaisted's, and Hawley's brigades moved along the east side of the railroad. West of the tracks marched Marston's XVIII Corps brigade, which represented the left flank of Benjamin Butler's infantry. Beyond Marston were only cavalry patrols of the 1st New York Mounted Rifles. Driving the Confederate skirmishers from a narrow belt of timber, Gillmore's men found themselves confronted by the Confederate second line that had already stopped Smith. Like their comrades in the XVIII Corps, the X Corps soldiers paused in front of the massive defenses.[49]

About the time that the outer Confederate line was falling to the Federals, Braxton Bragg arrived from Richmond to confer with Beauregard. Unable to see Jefferson Davis, Colonel Stevens had presented Beauregard's proposal to Bragg, who had thought it best to hear the plan from Beauregard in person. Not at all reticent about his brain child, Beauregard launched into a description of his proposal and closed with a fervent plea for its adoption. According to Beauregard's later testimony, Bragg agreed that the plan was the only one that would save Richmond and the Confederacy, and he expressed his "unreserved approval" of the proposal. Bragg, however, would not take upon himself the authority to issue the orders that would set the plan in motion. Over Beauregard's earnest entreaties he refused to do more than lay the proposal before the president, who would make the final decision.[50]

If the morning conference at the Drewry mansion had taken place the way Beauregard remembered it, Bragg had completely concealed his true opinion of Beauregard's scheme. Undoubtedly, the written analysis of the plan he prepared for Davis several days later was much more representative of his true feelings. Bragg believed the plan would require too much time to implement, would result in the loss of Petersburg, the Shenandoah Valley, and other productive territory, and would expose the Army of Northern Virginia to intolerable risks. In light of these objections, it is highly unlikely that Bragg had wholeheartedly approved the proposal on 14 May in the terms Beauregard ascribed to him. Perhaps Bragg voiced some of his objections at the conference, or perhaps he was noncommittal, but at any rate he refused to act on his own. Stepping out into the rain, he left Beauregard to await the pleasure of his old nemesis, Jefferson Davis. Marking time until he heard from Davis, Beauregard called Dearing's cavalry to Petersburg and ordered north the last mobile unit remaining in North Carolina, Walker's South Carolina Brigade.[51]

Slightly over a mile from where Beauregard sat drafting orders, the skirmishers of Brooks's division pushed forward into the field of stumps and abandoned log huts,

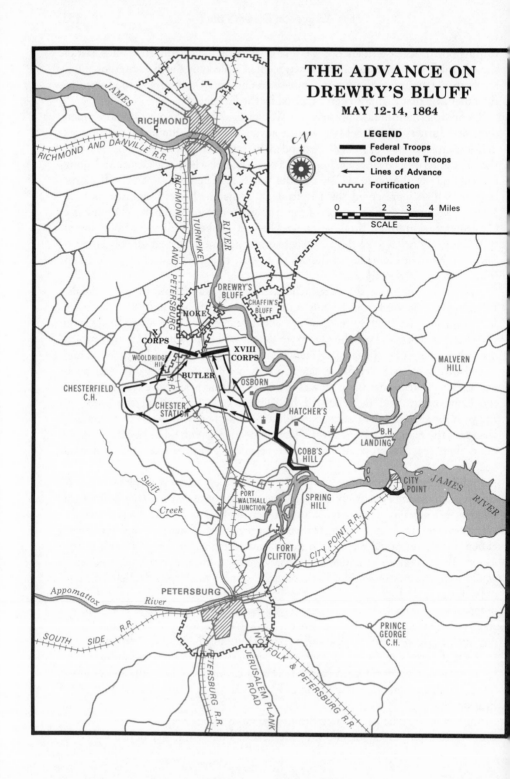

THE ADVANCE ON DREWRY'S BLUFF
MAY 12-14, 1864

LEGEND
- Federal Troops
- Confederate Troops
- Lines of Advance
- Fortification

0 1 2 3 4 Miles
SCALE

JAMES

RICHMOND

RICHMOND AND DANVILLE R.R.

RICHMOND AND PETERSBURG R.R.

TURNPIKE

RIVER

DREWRY'S BLUFF

CHAFFIN'S BLUFF

HOKE

X CORPS

XVIII CORPS

WOOLDRIDGE HILL

BUTLER

OSBORN

CHESTERFIELD C.H.

CHESTER STATION

HATCHER'S

B.H. LANDING

COBB'S HILL

CITY POINT

JAMES RIVER

MALVERN HILL

Swift

Creek

PORT WALTHALL JUNCTION

SPRING HILL

FORT CLIFTON

CITY POINT R.R.

Appomattox

River

PETERSBURG

PRINCE GEORGE C.H.

SOUTH SIDE R.R.

PETERSBURG R.R.

NORFOLK & PETERSBURG R.R.

JERUSALEM PLANK ROAD

while their parent units consolidated their positions behind the outer works. On the right of the turnpike Weitzel's men moved through a belt of timber until they came in sight of Fort Stevens. As a heavy thundershower passed overhead, firing broke out all along the two-mile line, from Heckman's brigade on the right of the XVIII Corps to Marston's brigade guarding Gillmore's left beyond the railroad. For a time the Confederate artillery in Fort Stevens did considerable damage to the advancing Federals. When several Federal batteries near the turnpike failed to suppress the Confederate fire, the skirmishers of Heckman's, Wistar's, and Burnham's brigades were detailed to the task. Darting from stump to stump, dashing across open spaces, or crawling through brush, the Federals finally reached the tangled tree branches serving as abattis just a few hundred yards from the fort. From there the sharpshooting skirmishers fired with marked success at any person showing himself over the parapet. In this way the accurate Confederate artillery fire was slowed but not entirely stilled.[52]

In the midst of the afternoon's commotion, Jefferson Davis arrived to confer with Beauregard. After commenting on some ungarrisoned earthworks he had seen, Davis shifted the discussion to Beauregard's plan of the morning. Try as he might, Beauregard could not get Davis to approve the idea of bringing Lee back to the Richmond defenses, although the President did authorize the use of Robert Ransom's five thousand men in an offensive against Butler. Nor did Davis favor Beauregard's proposed role for Whiting and the Petersburg garrison. He preferred to have them march around Butler and unite with the army at Drewry's Bluff, rather than strike Butler in the rear. In fact, Davis had wanted Whiting's troops to join the Drewry's Bluff forces for some time, and Bragg had already sent preliminary orders to Whiting to move northward around the Federal flank. Although Beauregard remonstrated with him at length, Davis insisted that Whiting's role be modified. Grudgingly accepting the inevitable, Beauregard mumbled something about preparing Whiting's new orders when he found the time, and the conference was over.[53]

After Davis's departure, Beauregard prepared Whiting's instructions. In no hurry to begin the battle that might determine his future career, Beauregard ordered Whiting to leave Petersburg at dawn on Monday, 16 May, with Wise's, Martin's, and the remainder of Colquitt's Brigades. Whiting was to march to Drewry's Bluff by an even more indirect route than Beauregard had taken, arriving there no later than Tuesday afternoon. Petersburg would be guarded by Dearing's cavalry and Walker's Brigade, which was en route from North Carolina. To ensure that the dispatch reached Petersburg, Beauregard sent it in multiple copies. Under separate cover he ordered D. H. Hill and Quartermaster Willis also to leave on Monday for Drewry's Bluff.[54]

In Petersburg Chase Whiting was well on his way toward losing his composure. So unfamiliar with his surroundings that he occasionally lost his way on Petersburg's streets, Whiting saw himself threatened on every hand. His telegraphic communication with Richmond via Burkeville had been cut by Kautz's raiders, who were again threatening the line to Weldon, his pickets at Swift Creek were in contact with enemy forces of unknown strength, and three brigades of Federals were reported advancing from City Point. In the meantime Bragg kept telling Whiting to abandon Petersburg and move north, which he was reluctant to do. A similar situation had caused George Pickett to break under the strain. Like Pickett, Whiting had concluded that Petersburg was too important to be abandoned for any reason. Besides, no matter what was happening around Drewry's Bluff, Whiting believed that Petersburg was the true Federal goal. As a result, his telegrams to Beauregard became increasingly frantic. Although everyone else was too busy to notice, Whiting was rapidly going to pieces.[55]

While Beauregard and Davis conversed at the Drewry mansion and Whiting fidgeted at Petersburg, the skirmishing continued unabated along the lines around Drewry's Bluff. On Weitzel's front the Federals maintained their harassing fire against the Confederate gunners in Fort Stevens. Twice the fort's large garrison flag fluttered to earth, only to be replaced each time. Across the turnpike Bushrod Johnson's Tennesseans struggled against Brooks's skirmishers around the abandoned log barracks between the lines. The Federals had seized the crude buildings earlier, but they had been driven out by artillery fire that reduced several of the barracks to a blizzard of jagged splinters. Despite the heavy bombardment, Brooks's casualties were few, as a lieutenant in the 13th New Hampshire explained: "On the whole a fortunate day; the enemy firing hastily and high—making a great deal of noise, but doing very little execution. A great many bullets may fly, but a man is a small thing on an acre of ground."[56]

On the X Corps front, Alfred Terry's division suffered much more heavily than the XVIII Corps to its right. At a cost of 117 casualties, Hawley's brigade spent the afternoon contending for a house and garden several hundred yards from the Confederate second line. Driving the defenders out with artillery fire, Hawley sent his skirmishers forward to the house, which had caught fire and was burning briskly. All attempts to advance beyond the house proved futile, and in the face of several countercharges by Matt Ransom's Brigade, Hawley's troops were barely able to hold the ground they had gained. On Hawley's left, Plaisted's brigade was also heavily engaged. Plaisted's goal was a rail fence stretching across a field in his immediate front. In a rapid advance the fence was gained, but like Hawley, Plaisted found it difficult to maintain his position. The ground was held, but it cost Plaisted ninety men.[57]

As the long day came to a close, the volume of fire slackened. All along the Federal line fresh regiments silently slipped forward to relieve those that had borne the brunt of the action. Using whatever tools they could find, the new arrivals dug the shallow fighting holes deeper. If no tools were available, bayonets and tin cups were used. In the XVIII Corps' sector, where part of the Federal line ran through the woods, logs were piled on top of the dirt mounds. Near the turnpike someone got the idea to string telegraph wire from stump to stump beyond the Federal positions. Several hundred yards away Confederate artillerymen worked all night filling sandbags to repair the damaged parapets in Fort Stevens. Behind them, the brigades of Gracie, Lewis, and Terry arrived from Richmond, where they were no longer needed against Sheridan.[58]

Throughout the day Baldy Smith had been busy studying the Confederate line. Butler's dependence upon him, coupled with Smith's belief in the futility of the campaign, had made the corps commander quite contemptuous of his superior.[59] Just after dark Smith sent Lieutenant Peter Michie to Butler's headquarters at the Friend house with orders to report on the results of the day's reconnaissances. Impetuously disregarding Smith's cynicism, Michie informed Butler that he knew of a place where the Confederate works could be carried by assault. At 9:00 P.M. Butler approved what he thought was Smith's proposal for an attack and promised to bring up four of Ames's regiments from Port Walthall Junction as a support. Smith replied an hour later, denying that he had proposed anything whatsoever, but stating his willingness to make an attack if Butler wished it. Butler let his letter of 9:00 P.M. stand and Smith reluctantly began to issue preliminary orders for the assault.[60]

At the same time that he wrote to Smith, Butler drafted a message to Philip Sheridan, who had appeared opposite Bermuda Hundred during the afternoon with twelve thousand cavalrymen. Sheridan wanted only to rest his command before returning to the Army of the Potomac, but Butler saw the horsemen as a useful adjunct to the Army of the James. In order to press upon Sheridan the advantages of such a merger, Butler asked the cavalry commander for an immediate personal meeting. At 11:00 P.M. Sheridan replied that he would call upon the commander of the Army of the James on the next day. Until then Butler's plans for Sheridan would have to wait.[61]

That night a soldier who had remained behind in the Bermuda Hundred camp because of sickness wrote in his diary: "The N. Y. papers praise Butler for his success. 'The Newark Daily Advertiser' says that Butler holds the key to Richmond. I wonder if he will unlock it."[62]

NOTES

1. Cunningham, *Adirondack Regiment*, 109; Roe, *Twenty-Fourth Massachusetts*, 280; Valentine, *Story of Co. F*, 111; Clark, *My Experience*, 58; Brady, *Eleventh Maine*, 178; Dickey, *Eighty-Fifth Pennsylvania*, 322; Eldredge, *Third New Hampshire*, 464; Walter S. Clemence Diary, 11 May 1864, NCC; Thompson, *Thirteenth New Hampshire*, 274; Drake, *Ninth New Jersey*, 351–352.

2. Butler, *Butler's Book*, 649–650. In a postwar letter, Butler also stated that he was adhering to the target date of 15 May to be near Richmond, as agreed upon with Grant. Butler to W. P. Darby [Derby], 26 June 1882, Butler Papers, LC.

3. Marshall, ed., *Butler's Correspondence*, 4:192. Emphasis added.

4. Beauregard to Bragg, 3:30 A.M., 11 May 1864, Official Telegrams, 22 April–9 June 1864, Beauregard Papers, LC; O.R.A., 51, pt. 2, 920.

5. Beauregard to Bragg, 3:00 A.M., 11 May 1864, and 3:30 A.M., 11 May 1864, Official Telegrams, 22 April–9 June 1864, Beauregard Papers, LC; O.R.A., 51, pt. 2, 921; Roman, *Military Operations*, 2:199. The 17th and 30th Virginia Regiments of Corse's Brigade were absent, being still en route to Petersburg on 11 May. Cabel, "Swift Creek," 223; Herbert, "Seventeenth Virginia," 290; Wise, *Seventeenth Virginia*, 174.

6. Beauregard to Hoke (four messages), Beauregard to Matt Ransom, Beauregard to Colquitt, Beauregard to Wise, all 11 May 1864, Letter Book, April–May 1864, Beauregard Papers, LC; Clark, ed., *North Carolina Regiments*, 2:4.

7. Beauregard to Bragg, 7:00 A.M., Beauregard to Whiting, 7:00 A.M., Beauregard to Major Willis,

and Beauregard to Dearing (two telegrams), all 11 May 1864, Official Telegrams, 22 April–9 June 1864, Beauregard Papers, LC; William Beavans Diary, 11 May 1864, SHC; Cary Whitaker Diary, 11 May 1864, SHC; Edward Phifer to his mother, 29 May 1864, Phifer Family Papers, SHC; Henry Chambers Diary, 11 May 1864, NCDAH.

8. Cary Whitaker Diary, 11 May 1864, SHC; Edward Phifer to his mother, 29 May 1864, Phifer Family Papers, SHC; Henry Chambers Diary, 11 May 1864, NCDAH; Hagood, *Memoirs*, 231–232; Owen, *Washington Artillery*, 312; Jones, *Surry Light Artillery*, 76; *O.R.A.*, 51, pt. 1, 222–223, 229, 231; William Henry Morgan, *Personal Reminiscences of the War of 1861–5* (Lynchburg, Va: J. P. Bell Company, 1911), 194–195; Bushrod R. Johnson Diary, 11 May 1864, Johnson Papers, NA.

9. Beauregard to Robert Ransom, 7:30 A.M., 11 May 1864, Official Telegrams, 22 April–9 June 1864, Beauregard Papers, LC; *O.R.A.*, 51, pt. 2, 919–921; Roman, *Military Operations*, 2:554–555; *O.R.A.*, 36, pt. 2, 991–992.

10. *O.R.A.*, 36, pt. 2, 986 (misdated 10 May); Roman, *Military Operations*, 2:554. There are minor variations in wording and punctuation between the two citations. The version in the *Official Records* is quoted here. Misled by the *O.R.A.*'s error in dating, D. S. Freeman mistakenly placed the time of this message on the night of 10–11 May. Freeman, *Lee's Lieutenants*, 3:472–473.

11. Roman, *Military Operations*, 2:555–556. The time of Bragg's message is given in *O.R.A.*, 51, pt. 2, 920.

12. Beauregard to Seddon, 2:00 P.M., 11 May 1864, Official Telegrams, 22 April–9 June 1864, Beauregard Papers, LC; *O.R.A.*, 36, pt. 2, 992.

13. *O.R.A.*, 36, pt. 2, 992; Beauregard to Davis, 5:15 P.M., 11 May 1864, Official Telegrams, 22 April–9 June 1864, Beauregard Papers, LC; *O.R.A.*, 51, pt. 2, 920; Roman, *Military Operations*, 2:199–200, 555, 556.

14. *O.R.A.*, 36, pt. 2, 218, 985, 986, 990; *O.R.A.*, 51, pt. 2, 921. The controversy between Barton and Ransom dragged on for months and was still creating paperwork on 20 March 1865. The relevant correspondence is in *O.R.A.*, 36, pt. 2, 213–235.

15. *O.R.A.*, 36, pt. 2, 991; Beauregard to Seddon, 7:45 P.M., 11 May 1864, Letter Book, April–May 1864, Beauregard Papers, LC; Shaver, *Sixtieth Alabama*, 47; W. B. Stansel, "Gracie's Brigade at Drury's Bluff," *Confederate Veteran* 12 (December, 1904):592.

16. Beauregard to Hoke, 7:00 P.M., and Beauregard to Seddon, 7:45 P.M., 11 May 1864, Letter Book, April–May 1864, Beauregard Papers, LC. Colquitt and one of his regiments, as well as one of Martin's had already arrived. The rest of Colquitt's units apparently reached Petersburg during the night. Beauregard to Wise, Beauregard to Colquitt, and Beauregard to Colonel Neal, 19th Georgia, all 11 May 1864, Letter Book, April–May 1864, Beauregard Papers, LC.

17. *O.R.A.*, 36, pt. 2, 173, 180; "Kautz in the Great Rebellion," Kautz Papers, LC; *Eleventh Pennsylvania Cavalry*, 111; Wall, "Raids," 81–82; Price, *Ninety-Seventh Pennsylvania*, 258; Dickey, *Eighty-Fifth Pennsylvania*, 322; Brady, *Eleventh Maine*, 178; Valentine, *Story of Co. F,* 111; Walter S. Clemence Diary, 11 May 1864, NCC; John Paris Diary, 11 May 1864, SHC; Edward Phifer to his mother, 29 May 1864, Phifer Family Papers, SHC; Henry Chambers Diary, 11 May 1864, NCDAH; R. M. Belo Reminiscences (typescript), Civil War Collection, Miscellaneous Records, North Carolina Division of Archives and History, Raleigh, N.C.; Edward Baker Loving Diary, 11 May 1864, VSL; Izlar, *Edisto Rifles*, 51.

18. *O.R.A.*, 36, pt. 2, 113, 647–648, 650.

19. *O.R.A.*, 36, pt. 2, 11–12. Butler's actions were successful in forcing the Confederates to withhold reinforcements from the Army of Northern Virginia. Ibid., 988–989.

20. Butler, *Butler's Book*, 651.

21. *O.R.A.*, 36, pt. 2, 93–94, 100, 127, 134, 139, 151, 157; Drake, *Ninth New Jersey*, 182, 200; Everts, *Comprehensive History*, 106; Valentine, *Story of Co. F.*, 111; Emmerton, *Twenty-Third Massachusetts*, 181; Derby, *Bearing Arms*, 265–266; Clark, *My Experience*, 58; Putnam, *Story of Company A*, 274; Bartlett, *Twelfth New Hampshire*, 178; *New York Times*, 14 May 1864; Mowris, *One Hundred and Seventeenth New York*, 104.

22. *O.R.A.*, 36, pt. 2, 122–123, 151, 157; Derby, *Bearing Arms*, 266; Emmerton, *Twenty-Third Massachusetts*, 181; Valentine, *Story of Co. F,* 111; Drake, *Ninth New Jersey*, 182; Everts, *Comprehensive History*, 106; Bartlett, *Twelfth New Hampshire*, 178; Kreutzer, *Ninety-Eighth New York*, 189; Clark, *Iron Hearted Regiment*, 111.

23. Thompson, *Thirteenth New Hampshire*, 281; Izlar, *Edisto Rifles*, 51; Loehr, *First Virginia*, 46; Owen, *Washington Artillery*, 312; *O.R.A.*, 51, pt. 1, 226, 229; John Paris Diary, 11 and 12 May 1864, SHC; Edward Phifer to his mother, 29 May 1864, Phifer Family Papers, SHC; William H. S. Burgwyn Diary, 11 [12] May 1864, NCDAH.

24. *O.R.A.*, 36, pt. 2, 113–114, 120, 123, 151, 157; Cunningham, *Adirondack Regiment*, 110; Philip

S. Chase, *Battery F, First Regiment Rhode Island Light Artillery, in the Civil War, 1861–1865* (Providence R.I.: Snow & Farnham, 1892), 156–158.

25. *O.R.A.*, 36, pt. 2, 36, 41, 94, 97, 102, 108, 127, 131, 134, 141, 151, 689–690.

26. *O.R.A.*, 36, pt. 2, 94, 98, 114, 134, 139; *O.R.A.*, 51, pt. 1, 226; Thompson, *Thirteenth New Hampshire*, 279–281; Cunningham, *Adirondack Regiment*, 110–111; Bartlett, *Twelfth New Hampshire*, 178; Derby, *Bearing Arms*, 266; Cabell, "Swift Creek," 223; Owen, *Washington Artillery*, 312–313; Harrill, *Reminiscences*, 21; R. M. Belo Reminiscences, NCDAH; John Washington Calton to his father, 24 May 1864, John Washington Calton Letters, NCDAH; Henry Chambers Diary, 12 May 1864, NCDAH; William H. S. Burgwyn Diary, 11 [12] May 1864, NCDAH; David Emmons Johnston, *Four Years a Soldier* (Princeton, W. Va., 1887), 304–305; Johnston, *Confederate Boy*, 246; Morgan, *Reminiscences*, 195; Loehr, *First Virginia*, 46; Edwin Baker Loving Diary, 12 May 1864, VSL; Izlar, *Edisto Rifles*, 51; Gregorie, ed., "Wescoat Diary," 85; William Beavans Diary, 12 May 1864, SHC; John Paris Diary, 12 May 1864, SHC; Cary Whitaker Diary, 12 May 1864, SHC.

27. *O.R.A.*, 36, pt. 2, 36, 114; Smith, *Battles and Leaders*, 4:209. After reaching the turnpike at midmorning, Smith had advanced less than two miles farther during the rest of the day.

28. *O.R.A.*, 36, pt. 2, 36, 78, 688, 689; Eldredge, *Third New Hampshire*, 464. Hawley and Plaisted marched with only three regiments each, their remaining regiments being on picket. *O.R.A.*, 36, pt. 2, 50; *O.R.A.*, 51, pt. 1, 1246.

29. *O.R.A.*, 36, pt. 2, 41, 50, 60, 67, 72, 85, 111–112, 114, 127; *O.R.A.*, 51, pt. 1, 1241; Roe, *Twenty-Fourth Massachusetts*, 280; Stowits, *One Hundredth New York*, 252–253; Little, *Seventh New Hampshire*, 247; Tourtellotte, *History of Company K*, 169; Waite, *New Hampshire in the Great Rebellion*, 240; Hyde, *One Hundred and Twelfth New York*, 75.

30. *O.R.A.*, 36, pt. 2, 114; Clark, *Iron Hearted Regiment*, 111; Nichols, *Perry's Saints*, 213; Cunningham, *Adirondack Regiment*, 111; Thompson, *Thirteenth New Hampshire*, 280–281; Cleveland, ed., "Campaign of Promise," 320; Drake, *Ninth New Jersey*, 182; Valentine, *Story of Co. F*, 111; Beecher, *First Connecticut Light Battery*, 1:393–394; Walter S. Clemence Memoranda, 12 May 1864, NCC; Samuel H. Putnam, Regimental Record—Co. A, 25th Mass. Vols., DU; Stowits, *One Hundredth New York*, 253; Emmerton, *Twenty-Third Massachusetts*, 181–182; Bartlett, *Twelfth New Hampshire*, 178.

31. Roman, *Military Operations*, 2:556.

32. Beauregard to Hoke, 5:15 A.M., 12 May 1864, Official Telegrams, 22 April–9 June 1864, Beauregard Papers, LC; Roman, *Military Operations*, 2:556 (mistimed here); *O.R.A.*, 36, pt. 2, 11, 691, 997; Cleveland, ed., "Campaign of Promise," 320; Marshall, ed., *Butler's Correspondence*, 4:198; *New York Times*, 16 May 1864. Hoke never received this message because the courier was captured by the advancing enemy, but he learned of its existence from captured Federals.

33. Beauregard to Bragg, 1:15 P.M., 12 May 1864, Official Telegrams, 22 April–9 June 1864, Beauregard Papers, LC; Beauregard to Wise, Beauregard to Colquitt, Beauregard to Hill, all 12 May 1864, Letter Book, April–May 1864, Beauregard Papers, LC; *O.R.A.*, 36, pt. 2, 998; Herbert, "Seventeenth Virginia," 290; Wise, *Seventeenth Virginia*, 175.

34. McGuire, *Southern Refugee*, 266; Jones, *War Clerk*, 2:206–207; *O.R.A.*, 36, pt. 2, 995; Shaver, *Sixtieth Alabama*, 47–50.

35. *O.R.A.*, 36, pt. 2, 994–997; *O.R.A.*, 51, pt. 2, 922, 924, 926; *O.R.N.*, 10:628, 630; Loehr, *First Virginia*, 46; Clark, ed., *North Carolina Regiments*, 3:275; William Beavans Diary, 12 May 1864, SHC; John Paris Diary, 12 May 1864, SHC; Cary Whitaker Diary, 12 May 1864, SHC.

36. Beauregard to Wise, 1:00 A.M., 13 May 1864, Beauregard to Colquitt, 13 May 1864, both in Letter Book, April–May 1864, Beauregard Papers, LC; Wise, *Seventeenth Virginia*, 175–176; Herbert, "Seventeenth Virginia," 290–291; Beauregard to Bragg, 5:30 A.M., 13 May 1864, Beauregard to Hoke, 13 May 1864, and Beauregard to Davis, 7:15 A.M., 13 May 1864, all in Official Telegrams, 22 April–9 June 1864, Beauregard Papers, LC; *O.R.A.*, 51, pt. 2, 927; Roman, *Military Operations*, 2:200, 557; *O.R.A.*, 36, pt. 2, 259; Beauregard, "Drury's Bluff," 249; Beauregard, *Battles and Leaders*, 4:197; G. T. Beauregard, "Drewry's Bluff. A Letter from General Beauregard to General Wise Regarding the Battle, and the Difference Between General Beauregard and General Bragg as to the War Policy at that Crisis," *Southern Historical Society Papers* 25 (1897):206; Manuscript of Gen. H. A. Wise Relative to Battle of Petersburg, Va. in June 1864, Beauregard papers, LC.

37. Butler, *Butler's Book*, 651; *O.R.A.*, 36, pt. 2, 36–37, 41, 50, 60, 78, 170; *O.R.A.*, 51, pt. 1, 1241; Stowits, *One Hundredth New York*, 253–254; Copp, *Reminiscences*, 374.

38. Smith, *Battles and Leaders*, 4:209; *O.R.A.*, 36, pt. 2, 94, 103, 114–115, 127, 134, 141, 151, 743; Drake, *Ninth New Jersey*, 182–183, 200; Thompson, *Thirteenth New Hampshire*, 282; Valentine, *Story of Co. F*, 111; Bartlett, *Twelfth New Hampshire*, 179; Kreutzer, *Ninety-Eighth New York*, 189–190; Bushrod R. Johnson Diary, 13 May 1864, Johnson Papers, NA.

39. *O.R.A.*, 36, pt. 2, 115, 134, 157; Smith, *Battles and Leaders*, 4:209; Thompson, *Thirteenth New*

Hampshire, 282; Drake, *Ninth New Jersey*, 200; Derby, *Bearing Arms*, 266; Clark, *My Experience*, 60. Staff officer George A. Bruce did not find the Confederate works so formidable. Bruce, "General Butler's Bermuda Campaign," 328.

40. *O.R.A.*, 36, pt. 2, 37, 41, 50–51, 67, 72, 78, 85; *O.R.A.*, 51, pt. 1, 1241–1242; Eldredge, *Third New Hampshire*, 465.

41. *O.R.A.*, 36, pt. 2, 51, 67; Eldredge, *Third New Hampshire*, 465; Copp, *Reminiscences*, 374–377; Waite, *New Hampshire in the Great Rebellion*, 203–204; Clark, ed., *North Carolina Regiments*, 3:136, 351–352; Harrill, *Reminiscences*, 21–22; R. M. Belo Reminiscences, John H. C. Burch Reminiscences, both in Civil War Collection, Miscellaneous Records, NCDAH; John Lane Stuart to his mother, 29 May 1864, John Lane Stuart Papers, Duke University, Durham, N.C.

42. *O.R.A.*, 36, pt. 2, 37, 41–42, 51–52, 60, 67, 72, 78, 85–86, 742; *O.R.A.*, 51, pt. 1, 1242; Eldredge, *Third New Hampshire*, 466–468; Little, *Seventh New Hampshire*, 248; Waite, *New Hampshire in the Great Rebellion*, 240–241; Stowits, *One Hundredth New York*, 254–255; Tourtellotte, *History of Company K*, 169; Joseph Hawley to his wife, 15 May 1864, and 17 May 1864, Hawley papers, LC; Clark, ed., *North Carolina Regiments*, 2:285, 619–620, 3:136–137, 352; Harrill, *Reminiscences*, 22; Edward Phifer to his mother, 29 May 1864, Phifer Family Papers, SHC; John Lane Stuart to his mother, 29 May 1864, John Lane Stuart Papers, DU.

43. Marshall, ed., *Butler's Correspondence*, 4:202; *O.R.A.*, 36, pt. 2, 127, 742; Thompson, *Thirteenth New Hampshire*, 283–285; Bartlett, *Twelfth New Hampshire*, 179; Valentine, *Story of Co. F*, 111–112; Beecher, *First Connecticut Light Battery*, 1:400; Drake, *Ninth New Jersey*, 184–185; Clark, *My Experience*, 60; Clark, *Iron Hearted Regiment*, 112; Eldredge, *Third New Hampshire*, 466–468; Stowits, *One Hundredth New York*, 255.

44. *O.R.A.*, 36, pt. 2, 999; *O.R.A.*, 51, pt. 1, 223, 226, 229, 231, pt. 2, 928; Izlar, *Edisto Rifles*, 52; Hagood, *Memoirs*, 232; Cabell, "Swift Creek," 224; Owen, *Washington Artillery*, 313; Jones, *Surry Light Artillery*, 179–181; William H. S. Burgwyn Diary, 12 [13] May 1864, NCDAH; Henry Machen Patrick to his wife, 19 May 1864, Henry Machen Patrick Letters, NCDAH; Shaver, *Sixtieth Alabama*, 50–51; Edwin Baker Loving Diary, 13 May 1864, VSL; William Beavans Diary, 13 May 1864, SHC; John Paris Diary, 13 May 1864, SHC; Cary Whitaker Diary, 13 May 1864, SHC; Beauregard, "Letter to Wise," 206.

45. Henry Machen Patrick to his wife, 19 May 1864, Henry Machen Patrick Letters, NCDAH; Beauregard, "Letter to Wise," 206; Roman, *Military Operations*, 2:200–201; *O.R.A.*, 36, pt. 2, 1002; Beauregard, *Battles and Leaders*, 4:197; Beauregard, "Drury's Bluff," 249.

46. *O.R.A*, 36, pt. 2, 1024; Beauregard, *Battles and Leaders*, 4:197–199; Beauregard, "Drury's Bluff," 249–250; Roman, *Military Operations*, 2:201; Williams, *Beauregard*, 213–215.

47. *O.R.A.*, 36, pt. 2, 94, 97, 103, 115, 121, 123, 127, 134, 139, 151, 157, 195; Thompson, *Thirteenth New Hampshire*, 284–287, 320; Hagood, *Memoirs*, 234; Captain David F. Dobie to "dear friend Hattie," 17 May 1864, David F. Dobie Letters, Virginia State Library, Richmond, Va.; Valentine, *Story of Co. F*, 112; Walter S. Clemence Memoranda, 14 May 1864, NCC; Clark, *Iron Hearted Regiment*, 112.

48. Thompson, *Thirteenth New Hampshire*, 285–287; *O.R.A.*, 36, pt. 2, 115; Smith, *Battles and Leaders*, 4:209–210; Cowles, ed., *O.R. Atlas*, plate 77, 3; Hagood, *Memoirs*, 232.

49. *O.R.A.*, 36, pt. 2, 37, 42, 52, 60, 78–79, 772, 773; *O.R.A.*, 51, pt. 1, 1242–1243; Eldredge, *Third New Hampshire*, 468; Stowits, *One Hundredth New York*, 256.

50. *O.R.A.*, 36, pt. 2, 1002; Beauregard, *Battles and Leaders*, 4:198–199; Beauregard, "Drury's Bluff," 250–251; Beauregard, "Letter to Wise," 207; Roman, *Military Operations*, 2:201–202, 557. Beauregard placed the time of Bragg's arrival at either 5:30 or 6:00 A.M., but this does not appear to allow enough time for the intervening events to have happened.

51. *O.R.A.*, 36, pt. 2, 1023–1025; Beauregard to Whiting, 10:00 A.M., 14 May 1864, and Beauregard to Walker at Kinston, 14 May 1864, both in Official Telegrams, 22 April–9 June 1864, Beauregard Papers, LC.

52. *O.R.A.*, 36, pt. 2, 127–128, 134, 142, 146, 148, 151, 157; 164; *O.R.A.*, 51, pt. 1, 223, 228, 229, 231–232; Owen, *Washington Artillery*, 313–314; Harrison, *Pickett's Men*, 161; Jones, *Surry Light Artillery*, 181–185; Haynes, *Second New Hampshire*, 169; Bartlett, *Twelfth New Hampshire*, 179–180, 185–186, 422–423; Foster, *New Jersey and the Rebellion*, 240; Drake, *Ninth New Jersey*, 185–188; Derby, *Bearing Arms*, 266–267; Clark, *My Experience*, 60; Putnam, *Story of Company A*, 275–276; Valentine, *Story of Co. F*, 112; Thompson, *Thirteenth New Hampshire*, 285–287, 289, 292; Walter S. Clemence Memoranda, 14 May 1864, NCC; Cunningham, *Adirondack Regiment*, 112; Clark, *Iron Hearted Regiment*, 113.

53. Davis, *Rise and Fall*, 2:511–513; Beauregard, *Battles and Leaders*, 4:199; Beauregard, "Drury's Bluff," 251–252; Roman, *Military Operations*, 2:202, 211–217, 220–221, 223; O.R.A., 51, pt. 2, 929; Whiting to Beauregard, 12:30 P.M., 14 May 1864, and untimed, 14 May 1864, P. G. T. Beauregard Papers, NCDAH; O.R.A., 36, pt. 2, 1002–1003. According to Beauregard, the conference took place in midmorning, but Davis stated that he had arrived during the afternoon. In terms of substantive issues, the chief point of difference between Beauregard's and Davis's versions concerns the "offer" of Ransom's 5,000 troops by Davis to join Beauregard during the coming offensive.

54. Beauregard to Whiting, Beauregard to D. H. Hill, Beauregard to Major Willis, all 14 May 1864, Official Telegrams, 22 April–9 June 1864, Beauregard Papers, LC; Roman, *Military Operations*, 2:217. No matter how many copies were sent, Beauregard's message outlining Whiting's participation already differed from President Davis's conception of the plan. Davis had left Drewry's Bluff believing that Whiting would move at once, arrive near daylight of Sunday, 15 May, and after a day's rest join the combined attack scheduled for Monday. Davis, *Rise and Fall*, 2:512. As Beauregard envisioned it, Whiting would not depart from Petersburg until Monday morning.

55. O.R.A., 36, pt. 2, 259; O.R.A., 51, pt. 2, 931; Whiting to Beauregard, untimed, 14 May 1864, and 9:00 P.M., 14 May 1864, Beauregard Papers, NCDAH.

56. Thompson, *Thirteenth New Hampshire*, 285–290; Bartlett, *Twelfth New Hampshire*, 180, 186; O.R.A., 51, pt. 1, 224; Owen, *Washington Artillery*, 319; Hagood, *Memoirs*, 234–235; O.R.A., 36, pt. 2, 139; Cunningham, *Adirondack Regiment*, 112; Bushrod R. Johnson Diary, 14 May 1864, Johnson Papers, NA.

57. O.R.A., 36, pt. 2, 52, 60, 67–68, 72, 78–79, 86, 90; Croffut and Morris, *Connecticut During the War*, 542–543; Eldredge, *Third New Hampshire*, 469–470; Tourtellotte, *History of Company K*, 169–171; Little, *Seventh New Hampshire*, 248–250, 253; Joseph Hawley to his wife, 15 May 1864, and 17 May 1864, Hawley Papers, LC; O.R.A., 51, pt. 1, 1243; Stowits, *One Hundredth New York*, 256–258; Roe, *Twenty-Fourth Massachusetts*, 282; Beecher, *First Connecticut Light Battery*, 1:406–425.

58. Eldredge, *Third New Hampshire*, 470; Roe, *Twenty-Fourth Massachusetts*, 282; Stowits, *One Hundredth New York*, 258; Clark, *Iron Hearted Regiment*, 115; O.R.A., 36, pt. 2, 98; Clark, *Thirty-Ninth Illinois*, 318–319; Haynes, *Second New Hampshire*, 169; Waite, *New Hampshire in the Great Rebellion*, 157; Derby, *Bearing Arms*, 289; Jones, *Surry Light Artillery*, 185–186; O.R.A., 51, pt. 1, 232; Shaver, *Sixtieth Alabama*, 51; Johnston, *Four Years*, 305; Edwin Baker Loving Diary, 14 May 1864, VSL; William G. Lewis to his wife, 14 May 1864, William G. Lewis Papers, Southern Historical Collection, University of North Carolina, Chapel Hill, N.C.; William Beavans Diary, 14 May 1864, SHC; John Paris Diary, 14 May 1864, SHC; Cary Whitaker Diary, 14 May 1864, SHC.

59. O.R.A., 36, pt. 2, 37, 115, 121, 123, 772–776; Smith, *Battles and Leaders*, 4:210, 212. Although Smith's memory failed him slightly in regard to the exact date of his conference with Philip Sheridan, the opinion he expressed at that time of Butler and the campaign had not materialized overnight. In fact, his views were already known in more distant circles, as evidenced by letters sent to him on 14 May by Brigadier Generals Israel Vogdes in Portsmouth, Virginia, and James H. Wilson with Sheridan's cavalry. O.R.A., 36, pt. 2, 777–778.

60. O.R.A., 36, pt. 2, 776–777.

61. O.R.A., 36, pt. 2, 765–766, 771–772; Butler, *Butler's Book*, 652–653.

62. Cleveland, ed., "Campaign of Promise," 321.

☆ 11 ☆

Kautz's Second Raid
12–18 May 1864

With the line to Weldon cut on both sides of Petersburg, Richmond's one remaining rail link with the deep South was the Richmond and Danville Railroad. If it were to be severed, both the Confederate capital and Lee's army would face a difficult supply situation. Therefore a successful attack upon the Richmond and Danville was much desired by Federal strategists and feared in equal degree by the Confederate government. Well aware of the importance of the Richmond and Danville, Butler had resolved to break it as part of his campaign to aid the Army of the Potomac. With Grant on his way to Richmond, the railroad should be struck quickly and severely. So Butler assigned the task to August Kautz and his cavalry.[1]

Kautz had serious reservations about beginning another raid so soon, but he ordered his weary men to prepare for immediate departure. Although they worked throughout the night, the troopers were so delayed by the short notice and the inclement weather that it was 9:00 A.M., 12 May, before they were ready to leave. At that hour the column passed through the Bermuda Hundred entrenchments in the wake of Weitzel's division of the XVIII Corps. Reaching the Richmond turnpike at the site of Terry's battle on 10 May, the troopers were momentarily sickened by the sights and stench of the crossroads, before continuing westward toward Chester Station. Soon they were beyond the sheltering flank of Weitzel's infantrymen, who were beginning their own push northward toward Proctor's Creek. When the advance guard suddenly met and dispersed a handful of Confederate pickets, Kautz's men knew they were once more alone in the enemy's country.[2]

With Weitzel's guns booming behind them, the Federal horsemen entered Chester Station. Finding little of significance to destroy, the column continued through the pouring rain toward Chesterfield Court House, four miles away. There a small quantity of Confederate supplies was located and burned, and several Union sympathizers in the jail were released. Leaving the common criminals behind bars, the cavalrymen headed toward the Richmond and Danville Railroad at Coalfield Station, thirteen miles from Chesterfield Court House and little more than ten from Richmond. Moving slowly through the driving rain, the column did not reach Coalfield until 11:00 P.M. The telegraph office was first to be wrecked. While

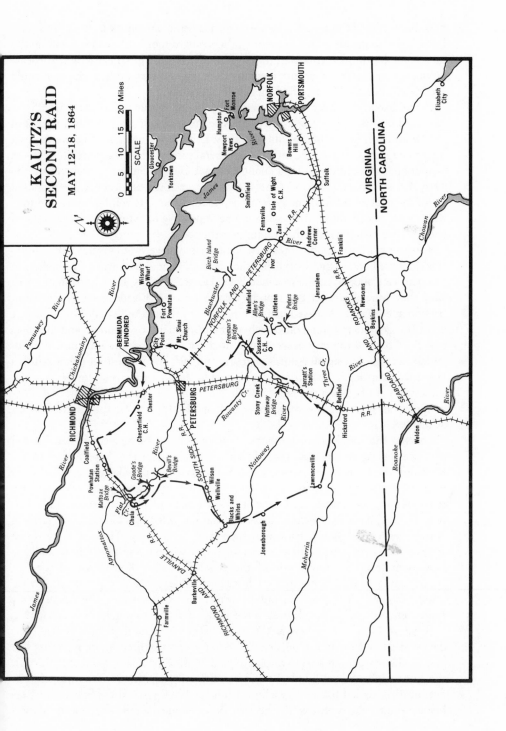

KAUTZ'S
SECOND RAID

MAY 12-18, 1864

SCALE

0   5   10   15   20 Miles

N

VIRGINIA

NORTH CAROLINA

NORFOLK

PORTSMOUTH

Elizabeth
City

Fort
Monroe

Hampton

Newport
News

Gloucester

Yorktown

Smithfield

Fernsville

Isle of Wight
C.H.

Zuni

Ivor

Andrews
Corner

Franklin

Suffolk

Bowers
Hill

Chowan
River

James River

Wilson's
Wharf

Fort
Powhatan

Birch Island
Bridge

Wakefield

Allen's
Bridge

Littleton

Peters
Bridge

Jerusalem

Newsoms

Boykins

BERMUDA
HUNDRED

City
Point

Mt. Sinai
Church

Freeman's
Bridge

Sussex
C.H.

Jarratt's
Station

Belfield

Hicksford

Weldon

Pamunkey River

Chickahominy River

RICHMOND

Coalfield

Chesterfield
C.H.

Chester

PETERSBURG

Rowanty Cr.

Stony Creek

Nottoway
Bridge

Three Cr.

Roanoke River

Powhatan
Station

Goode's
Bridge

Bevill's
Bridge

Wilson

Wellville

Blacks and
Whites

Lawrenceville

Mattoax
Bridge

Flat Cr.

Chula

Appomattox River

Jonesborough

Meherrin River

Burkeville

Farmville

James River

NORFOLK AND PETERSBURG

SOUTH SIDE R.R.

DANVILLE

RICHMOND AND DANVILLE

SEABOARD

ROANOKE AND

R.R.

R.R.

Nottoway River

detachments fired the station, wood-storage facilities, a water tank, six railroad cars loaded with munitions, and a tannery, others sought tools with which to pry up the rails. Suitable implements were discovered at the coal pits nearby and the cavalrymen were soon hard at work breaking the track. As they worked, the men could see the glow of the lights of Richmond off to the east.[3]

Before leaving Coalfield with its railroad property in ruins, Kautz and his officers discussed making a dash toward Bellona Arsenal, a munitions plant on the bank of the James River less than four miles away. When inquiry revealed that the Arsenal might be too heavily guarded for a quick Federal success, the idea of attacking it was abandoned. According to Lieutenant Colonel George Stetzel, commanding the 11th Pennsylvania Cavalry, Colonel Samuel Spear of the Second Brigade proposed to set the coal pits afire as the Federals departed. When Stetzel, however, informed Kautz that, once ignited, the coal would be impossible to extinguish, Kautz ordered the coal pits guarded until the column left the scene.[4]

After destroying all public property, Kautz marched westward several miles on the Buckingham Road, which paralleled the railroad. Four miles beyond Coalfield, the troopers were allowed to rest in a muddy field for a few hours, but by first light on 13 May they were again on the march. Spear's Second Brigade reached Powhatan Station at 8:30 A.M., followed half an hour later by the rest of the division. The first arrivals seized the telegraph office, where the instrument was removed and the wires cut. Piled around the station were large stocks of forage, bacon, and corn, some of which were used to supply Kautz's men and animals, and the rest set ablaze. In this way fifteen cars loaded with hay were burned to their running gear, followed by the station, freight house, and water tank. To make the damage at Powhatan Station as complete as possible, the troopers ripped up the track with the limited means available.[5]

Leaving the wreckage of Powhatan Station behind them, Kautz's men headed southwest along the railroad toward Mattoax Bridge over the Appomattox River. Reaching the bridge approaches, the 5th Pennsylvania Cavalry made two discoveries. First, the span could not be burned because it was made of iron. It would have to be taken apart in sections, a difficult task without the proper tools. Second, even if tools could have been found, the bridge was protected by a Confederate garrison entrenched on the south bank and supported by artillery. The defending force appeared too strong to permit access to the bridge without a stiff fight and a flanking movement from the south side of the river. Therefore Kautz ordered the 5th Pennsylvania to hold the garrison's attention while the rest of the division rode toward Goode's Bridge several miles downstream. Unknown to the cavalrymen, there were only 175 Confederates in the bridge defenses to watch them depart.[6]

Reaching Goode's Bridge at 5:00 P.M., the Federals found that the span had been damaged so as to make it impassable. After spending three hours repairing the bridge, the troopers crossed to the south bank of the Appomattox and rode through the rainy night toward Chula Station on the railroad, three miles away. Spear's Second Brigade led the way, reaching Chula at 10:00 P.M. There Spear's troopers bivouacked for the night, while the First Brigade halted a mile short of the station on the Goode's Bridge road. Seeking information about the force at Mattoax Bridge, Kautz learned that three trainloads of reinforcements had passed Chula that afternoon on their way to the bridge. Two of the trains had returned southward empty, but the third was still somewhere north of the station. Lining a switch so as to derail any southbound train, Kautz's troopers awaited events.[7]

Soon out of the darkness came the sound of a locomotive and, before long, a headlight appeared bearing down upon the station. Riding on the locomotive were Charles Talcott and J. L. Morrow, superintendents of the railroad and telegraph line respectively. Talcott and Morrow had been following the Federals all day. Reaching Coalfield that afternoon at 1:00 P.M., they had reconstructed the telegraph line and noted that track damage there could be repaired in an hour. Pushing on to Powhatan Station by 5:00 P.M., they had quickly restored telegraph service to Richmond and estimated that the railroad could be reopened in a half-day's time. The noise of firing in the direction of Mattoax Bridge caused the two supervisors to continue southward. Finding the bridge guarded by a regiment sent from Petersburg by Beauregard, Talcott and Morrow boarded the engine of the last troop train to arrive and headed toward Chula Station. At Chula the locomotive struck the open switch and derailed. Covered by darkness, Talcott, Morrow, and the engineer made good their escape as the cavalrymen closed in, leaving the Negro fireman to be taken by the Federals. The relatively undamaged engine was also left to the Federals, who gleefully destroyed it.[8]

At daybreak on 14 May, Major Ferris Jacobs's First Brigade joined the rest of the division at Chula Station. Unwilling to leave the vicinity without destroying any bridges, Kautz decided to send a detachment up the railroad to a wooden span over Flat Creek, between Chula Station and Mattoax Bridge. Selected for this duty were the 11th Pennsylvania Cavalry and 120 men of the 3rd New York, supported by one mountain howitzer, all under the command of Samuel Spear. Spear was to capture the bridge if the garrison was weak, but under no circumstance was he to become heavily engaged with a large force. As Spear's troopers moved out, the rest of the command began to destroy all of the railroad property at Chula.[9]

Guarding the Flat Creek bridge was the 17th Virginia Infantry of Corse's Brigade, commanded by Lieutenant Colonel Arthur Herbert. Like the 30th Virginia at Mattoax Bridge, the 17th had been transported early on 13 May to Burkeville via the South Side Railroad and thence toward Richmond on the Richmond and Danville. Arriving at Mattoax Bridge after Kautz's departure on the previous day, the 30th Virginia had remained at the iron span, while the 17th Virginia had returned to the wooden bridge over Flat Creek. One company barricaded the highway bridge nearby, while two companies took position at the north end of the railroad bridge with the rest of the regiment in reserve. The night passed uneventfully except for the arrival of Talcott and Morrow from their narrow escape at Chula.[10]

Not long after dawn, shots were exchanged between Herbert's pickets south of the creek and Spear's advancing skirmishers. The Confederates retreated across the bridge as Spear deployed the 11th Pennsylvania west of the track and the 3rd New

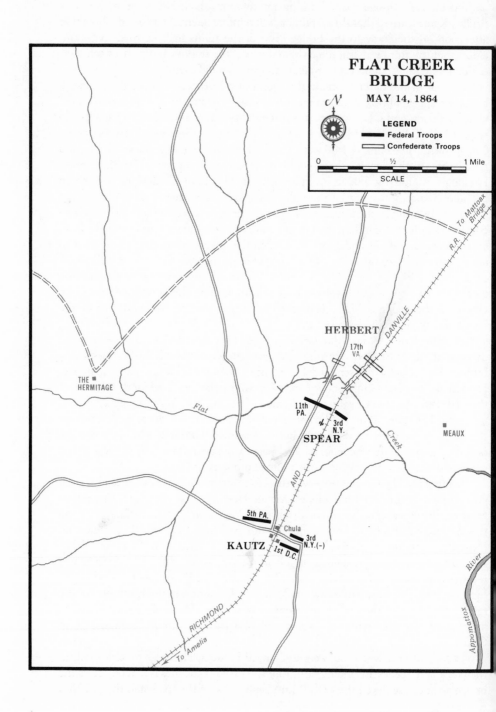

FLAT CREEK
BRIDGE
MAY 14, 1864

LEGEND
Federal Troops
Confederate Troops

0   ½   1 Mile
SCALE

To Mattoax Bridge

R.R.

DANVILLE

HERBERT

17th VA

THE HERMITAGE

Flat

11th PA.

3rd N.Y.

SPEAR

Creek

MEAUX

AND

5th PA.

Chula

3rd N.Y.(-)

KAUTZ

1st D.C.

RICHMOND

To Amelia

Appomattox River

York to the east. A dash toward the highway bridge by part of the 11th Pennsylvania collapsed at the barricade and the Federals recoiled with several casualties. Next, a dismounted charge was made toward the railroad bridge, but it too was repulsed. Nevertheless, Spear resolved to continue the fight, disregarding the mounting Federal casualties and showing, as Kautz later wrote, "that his judgment was not on a par with his bravery." Although he lacked the means to burn the rain-soaked span, Spear doggedly kept pushing his men forward. For many it was their last charge, as an officer of the 3rd New York lamented: "I took thirty of my men down, dismounted as carabineers, and brought back 22 unhurt. Six were killed before my face, two I brought back wounded."[11]

Back at Chula Station, Kautz supervised the destruction of the depot, the freight warehouse, a water tank, several cars, and sections of the track and telegraph line. When the distant firing grew in volume, he sent a courier to determine the cause. Finding that Spear had already lost more men than the small bridge was worth, Kautz ordered the detachment to rejoin the main body at Chula. Obeying promptly, Spear withdrew his men from the vicinity of the bridge. No order was given to recover either the wounded or the slain, although several troopers remained behind trying to rescue injured comrades. Some of these men were captured by the 17th Virginia, which crossed the creek and followed the retreating Federals. Colonel Herbert's losses had been only two killed and two wounded, but Spear's men had suffered severely. The detachment of the 3rd New York lost twenty-five men killed, wounded and missing, while the 11th Pennsylvania lost several more.[12]

After Spear's men returned to Chula Station, Kautz ordered the reunited column to ride southward. Believing the Richmond and Danville Railroad to be seriously damaged, the troopers headed for the South Side Railroad, twenty miles away. For a while the column paralleled the Appomattox River, feinting at Goode's and Bevill's Bridges with the rear-guard 5th Pennsylvania Cavalry. As they passed large and prosperous plantations, many of the men broke ranks to plunder the premises, apparently with the connivance of their regimental officers. Kautz abhorred this practice and had already issued stern orders against it, but he could not be everywhere at once and the civilians paid the price. In this way the Federals traveled through the lush countryside, gathering booty and crowds of escaping slaves as they marched.[13]

Near the village of Wellville, Kautz divided his command, sending Jacobs's First Brigade to wreck the South Side Railroad there, while Spear's Second Brigade struck the tracks at Wilson's Station, two miles to the east. At Wellville the first Brigade burned a freight station and an empty railroad car and tore up approximately a mile of track. The results were similarly meager at Wilson's, where Spear's troopers fired the depot and large stocks of locomotive fuel, then pulled up some rails. Both columns then headed westward toward Black's and White's, a station on the South Side Railroad named for two well-known taverns. Arriving at 8:00 P.M., the First Brigade found the station to be a collection point for forage and provisions of all sorts. After the cavalrymen replenished their dwindling stocks, the remaining grain, bacon, and hay were all "resolved into their original elements," along with the depot, warehouses, water tanks, woodshed, and thirteen freight cars. In addition, sections of track and telegraph line were ripped up, severing the South Side Railroad in yet a third place. Leaving Black's and White's in ruins, the column marched southward until 2:00 A.M., when the men were finally allowed to rest in a roadside field. It had been twenty-two hours since Spear had first moved against Flat Creek Bridge.[14]

A heavy shower during the night served to make the roads muddy, but by the time Kautz's division resumed its march the rain had ceased. The fifteenth of May was spent traveling southward toward the town of Lawrenceville, twenty-five miles away. The division moved without a guide, relying instead upon compasses and captured county maps to show the way. The cavalrymen reached Lawrenceville at 8:00 P.M. and the customary hunt for Confederate property began. As there was no railroad, the search revealed little except stockpiles of corn, bacon, and salt. Part of these were appropriated for the column's needs, and the remainder destroyed. A few Confederate soldiers also turned up and were taken prisoner, but otherwise Lawrenceville represented a peaceful interlude. Making the most of the relative calm, Kautz's men camped near the town for the night. Behind them, detachments of the 5th and 7th South Carolina Cavalry were on their trail, fanning out from Black's and White's.[15]

Early on the morning of 16 May, Kautz's division headed eastward toward the twin villages of Belfield and Hicksford. The two hamlets straddled the Meherrin River and were the site of a large bridge carrying the Petersburg Railroad over that stream. More than a week before, Beauregard had believed Belfield and Hicksford to be the goals of Kautz's first raid and had halted some of Henry Wise's men there to defend the bridge. But Kautz had not then appeared at the Meherrin crossing and Wise's men had eventually gone on to Petersburg. Now Kautz was nearing the villages from the opposite direction. Approaching Belfield in the early afternoon, he learned that two earthworks covered the bridge and that the garrison was large and heavily armed. After checking his division's ammunition supply, Kautz concluded that Belfield-Hicksford was impossible to capture with the force at hand. Sadly, he turned the column northward four miles short of the towns.[16]

The direction of march now pointed toward Jarratt's Station on the Petersburg Railroad, the same place that had been stormed by the 5th Pennsylvania Cavalry on 8 May. Many of the men were curious to see how much of the destruction there had been repaired. Entering Jarratt's at 5:00 P.M., the troopers found that the tracks had been relaid and most of the railroad buildings had been reconstructed. In the distance a train could be seen disappearing northward, evidence that Nottoway Bridge had been rebuilt in only a week. Chagrined to find that the damage created during the first raid had been so quickly repaired, the First Brigade commenced to wreck Jarratt's Station a second time. The men worked without spirit, for it seemed the Confederates could create passable substitutes for bent rails and burned bridges out of thin air. Besides, the vacant camps, broken wagons, and well-trodden roads were mute testimony that breaks in the railroad could be surmounted. Tired and discouraged, the Federals did no more than burn the new water tank and lift a few rails before leaving Jarratt's. On their way out they also destroyed a pontoon train and some piles of baggage left behind by Hoke's brigades, but that was all.[17]

After scouts reported that Nottoway Bridge was heavily guarded, Kautz briefly considered his options. With darkness approaching and his command "in no condition to make a fight," he saw no alternative but to return to the Army of the James. The column paralleled the Nottoway River until it reached Freeman's Bridge around midnight. The bridge was being destroyed by a party of Confederates, who dropped two of the three spans before the 1st District of Columbia Cavalry drove them away. That left forty feet of unfordable river to be bridged before the weary horsemen could feel relatively secure from pursuit. Under the guidance of Major J. S. Baker, the Maine woodsmen of the 1st District of Columbia rebuilt the bridge in less than three hours while the remainder of the column rested.[18]

Although they had been in contact with small detachments all afternoon, Kautz's men need not have worried about their pursuers. The chase was being directed from Burkeville, sixteen miles west of Black's and White's. There Major General Lafayette McLaws was attempting to guide Confederate cavalry detachments to an interception of Kautz's column. He was hindered by a series of irrelevant telegrams from Secretary of War Seddon, who believed Kautz to be heading west toward the Richmond and Danville's big Staunton River bridge. Further, McLaw's field commanders felt compelled to shield the South Side Railroad from new attacks, which limited their freedom of movement. They were also delayed by wildly inaccurate sighting reports furnished by well-meaning but misinformed citizens. Operating under such handicaps, the Confederate pursuit never really got started.[19]

Just before dawn on 17 May the Federals cautiously crossed the Nottoway River on Major Baker's handiwork. Less than a mile beyond, they reached the Jerusalem Plank Road and headed northward toward Petersburg. Following the path he had taken on the previous raid, Kautz next ordered a turn to the east to bypass the city. At the Norfolk and Petersburg Railroad, the troopers discovered a crew busily repairing the damage done more than a week before. Scattering the workers, the Federals paused to tear up the track again, then continued their march. Shortly before 6:00 P.M. the advance guard entered the City Point fortifications and two hours later the Second Brigade filed in, safe at last. Far behind them, their pursuers had long since given up the chase. August Kautz's second raid was over.[20]

On 18 May Butler telegraphed Stanton a summary of Kautz's achievements. On the surface they appeared impressive: the Richmond and Danville Railroad broken at Coalfield, Powhatan, and Chula Stations, with accompanying destruction of depots, water tanks, freight houses, railroad cars, and a locomotive; the South Side Railroad severed at Wilson's Station, Wellville, and Black's and White's, with similar damage to its facilities; the Petersburg Railroad cut again at Jarratt's Station; and finally the destruction of large quantities of Confederate commissary stores. In a report filed after the raid, Kautz found additional benefits in the several hundred mules captured and the hundred of slaves freed. The cost in his opinion had been surprisingly light. Casualty figures for both raids were lumped together but, even so, they amounted to only 101 men killed, wounded, and missing.[21]

In assessing both raids years later, Chaplain Edward Wall of the 3rd New York Cavalry found five beneficial results. First was the physical breaking of communication lines, both rail and telegraph. Second was the destruction of stocks of provisions, the most important accomplishment in Wall's opinion. Third, the raids permitted Kautz's division to subsist in the enemy's country for days at the enemy's expense. Fourth, the raids took Confederate troops away from other duties in order to protect the railroads and follow the raiders. Finally, the chaplain identified a psychological effect created by the raids, the fear among Confederates that thousands of Federal horsemen might be sweeping down upon them at any moment. Wall was well aware that most of the physical damage caused by the raiders was temporary in nature. The same realization had forcibly struck Kautz at Jarratt's Station, when he saw the train disappearing over a newly reconstructed Nottoway Bridge. Although they suffered from mortal shortages of rails and locomotives, the Virginia railroads proved remarkably resilient in recovering from the damage inflicted by Kautz's cavalry.[22]

Because of surprise and the poor tactics of Confederate defenders, Kautz's first raid had been much more successful than the second. Even then, Confederate units moving northward lost less than a day traversing the gap between Jarratt's Station and Stony Creek. Beauregard's foresight in stockpiling bridging material and the ingenuity of his quartermasters in improvising means to bypass the gap contributed mightily toward undoing the raiders' work. Hindered by the lack of surprise, the second raid achieved even less. Due to the rapid movement of two Confederate regiments by rail and the nature of one of the spans, not a single railroad bridge was destroyed by the raiders. Nor was the damage to track and telegraph lines significant, because Superintendents Talcott and Morrow had crews repairing the damage almost as fast as Kautz's men created it and certainly long before the Federals reached City Point. In sum, Kautz's experience proved once again that mounted raids could temporarily disrupt Richmond's iron lifelines, but that different techniques would have to be employed to destroy them permanently.[23]

NOTES

1. O.R.A., 36, pt. 2, 11–12.
2. Ibid., 173, 180; Eleventh Pennsylvania Cavalry, 111–112; Wall, "Raids," 147; "Kautz in the Great Rebellion," Kautz Papers, LC; Rowland Minturn Hall to his father, 20 May 1864, Julia Ward Stickley Collection, NCDAH.
3. O.R.A., 36, pt. 2, 173, 177–178, 180, 183, 185; Eleventh Pennsylvania Cavalry, 112, 116–117; Wall, "Raids," 147–148, 159; "Kautz in the Great Rebellion," Kautz Papers, LC; Merrill, First District of Columbia, 238–239.
4. Wall, "Raids," 148; Eleventh Pennsylvania Cavalry, 117.
5. O.R.A., 36, pt. 2, 173, 183, 185, 190; Eleventh Pennsylvania Cavalry, 112, 117; Wall, "Raids," 148–149; "Kautz in the Great Rebellion," Kautz Papers, LC.
6. O.R.A., 36, pt. 2, 173, 183, 185–186, 1003; Eleventh Pennsylvania Cavalry, 112, 117; Wall, "Raids," 149; "Kautz in the Great Rebellion," Kautz Papers, LC.
7. O.R.A., 36, pt. 2, 173, 178, 183, 186, 190; Eleventh Pennsylvania Cavalry, 112, 117; "Kautz in the Great Rebellion," Kautz Papers, LC; Wall, "Raids," 149.
8. O.R.A., 36, pt. 2, 173, 186, 190, 1000–1001, 1003; Eleventh Pennsylvania Cavalry, 112, 117; Wall, "Raids," 150; "Kautz in the Great Rebellion," Kautz Papers, LC.

9. *O.R.A.*, 36, pt. 2, 174, 178, 183, 186; *Eleventh Pennsylvania Cavalry*, 113, 117; "Kautz in the Great Rebellion," Kautz Papers, LC.

10. Wise, *Seventeenth Virginia*, 175–176; Herbert, "Seventeenth Virginia," 290–292.

11. *O.R.A.*, 36, pt. 2, 178, 186, 190; *Eleventh Pennsylvania Cavalry*, 112–113, 117–118; Wise, *Seventeenth Virginia*, 176; Herbert, "Seventeenth Virginia," 292; Warfield, *Memoirs*, 168–169; Rowland Minturn Hall to his father, 20 May 1864, Julia Ward Stickley Collection, NCDAH.

12. *O.R.A.*, 36, pt. 2, 174, 178, 183, 186, 190; *O.R.A.*, 51, pt. 2, 933; Wall, "Raids," 150; "Kautz in the Great Rebellion," Kautz Papers, LC; *Eleventh Pennsylvania Cavalry*, 113, 118; Wise, *Seventeenth Virginia*, 176–177; Herbert, "Seventeenth Virginia," 292.

13. *O.R.A.*, 36, pt. 2, 175, 186, pt. 3, 596; *Eleventh Pennsylvania Cavalry*, 113–115, 118; Wall, "Raids," 151, 158–159.

14. *O.R.A.*, 36, pt. 2, 174, 180, 183, 186, 190; *Eleventh Pennsylvania Cavalry*, 113, 118; Wall, "Raids," 151–152; Merrill, *First District of Columbia*, 239–240; "Kautz in the Great Rebellion," Kautz Papers, LC.

15. *O.R.A.*, 36, pt. 2, 174, 178, 180–181, 183, 186, 266; *Eleventh Pennsylvania Cavalry*, 113, 118; Wall, "Raids," 152; "Kautz in the Great Rebellion," Kautz Papers, LC.

16. *O.R.A.*, 36, pt. 2, 174, 186; *Eleventh Pennsylvania Cavalry*, 113, 114, 118; "Kautz in the Great Rebellion," Kautz Papers, LC; Wall, "Raids," 152–153.

17. *O.R.A.*, 36, pt. 2, 174, 178, 181, 183, 186; *Eleventh Pennsylvania Cavalry*, 114; Wall, "Raids," 152–154; "Kautz in the Great Rebellion," Kautz Papers, LC.

18. *O.R.A.*, 36, pt. 2, 174, 178, 181, 183–184, 190; *Eleventh Pennsylvania Cavalry*, 118–119; Wall, "Raids," 154; Merrill, *First District of Columbia*, 240–243; "Kautz in the Great Rebellion," Kautz Papers, LC. Eight companies of the regiment had been recruited in Maine.

19. Wall, "Raids," 153; *O.R.A.*, 36, pt. 2, 266–268, 1014–1015.

20. *O.R.A.*, 36, pt. 2, 174, 178, 181, 184, 186, 190, 863, 1018, 1019; *Eleventh Pennsylvania Cavalry*, 114, 119; Wall, "Raids," 154–155; "Kautz in the Great Rebellion," Kautz Papers, LC.

21. *O.R.A.*, 36, pt. 2, 12, 174, 175, 178, 181, 186, 188, 190–191, 191n; *Eleventh Pennsylvania Cavalry*, 115; "Kautz in the Great Rebellion," Kautz Papers, LC; Rowland Minturn Hall to his mother, 5 June 1864, Julia Ward Stickley Collection, NCDAH.

22. Wall, "Raids," 156–157. For the psychological effect, see also Kautz, *Battles and Leaders*, 4:534.

23. Johnston, *Virginia Railroads*, 298, note 33.

12

Beauregard's Offensive Plan
15 May 1864

Long before dawn on 15 May, Baldy Smith's preparations for an assault on the Confederate works were well underway. Smith planned to use a brigade each from Ames's and Weitzel's divisions for the storming column, along with two regiments from Brooks's division. Because he had no reserves, Smith proposed to guard against a repulse by ordering Turner's division to cover the flank of the attacking column. Turner, however, had reverted to Gillmore's control on the previous day. When informed of this, Smith sought the return of Marston's brigade from the army's extreme left flank, but it could not be transferred in time. The lack of troops to provide flank protection gave Smith an excuse to argue that the attack should be cancelled, or at least postponed until reserves could be accumulated. In a conference with Butler, Smith persuaded the army commander that an attack would be unwise, and the idea was abandoned. With that decision, the Army of the James passed to the defensive.[1]

In the Drewry mansion, less than two miles from Butler's headquarters, P. G. T. Beauregard was working on plans for an offensive of his own. Unlike Smith, Beauregard ardently wished to attack the enemy. Unlike Butler, he was operating in proximity to his civilian superiors and was feeling increasingly hampered by their interference. Beauregard probably had expected Jefferson Davis to veto the idea of taking units from Lee, but he resented the restrictions Davis had placed on the use of Chase Whiting's troops. In response to a message from D. H. Hill at Petersburg, Beauregard agreed that another course of action would have been preferable, but that since the order to concentrate at Drewry's Bluff still stood, "the sooner he [Whiting] comes the better." As a result, Beauregard wrote Whiting to accelerate his departure time to Sunday, if possible. The grand attack still would not take place before Wednesday morning, since Whiting could hardly join Beauregard before Tuesday afternoon.[2]

In a 6:45 A.M. telegram to Braxton Bragg, Beauregard mentioned that the attack would take place on Wednesday, 18 May. This news met with instant disapproval from Secretary of War Seddon, who vigorously endorsed his objection: "May I be pardoned for saying that this proposed delay seems to me fatal. By Wednesday our fate will in all probability be settled." Jefferson Davis strongly agreed with Seddon and expressed the hope that Whiting could arrive that very night, so that the attack could take place the next morning.[3] Acting under instructions from Davis and Seddon, Bragg drafted another message for Whiting, which unfortunately is not extant. According to Henry Wise, the telegram stated that the situation north of Richmond required that all troops, including Whiting's, converge upon the capital, because Richmond's safety was more important than Petersburg's.[4] Bragg then informed Beauregard of the dispatch to Whiting, and he suggested that the attack begin in the morning.[5]

At Drewry's Bluff Beauregard considered the idea of advancing the attack date. His superiors seemed to want an attack on the following morning as well as Whiting's arrival to join Beauregard beforehand, but these were mutually exclusive. There could be either an attack on Monday morning without Whiting or there would have to be a delay until Wednesday. The dilemma could only be resolved by returning to Beauregard's original proposal in which Whiting would not join Beauregard, but would move directly upon the Federal flank and rear. The Davis administration would have its immediate attack, while Beauregard could still fight the battle in the way he had initially envisioned.[6]

By 10:45 A.M. Beauregard had made up his mind. The attack would begin at daybreak the next morning, and Whiting would attack north toward the Federal rear from Petersburg. Instructions were drafted ordering Whiting to move during the night to Swift Creek with Wise's and Martin's Brigades, the remainder of Colquitt's Brigade, Dearing's cavalry, and twenty guns:

> At daybreak you will march to Port Walthall Junction, and when you hear an engagement in your front you will advance boldly and rapidly by the shortest road in the direction of heaviest firing, to attack enemy in rear or flank. . . . This revokes all former orders of movements.
> P.S.—I have just received a telegram from General Bragg, informing me that he has sent you orders to join me at this place. You need not do so, but follow to the letter the above instructions.[7]

Whiting's orders, accompanied by a rough draft of Beauregard's attack instructions to the units at Drewry's Bluff, were entrusted to Colonel Thomas Logan, a young officer serving temporarily on Beauregard's staff. Logan was to deliver the dispatches personally to Whiting by riding around the Federal left flank. In case he found it necessary to destroy the papers, he was informed of their contents in detail. Procuring an escort, Logan rode off before 11:00 A.M. on his circuitous journey through Chesterfield County.[8]

Aware that Jefferson Davis would not approve of the change in plans, Beauregard carefully composed a defense of his actions for the president. First he explained that Whiting could not possibly join him in time to take part in a Monday morning attack because the route around the Federal flank was thirty-four miles long. Then Beauregard bolstered his case with a telegram from Whiting forecasting an attack on Petersburg, a report from the Confederate Navy suggesting that Butler was being reinforced, and a statement that the Army of the James was fortifying its position in his front. Therefore, the offensive would begin in the morning "with the forces at present available here increased by Barton's brigade, as authorized by you. I have ordered Major General Whiting to co-operate with all his forces by attacking the enemy in rear from Swift Creek."[9] Colonel Samuel Melton of Beauregard's staff took the message to Richmond, where he delivered it personally to the president. Davis at once noted the change in Whiting's orders and commented that he had already prohibited such a course of action. Melton then informed the president that Beuaregard "upon a further examination . . . found his force sufficient; that his operations, therefore, did not depend upon making a junction with Whiting." Confronted with a *fait accompli* unless he wanted to postpone the offensive, Davis chose to allow Beauregard to have his way.[10]

In Petersburg, Whiting was becoming increasingly anxious. Convinced that the city was the real target of the Federal advance, no matter how much Butler feinted at Drewry's Bluff, he openly expressed his fears in a morning telegram to Beauregard and in a long letter to Bragg. With Kautz's cavalry deep in his rear, wrecking communication lines, Whiting believed that an attack on his position was imminent. Should an assault occur, he told Bragg, "it will not be probable that I can save the town—hardly the troops." Just before 11:00 a.m., a message from Beauregard arrived. This was not the dispatch handed Colonel Logan just fifteen minutes before, nor was it Beauregard's earlier message of the morning, since neither of these reached Petersburg for several hours. It was apparently Beauregard's order calling for Whiting to depart for Drewry's Bluff on Monday morning, which had been drafted the previous afternoon as a result of Beauregard's conference with Davis. Whiting acknowledged the message at 11:00 a.m.: "Time is rather short, but will do my best." He then wired Bragg, asking him to tell Beauregard that he would be at least halfway by Monday night.[11]

Orders in hand, Whiting began to prepare for the move. Henry Wise relinquished command of the First Military District to still another of the Confederacy's unemployed general officers, Brigadier General Raleigh Colston, then supplied his troops with sixty rounds of ammunition and five day's rations per man. Dearing's cavalry was recalled to garrison Petersburg until the arrival of Walker's Brigade from North Carolina. In order to meet Beauregard's timetable, Whiting fixed the time of his departure at 3:00 a.m., 16 May. Still unwell and burdened by what he considered to be the greatest of responsibilities, Whiting disregarded his need for rest and plunged into preparations for the next morning's advance.[12]

Between Whiting and Beauregard, the Army of the James lay quiescent after the planned dawn assault was abandoned. All along the lines there was little activity except for light skirmishing. On the left flank of the X Corps, Alfred Terry advanced Marston's brigade slightly, while several of his batteries commenced a slow desultory cannonade. Eastward, Turner's division received permission from Gillmore at noon to bring its supply trains forward and establish depots of issue. In the XVIII Corps affairs were equally languid. The steady rain that had been falling since the night of 11 May had dissipated into intermittent showers, so by carefully picking their spots the troops could occasionally lie in the sun and dry their uniforms. In Brooks's division the men of Burnham's brigade widened the fire-step they had cut in the face of the captured Confederate works and sought additional logs and boards to facilitate passage over the ditch. Across the turnpike in Weitzel's division, Wistar's and Heckman's brigades labored to improve their own makeshift breastworks.[13]

Brigadier General Charles Heckman, whose brigade guarded the right flank of the Army of the James, spent the early morning hours scouting toward the James River. Not far beyond his last regiment he stumbled upon a good road running deep into the Federal rear. Although the highway, known as the Old Stage Road, represented the quickest route back to the Federal base at Bermuda Hundred, it was completely unguarded, except for scattered pickets of the 2nd U.S. Colored Cavalry. Upon reporting his discovery to Godfrey Weitzel, Heckman was sent to corps headquarters to inform Baldy Smith. Although Smith was momentarily absent, Heckman found Butler there and told him of the unguarded road on the army's right. When Smith appeared, Heckman repeated his message. Although displeased that Heckman had gone outside the normal chain of command in making his report, Smith agreed to investigate the situation himself. He found not only the Old Stage Road unguarded but also a mile of relatively open ground stretching to the banks of the James River. To close the gap, Butler released to Smith's control the 21st Connecticut Infantry, which had just arrived at Bermuda Hundred, and the 8th Maine Infantry, one of Ames's regiments earmarked for the abortive morning attack. Until their arrival, Smith reinforced his right flank with two artillery batteries and another company of cavalry.[14]

Later in the day, Butler entertained Major General Philip Sheridan at the Friend house. With Sheridan were several of his officers, including Brigadier General James H. Wilson, Smith's friend and protégé. Responding to Butler's initial question about Grant's progress, Sheridan described the battle of the Wilderness and other events prior to his departure from the Army of the Potomac. Butler then asked how long it would take for Sheridan's command to be restored to peak fighting efficiency. According to Butler, Sheridan replied that seven or eight days were needed. Seizing this opening, Butler suggested that because Grant would have reached Richmond by then, Sheridan might just as well cross to Bermuda Hundred and there await the arrival of the Army of the Potomac. Sheridan demurred, promising only to clear the east bank of the river of torpedoes. Meanwhile, Wilson visited his old mentor Smith and received much confidential information regarding the internal affairs of the Army of the James. Sheridan also saw Smith privately during his visit, at which time Smith expressed his disgust at the tangled command relationships within the Army of the James. Smith requested that Grant be informed of the situation as soon as possible, and bluntly recommended that the campaign be terminated.[15]

Within the Confederate lines Beauregard spent the afternoon preparing a circular containing his battle plan for personal delivery to Generals Ransom, Hoke, and Colquitt. Beauregard wanted his chief subordinates to know their roles beforehand, so that any misunderstandings might be resolved at a 6:00 P.M. conference rather than on the battlefield the next morning. As outlined in the circular, Beauregard's army was to separate the Army of the James from its Bermuda Hundred base, then fall heavily upon it, capturing or destroying Butler's entire mobile force. Beauregard proposed to accomplish this goal by turning the Federal right via the Old Stage Road, while fixing the Federal center and left with holding attacks. [16]

According to the circular, Robert Ransom would be responsible for turning the Federal flank. To accomplish this task he would have Gracie's and Barton's Brigades from his own department, along with Lewis's and Terry's Brigades from North Carolina. Ransom was to transfer his 6,400 infantry to the Confederate left after nightfall, form them into two lines, and advance toward the enemy at daybreak. Once engaged, Ransom was to pivot on his right, roll up the Federal flank, and seize the spot where the Old Stage Road crossed Proctor's Creek. Supporting Ransom would be Lieutenant Colonel C. E. Lightfoot's Artillery Battalion (three batteries) and part of Colonel John Dunovant's 5th South Carolina Cavalry. [17]

Robert Hoke's task was to hold the attention of the Federal center and left with the 7,100 infantrymen of Hagood, Johnson, Clingman, and Corse. According to the plan, Hoke was to send a heavy line of skirmishers forward at daylight to drive in the Federal pickets. Meanwhile, his brigades would leave their trenches and form two assault waves with a 400-yard interval between them. As soon as Ransom was "fairly engaged," Hoke would advance with his four brigades. Supporting Hoke in his holding action would be the Washington Artillery Battalion, while Colonel John Baker's 3rd North Carolina Cavalry screened his right flank. [18] Five hundred yards in rear Alfred Colquitt would hold the 4,000 infantrymen of his own and Matt Ransom's Brigades on the turnpike as a general reserve. With Colquitt would be Captain S. T. Martin's Artillery Battalion and part of Colonel William Shingler's 7th South Carolina Cavalry. [19]

While their officers studied the plan, the troops lay within the works under constant fire from Federal snipers and random shots from the Federal artillery. At Fort Stevens, enfilading fire from some Federal guns on the turnpike drove part of Hagood's Brigade over the parapet and into the ditch to escape the rain of missiles. On Hagood's right, Johnson's Tennessee Brigade clung to its section of the works facing Burnham's skirmishers. Beyond Johnson, Clingman's North Carolinians extended the Confederate line to the right. West of Clingman, the brigades of Corse, Colquitt, and Matt Ransom completed the Confederate defensive alignment. During the day Colonel William Clarke, the new commander of Ransom's Brigade, was badly wounded and command of the unit devolved upon Colonel Leroy McAfee. In the 43rd North Carolina Infantry a soldier concluded his daily diary entry on a note of optimism: "Every body seems to think if we can drive the Yankees back this time that they will give it up, at least that the crisis of the country will have been passed and the most of the fighting will be over." [20]

Within the Federal position many soldiers sensed that the Army of the James had lost the initiative. On Gillmore's front Colonel Harris Plaisted was astonished to see his brigade's camp equipage transported to the front under division order.

Convinced that something unusual was happening inside the Confederate lines, Plaisted abruptly ordered the teamsters to take their loads to the rear, and began to issue extra ammunition and rations to his regiments. Like the men of the 7th New Hampshire Infantry of Hawley's brigade, Plaisted could see far down the railroad where trains seemed to be arriving regularly within the Confederate works. It was an ominous sign and, as the firing strangely began to slacken, the men of Terry's four brigades either improved their makeshift trenches or scratched out new ones. They were joined in their preparations by Alford's brigade of Turner's division. By contrast, many of the men in Turner's other brigade, Barton's, spent most of the day holding religious services.[21]

In the XVIII Corps, Burnham's brigade of Brooks's division labored all day to reverse the trenches they had occupied the previous morning. As evening neared, working parties collected lengths of telegraph wire from the turnpike and created an entanglement fifty yards in front of their position. Burnham's men had seen much riding to and fro within the Confederate lines and suspected that something was about to happen. Across the turnpike Wistar's brigade of Weitzel's division threw up relatively substantial breastworks of earth and logs, and finished by covering their front with some of the same wire that Brooks's division was stringing. Beyond Wistar, Heckman's brigade also created defenses of earth, logs, and boards. Unfortunately, Heckman's men failed to procure any of the telegraph wire the other units were using to protect their positions.[22] The wire itself had been Baldy Smith's idea, and he had suggested it to Brooks and Weitzel.[23]

Late in the afternoon, Smith, Weitzel, and Heckman crept out to the farmhouse of R. A. Willis, located on a slight rise several hundred yards to the right of Heckman's line and more than one hundred yards beyond the Federal pickets. All three officers agreed that the house should be occupied by a strong picket force after nightfall, in order to provide an early warning if the Confederates attacked from that direction. Upon his return, Smith told Butler that the XVIII Corps had no units available for a reserve in case of attack. Butler replied that three of Ames's regiments from Port Walthall Junction had been stationed at the Half-Way House as a general reserve. As darkness began to fall, the 21st Connecticut and 8th Maine, allocated to Smith during the morning for the purpose of covering the Old Stage Road, reported for duty. To make a place for the new arrivals, Heckman pulled his brigade out of line and shifted the temporarily attached 98th New York slightly to the left. The two new regiments were then deployed behind the defenses laboriously constructed by Heckman's four regiments. As they left their defensive handiwork, Heckman's men joked with the newcomers about building works for others to fight behind, then passed on through the woods to the right. At the same time, the artillery batteries that had covered the flank during the afternoon retired to the turnpike for the night.[24]

In their new positions Heckman's regiments found no works at all. Even with the extra units in line, only seven companies of Heckman's right regiment, the 9th New Jersey, were stationed beyond the Old Stage Road. With no more reinforcements available, Heckman had to make the best of the situation as he found it, and he once more ordered his regiments to entrench. This was a difficult task in the gathering darkness, without proper tools, and with muscles aching from the previous set of works constructed and left behind. As a result, in many instances the defensive preparations were half-hearted. This was particularly true in the sector of the 9th New Jersey, where the men had believed they were being relieved when the line was altered and were disgruntled upon learning the truth.[25]

After Heckman's shift, no further alterations were made in the positions held by Weitzel's division on the extreme right of the Army of the James. Beginning at the turnpike and extending to the east were the four regiments of Isaac Wistar's brigade, protected by a log-and-earth barricade and an entanglement of telegraph wire. Beyond Wistar's right were seven additional regiments, all under the control of Charles Heckman. First were the three temporarily attached units, the 21st Connecticut, 8th Maine, and 98th New York. All of these regiments were also covered by rough breastworks of earth and logs, but their front was not protected by wire. To the right of the 98th New York were the four original regiments of Heckman's brigade, the 25th, 27th, and 23rd Massachusetts, and the 9th New Jersey. These regiments had only begun to entrench and had no protective wire entanglements. In front of the 9th New Jersey there was a small stream and pond, and running along the front of the 23rd and part of the 27th Massachusetts was a slightly depressed wagon road. Otherwise there was nothing but the forest for protection. In front of the woods an open field stretched all the way to the ravine sheltering Kingsland Creek, beyond which lay rising ground and the enemy.[26]

At sundown Lieutenant Colonel James Stewart of the 9th New Jersey established Heckman's picket line. From each of the three attached regiments, Stewart ordered two companies to advance one hundred yards and spread out to form a chain of individual picket posts. These connected on their left with Wistar's pickets. From Heckman's original regiments Stewart drew four more companies. Three companies covered the front of the four regiments, while Captain Joseph Lawrence's Company H of the 9th New Jersey was posted in the Willis house. On Stewart's right, although not under his control, one company of the 8th Maine extended the infantry picket line toward the river. From there vedettes of Colonel George Cole's 2nd U. S. Colored Cavalry patrolled to the bank of the James.[27]

Within the Confederate works Beauregard made his final preparations for the next morning's offensive. At 4:00 P.M. he wired Bragg:

> I have already sent General Whiting his instructions to co-operate with me. Please telegraph him to follow them as delivered by Colonel Logan. Yours may conflict with mine.

At 6:00 P.M. he met with his division commanders for a final check of the plan. Colquitt was the only officer with whom he was really acquainted, but Hoke and Robert Ransom had good reputations, so Beauregard hoped for the best.[28] After dark Colquitt's and Matt Ransom's Brigades were withdrawn from the right of the Confederate line, and Hoke stretched his four brigades westward to fill the gap.

Colquitt then marched the two units back to their reserve positions on the turnpike. East of Fort Stevens, Robert Ransom stealthily moved his four brigades from the fortifications to the open ground north of Kingsland Creek. There Gracie's Alabama Brigade and Lewis's North Carolina Brigade took positions in the first line, while Terry's and Barton's Virginia Brigades occupied the second line. Ransom's troops were in position by 10:00 P.M. and the distribution of extra ammunition and rations began. In Terry's Brigade the company commanders were told of the task ahead and authorized to inform their men. This was a highly unusual procedure, and many of the troops did not credit the information they received. Others, who did, found it difficult to sleep.[29]

At 9:30 P.M. Beauregard telegraphed Bragg that Whiting's orders had been altered, although Bragg was doubtless already aware of the change. With all of his superiors formally notified of his new plan, Beauregard whiled away the hours before its execution by arranging details, such as guides for the attacking troops and the placement of railroad guards below Petersburg. Impatient for dawn to break, he then went outside to visit some of the men who would be advancing in a few hours. Touring Fort Stevens, he spoke to some of Hagood's South Carolinians and assured them they would not be confined behind earthworks much longer. At 10:00 P.M. Hagood himself went off to a meeting of Hoke's brigade commanders, one of a series of such conferences that took place throughout the night.[30]

Twelve miles away in Petersburg, Whiting was hindered in his preparations by a flood of contradictory orders. Throughout the day Whiting had assumed that he would begin his circuitous march to Drewry's Bluff on the following morning in order to arrive in time for the battle on Wednesday. Near nightfall, however, he had received Bragg's morning telegram calling upon him to abandon Petersburg and march with all his units to the defense of Richmond. This order was contrary to Whiting's granite-like conviction that Petersburg was vital to the safety of the capital and was the actual goal of the Army of the James. Calling to his headquarters both Roger Pryor and Henry Wise, Whiting had the two officers read Bragg's message. He then asked Wise for his opinion of the order. As Wise later recalled, he replied, "The man who issued this order ought to be shot, and the officer who executes it ought to be cashiered!" Whiting then asked if Wise would support him in disobeying Bragg's order and the fiery former governor of Virginia readily agreed. This account is contradicted by the testimony of Colonel Walter Harrison, who was temporarily serving on Whiting's staff and was also present at the meeting. According to Harrison, Bragg's order depressed and disgusted Whiting, but he nevertheless prepared to implement Bragg's wishes.[31]

No matter what Whiting had decided to do about Bragg's directive, he soon received further orders from Beauregard. Several hours after the arrival of Bragg's message, Henry Wise was again called to Whiting's headquarters, this time to read a dispatch from Beauregard. This was probably Beauregard's morning message advising Whiting to speed his departure for Drewry's Bluff. After discussing the situation, Whiting and Wise agreed to obey Beauregard's directive, although it would leave Petersburg almost as defenseless as if Bragg's order had been implemented. At 11:00 P.M. still another order from Beauregard arrived, in the hands of Colonel Logan. This was Beauregard's 10:45 A.M. order for Whiting to advance from Swift Creek directly against the Federal rear. Overjoyed at the latest change in plans, Whiting and Wise altered their preparations accordingly. At Swift Creek, D. H. Hill received a message from Whiting explaining the new course of action, along with the comment that "This suits better." At the same time, a telegram from Whiting was dispatched to Braxton Bragg: "All right. Got the orders I want now. Will try my best."[32]

Unaware of the trap set to close upon them, the Federal pickets in front of the Army of the James peered into the darkness. On the X Corps' front a brief charge by the Confederate pickets was repulsed easily by Hawley's brigade, while in the rear the surgeons of the 39th Illinois moved their equipment closer to the front. A mile away, soldiers in Brooks's division of the XVIII Corps, holding the old Confederate works in front of the Friend house, could hear a group of officers carousing at corps headquarters in their rear. Across the turnpike in Weitzel's division, two officers of the 98th New York Infantry consumed some cheese and crackers in a makeshift hut created from the remnants of a board fence, then retired for the night. All around them, cold and hungry, the men in the ranks sought sleep on the damp ground, thankful for the stillness that lay over the countryside.[33]

Sometime before 10:00 P.M. wisps of fog began to roll up from the river, making the already dark night even more impenetrable. At the Willis house beyond the picket line, Captain Lawrence's company of the 9th New Jersey watched quietly until suddenly the outpost was charged by a company of Confederate cavalry. Straining to find their targets in the swirling mist, the Federals unleased a volley that succeeded in driving off the attackers. Informed of the enemy activity around the Willis house, Heckman requested reinforcements from corps headquarters through his aide Lieutenant Richard Wheeler. The message bypassed Weitzel, and Smith claimed he never received it, but from somewhere Heckman received thirty cavalrymen. Because the ground in front of Heckman's troops was covered with numerous holes dug by the pickets, Lieutenant Colonel Stewart concluded that the horsemen would be useless in the darkness and sent them off toward the river.[34]

On the picket line the sentinels could hear sounds of trees being felled and the creaking of artillery wheels. Occasionally shots were exchanged across the no man's land separating the opposing lines. Now and then a hideous, bloodcurdling screech ripped through the fog, the effort of some Southerner to spoil the Yankees' peaceful dreams. Not long after midnight, the pickets covering the front of the 9th New Jersey were driven from their pits by more Confederate cavalry and cut off from their lines. To the west the pickets of Wistar's brigade lost contact with Heckman's men. Wistar and his staff spent several anxious hours creeping about in the underbrush trying to reconnect the line but met with no success. Word of the failure was dispatched to division headquarters, but no answer was returned.[35]

As the fog continued to cast its heavy blanket over the landscape, Captain Lawrence's men in the Willis house faced a new threat. Although the Federals had stationed themselves in the dwelling itself, the garden and outbuildings to the north were not occupied, and it soon became apparent that small groups of Confederates were creeping toward the house. During one of his trips to the front, Stewart advised Lawrence to push a few men forward to a fence beyond the garden, and Lawrence chose Private Henry Keenan for the task. Taking only one other man, Keenan crawled forward through the fog to the fence. As Keenan lay on the damp earth, the pickets of Heckman's brigade gave the general alarm three times because of threats of Confederate infiltration, the last time at 3:00 A.M., 16 May. None of these reports reached William F. Smith sleeping at the Friend house on the turnpike.[36] Unlike Henry Keenan and many more of the 18,590 Federal soldiers scattered from Drewry's Bluff to Port Walthall Junction, Baldy Smith passed the night peacefully.[37]

NOTES

1. *O.R.A.*, 36, pt. 2, 48, 115, 776–777, 805–807.

2. Williams, *Beauregard*, 94; Beauregard to Hill, Beauregard to Whiting, and Beauregard to Dearing, all 7:00 A.M., 15 May 1864, Official Telegrams, 22 April–9 June 1864, Beauregard Papers, LC; Roman, *Military Operations*, 2:217.

3. Beauregard to Bragg, 6:45 A.M., 15 May 1864, Official Telegrams, 22 April–9 June 1864, Beauregard Papers, LC; Roman, *Military Operations*, 2:560; *O.R.A.*, 36, pt. 2, 1004.

4. Harrison, *Pickett's Men*, 126; Wise MS, Beauregard Papers, LC. Beauregard himself annotated Wise's account and after Wise's summary of the message wrote "Correct—GTB." Although Wise stated that the message was dated 14 May, it is much more likely that Bragg sent the dispatch on 15 May as a result of Davis's and Seddon's concern that Beauregard's attack would be delayed. Cf. Bragg to Beauregard, *O.R.A.*, 51, pt. 2, 934. Much controversy later ensued regarding Bragg's order. *O.R.A.*, 36, pt. 2, 859–860. See also Freeman, *Lee's Lieutenants*, 3:485n, and Henry A. Wise to D. H. Hill, 31 May 1864, D. H. Hill Papers, VSL.

5. *O.R.A.*, 51, pt. 2, 934.

6. Beauregard to Bragg, 15 May 1864, Official Telegrams, 22 April–9 June 1864, Beauregard Papers, LC; *O.R.A.*, 51, pt. 2, 934.

7. Beauregard to Whiting, 15 May 1864, Official Telegrams, 22 April–9 June 1864, Beauregard Papers, LC; *O.R.A.*, 36, pt. 2, 200; Roman, *Military Operations*, 2:203–204; Beauregard, "Drury's Bluff," 252–253.

8. T. M. Logan to Beauregard, 2 January 1882, in Roman, *Military Operations*, 2:557–558; Beauregard, *Battles and Leaders*, 4:200; Beauregard, "Drury's Bluff," 253; Roman, *Military Operations*, 2:217–220; *O.R.A.*, 36, pt. 2, 256.

9. *O.R.A.*, 51, pt. 2, 1077; Roman, *Military Operations*, 2:218.

10. Davis, *Rise and Fall*, 2:513; *O.R.A.*, 51, pt. 2, 951. The quotation is Davis's and Beauregard took great pains, in Roman, *Military Operations*, 2:218–220, to prove that Melton could not have said such a thing. Apparently Beauregard had argued in his previous meeting with Davis that he could not attack the Federals without the aid of Whiting's force. Davis must have interpreted this to mean there would be no attack until after Whiting had joined Beauregard. To soften the blow of the new orders upon Davis, Beauregard probably authorized Melton to say that Beauregard no longer required Whiting's junction with him before the battle, although he was still counting heavily on Whiting's participation.

11. *O.R.A.*, 36, pt. 2, 1005–1007; Whiting to Beauregard, 15 May 1864, Beauregard Papers, NCDAH.

12. *O.R.A.*, 36, pt. 2, 1007–1009.

13. *O.R.A.*, 36, pt. 2, 42, 134–135, 157, 807; Thompson, *Thirteenth New Hampshire*, 291–292; Cunningham, *Adirondack Regiment*, 112; Walter S. Clemence Memoranda, 15 May 1864, NCC; Haynes, *Second New Hampshire* (2), 224; Valentine, *Story of Co. F*, 112; Derby, *Bearing Arms*, 250; Drake, *Ninth New Jersey*, 189.

14. Heckman, quoted in Derby, *Bearing Arms*, 249–250; Heckman, quoted in Drake, *Ninth New Jersey*, 205; *O.R.A.*, 36, pt. 2, 116, 143; Smith, *Battles and Leaders*, 4:210. Smith blamed Butler totally

for the situation on the right. Smith to W. P. Derby, 30 March 1883, quoted in Derby, *Bearing Arms*, 288.

15. *O.R.A.*, 36, pt. 2, 798, 803; Butler, *Butler's Book*, 653, 655–656; Wilson, *Old Flag*, 1:416; Memorandum, 8 January 1879, Butler Papers, LC; Smith, *Battles and Leaders*, 4:212. The meeting between Sheridan and Smith was unknown to Butler until years later. Butler, *Butler's Book*, 654n.

16. *O.R.A.*, 36, pt. 2, 199–201; Roman, *Military Operations*, 2:205; Beauregard, *Battles and Leaders*, 4:200–201.

17. *O.R.A.*, 36, pt. 2, 200–201, 1004–1005; Roman, *Military Operations*, 2:204; Beauregard, *Battles and Leaders*, 4:200–201; Beauregard, "Drury's Bluff," 253. The figure given in the text represents the aggregate present, a category that includes noncombatants of all descriptions. In terms of effective infantry strength (men actually carrying muskets), Ransom could probably deploy little more than 5,000 men. (Two of his four brigades were each lacking a regiment.) The attached artillery and cavalry units added 860 men to the total. *O.R.A.*, 33:1201; *O.R.A.*, 36, pt. 2, 254, 988; Charles T. Loehr, "Battle of Drewry's Bluff," *Southern Historical Society Papers* 19 (1891):102. Attempts at strength determination are usually very inexact, consisting as they must of a combination of outdated figures and modern estimates. For discussions of this problem see Thomas L. Livermore, *Numbers and Losses in the Civil War in America: 1861–65*, Reprint ed. (Bloomington: Indiana University Press, 1957), 66–70, and Dowdey, *Lee's Last Campaign*, 379–380. Both Livermore, *Numbers and Losses*, 113–114, and Humphreys, *Virginia Campaign*, 150n, give slightly different figures for all three Confederate divisions.

18. *O.R.A.*, 36, pt. 2, 201, 236–237, 1004–1005; Roman, *Military Operations*, 2:204; Beauregard, *Battles and Leaders*, 4:201; Beauregard, "Drury's Bluff," 253. Hoke's infantry strength is also stated in terms of the aggregate present. His effective strength was approximately 6,100 muskets. Artillery and cavalry contingents added 830 men to the total. *O.R.A.*, 33:1201; *O.R.A.*, 36, pt. 2, 205, 254, 1010, pt. 3, 817, 819.

19. *O.R.A.*, 36, pt. 2, 201, 1005; Roman, *Military Operations*, 2:204–205; Beauregard, *Battles and Leaders*, 4:201; Beauregard, "Drury's Bluff," 254. Like Ransom's and Hoke's divisions, Colquitt's infantry strength is given as the aggregate present. Effective infantry strength was an estimated 3,700. Attached artillery and cavalry units added 500 more men to the total. *O.R.A.*, 33:1201; *O.R.A.*, 36, pt. 2, 205, 988, pt. 3, 817, 819.

20. Hagood, *Memoirs*, 235; *O.R.A.*, 36, pt. 2, 247, 1010; William H. S. Burgwyn Diary, 15 May 1864, NCDAH; Clark, ed., *North Carolina Regiments*, 2:285, 3:353; Edward Phifer to his mother, 29 May 1864, Phifer Family Papers, SHC; Cary Whitaker Diary, 15 May 1864, SHC.

21. *O.R.A.*, 36, pt. 2, 48, 79, 100; *O.R.A.*, 5, pt. 1, 1243; Little, *Seventh New Hampshire*, 250; Clark, *Thirty-Ninth Illinois*, 180, 184; De Forest, *Random Sketches*, 242; Clark, *Iron Hearted Regiment*, 115–116.

22. *O.R.A.*, 36, pt. 2, 131, 134–135, 140, 157; Thompson, *Thirteenth New Hampshire*, 291–292, 319; Cunningham, *Adirondack Regiment*, 112–113; Haynes, *Second New Hampshire* (2), 224–225; Wistar, *Autobiography*, 451; Valentine, *Story of Co. F*, 112; Derby, *Bearing Arms*, 269.

23. Much controversy arose regarding this first large-scale use of wire entanglements in warfare. (A smaller amount of wire had been strung around the Federal Fort Sanders during the Knoxville Campaign and played some part in the Confederate repulse there on 29 November 1863.) Butler claimed that the inspiration for the use of the telegraph wire came from Godfrey Weitzel (Butler, *Butler's Book*, 658), but Weitzel and William F. Smith both agreed that the wire was emplaced as the result of a suggestion by Smith (*O.R.A.*, 36, pt. 2, 150–152; Weitzel to W. P. Derby, 2 May 1883, and Smith to W. P. Derby, 30 March 1883, both quoted in Derby, *Bearing Arms*, 289; Smith, *From Chattanooga to Petersburg*, 163; Smith, *Battles and Leaders*, 4:210). Smith had been in Tennessee during the Knoxville Campaign and may have learned of the use of wire at Fort Sanders at that time.

Weitzel wrote in his battle report that Heckman had received the order regarding the wire (*O.R.A.*, 36, pt. 2, 152), but Heckman stated years later that he had "no recollection of any order for the use of wire." Heckman to W. P. Derby, 23 March 1883, quoted in Derby, *Bearing Arms*, 290. If Heckman had received Weitzel's order, he transmitted it no further, for two of his regimental commanders, the colonels of the 25th and 27th Massachusetts Regiments, were positive that they "received no order for the use of wire." Ibid., 291. Heckman did recall that he attempted to procure a supply of wire on his own initiative on the morning of 15 May, but he was unable to obtain any. This was contradicted by Butler who stated that several miles of wire were available for the taking. Butler, *Butler's Book*, 658. Smith in *Battles and Leaders*, 4:210n, absolved Heckman of blame by agreeing that the wire was in short supply and was therefore allocated to those units closest to the Confederates. Several years later, however, in his book *From Chattanooga to Petersburg*, 163, Smith reversed his position and stated explicitly that Heckman had failed to obey Weitzel's order regarding the wire.

24. Smith, *Battles and Leaders*, 4:210; Butler, *Butler's Book*, 658; *O.R.A.*, 36, pt. 2, 116, 129, 131, 143–144, 148, 157, 164; Denny, *Wearing the Blue*, 289; Valentine, *Story of Co. F*, 112–113; Walter S. Clemence Diary and Memoranda, 15 May 1864, NCC; Clark, *My Experience*, 61; Emmerton, *Twenty-Third Massachusetts*, 183; Derby, *Bearing Arms*, 267–268; Drake, *Ninth New Jersey*, 189–191; Kreutzer, *Ninety-Eighth New York*, 191; *Twenty-First Connecticut*, 181, 189, 202.

25. Drake, *Ninth New Jersey*, 190–192, 201; Foster, *New Jersey and the Rebellion*, 241; Valentine, *Story of Co. F*, 113; Emmerton, *Twenty-Third Massachusetts*, 183; Derby, *Bearing Arms*, 268.

26. Wistar, *Autobiography*, 451; *O.R.A.*, 36, pt. 2, 131, 151; Emmerton, *Twenty-Third Massachusetts*, 183–184; Putnam, *Story of Company A*, 276; Derby, *Bearing Arms*, 268.

27. *O.R.A.*, 36, pt. 2, 129, 159, 160, 161, 195; Derby, *Bearing Arms*, 269; *Twenty-First Connecticut*, 181; Henry Keenan, quoted in Drake, *Ninth New Jersey*, 353.

28. *O.R.A.*, 51, pt. 2, 934; Roman, *Military Operations*, 2:203, 560.

29. *O.R.A.*, 36, pt. 2, 212, 236–237; Loehr, *First Virginia*, 46; Johnston, *Four years*, 305-309; Jones, *Surry Light Artillery*, 186–187; Edwin Baker Loving Diary, 15 May 1864, VSL; Johnston, *Confederate Boy*, 249-251; Morgan, *Reminiscences*, 195–196; Shaver, *Sixtieth Alabama*, 51; John U. Sumpter, "Fighting that Was Close by Us. One Who Was There Tells About the Battle of Drewry's Bluff—Many Errors Corrected," *Southern Historical Society Papers* 37 (1909):181–182.

30. Beauregard to Bragg, 9:30 P.M., 15 May 1864, Official Telegrams, 22 April–9 June 1864, Beauregard Papers, LC; Roman, *Military Operations*, 2:560; *O.R.A.*, 51, pt. 2, 934; Beauregard to Major F. W. Smith, 15 May 1864, and Beauregard to Wise, 15 May 1864, both in Letter Book, April–May 1864, Beauregard Papers, LC; Hagood, *Memoirs*, 235–236.

31. Wise MS, Beauregard Papers, LC; Henry Wise, quoted in B. H. Wise, *Life of H. A. Wise*, 337–338; Harrison, *Pickett's Men*, 126. Harrison's testimony is indirectly corroborated by telegrams from Whiting to Bragg and Beauregard. *O.R.A.*, 36, pt. 2, 1006; *O.R.A.*, 51, pt. 2, 935.

32. Wise MS, Beauregard Papers, LC; Henry Wise, quoted in B. H. Wise, *Life of H. A. Wise*, 338; Logan to Beauregard, 2 January 1882, quoted in Roman, *Military Operations*, 2:558; Beauregard, *Battles and Leaders*, 4:200n; Harrison, *Pickett's Men*, 126–127; *O.R.A.*, 36, pt. 2, 256, 1009; *O.R.A.*, 51, pt. 2, 935. Whiting claimed that Logan had arrived at 11:00 A.M., but this must have resulted from a copying error.

33. *O.R.A.*, 36, pt. 2, 43; Clark, *Thirty-Ninth Illinois*, 180–181; Cunningham, *Adirondack Regiment*, 113; Kreutzer, *Ninety-Eighth New York*, 191; *Twenty-First Connecticut*, 189.

34. *O.R.A.*, 36, pt. 2, 116, 152, 161–162; Emmerton, *Twenty-Third Massachusetts*, 182–183; James Stewart, quoted in Drake, *Ninth New Jersey*, 201, and Henry Keenan, quoted in same, 353. Many years later, William F. Smith claimed to have been at the Willis house until midnight, after which he returned to his headquarters in bright moonlight. This testimony, with regard both to the time of Smith's presence and to the night's visibility, is totally at variance with all other sources and must be discounted. Smith, *Battles and Leaders*, 4:210; Smith to W. P. Derby, 30 March 1883, quoted in Derby, *Bearing Arms*, 288.

35. Derby, *Bearing Arms*, 269; Valentine, *Story of Co. F*, 113–114; Drake, *Ninth New Jersey*, 191–192; Walter S. Clemence Memoranda, 15 May 1864, NCC; *O.R.A.*, 36, pt. 2, 160–161; Wistar, *Autobiography*, 451.

36. Henry Keenan, quoted in Drake, *Ninth New Jersey*, 353–354; *O.R.A.*, 36, pt. 2, 116, 152, 157, 162, 265.

37. Ironically, Federal strength on 16 May 1864 is more difficult to compute than Confederate, because Federal casualties for the entire month of May are lumped together. The strength of the Army of the James on 16 May can be computed by taking the strength figures for 31 May 1864 (*O.R.A.*, 36, pt. 3, 427) plus casualties 5–31 May (*O.R.A.*, 36, pt. 2, 13–18) minus losses 5–15 May (6 May—68, 7 May—305, 9 May—145, 10 May—280, 12–15 May—approximately 900) multiplied by 0.88. (Of the fifty infantry regiments in the Army of the James, six, or 0.12, had been left to guard the Bermuda Hundred entrenchments. Of the forty-four available infantry regiments, thirty-nine were in line, three were in reserve, and two were at Port Walthall Junction.) Using "aggregate present" figures, Butler's mobile force (excluding the Bermuda Hundred garrison, Hincks's division at City Point, and Kautz's cavalry) totalled appxoimately 21,000. Since most regiments had left camp guards and other detailed men behind, as well as their sick, the figure used in the text is the number "present for duty." If Thomas L. Livermore's measurement of effective strength (93 percent of those present for duty) is utilized, Butler's effective strength was 17,289. Livermore, *Numbers and Losses*, 113, places Butler's effective strength at 15,800, but he appears to have omitted consideration of the Negro cavalry regiments serving with the infantry, and to have computed casualties differently.

13

The Battle of Drewry's Bluff—First Phase
16 May 1864

At 2:00 A.M., 16 May, Confederate officers roused their sleeping troops. By then the fog rolling up from the river had seeped into every hollow, covering everything in a thick white mist. The clammy dampness of the fog, coupled with the darkness and knowledge of the task ahead, depressed many of Robert Ransom's men as their officers guided them toward their designated positions. Visibility was nil; a man standing in the center of his regiment could see neither end of the regimental line, and the presence of adjacent units was indicated only by muffled commands uttered by strange voices or by the shuffling of hundreds of feet. Reaching the ravine of Kingsland Creek, the men piled their blanket rolls on the ground, then crossed to the south side of the stream. There final adjustments in the formations were made. As the troops waited in the fog they could hear the guns of Lightfoot's Artillery Battalion being drawn through the woods until they were halted just in rear of the infantry.[1]

Not long after 4:00 A.M., a faint gray tinge in the sky heralded the coming of dawn, although on the ground the fog continued to limit visibility to fifteen yards. All along the line regimental and company commanders checked the alignment of their troops, while junior officers and sergeants took their positions in the rear as file closers. At 4:45 A.M., Major General Robert Ransom ordered his division to advance. On the left the command was passed to Brigadier General Archibald Gracie, whose stentorian voice reverbrated down the ravine: "Skirmishers forward, march! second the battalion of direction; battalions forward; guide right, march!" As the Alabamians swarmed up the slope they were joined on their right by Lewis's North Carolinians, while the two Virginia brigades brought up the rear. Ahead, skirmishers probed ghostlike through the mist, seeking the enemy's pickets.[2]

Directly in line with Gracie's advancing left flank stood the Willis house, garrisoned by Company H of the 9th New Jersey Infantry. Lying behind a fence at the rear of the garden was Private Henry Keenan. As the Confederate advance began, Keenan suddenly detected indistinct forms filtering around the fence and nearby outbuildings. Firing his gun, he crawled rapidly back to the house and reported to his commanding officer. Captain Joseph Lawrence then ordered Keenan

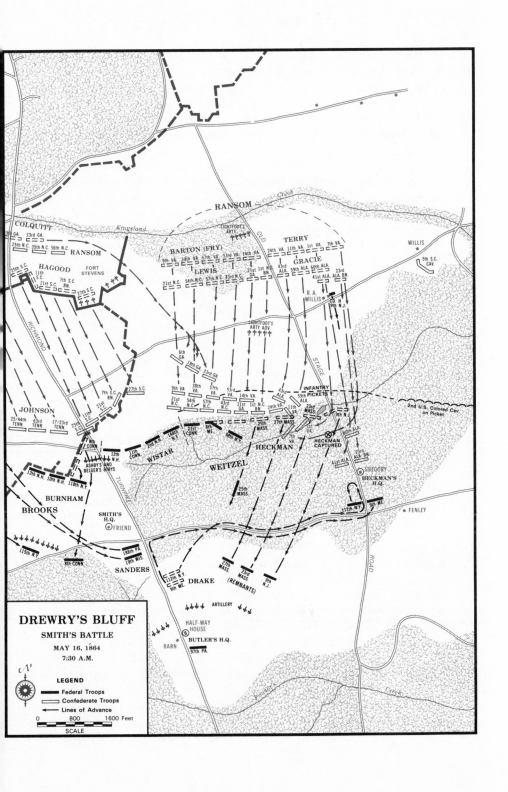

COLQUITT

RANSOM

9th GA. 23rd GA.
25th N.C. 35th N.C. 56th N.C.
RANSOM

HAGOOD
25th S.C.
11th S.C.
7th S.C. BN
21st S.C.
27th S.C.

FORT STEVENS

Kingsland

LIGHTFOOT'S ARTY.

BARTON (FRY)
9th VA. 38th VA. 57th VA. 53rd VA. 14th VA.
21st N.C. 54th N.C. 57th N.C. 43rd N.C.

LEWIS

TERRY
24th VA. 11th VA. 1st VA. 7th VA.
7th N.C. 1st N.C. BN

GRACIE
43rd ALA. 59th ALA. 60th ALA.
41st ALA. ALA. BN 23rd

WILLIS

5th S.C. CAV.

R. A. WILLIS

CO. H 9th N.J.

6th GA.
19th GA. 23rd GA.

LIGHTFOOT'S ARTY ADV

9th VA.
38th VA. 57th VA. 53rd VA. 14th VA.
21st N.C. 54th N.C. 57th N.C. 43rd 21st 1st N.C. N.C. GA. N.C. BN
24th VA. 11th VA.

43rd ALA.

INFANTRY 59th PICKETS ALA.

23rd MASS.

CO. H 9th N.J.

2nd U.S. Colored Cav. on Picket

JOHNSON
25/44th TENN. 63rd TENN. 17/23rd TENN.
11th S.C.
21st S.C.
25th S.C.
8th CONN.

12th N.H.
11th CONN.
2nd N.H.
21st CONN.
8th ME.
3rd N.Y.

WISTAR

WEITZEL

25th MASS.
27th MASS.
7th VA.

HECKMAN

60th ALA.

HECKMAN CAPTURED

GREGORY

HECKMAN'S H.Q.

23rd ALA. BN
41st ALA.

13th N.H. 10th N.H. 118th N.Y.
ASHBY'S AND BELGER'S B'RYS

TURNPIKE

25th MASS.

112th N.Y. 9th ME.

FENLEY

BURNHAM

BROOKS

SMITH'S H.Q.
FRIEND

115th N.Y.

8th CONN.

188th PA.
19th WIS.

SANDERS

112th N.Y.
9th ME.

DRAKE

27th MASS.
23rd MASS.
8th N.J.

(REMNANTS)

ARTILLERY

HALF-WAY HOUSE

BARN

BUTLER'S H.Q.

97th PA.

DREWRY'S BLUFF

SMITH'S BATTLE

MAY 16, 1864

7:30 A.M.

N

LEGEND

Federal Troops
Confederate Troops
Lines of Advance

0   800   1600 Feet

SCALE

and the rest of the company out of the house, a poor defensive position surrounded by fences, outbuildings, and the impenetrable fog, but matters were little better outside. Thereupon Keenan and the other pickets unanimously decided it was time to go, and they all scattered in the direction of the Federal lines.[3]

Within the Federal position, Heckman's regiments were alert, since picket firing had become general across the front. Picket supervisor James Stewart rushed forward through the fog to determine the cause of the firing. Meeting the pickets coming back, he was told the Confederates were advancing in force and the stream of bullets zipping through the mist corroborated their story. Stewart then returned to the brigade and joined his regiment. Behind him, the pickets in front of Heckman's seven regiments had abandoned their rifle pits and were making their way to safety. Until all of the pickets entered the lines, the regiments could not open fire for fear of hitting their own men. Soon the pickets appeared at the edge of the woods, where they halted briefly and then came within the works. Waiting a few seconds more for stragglers, the Federals then sent a thunderous volley into the mist.[4]

Once Gracie's and Lewis's men reached the top of the ravine, they found themselves in an open field that sloped slightly downward for 650 yards toward the Federals in the woods. The land was devoid of natural cover, but the dense fog provided concealment as the men advanced. Suddenly from out of the mist came the volley fired by Heckman's regiments. Withstanding the first fire, Gracie's men cheered and swept forward to the attack. On Gracie's right Colonel William Lewis's North Carolinians pressed ahead into an equally devastating fire from the 98th New York, 8th Maine, and 21st Connecticut. In the second line Terry's and Barton's regiments stumbled through the mist, trying desperately to maintain their alignment several hundred yards behind the leading brigades. Behind the Virginians Colonel Lightfoot moved his batteries to the edge of the plateau, where they went into action over the heads of the advancing infantry.[5]

The necessity of waiting for the pickets had forced the Federals to hold their fire until the charging Confederates were quite close. In the 23rd Massachusetts, the left of the regiment was given its target when a momentary rift in the fog disclosed hundreds of massed feet just a few yards in front, while the right was warned by sounds of men splashing through a small pond beyond the line. In both cases the Federals responded with a heavy volley, then loaded and fired individually as fast as they could, sending shot after shot into the mist. Behind the Federal line regimental commanders and Heckman himself passed slowly along, cautioning the men to fire low so as not to waste their ammunition. While encouraging his troops, Colonel Abraham Zabriskie of the 9th New Jersey early received a mortal wound in the throat. As Zabriskie, only twenty-three years old, was borne from the field, Lieutenant Colonel Stewart took command of Heckman's right regiment.[6]

In the face of the heavy fire from the aroused Federals, Ransom's attack began to stall. On the Confederate left, all attempts by Gracie to crack the Federal line failed. On Gracie's right, Lewis's Brigade found the going even more difficult. Lewis's regiments had gotten off to a slightly slower start than Gracie's and they had also become separated in the fog, with a wide gap opening in the center of the brigade. Lewis's left regiments advanced against the three attached regiments of Heckman's command and began to suffer fearfully from the accurate Federal fire. His remaining troops blundered to the right in the mist and ended up in front of Wistar's brigade. There they became entangled in the telegraph wire cunningly stretched a foot from the ground, and there they remained, firing blindly into the fog. In less than half an hour they were out of ammunition.[7]

If the impasse were to be broken, Gracie's men would have to do it. The left regiment of the brigade had begun its advance 200 yards east of the Old Stage Road, yet the Federal defenders there consisted of only seven companies of the 9th New Jersey. Although the fog hid this fact for a time, Gracie's left regiment eventually discovered that the Federal flank could be turned. Taking heavy casualties, the 41st Alabama began to edge around the opposing Jerseymen. To counter this threat, Lieutenant Colonel Stewart bent back the three right companies of his regiment. This checked the Confederates briefly, although they did not slacken their fire. As a result, casualties became heavy in Stewart's command, among them Captain Lawrence, whose company had begun the battle, and Private Henry Keenan.[8]

Soon Stewart found that he was still in danger of being flanked and once more he altered the direction of his three right companies. At this juncture Charles Heckman arrived on the scene. Told by Stewart that the regiment had suffered heavily, was almost out of ammunition, and was being attacked on three sides, Heckman ordered the 9th New Jersey to retreat. As the general disappeared into the mist and smoke drifting among the trees, the Jerseymen fell back singly or in small groups, with the Alabamians pressing hard behind them. Fearing capture of the regiment's national and state colors, the color bearers ripped the flags from the staffs and stuffed them into their shirts before making their way to the rear. Nor did the retreating men stop until they emerged from the woods into a large field. Behind them, two companies west of the road did not receive the order to retreat and they remained in position until advancing Confederates ordered them to surrender. Refusing this "rude and ill-mannered request," the companies broke and fled rearward through the woods until they were captured by a Confederate line-of-battle. With their retreat, the Old Stage Road was left wide open.[9]

The success of his left regiment was unknown to Archibald Gracie, who saw only that the rest of his brigade had suffered heavy casualties, yet had made no headway. Even as the 41st Alabama was entering the position just vacated by the 9th New Jersey, Gracie's right regiments were lying down, contenting themselves with firing into the fog toward the Federal line. Riding among the troops, Gracie realized that his men had gone as far as they could without help and he rode back toward Ransom's second line in search of Colonel William Terry. Terry's men were waiting several hundred yards to the rear of where Gracie's regiments had stalled. Unable to see what was happening because of the blinding fog, they had come under fire from stray bullets, and these random missiles were having an unnerving effect on the troops. Soon the wounded and stragglers of Gracie's command appeared, crawling or hobbling to safety. As they passed through the Virginians' lines, several cried, "Boys, go in there; they need you." Behind them came Gracie, "cursing and swearing like a sailor, apparently oblivious of the danger from the balls that were flying through the air, calling his men 'd———d cowards,' and using much strong language."[10]

Riding up to Terry, Gracie asked for the loan of a regiment or two to replace his faltering men. Rather than commit his units piecemeal, Terry preferred to use his entire brigade. Giving the necessary orders, he led the 7th, 1st, 11th, and 24th Virginia Regiments, less than 900 muskets all told, forward into the fog. In the 24th Virginia, Lieutenant Colonel R. L. Maury stepped forward of the line and walked backwards, sword in hand, while urging his men on. Here and there individual soldiers would run out in front of the advancing lines, turn their heads and release the wild scream known as the "rebel yell." The peculiar cheer was then taken up by hundreds of men in the ranks, as they plunged ahead, bodies bent slightly forward as if breasting a heavy wind. Almost at once they passed through the Alabamians lying on the ground, one of whom called out, "Hurry up, boys, they are tearing us all to pieces."[11]

Once beyond Gracie's men, Terry's regiments met varied opposition. On the right the 11th and 24th Virginia ran into the same hail of fire that had halted the Alabamians. The three Massachusetts regiments of Heckman's brigade were still standing to their work, and the Virginians could make no progress. Lieutenant Colonel Maury of the 24th was soon shot down, as were seven members of the color guard who followed him. Before the fight was over, the 24th Virginia lost more than half of the men it had taken into action. Yet, on the left there was an entirely different situation. The 7th Virginia on the flank swung wide, for it met no Alabamians, nor was it opposed by any Federals. The 1st Virginia advanced along the Old Stage Road beyond Gracie's position, also without opposition. After passing the pond on their right, the men of the 1st Virginia continued south for one hundred yards then swerved into the woods to the west. Almost at once in the mist and smoke-filled forest they came upon several small fires with untended coffee pots, an obvious clue that they were behind the Federal line.[12]

While the 1st Virginia sampled the Yankee coffee, the 7th Virginia met an officer wearing a nondescript overcoat riding through the woods. The officer was General Heckman, who had apparently lost his way in the fog. Realizing that he was surrounded by Confederates, Heckman attempted to bluff his way to safety by claiming to be one of Robert Hoke's staff officers. This and other ruses succeeded, until a sergeant of the 7th Virginia, suspicious of an officer alone in the woods, asked Heckman the number of his regiment. Unable to think of a reply, Heckman repeated his earlier bluffs, to which the sergeant answered, "You are my prisoner." Realizing there was no escape, Heckman surrendered, but asked to be permitted to yield his sidearms to a field officer. After Colonel C. C. Flowerree of the 7th Virginia accepted the weapons, Heckman was sent to the rear. There, after a friendly chat with Archibald Gracie, he was marched to Fort Darling, carried by boat to Richmond, and registered in Libby Prison by 9:00 A.M.[13]

After the rapid withdrawal of the 9th New Jersey, the last regiment on the right flank of the Army of the James was the 23rd Massachusetts. This regiment had already lost its commander, Lieutenant Colonel John Chambers, who had been mortally wounded while encouraging his men. Unable to find the major, the senior captain had assumed command and it was he who discovered the 1st Virginia Infantry pushing through the woods behind his position. At once he ordered the 23rd Massachusetts to fix bayonets, face to the rear, and fall back, but for many it was too late. As the Confederates rushed upon them, the Massachusetts troops lost all organization, with every man scrambling to reach safety on his own. The bearer of the national colors managed to carry away his standard, but the bearer of the state colors blundered into the arms of the Confederates. He joined fifty other members of the regiment as prisoners, while forty more lay in the woods killed and wounded, ninety-one casualties out of only 220 engaged.[14]

To the left of the 23rd stood the 27th Massachusetts. Its right flank was now open and it also found Confederate troops storming through the woods in its rear. In response to a demand for surrender, the Massachusetts men released a point-blank volley that struck down nine Virginians. But there was no time to reload and repeat the trick, because the Confederates were too close and the 7th Virginia was already crossing the Federal escape route. Disgusted at having been trapped in such ignominious fashion after repulsing three heavy charges against their front, many soldiers smashed their weapons against trees before being taken prisoner. Captured were 249 men, including Colonel Horace Lee, and all of the regiment's flags. Besides the captured, the 27th lost ten killed and forty-two wounded, while the survivors fled through the woods.[15]

The collapse of the 27th Massachusetts exposed the flank of the 25th Massachusetts on its left. Although Colonel Josiah Pickett was present, he was ill and had relinquished command to Lieutenant Colonel Orson Moulton. To meet the new threat, Moulton decided to face his regiment to the rear and, upon the approach of the Confederates, charge through them. This tactic was opposed by Colonel Frederick Wead of the 98th New York on Moulton's left, who favored forming the two regiments at right angles to their original position. Adamantly refusing Wead's suggestion, Moulton waited until the Confederates approached, then he ordered his regiment to reverse its front and charge. As Wead had expected, the Massachusetts men completely lost their organization in the fog and the smoke-filled forest, and before the regiment could escape it had lost 140 men. Its bold action, however, checked the Confederate advance and gave the 98th New York time to complete its change of front from north to east. There the New Yorkers held off further attacks and momentarily stabilized the right of the line.[16]

By the time Colonel Wead had halted the deterioration of the Federal right flank, approximately one hour had elapsed since Ransom's Division had begun its advance. With his brigades in confusion and with many of the troops out of ammunition, Ransom halted offensive operations while he sought more cartridges from the reserve train and fresh units from Beauregard.[17] There is no doubt that his four assaulting brigades had gotten themselves hopelessly out of position due to the fog, the relative inexperience of their brigade commanders, and the stubborn Federal resistance. On the left Gracie's Brigade had remained inert after pushing back the 9th New Jersey, while Terry's Brigade, which had advanced through the Alabamians, ended up with its right wing facing south and its left wing facing north.[18] On Ransom's right, Lewis's Brigade had split into two halves in the dense fog, and Colonel B. D. Fry had unknowingly led Barton's Brigade into the gap, where it blundered into the deadly volleys of the 8th Maine and 21st Connecticut. Falling back into the mist after taking heavy casualties, Fry's men had joined Lewis's North Carolinians in blindly blasting away their ammunition stocks.[19]

Ransom's halt gave the Federals additional time to reinforce the right flank of the Army of the James. Although Weitzel had been awake drinking coffee when Ransom's men burst out of the fog, Smith and Butler had been asleep at the Friend and Half-Way Houses, respectively. Awakened by the first heavy volleys, Smith rushed outside and discovered visibility to be minimal. Moving to the turnpike, he established his headquarters in a central location, reported the attack to Butler, and opened communication with Brooks and Weitzel. At 5:20 A.M., as Heckman's line was being assailed from two sides, Smith called to Butler for aid.[20] His message was relayed to Adelbert Ames, who was holding several regiments at the Half-Way House as a general reserve. In reply to Smith's call, Ames started the 112th New York Infantry toward the Federal right.[21]

While waiting for Ames's men to arrive, Smith ordered the corps artillery batteries and supply trains to be withdrawn so as to avoid capture in the fog. In the case of the guns, this decision seemed eminently sensible, if the further assumption were made that the fog was not going to dissipate any time soon. In the swirling mist the guns had few targets to fire upon and could be approached easily by the enemy. Once taken to the rear, however, the guns might find it difficult to return to action if the visibility improved. Giving no thought to the possible duration of the fog, Smith ordered the guns removed and the majority of them were taken to the rear.[22]

At the same time, Smith sent Colonel Arthur Dutton to Adelbert Ames for more reinforcements. The officer in immediate charge of Ames's regiments, Colonel J. C. Drake, had expected that the remaining regiment, the 9th Maine, would be needed and it was ready to move upon Dutton's arrival. Together Drake and Dutton guided the 9th Maine eastward along a side road leading to the Old Stage Road. Before reaching the junction they met the 112th New York retreating from the woods on their left. A few minutes earlier this regiment had pushed forward to the Gregory house on the Old Stage Road, where it had stumbled into an alert Confederate unit that had driven it back in disarray. The lieutenant colonel commanding the New Yorkers was mortally wounded and he had been carried by his frightened horse through the ranks, thus adding to the panic. As had already happened several times that morning, the senior captain was forced to assume command and rally the regiment.[23]

Realizing that possession of the Old Stage Road was vital for the Army of the James, Drake and Dutton began to deploy the 112th New York and the 9th Maine so as to control the crossroads ahead of them. They were joined by Godfrey Weitzel, who had learned with some difficulty of the debacle befalling Heckman and who now assumed the task of rebuilding the army's right flank. Seeing the shattered remnants of Heckman's brigade retreating out of the woods, Weitzel placed them under the command of the surviving senior officer, Colonel Josiah Pickett of the 25th Massachusetts. Pickett could find only four hundred men but he formed a provisional organization with those and took position with Drake's units guarding the crossroads. After deploying the reserves, Weitzel rode back to see what was happening to the rest of his line, where the sound of heavy firing could be heard through the fog. Before leaving, he warned Baldy Smith by messenger that there was some danger of Confederate movement around his right.[24]

In order to relieve the pressure on Smith, at 6:00 A.M. Butler wrote to Gillmore:

> The enemy has advanced from his works on our right and made a vigorous demonstration there; a rapid movement on the left would, I think, carry his lines in your front. Make it at once.[25]

This message presumed that Confederate strength was finite and that if Beauregard had concentrated heavily on Butler's right, the units facing Gillmore must be stretched thin and therefore were vulnerable. Delivery of the attack order took twenty minutes and its implementation would require some time longer. It remained to be seen whether the notoriously tardy Gillmore could bring his corps into action fast enough and hard enough to make a difference before Smith's fears for the army's escape route became the overriding consideration at Butler's headquarters.

Although Butler's attention had been concentrated on his flanks, the next Confederate blow had already begun to strike the Federal center. There Robert Hoke had spread Hagood's, Johnson's, Clingman's, and Corse's Brigades to cover the entire front from Fort Stevens to the railroad. Because his line was thin, Hoke was only supposed to demonstrate against the Federal center until Ransom had crushed the Federal right, after which he would advance in coordination with Ransom's continuing drive into the Federal rear. Hearing Ransom's assault begin at 4:45 A.M., Hoke opened fire with his artillery and sent his skirmishers forward. For more than an hour he waited in the fog, unable to discern either Ransom's exact location or the degree of his success. At last, around 6:00 A.M., Hoke ordered Hagood's and Johnson's Brigades to advance on both sides of the turnpike, supported by part of the Washington Artillery. Very soon both brigades were heavily engaged.[26]

Hoke sent his men forward in the expectation of connecting with Ransom's right, advancing triumphantly against a beaten enemy. But something had gone wrong; the Federals met by Hagood and Johnson showed no signs of being beaten. Finding an unshaken force in his front, Hoke thought he had no choice but to press forward with the two brigades in the hope of driving the Federals back. On the east side of the turnpike Hagood managed to gain the relative safety of a line of entrenchments that linked the outer works taken by the Federals and the inner line held by the Confederates. Just beyond, Hagood could see another line of works occupied by the enemy, and he hesitated to move against the second position without further orders.

When he arrived at Hagood's position, Hoke ordered Hagood to face his regiments westward, parallel with the turnpike, so as to meet Ransom's advance, which Hoke thought was nearby. Although Hagood believed Ransom's troops were yet some distance away, he reluctantly ordered the 27th, 11th, and 7th South Carolina to leave the works and wheel around toward the west. As Hoke turned away, the movement commenced, and immediately ran into trouble. The South Carolinians stumbled into Wistar's brigade, which had not been flanked, was full of fight, and whose front was covered by the entanglement of telegraph wire. The wire tripped a good many Confederates and hindered the movements of all of them, making them easier targets for the Federals. Fired into from three sides and taking fearful casualties, Hagood's regiments began to waver. Since it was quite obvious that Ransom's Division was not sweeping triumphantly toward the turnpike, Hagood recalled his entire command to the first line of works captured.[27]

West of the turnpike, Johnson's Brigade fared even worse than Hagood's men. Weak in numbers, the Tennesseans advanced against the larger Federal brigade of Hiram Burnham, which was also protected by a wire entanglement. Burnham's men were ready for the onslaught, and as soon as their pickets had cleared the front and targets could be distinguished in the fog, they poured a heavy volume of fire into the charging Tennesseans. Yet Johnson's men still came on until, reaching the wire, they stumbled and faltered. Even this did not stop the left of the brigade, which pressed forward near the turnpike against Burnham's right regiment, the 8th Connecticut. Fearing a flank move due to Hagood's maneuvers beyond the pike, the commander of the Connecticut troops withdrew his regiment some distance to the rear, leaving a gap in the line. Part of Johnson's command promptly occupied the vacant section of works, while the rest of the brigade hung on as best it could in front of Burnham.[28]

Just behind Burnham's right were Captain James Belger's Battery F, 1st Rhode Island Light Artillery, and Captain George Ashby's Battery E, 3rd New York Light Artillery. Neither of these batteries had received Smith's order to withdraw and the guns had remained in position until it was too late to remove all of them. Dueling first with the Washington Artillery and later with the onrushing infantry, the Federal gunners at length retired with whatever they could salvage. Left behind for want of horses were two twelve-pounder Napoleons and three twenty-pounder Parrotts. Two officers and several men of the 12th New Hampshire Infantry then dashed from cover and briefly manned one of the Napoleons. Forced to withdraw because of Confederate fire, the infantrymen dragged one of the heavy Parrotts rearward for a short distance, but were unable to save it from capture.[29]

Although the Federal artillery near the pike had been silenced, the two brigades Hoke had sent forward remained in danger. Both Hagood's left and Johnson's right were open to flank attacks that might force them to give up their hard-won toeholds near the Federal line. Relief for Hoke's left was already on the way, as Beauregard had responded to Robert Ransom's earlier call for reinforcements by detaching Colquitt's Brigade from the reserve at 6:30 A.M. and sending it to the left. Even before Colquitt arrived, Ransom had somehow noted the distress of Hagood's South Carolinians and had dispatched one of Lewis's regiments to their support. Although Hagood emphatically denied having seen either the North Carolina regiment or Colquitt's Georgians, these units apparently did engage the three Federal regiments on Wistar's right, thus closing the dangerous gap developing between Ransom and Hoke.[30]

With his left flank reasonably secure, Hoke turned his attention to Bushrod Johnson's Tennesseans, who were hanging on grimly west of the turnpike in the face of heavy fire from Burnham's Federals. Because of the withdrawal of the 8th Connecticut, some of Johnson's men had been able to occupy a short section of the works near the pike, but the Federals were only a few yards away around a bend in the line. The position appeared untenable for the Confederates and a call was made for the 17th/23rd Tennessee to surrender. The offer was vehemently refused by the majority, but several stragglers in a ditch raised a white flag. With cries of "Tear it down" ringing in his ears, a lieutenant ran over and snatched away the offending banner, at the cost of a disabling wound. To the right of the 17th/23rd, fifty men of the 25th/44th Tennessee did surrender. With two commanding officers shot down, command of the regiment devolved upon a captain who strove to protect his right flank from groups of Federals persistently trying to enfilade his line.[31]

Realizing he was in danger of losing his brigade, Johnson called loudly for help. Hoke was reluctant to send reinforcements from his two remaining brigades, since he wished to use Clingman's and Corse's troops to try to turn the Federal left flank. To relieve the pressure on Johnson, two regiments from Matt Ransom's Brigade in reserve were released to Hoke by Beauregard. The North Carolinians went forward yelling wildly, but they had been mistakenly placed by their guide and consequently veered too far to the right to be of any great service to Johnson. Crashing into what probably was Barton's brigade of Turner's division, they drove the Federals briefly out of a slight line of works, but then were themselves flanked and forced into a disorganized retreat to their starting point.[32]

Finding that Johnson's Tennesseans were still without support, Hoke reluctantly sent forward two regiments of Clingman's Brigade. These two units also miscarried on the fog-shrouded field, forcing Beauregard to order Hoke to commit the rest of Clingman's Brigade and Corse's as well. Just before the charge, Corse's Brigade was strengthened by the 17th Virginia Infantry, which had just reached the field after defending Flat Creek Bridge against Kautz's cavalry. Both brigades advanced with spirit, but the effort was sadly lacking in coordination. Led by staff officer William Burgwyn, the 51st North Carolina routed the Federals from two positions before it was hit hard by counterattacks. Without support, the 51st was forced to give ground. Because Corse feared an attack on his open right flank and Clingman was unable to connect with any friendly troops on his left, both brigades fell back exhausted almost to their original positions. Although it was just midmorning, Clingman's and Corse's retirement signaled the end of Confederate offensive operations on Beauregard's front.[33]

While Hoke mounted his piecemeal assaults against the Federal center and Robert Ransom realigned his disorganized brigades, Baldy Smith was losing his nerve. His inability to survey the field because of the fog had so rattled Smith that he could think of little except covering his route of retreat to the Bermuda Hundred base. Actually, only Heckman's four regiments on the extreme right had been crushed, while the remaining seven regiments of Weitzel's division were still holding their ground east of the turnpike. West of the highway Burnham's brigade of Brooks's division was maintaining its position, while Brooks's other brigade, Sanders's, had been moved behind Burnham as a reserve. Thus ten regiments were still firmly holding the original XVIII Corps line, with two more in reserve, and even on the threatened right flank, two fresh regiments and the survivors of Heckman's shattered command were guarding the Old Stage Road.[34]

Blinded by the fog, Smith conjured up visions of disaster striking on his right. Although Ransom's disorganized infantry was not pressing beyond Heckman's original position, his cavalry did probe the new Federal line along the Old Stage Road. Apparently these probes prompted Godfrey Weitzel's passing reference to Confederate activity on his right flank in one of his early morning dispatches to Smith. Although Weitzel gave no more thought to what he probably considered a minor threat, Smith reasoned that a new Confederate assault was imminent against the regiments holding the Old Stage Road. This danger, coupled with Hoke's assaults, caused Smith at last to order a withdrawal. At 7:45 A.M. Brooks was ordered to retire slowly, while maintaining contact with Weitzel's men falling back east of the pike. Weitzel received a similar message as he returned to his headquarters after completing the deployment of Drake's regiments on his right. Both officers sent the order forward to the troops still vigorously defending themselves.[35]

The three regiments formerly attached to Heckman had meanwhile been holding their own as the right flank of the original XVIII Corps line, although the 98th New York and 8th Maine had had to maneuver slightly in order to stand their ground. Unfortunately, these three regiments had no central direction after Heckman's capture and they acted independently during the retreat. Although Wistar's brigade still had its commander, it also retired independently of the three regiments on its right. Wistar's men had repelled every attack upon their line with the aid of the wire and were greatly displeased at being ordered to retreat, yet the command was peremptory and Wistar obeyed. Hagood's South Carolinians were not sorry to see the Federals depart and did not molest them except by means of sporadic long-range rifle fire. Coupled with the disorganization inherent in the retreat through the foggy woods, this fire served to aid the escape of many of the Confederates taken prisoner by Wistar.[36]

As Weitzel's seven regiments disengaged and made their way rearward through the woods, the fog finally lifted, giving Smith a better view of the field of action. Realizing that he had been too hasty in ordering a precipitate retreat, Smith countermanded the order, but what was done could not be undone so easily. When the new order reached Weitzel he tried to reverse the flow of his troops, which resulted in considerable confusion. Only Wistar's brigade was well enough in hand to advance again, and only two of its regiments could be readily turned around. Believing that an advance with such a small force was futile, Wistar ordered the retreat to continue. To cover the retirement, he detached the 11th Connecticut and 2nd New Hampshire Regiments and sent them back to the brigade's original position. Unexpectedly, the units reoccupied their defenses near the turnpike without difficulty and even managed to spike with horseshoe nails several of the abandoned cannon standing in the road.[37]

Their mission accomplished, the New Englanders rejoined their parent unit. By this time Wistar's brigade, as well as the 21st Connecticut, 8th Maine, and 98th New York, had emerged from the woods into the clearing that stretched from the Half-Way House to the crossroads on the Old Stage Road. There Weitzel organized the new defensive line for his division. Wistar retained his position as Weitzel's left brigade, and Colonel Wead of the 98th New York was given a provisional brigade composed of his own regiment, the 8th Maine, the 21st Connecticut, and any fragments of Heckman's old command that could be found. Throughout the rest of the morning this position was perfected and strengthened with a few artillery pieces. The Old Stage Road, which had so concerned Smith, was at last secured.[38]

The order that brought Weitzel's division back had also been sent to Brooks west of the turnpike. At 8:00 A.M., as the fog was dissipating, Brooks sent a staff officer to Burnham's brigade with the order to withdraw. Although the unauthorized retreat of the 8th Connecticut near the turnpike had caused the 118th New York to be flanked and also forced back, Burnham's two remaining regiments had steadfastly maintained their positions. Aided greatly by the wire in front and the zigzag nature of the trench they were holding, the 10th and 13th New Hampshire Regiments had repulsed every charge against them. When the fog lifted, the Federals could see hundreds of Confederates entangled in the wire, living and dead, many of the prostrate forms having been bayonetted by their comrades as they fell. Seizing the opportunity, the Federals gathered in more than fifty prisoners, and took unspecified vengeance upon men of the 25th/44th Tennessee, the alleged culprits of the Port Walthall atrocities on 7 May.[39]

On his way to the front with Brooks's order, staff officer George Bruce could see thousands of Confederates in the open, perfect targets for artillery had it not been in the rear. Reaching Burnham's regiments, he found their commanders unwilling to exchange the relative safety of the earthworks for a retreat across an open field in full view of the enemy. Volunteering to try to get the order rescinded, Bruce returned to Brooks, but received only a sulphurous dressing down for his pains. Around 9:00 A.M. Burnham's two New Hampshire units at last withdrew from the trenches, having fired an estimated 50,000 rounds of ammunition between them. The men were angry at having to run the gauntlet of fire already flailing the open field behind them, and they became more incensed upon passing the abandoned piles of regimental record books and baggage brought up to the line the day before.

As the 10th New Hampshire covered the retreat of the 13th, Lieutenant Colonel John Coughlin detected signs that his men were wavering and retiring entirely too rapidly. Halting the regiment, he faced it toward the enemy, dressed its ranks, and had the men fix bayonets before joining the 13th in the woods. There the two regiments remained until further instructions brought them nearer the Half-Way House, where they took position as the westernmost units of the XVIII Corps.[40]

As the XVIII Corps began to give ground, Beauregard attempted to breathe new life into his stalled offensive. In order to strengthen Hoke's thinly spread division, Beauregard recalled Colquitt's Brigade from Ransom. Since Colquitt's regiments were in contact with the Federals, Ransom sent Barton's Brigade to Beauregard instead. At the same time Beauregard directed Ransom to form his brigades *en echelon* and continue the flank attack toward the Old Stage Road crossing of Proctor's Creek. Trying to implement the order, Ransom discovered that Colquitt and Lewis overlapped Hoke's position instead of merging smoothly with his left, and more time was spent in perfecting the alignment. By 10:00 A.M. Ransom's men were satisfactorily positioned, with Dunovant's cavalry screening the front and flank of his four brigades. Ransom rode over to inform Beauregard in person, expecting to be told to continue the advance, but the commanding general withheld the order to go forward.[41]

Beauregard had several reasons for halting Ransom. First, Hoke was still heavily engaged and might need further reinforcements. Second, the reserve force was down to only three small regiments. Third, Beauregard wanted to give Chase Whiting's two brigades a chance to arrive from Petersburg. Finally, Ransom himself reported strong Federal forces in his front, who might handle his depleted regiments severely. Of all of these factors that influenced Beauregard's decision, the possibility of Whiting's arrival in the Federal rear played a most significant role. A few sounds of firing in Whiting's direction had been heard by Beauregard at 8:00 A.M. as he waited near the reserve artillery on the turnpike, but these harbingers of Whiting's approach soon became inaudible. At 9:00 A.M. Beauregard had dispatched a message to Whiting that told of Ransom's progress and predicted that an advance by Whiting would make the victory complete. This was followed by a similar message half an hour later, in which an increasingly impatient Beauregard begged Whiting to "try and join us." Since the messages would be several hours in transit, Beauregard could only hope that Whiting would make his appearance on the battlefield without further prompting.[42]

On the Federal side, the hard-pressed men of the XVIII Corps faced a mystery of their own. Where was the X Corps and the attack Butler had ordered Gillmore to make at 6:00 A.M.? As Brooks's and Weitzel's weary soldiers cobbled together a line covering the turnpike and the Old Stage Road, Gillmore's nonarrival began to assume for the Federals the same enigmatic character as Whiting's for the Confederates. Aware of the X Corps' position by means of a series of messages from Gillmore, Butler became increasingly disgusted with that officer's performance as the morning wore along. Thus as the sun climbed toward its zenith, burning away the last wisps of fog, the commanders of both armies waited anxiously for subordinates to perform maneuvers of vital significance for their respective hopes of success. The battered and bloody combatants of the fog-shrouded morning could only wait for either Quincy Gillmore or Chase Whiting to decisively alter the course of the battle.[43]

NOTES

1. *O.R.A.*, 36, pt. 2, 212; Cary Whitaker Diary, 16 May 1864, SHC; Loehr, *First Virginia*, 46; Loehr, "Battle of Drewry's Bluff," 103; Morgan, *Reminiscences*, 196–197; Sumpter, "Fighting," 182; Shaver, *Sixtieth Alabama*, 51; Johnston, *Four Years*, 309–310.

2. *O.R.A.*, 36, pt. 2, 212; Shaver, *Sixtieth Alabama*, 52; Johnston, *Four Years*, 311; Loehr, "Battle of Drewry's Bluff," 103.

3. Keenan, quoted in Drake, *Ninth New Jersey*, 354–356.

4. *O.R.A.*, 36, pt. 2, 162; Drake, *Ninth New Jersey*, 192–193; Valentine, *Story of Co. F*, 114.

5. Loehr, "Battle of Drewry's Bluff," 101–104; Johnston, *Four Years*, 311–313; Johnston, *Confederate Boy*, 251–252; Shaver, *Sixtieth Alabama*, 52; Cary Whitaker Diary, 16 May 1864, SHC; *O.R.A.*, 36, pt. 2, 236; Morgan, *Reminiscences*, 197.

6. Emmerton, *Twenty-Third Massachusetts*, 185, 187; Valentine, *Story of Co. F*, 114; Derby, *Bearing Arms*, 271–272; *O.R.A.*, 36, pt. 2, 157; Drake, *Ninth New Jersey*, 193–194, 201, 356–357, 379; Foster, *New Jersey and the Rebellion*, 243–244; Everts, *Comprehensive History*, 109–110.

7. Clark, ed., *North Carolina Regiments*, 3:10, 276; Kenan, *Forty-Third North Carolina*, 14; Cary Whitaker Diary, 16 May 1864, SHC.

8. Stansel, "Gracie's Brigade," 592; Drake, *Ninth New Jersey*, 194–195, 202, 357.

9. Drake, *Ninth New Jersey*, 194–197, 202, 398–399; Foster, *New Jersey and the Rebellion*, 243; Cleveland, ed., "Campaign of Promise," 322–323; Everts, *Comprehensive History*, 108.

10. Stansel, "Gracie's Brigade," 592; Shaver, *Sixtieth Alabama*, 54; Owen, *Washington Artillery*, 325n; Loehr, "Battle of Drewry's Bluff," 104; Johnston, *Four Years*, 313; Johnston, *Confederate Boy*, 252; W. M. Seay, "Vivid Story of Drury's Bluff Battle," *Confederate Veteran* 12 (1904):229. Gracie's description is in Morgan, *Reminiscences*, 199.

11. Loehr, *First Virginia*, 47; Loehr, "Battle of Drewry's Bluff," 102–105; Edwin Baker Loving Diary, 16 May 1864, VSL; Johnston, *Four Years*, 313–314; Johnston, *Confederate Boy*, 252–253; Morgan, *Reminiscences*, 199–200; E. F. Compton, "About the Battle at Drury's Bluff," *Confederate Veteran* 12 (1904):123; Sumpter, "Fighting," 182.

12. Morgan, *Reminiscences*, 200–202; Sumpter, "Fighting," 182; Memorandum of Lieutenant Colonel R. L. Maury, Richard L. Maury Papers, Duke University, Durham, N.C.; Loehr, *First Virginia*, 47; Loehr, "Battle of Drewry's Bluff," 104–105; Johnston, *Four Years*, 314; Johnston, *Confederate Boy*, 253.

13. Johnston, *Four Years*, 316–317; Johnston, *Confederate Boy*, 254; Loehr, *First Virginia*, 47; Loehr, "Battle of Drewry's Bluff," 107–108; Compton, "About the Battle," 123; Heckman, quoted in Drake, *Ninth New Jersey*, 206; Foster, *New Jersey and the Rebellion*, 242. Heckman in later years claimed he was taken by Gracie's Brigade, and a similar account can be found in Owen, *Washington Artillery*, 319, but the preponderance of evidence gives credit for the capture to Sergeant Blakey of Company F, 7th Virginia Infantry.

14. Emmerton, *Twenty-Third Massachusetts*, 187–191, 194–198; Valentine, *Story of Co. F*, 114–117; Alfred Otis Chamberlin to his parents, 18 May 1864, Alfred Otis Chamberlin Papers, DU.

15. Derby, *Bearing Arms*, 272–284, 522; Loehr, *First Virginia*, 47; Loehr, "Battle of Drewry's Bluff," 106–107.

16. Clark, *My Experience*, 61–62; Putnam, *Story of Company A*, 276–279; Samuel H. Putnam, *Regimental Record—Co. A, 25th Mass. Vols*, DU; *O.R.A.*, 36, pt. 2, 129–132, 157–158; Walter S. Clemence Memoranda, 16 May 1864, NCC; Kreutzer, *Ninety-Eighth New York*, 192. Colonel Pickett later denied that his regiment withdrew in disorder. Pickett, quoted in Denny, *Wearing the Blue*, 290.

17. *O.R.A.*, 36, pt. 2, 212.

18. Shaver, *Sixtieth Alabama*, 52–54; Loehr, "Battle of Drewry's Bluff," 107, 109–110; Johnston, *Four Years*, 314–318; Johnston, *Confederate Boy*, 253–257; Morgan, *Reminiscences*, 202–203; Sumpter, "Fighting," 182; Seay, "Vivid Story," 229. Gracie's Brigade suffered casualties of 34 killed, 276 wounded, and 4 missing, for a total of 314. *O.R.A.*, 36, pt. 2, 205. Terry's Brigade lost 57 killed and 264 wounded, a

total of 321 out of little more than 900 engaged. Most of Terry's casualties were sustained by the 11th and 24th Virginia Regiments. Loehr, *First Virginia*, 48.

19. Kenan, *Forty-Third North Carolina*, 14; Clark, ed., *North Carolina Regiments*, 3:10; William Beavans Diary, 16 May 1864, SHC; Cary Whitaker Diary, 16 May and 20 May 1864, SHC; John Paris Diary, 16 May 1864, SHC; Henry M. Talley to his mother, 21 May 1864, Henry C. Brown Papers, NCDAH; O.R.A., 36, pt. 2, 236; Griggs, "Memoranda," 255. Casualties in Lewis's Brigade were 25 killed, 137 wounded, and 25 missing, making a total of 187. Barton's Brigade sustained the heaviest loss of any of Ransom's units, losing 43 killed, 292 wounded, and 10 captured, for a total of 345. O.R.A., 36, pt. 2, 205.

20. Weitzel to W. P. Derby, 11 May 1883, quoted in Derby, *Bearing Arms*, 290; Butler, *Butler's Book*, 655; O.R.A., 36, pt. 2, 116, 122, 123; Smith, *Battles and Leaders*, 4:210. Smith's 5:20 A.M. message is timed at 4:20 A.M. by the aide who carried it, but this is in error because the Confederate attack did not begin until 4:45 A.M.

21. O.R.A., 36, pt. 2, 108–109, 806. Of the four regiments originally brought forward by Ames on 15 May, the 8th Maine had been assigned to Heckman during the afternoon of 15 May, while the 97th Pennsylvania was held under Butler's personal control at the Half-Way House.

22. O.R.A., 36, pt. 2, 116, 123, 147, 148; Smith, *Battles and Leaders*, 4:210–211.

23. O.R.A., 36, pt. 2, 108–109, 112, 143; Hyde, *One Hundred and Twelfth New York*, 76–77; Whitman and True, *Maine in the War*, 221.

24. O.R.A., 36, pt. 2, 109, 112, 117, 143, 152, 153; Hyde, *One Hundred and Twelfth New York*, 77–78; Whitman and True, *Maine in the War*, 221; Putnam, *Story of Company A*, 280; Walter S. Clemence Memoranda, 16 May 1864, NCC; Denny, *Wearing the Blue*, 290.

25. O.R.A., 36, pt. 2, 37, 834.

26. Ibid., 236–237, 247–248, 253–254; O.R.A., 51, pt. 1, 223–224, 226–227; Owen, *Washington Artillery*, 316; Hagood, *Memoirs*, 245.

27. O.R.A., 36, pt. 2, 237, 253–254; Hagood, *Memoirs*, 245–248; Izlar, *Edisto Rifles*, 54–57; DuBose, *History of Company B*, 61–62.

28. O.R.A., 36, pt. 2, 128, 135, 137, 139, 247, 248; Thompson, *Thirteenth New Hampshire*, 293–296, 321; Waite, *New Hampshire in the Great Rebellion*, 436, 490; Croffut and Morris, *Connecticut During the War*, 547; Cunningham, *Adirondack Regiment*, 113; David F. Dobie to "Dear Friend Hattie," 17 May 1864, David F. Dobie Letters, VSL; Bruce, "General Butler's Bermuda Campaign," 329; Smith to W. P. Derby, 30 March 1883, quoted in Derby, *Bearing Arms*, 289.

29. O.R.A., 36, pt. 2, 116, 153, 164, 203, 206, 247; Smith, *Battles and Leaders*, 4:211; Bartlett, *Twelfth New Hampshire*, 183, 187, 194. The version of the incident reported by the New Hampshiremen is strongly but inconclusively disputed in Chase, *Battery F*, 165–190.

30. O.R.A., 36, pt. 2, 201–202, 212; Hagood, *Memoirs*, 244–245.

31. O.R.A., 36, pt. 2, 203, 237, 247–249.

32. Ibid., 203; Clark, ed., *North Carolina Regiments*, 2:285–286, 3:138; Henry A. Chambers Diary, 16 May 1864, NCDAH.

33. O.R.A., 36, pt. 2, 203, 237–238; Wise, *Seventeenth Virginia*, 177–179; Warfield, *Memoirs*, 170; Herbert, "Seventeenth Virginia," 292–294; Clark, ed., *North Carolina Regiments*, 1:403, 2:515–516, 3:211; William H. S. Burgwyn Diary, 16 May 1864, NCDAH.

34. O.R.A., 36, pt. 2, 125–126, 128, 135, 142; Wistar, *Autobiography*, 452; Bartlett, *Twelfth New Hampshire*, 184, 187; Haynes, *Second New Hampshire*, 169–170; Haynes, *Second New Hampshire* (2), 225–227; Whitman and True, *Maine in the War*, 202–203; *Twenty-First Connecticut*, 189–190.

35. Beauregard, *Battles and Leaders*, 4:202; Beauregard, "Drury's Bluff," 255; O.R.A., 36, pt. 2, 116–117, 122, 151, 152, 202, 213; Smith, *Battles and Leaders*, 4:211. If Butler had any role in this decision of Smith's, it is nowhere recorded. Years later, in a letter to Smith, Isaac Wistar claimed that Butler never appeared near the front during the battle (Wistar to Smith, 23 January 1893, quoted in Smith, *From Chattanooga to Petersburg*, 194), yet reporter Henry J. Winser placed Butler in the thick of the fighting (*New York Times*, 20 May 1864).

36. O.R.A., 36, pt. 2, 130, 132, 144, 162; *Twenty-First Connecticut*, 187–192, 203; Croffut and Morris, *Connecticut During the War*, 551–552; Bartlett, *Twelfth New Hampshire*, 183–184, 187, 425–426; Haynes, *Second New Hampshire*, 171; Haynes, *Second New Hampshire* (2), 228; Wistar, *Autobiography*, 442–443, 452–455.

37. O.R.A., 36, pt. 2, 117, 152, 162–163; Smith, *Battles and Leaders*, 4:211; Wistar, *Autobiography*, 453–454; Haynes, *Second New Hampshire*, 170.

38. O.R.A., 36, pt. 2, 130, 132, 144, 152, 158, 195–196; Bartlett, *Twelfth New Hampshire*, 184, 425;

Haynes, *Second New Hampshire*, 170–171; Haynes, *Second New Hampshire* (2), 228; Kreutzer, *Ninety-Eighth New York*, 192–193; Croffut and Morris, *Connecticut During the War*, 552; *Twenty-First Connecticut*, 192; Drake, *Ninth New Jersey*, 195–196, 202–203, 207–208; Cleveland, ed., "Campaign of Promise," 322–325; Emmerton, *Twenty-Third Massachusetts*, 192–194; Valentine, *Story of Co. F*, 115–116; Derby, *Bearing Arms*, 273–274.

    39. Cunningham, *Adirondack Regiment*, 113–115, 121–122; David F. Dobie to "Dear Friend Hattie," 17 May 1864, and Lists of Ordnance, Stores, Clothing, Camp and Garrison Equippage Lost or Destroyed in Second Quarter of 1864, David F. Dobie Letters, VSL; Thompson, *Thirteenth New Hampshire*, 296–298, 307–310, 312–315, 321–322; Waite, *New Hampshire in the Great Rebellion*, 490; Bruce, "General Butler's Bermuda Campaign," 337–338.

    40. Bruce, "General Butler's Bermuda Campaign," 338–339; O.R.A., 36, pt. 2, 135, 139–140; Thompson, *Thirteenth New Hampshire*, 298–301, 303, 307–308, 310, 312, 315–320; Waite, *New Hampshire in the Great Rebellion*, 436–437, 490.

    41. O.R.A., 36, pt. 2, 202, 212–213; Beauregard, *Battles and Leaders*, 4:202; Beauregard, "Drury's Bluff," 255. Beauregard's postwar accounts are much more critical of Ransom than is his battle report, and even his official views changed rather quickly. After commending Ransom on 17 May 1864 in Special Orders, No. 11, Beauregard had a change of heart, writing on 14 June 1864 that "Subsequent investigation, necessarily requiring time, has, I regret to say, brought me to a different conviction." O.R.A., 36, pt. 2, 205, 1017–1018.

    42. O.R.A., 36, pt. 2, 202; Roman, *Military Operations*, 2:560; Beauregard to Whiting, 9:00 A.M., 16 May 1864, and G. W. Lay to Whiting, 9:30 A.M., 16 May 1864, both in Official Telegrams, 22 April–9 June 1864, Beauregard Papers, LC; Clark, ed., *North Carolina Regiments*, 2:298, 620, 3:353–354; Harrill, *Reminiscences*, 23.

    43. O.R.A., 36, pt. 2, 835; Butler, *Butler's Book*, 655.

14

The Battle Of Drewry's Bluff—Second Phase
16 May 1864

For Quincy Gillmore and the X Corps, the Battle of Drewry's Bluff opened with light skirmishing in the fog, as Robert Hoke tried to divert attention from the Federal right. The men of Gillmore's six brigades had long been awake listening to the progress of the action, and as the sounds of combat drew nearer, they gathered up their knapsacks in anticipation of an order to move. Benjamin Butler had sent such an order at 6:00 A.M. but Gillmore, who had incurred some bloody repulses at Charleston, was not a man to rush impetuously forward. Upon receiving Butler's message at 6:20 A.M., Gillmore pondered it briefly, then directed Alfred Terry and John Turner to prepare to advance. Before the order could be implemented, Terry's front was probed by Confederate skirmishers. Although the Federals easily repulsed the effort, Gillmore reported to Butler that his troops were under assault. [1]

Unlike their commander, many of the Federals were eager to charge. This was particularly true in Terry's division, which was posted on the left of the X Corps line. West of the railroad was Marston's brigade, still operating under X Corps control. East of the tracks were the brigades of White, Plaisted, and Hawley. On Terry's right stood Turner's division, which consisted of only two brigades. Brigade commanders Samuel Alford and William Barton had their lines spread thinly over a wide front in order to preserve the connection with the XVIII Corps. While making preparations to advance in conjunction with Terry, Turner learned that W. T. H. Brooks's division of the XVIII Corps was going to move to the right, leaving a gap. Actually, Brooks only moved Sanders's brigade behind Burnham's brigade as a reserve, but the gap thus created was real enough. To cover it, Turner ordered Barton to shift his regiments to the right, thereby maintaining the connection with Brooks. [2]

In the midst of his own attack preparations, Terry was forced to detach a regiment each from Plaisted and Hawley to reinforce the XVIII Corps. At the same time he faced persistent though relatively weak Confederate probes. Exaggerated by the fog, the Confederate activity on Terry's front influenced Gillmore to inform Butler at 7:01 A.M. that the Confederates had attacked him three times "in force." He concluded: "If I move to the assault and meet a repulse, our loss would be

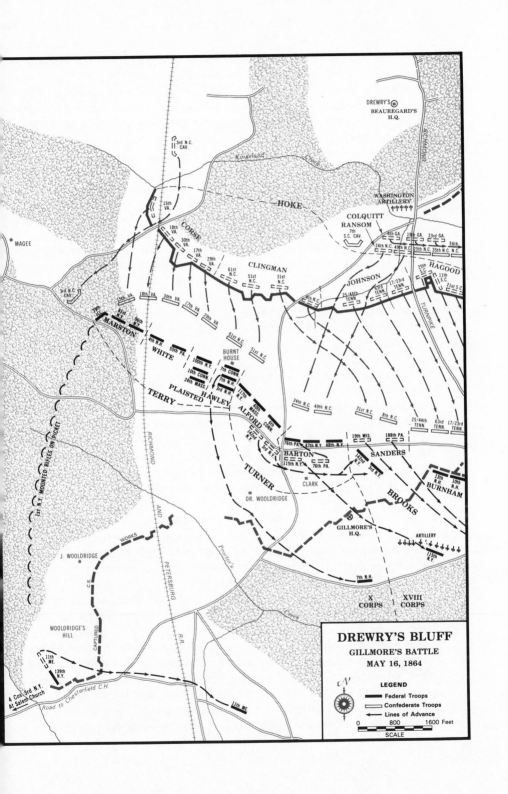

DREWRY'S
BEAUREGARD'S
H.Q.

3rd N.C.
CAV.

Kingsland

HOKE

15th
VA.

WASHINGTON
ARTILLERY

18th
VA. CORSE

COLQUITT
RANSOM

7th
S.C. CAV.

8th GA. 19th GA. 23rd GA.

30th
VA.

17th
VA. 29th
VA.

CLINGMAN

24th N.C. 49th N.C. 25th 35th N.C. N.C. 56th.

61st
N.C. 51st
N.C. 31st
N.C.

JOHNSON

25th
N.C. HAGOOD

11th
S.C.

3rd N.C.
CAV.

50th VA. 18th VA.

MARSTON

31st
86th

30th VA. 17th VA.

29th VA.

61st N.C.

27th N.C.

63rd
TENN. 17/23rd
TENN.

17/23rd
TENN.

21st S.C.

4th N.H.

WHITE 55th PA.

100th N.Y.

10th CONN.

24th MASS. 3rd N.H.

BURNT
HOUSE

7th CONN.

3rd N.H.

51st N.C.

61st N.C.

TERRY PLAISTED HAWLEY

ALFORD

117th
N.Y.

6th
MASS.

6th
CONN.

24th N.C. 49th N.C.

31st N.C.

8th N.C.

25/44th
TENN. 63rd
TENN. 17/23rd
TENN.

112th
N.Y.

76th PA. 47th N.Y. 48th N.Y.

19th WIS.

188th PA.

TURNER

BARTON

142nd
N.Y.

50 N.Y.

115th N.Y.

76th PA.

CLARK

SANDERS

142nd
N.Y. 3rd N.Y.

13th
N.H. 10th
N.H.

BURNHAM

BROOKS

1st N.Y. MOUNTED RIFLES ON PICKET

DR. WOOLDRIDGE

GILLMORE'S
H.Q.

ARTILLERY

115th
N.Y.

J. WOOLDRIDGE

WORKS

C.S.

CAPTURED

RICHMOND AND PETERSBURG

Proctor's

7th N.H.

R.R.

WOOLDRIDGE'S
HILL

X
CORPS XVIII
CORPS

11th
ME.

139th
N.Y.

4 Cos. 3rd N.Y.
At Salem Church

Road to Chesterfield C.H.

Creek

11th ME.

DREWRY'S BLUFF
GILLMORE'S BATTLE
MAY 16, 1864

N

LEGEND

▬▬▬ Federal Troops

▭▭▭ Confederate Troops

◀━━ Lines of Advance

0   800   1600 Feet

SCALE

MAGEE

fearful." Six minutes later, in another dispatch to Butler, Gillmore repeated his account of the Confederate probes and emphatically stated that "No troops have been taken from my front." More than one hour had elapsed since Butler had first ordered an attack by the X Corps to relieve pressure on Smith's beleaguered troops, and although Butler's order permitted no discretion in timing the move, Gillmore still had not acted.[3]

As the minutes passed, Gillmore continued to delay his assault, almost as if he were awaiting news that would permit him to cancel it altogether. At 7:25 A.M. he sent Butler a report from Turner that claimed that Brooks's right flank had been turned and some artillery lost. Sensing that this might be the clinching argument against an assault by the X Corps, Gillmore closed: "I am ready to assault, but shall wait until I hear from you, as I may have to support Smith. Please answer soon." In a short while, as the battle raged around the turnpike, Gillmore's message to Butler was returned with an endorsement denying that Brooks was flanked, but giving Gillmore permission to "use discretion as to assault." With the decision now resting in his own hands, Gillmore could withhold the attack without fear of violating a direct order from a superior. Characteristically, he decided to await further news from Smith before moving. He seemed totally unaware that an early attack by his troops not only might have clarified the situation on his right but significantly altered it as well.[4]

John Turner, meanwhile, was finding it difficult to maintain the connection with the XVIII Corps. As the action waxed along the turnpike, Brooks kept sending Turner messages that he was moving to the right. In order to fill the widening gap, Turner was forced to pull two of Alford's regiments from the left of the division line and rush them eastward to extend Barton's right. Before this could be accomplished, Confederate units pushed into the gap and endangered Barton's right flank, until Alford's two regiments arrived and forcibly ejected them from the position. Fearing that the Confederates would charge once more and break his tenuous connection with Brooks, Turner detached still another of Alford's regiments to serve as a reserve for Barton's right. This meant that two of Alford's regiments were operating on the left of Barton's brigade and three on the right, a difficult position for any brigade commander wishing to maintain control of his units. In Alford's case it hardly mattered, as he was somewhere in the rear suffering from what one soldier termed a "severe attack of discretion."[5]

As Turner juggled regiments in a desperate effort to maintain contact with the XVIII Corps, Butler informed Gillmore that Smith was moving to the right to protect his flank and that the X Corps should conform. This order was sent in both written and verbal editions, which were acknowledged by Gillmore at 8:34 A.M. Now, two-and-one-half hours after Butler had first ordered it, Gillmore decided to make the long-awaited assault. Reasoning that if the Confederates were concentrating against Smith's right, an advance by the X Corps would strike them in flank, Gillmore issued attack orders to his division commanders. Terry was to leave his skirmishers in position so as to fool the Confederates facing them, then move his men to the right and attack in a northeasterly direction. Turner, already in a precarious position, was to do the same.[6]

None of Terry's three brigades made the transition from defense to offense without difficulty. On the left, White's brigade, reduced by detachments to only two regiments, apparently never received the order at all. Finding themselves alone after the departure of the rest of the division, the regiments advanced to meet the oncoming Confederates, were flanked, and sent reeling backwards. Colonel Richard White was taken prisoner and was joined by many of his men. In the center Colonel Harris Plaisted was confused by the vagueness of the order and allowed his units to become widely separated. Punished severely by the Confederates, who followed them closely, Plaisted's regiments required considerable time to regain their brigade organization. On Plaisted's right, Colonel Joseph Hawley withdrew his two remaining regiments after detaching 150 men of the 7th Connecticut to serve as a rear guard. Left on the field by mistake, the detachment was eventually overrun by the charging Confederates.[7]

If Terry's attempts to disengage and move to the right were marked by confusion, Turner's were characterized by desperation. Before he could execute Gillmore's order, Turner was assaulted heavily by Confederate infantry. One of Alford's regiments on Barton's left gave way, which resulted in the loss of part of the Federal field works and scores of prisoners. At the same time Barton's brigade was assailed both in front and on its right flank. With the aid of staff officers, Turner managed to close the gap on his left, while Barton's men held firm on the right. The Confederates were dislodged from the rifle pits they had taken and some of the Federals taken prisoner earlier were freed. In the distance the head of Terry's division could at last be seen moving toward Turner's position. Still, Turner was not out of difficulty, because Brooks's continuing withdrawal on his right permitted Confederate units to creep around his flank. Instead of taking part in an assault, Turner had been lucky to hold his ground.[8]

As Terry and Turner struggled to disengage and displace to the right, Gillmore received a message from Colonel J. W. Shaffer, Butler's chief of staff. Shaffer reported that both Brooks and Weitzel were falling back and he advised Gillmore: "You must govern your line according to movements on your right." Gillmore found that the XVIII Corps was retreating beyond Smith's former headquarters at the Friend house. If this movement continued, the X Corps might not be able to use the turnpike in case its own retreat became necessary. To hold an alternate escape route open, Gillmore decided to use Marston's brigade, just leaving its position on the extreme left of the X Corps. Marston was ordered to bring two regiments and the remnants of White's brigade to a new location behind the center of the X Corps line covering a road to the south. Leaving the 39th Illinois to hold the brigade's position west of the railroad, Marston obeyed.[9]

By 9:30 A.M. Marston was in position and Gillmore informed Butler: "I am forming line of battle in the brush in rear of my old position." At the same time that Gillmore was transmitting this ambiguous and misleading message, Butler's chief of staff was drafting another dispatch informing Gillmore of developments on the army's right and giving him new instructions. The message read:

> The enemy is pressing around our right. Smith has fallen back to near Half-Way House. The enemy is near Dr. Howlett's. You must fall back, press to right, and get in rear of Smith's corps. He will try and hold his ground until you get in his rear and clear the road to the intrenchments, so that we may get back behind the defenses. Push vigorously.
> [PS] Smith will have to fall back and hold road in rear of his right. Gillmore must hold pike. Information is clear that they are pressing across river fast.[10]

Although Shaffer's dispatch seemed to leave no doubt that Confederate troops were already deep in the Federal rear, Butler delayed sending the message to Gillmore until a staff officer could make a visual confirmation. While Butler waited, Gillmore's dispatch of 9:30 A.M., in which he reported forming a new line to his rear, arrived at headquarters. Butler immediately concluded that the entire X Corps was retreating, an obvious interpretation from the loose wording Gillmore had employed. When the staff officer reported seeing no Confederates in the Federal rear, Butler drafted a reply to Gillmore: "Why falling back? Lieutenant Davenport reports no fighting at Ware Bottom Church nor on our right. I sent him back to see and report." Since Shaffer's order to "fall back" and Butler's message asking Gillmore why he was "falling back" seemed quite contradictory, Butler's original message was replaced by a second version:

> Lieutenant Davenport reports no fighting at Ware Bottom Church, nor on our right. I sent him back to see and report. Hold the road to intrenchments at all hazards. I send Shaffer's dispatch. No prisoners have been captured but from the North Carolina brigades.

The two dispatches, Shaffer's and Butler's second draft, were then entrusted to Lieutenant Colonel George Kensel, who rode to find Gillmore.[11]

Gillmore's command post was in a house behind the center of his line. The corps commander and his staff had just finished a late breakfast and were standing in the yard when Kensel arrived at 9:50 A.M. The initial part of Shaffer's message was readily understandable, as Gillmore had already been told by Lieutenant Peter Michie that Confederates were in the Federal rear at Ware Bottom Church. Gillmore, however, was confused by the postscript about Confederates crossing the James River and he asked Kensel for clarification. Kensel replied "that the enemy was receiving re-enforcements from the other side of James River, and that it was feared that our retreat to the intrenchments would be cut off." Thus Gillmore had a verbal report from Michie, a written dispatch from Shaffer, and a verbal explanation from Kensel, all describing Confederate activity in the Federal right rear. On the other hand, there was Butler's message denying the rumors that the Federal rear was in danger, but also directing that the X Corps cover the army's routes of retreat.[12]

The confusion about events in the army's rear notwithstanding, Gillmore decided to move toward the Half-Way House. He was strengthened in his decision when his original message of 9:30 A.M. was returned with Butler's endorsement: "General Gillmore is ordered to hold the roads and left on turnpike." There was also an endorsement from Smith, who noted that his men had lost connection with the X Corps and repeated the reports of Confederate reinforcements crossing the river. Finding in these diverse comments justification for his decision to withdraw, Gillmore added a third endorsement to the scrap of paper and sent it once more to Butler. Unlike most of the poorly worded messages of this series, Gillmore's final statement was direct: "I am falling back on two roads between the railroad and pike." As his troops began to move, Gillmore received an order from Shaffer to hurry, because Ames was being pressed at Port Walthall Junction. Because the X Corps was already heading in the direction required, Gillmore continued leisurely toward the Half-Way House, which he reached at noon.[13]

When the order to retreat reached Turner's division it was being flanked on the right by Confederate infantry moving into the gap left by the XVIII Corps. Hit hard, the 142nd New York had already fallen back in disorder. Pleased to be leaving his increasingly untenable position, Colonel William Barton led his brigade and Alford's scattered regiments to the rear. The withdrawal was covered by the 117th New York, which remained in position long enough for the rest of Turner's division to move off the field. At last it was the turn of the 117th and it retired also, passing an aid station where surgeons were hurriedly burying battle fatalities before falling back themselves. Turner's troops did not stop until they were beyond Proctor's Creek, where they occupied positions east of the turnpike.[14]

Terry's division had mixed success in obeying Gillmore's order to retire. Joseph Hawley's two regiments withdrew unmolested to the south side of Proctor's Creek, then recrossed the creek to the Half-Way House, where they served as a support during the afternoon. Plaisted's brigade was not so fortunate, since the three regiments had become separated earlier in the morning. Before Plaisted could collect his units, the Confederates rushed in upon the flank of the 100th New York Infantry and shattered the regiment, while the 24th Massachusetts wandered away to join Marston's reserve line some distance to the east. Eventually the 24th rejoined Plaisted and the 10th Connecticut, and together they moved to the rear. On the way Plaisted's men passed another field hospital where surgeons continued to process casualties, even as the last organized Federal units passed them in retreat. Leaving this pitiful scene behind, Plaisted's men continued on their way toward the Half-Way House.[15]

With the remnants of White's brigade either under Marston's command, or scattered into the woods, or marching to Confederate prisons, the only unit remaining on the original line of the X Corps was the 39th Illinois Infantry west of the railroad. Left to hold the position alone when Marston's other regiments had been called to the right, the 550 soldiers from Illinois had been forgotten in the general confusion. Isolated by Terry's departure, the regiment was soon flanked by Confederates advancing within the security of a deep railroad cut. After the major in command suffered multiple wounds, the various companies fought disjointedly until they were overrun. The survivors fled south along the railroad toward Chester Station. On the way some coal cars were commandeered to haul away the wounded, with unhurt soldiers providing the motive power. Yet there was no safety even in the vicinity of Chester Station, toward which hundreds of wounded and unwounded stragglers from the 39th Illinois, 100th New York, and other crushed units were converging. As if from nowhere a detachment of Confederate cavalry appeared, slashing its way through the mob and rounding up scores of prisoners, including the wounded trapped in the cars. A few Federals managed to escape by dashing into the thick underbrush, but most were not so fortunate.[16]

Between noon and 2:00 P.M. the X Corps completed its retrograde movement to the Half-Way House on the turnpike. While Turner's division crossed to the south side of Proctor's Creek, Butler ordered Terry to take personal command of the line around the Half-Way House and to cover the withdrawal of Brooks's division of the XVIII Corps. Utilizing regiments from both Hawley's and Plaisted's brigades as well as some artillery units, Terry stabilized the left flank of the Army of the James. He was not molested by Confederate infantry, which could be seen occupying the positions held by the Federals early in the morning. By 2:00 P.M., except for a few remnants, the entire Federal army had been consolidated around the Half-Way House. West of the turnpike was Terry's command, with the rest of the X Corps in reserve beyond Proctor's Creek. East of the pike were the divisions of Brooks and Weitzel, comprising the XVIII Corps.[17]

With his line reestablished, Butler decided to send the XVIII Corps forward to recover the wounded from the morning's fight and to learn the position of Confederate units in Smith's front. At 2:15 P.M. Gillmore was ordered to relieve some of Brooks's regiments near the turnpike and to protect Smith's flank as the XVIII Corps advanced. Smith in turn directed Brooks to probe forward, supported on the right by Weitzel's division, which was also to maintain its hold on the Old Stage Road. This advance, the last made by the Army of the James on the field of Drewry's Bluff, was short-lived. Between 2:00 and 3:00 P.M. Smith's five brigades pushed gingerly into the woods. Before reaching the Federal positions of the morning where most of the casualties lay, Smith's men once more encountered Confederate fire. After collecting the wounded men they could reach, the soldiers were ordered to withdraw by Smith, who considered the Confederate force too large for the XVIII Corps to engage. Nothing had been gained, because the wounded recovered were offset by new casualties sustained during the advance.[18]

While he awaited the results of Smith's probe, Butler received a message from Gillmore in which the commander of the X Corps commented "that the intrenchments which I was ordered to fall back upon this morning have been reoccupied by the enemy." At 3:05 P.M. Butler angrily responded that he had not ordered Gillmore to retreat until Gillmore himself had reported that the X Corps was withdrawing. Thus Butler openly accused Gillmore of having retreated without orders. The charge was untrue; it stemmed from a misunderstanding of Gillmore's 9:30 A.M. message concerning Marston's brigade and the endorsements added to it later. Given time for reflection and goodwill among the principals, the actual sequence of events could have been untangled easily, but both Butler and Gillmore were operating under considerable pressure. Upon receiving Butler's accusation, Gillmore hastened to army headquarters in person, but the heated discussion that ensued resolved nothing.[19]

While Butler and Gillmore argued fruitlessly, Baldy Smith's abortive advance came to an end. Influenced by Smith's opinion that a large Confederate force still threatened the Army of the James, Butler decided to order a general withdrawal to the Bermuda Hundred base. He later claimed that he had retreated because Grant and the Army of the Potomac had not fulfilled their part of the bargain by meeting the Army of the James within ten days. With Grant still far away, the Confederates might combine part of Lee's army with Beauregard's troops and drive the Army of the James out of the uncompleted Bermuda Hundred defenses, thereby seizing the base Butler was preparing for Grant's arrival. Butler argued therefore that the Army of the James could best serve the Union cause by withdrawing behind the Bermuda Hundred fortifications and strengthening them until they were impregnable. This move would guarantee Grant and the Army of the Potomac a secure base area whenever they arrived.[20]

Undoubtedly Grant's absence played a part in Butler's decision, but at least equally compelling must have been the vigorous Confederate attacks of the morning. Also, the threat posed by the Confederate force facing Ames at Port Walthall Junction must have influenced Butler's thinking. Certainly the two corps commanders were not in favor of returning to the offensive. Smith, who had bitterly opposed the campaign from the beginning, proved by his feeble advance in mid-afternoon that he was no longer offensive-minded, if indeed he ever had been. Likewise, Gillmore had shown little desire to advance during the early morning, when his corps had faced only two Confederate brigades and when a bold assault might have turned the tide of battle. Thus, with Grant still far away, with his base relatively undefended, with strong enemy forces in both front and rear, with one corps commander shaken by the morning's fight and the other accused of having retreated without orders, the inexperienced Butler believed he had no choice but to withdraw to Bermuda Hundred.

Although Butler's generals had had difficulty maintaining control of their units throughout the morning, they conducted the retreat professionally. As the afternoon waned, Terry's division masked Turner's withdrawal on the turnpike, while Weitzel covered Brooks on the Old Stage Road. At last, between 8:00 and 9:00 P.M., the weary, dispirited soldiers of the Army of the James trudged within the Bermuda Hundred lines. At no time during the afternoon had they been molested by the Confederates, a fact that partially explains the ease of the retreat. Strangely, the Confederate forces had been inactive since late morning, a state of affairs that proved beneficial to the Army of the James but one that had not been a part of the Confederate battle plan.[21]

Although Butler's withdrawal to the Half-Way House had given the Confederates control of the original Federal positions as well as five captured cannon, most of Beauregard's units had been fought to a frazzle in the process. Rather than continue his costly frontal attacks and risk precipitating a Federal retreat into the Bermuda Hundred lines before Whiting arrived, Beauregard ordered Ransom and Hoke to halt until Whiting's position could be ascertained. The distant sounds of the morning had long since faded and, try as he might, Beauregard could hear nothing further from Whiting's direction. During the afternoon, the already embarrassing hiatus in the action became even more unbearable with the arrival of President Davis, who met Beauregard behind the forward Confederate positions near the turnpike. There they were joined by another party of official sightseers, led by Postmaster General John Reagan and Congressman Eli Bruce of Kentucky.[22]

Except for light skirmishing, the fighting had ceased on Beauregard's front as he strained to detect any sign that Whiting might be approaching. The presence of Davis, who had bitterly opposed the plan to have Whiting join the battle from the south, must have made the wait especially excruciating for Beauregard. Just after 1:00 P.M. a message arrived from Bragg suggesting that Beauregard send part of his forces around the Federal left. Fearing that such a movement would cause the Federals to retire within the Bermuda Hundred lines before Whiting could strike them from the rear, Beauregard replied that he did not feel justified in taking such a step. His judgment seemed vindicated for a brief instant around 1:45 P.M. when faint sounds of firing were heard from the south. Standing on a parapet, Davis exclaimed "At last!" Yet the firing immediately ceased and silence descended upon the battlefield once more.[23]

Around 4:00 P.M., as the Federals began to withdraw to their base, Colonel Thomas Logan reached Beauregard with a first-hand report on Whiting's movements. According to Logan, Whiting's force was halted at Port Walthall Junction and could not be counted upon to advance farther that day because of Whiting's confused state of mind. Beauregard, who had already begun to doubt that Whiting would appear in time to trap the Federals, now had to revise his plans. Giving up on Whiting, he ordered Robert Hoke to send Corse's and Clingman's Brigades across Proctor's Creek to Wooldridge's Hill, where they might threaten the Federal flank. At 4:15 P.M. notice of these dispositions was sent to Whiting along with a plaintive request that he join in the movement. Before sunset the request was repeated, but to no avail.[24]

With the remaining hours of daylight slipping away, Beauregard ordered Corse and Clingman to follow the retreating Army of the James, but he did not push forward the rest of his brigades. Even this cursory attempt at pursuit was delayed by a heavy thunderstorm, and by the time the two brigades were ready to advance, darkness prevented any further activity. At 6:45 P.M. Beauregard sent a message to Whiting announcing a new offensive movement for daybreak and ordering Whiting to meet the main army three miles north of Port Walthall Junction. In a 9:15 P.M. telegram to Bragg, Beauregard reported that he would advance at dawn and that he hoped "to have the co-operation of General Whiting." The inference was clear. Whether Whiting moved or not, Beauregard would no longer squander precious hours waiting for him.[25]

NOTES

1. Little, *Seventh New Hampshire*, 251; Eldredge, *Third New Hampshire*, 471; *O.R.A.*, 36, pt. 2, 37, 43, 53, 94, 834; *O.R.A.*, 51, pt. 1, 1243. Gillmore's worst fiasco had been the ill-planned assault on Fort Wagner on 18 July 1863. Kreutzer, *Ninety-Eighth New York*, 159; Gordon, *War Diary*, 188. Of Gillmore's tour of duty at Charleston, Bruce Catton wrote: "He had failed there through no especial fault of his own. The experience had left him highly distrustful of any operation that involved attacking entrenched Confederates, but there was no way to know that it had left him very reluctant to make any attack at all." Catton, *Never Call Retreat*, 346–347.

2. *O.R.A.*, 36, pt. 2, 53, 94, 126; *O.R.A.*, 51, pt. 1, 1243; Little, *Seventh New Hampshire*, 251; Eldredge, *Third New Hampshire*, 471; Clark, *Thirty-Ninth Illinois*, 182, 184; Thompson, *Thirteenth New Hampshire*, 300–301.

3. *O.R.A.*, 36, pt. 2, 38, 43, 53, 72–73, 83, 834; *O.R.A.*, 51, pt. 1, 1246; Little, *Seventh New Hampshire*, 251; Brady, *Eleventh Maine*, 185.

4. *O.R.A.*, 36, pt. 2, 38, 94; Clark, *Iron Hearted Regiment*, 118.

5. *O.R.A.*, 36, pt. 2, 94–95, 100; Nichols, *Perry's Saints*, 215–216; Mowris, *One Hundred and Seventeenth New York*, 105–107.

6. *O.R.A.*, 36, pt. 2, 38, 43, 95.

7. Waite, *New Hampshire in the Great Rebellion*, 205, 242–243; *O.R.A.*, 36, pt. 2, 53–54, 62–63, 68, 79, 86; *O.R.A.*, 51, pt. 1, 1244; Roe, *Twenty-Fourth Massachusetts*, 286; Joseph Hawley to his wife, 17 May 1864, Hawley Papers, LC; Eldredge, *Third New Hampshire*, 471–472; Walkley, *Seventh Connecticut*, 136–137, 224–225; Croffut and Morris, *Connecticut During the War*, 545–546.

8. *O.R.A.*, 36, pt. 2, 95, 98, 100–101, 103, 104; Nichols, *Perry's Saints*, 215–219; Cadwell, *Old Sixth*, 91; Croffut and Morris, *Connecticut During the War*, 542; Charles A. Currier, "Recollections of service with the Fortieth Massachusetts Infantry Volunteers," United States Army Military History Institute, Carlisle Barracks, Pa.

9. *O.R.A.*, 36, pt. 2, 38–39, 48; Clark, *Thirty-Ninth Illinois*, 184.

10. *O.R.A.*, 36, pt. 2, 39, 834.

11. Ibid., 39, 835.

12. *O.R.A.*, 36, pt. 2, 38–39, 836; *O.R.A.*, 51, pt. 1, 1163–1165, 1168.

13. *O.R.A.*, 36, pt. 2, 39–40, 834–835.

14. Ibid., 95, 97, 98, 101, 103; Nichols, *Perry's Saints*, 219–220; Mowris, *One Hundred and Seventeenth New York*, 106–107; Charles Lafferty to his sister, 26 May 1864, Fort Pulaski Papers, Southern Historical Collection, University of North Carolina, Chapel Hill, N.C.; John B. Foote to his mother, 18 May 1864, John B. Foote Papers, DU.

15. *O.R.A.*, 36, pt. 2, 54, 63, 79, 86; Walkley, *Seventh Connecticut*, 139; Eldredge, *Third New Hampshire*, 472–476; Waite, *New Hampshire in the Great Rebellion*, 205; *O.R.A.*, 51, pt. 1, 1244–1246; Roe, *Twenty-Fourth Massachusetts*, 284–287, 289; Stowits, *One Hundredth New York*, 258–261.

16. *O.R.A.*, 36, pt. 2, 48; Clark, *Thirty-Ninth Illinois*, 179, 182–190, 319–322, 334–335, 341, 407, 410.

17. *O.R.A.*, 36, pt. 2, 43, 53, 72–73, 79–80, 95, 98, 101, 109, 132, 135, 142, 147, 148, 837; *O.R.A.*, 51, pt. 1, 1245; Little, *Seventh New Hampshire*, 251–252; Beecher, *First Connecticut Light Battery*, 1:444–449; Henry Clay Trumbull, *The Knightly Soldier: A Biography of Major Henry Ward Camp, Tenth Conn. Vols.* (Boston: Nichols and Noyes, 1865), 225–226; Thompson, *Thirteenth New Hampshire*, 300, 305–306.

18. *O.R.A.*, 36, pt. 2, 109, 112, 117, 122, 123, 132, 135, 137, 142, 150–152, 835; Smith, *Battles and Leaders*, 4:211; Thompson, *Thirteenth New Hampshire*, 300; Wistar, *Autobiography*, 455–456; Haynes, *Second New Hampshire* (2), 228; Whitman and True, *Maine in the War*, 203; Hyde, *One Hundred and Twelfth New York*, 78; Stewart, quoted in Drake, *Ninth New Jersey*, 202–203.

19. *O.R.A.*, 36, pt. 2, 835, 836; *O.R.A.*, 51, pt. 1, 1163–1165, 1168–1169. In this particular instance, Butler was clearly mistaken, as shown by the testimony of various staff officers. Gillmore, however, had contributed to the misunderstanding by the poor phrasing of his original message to Butler regarding Marston.

20. Butler, *Butler's Book*, 655–657, 664; Memorandum of 8 January 1879, and Butler to W. P. Darby [Derby], 26 June 1882, both in Butler Papers, LC; Butler to Surgeon Gillette, 1887, quoted in Drake, *Ninth New Jersey*, 209.

21. *O.R.A.*, 36, pt. 2, 40, 43–44, 80, 97, 98, 122, 123, 137, 148, 152, 170–171, 836, 837; Roe,

Twenty-Fourth Massachusetts, 289; Stowits, *One Hundredth New York*, 261; De Forest, *Random Sketches*, 151; Cadwell, *Old Sixth*, 91–92; Thompson, *Thirteenth New Hampshire*, 300, 306, 308, 310; Cunningham, *Adirondack Regiment*, 115; Bartlett, *Twelfth New Hampshire*, 184–185, 194–195; Derby, *Bearing Arms*, 273–274; Putnam, *Story of Company A*, 280; *Twenty-First Connecticut*, 195; Beecher, *First Connecticut Light Battery*, 1:448–451.

22. O.R.A., 36, pt. 2, 196–197, 203, 249, 254; O.R.A., 51, pt. 2, 938; Roman, *Military Operations*, 2:560; Beauregard to Bragg, 11:00 A.M., 16 May 1864, and Beauregard to General John Winder, 11:00 A.M., 16 May 1864, both in Official Telegrams, 22 April–9 June 1864, Beauregard Papers, LC; Beauregard, *Battles and Leaders*, 4:203; Beauregard, "Drury's Bluff," 257; Owen, *Washington Artillery*, 316–318; Jones, *Surry Light Artillery*, 190, 193; Davis, *Rise and Fall*, 2:513; John H. Reagan, *Memoirs* (New York: The Neale Publishing Company, 1906), 189–191; Jones, *War Clerk*, 2:212–213.

23. O.R.A., 36, pt. 2, 197, 203–204; Beauregard, *Battles and Leaders*, 4:203; Beauregard, "Drury's Bluff," 257; Owen, *Washington Artillery*, 318. Bragg's message to Beauregard has not been found. Beauregard later surmised that the distant firing came from James Dearing's cavalry, which was operating between Whiting's force and the main army.

24. O.R.A., 36, pt. 2, 204, 1014; Beauregard, *Battles and Leaders*, 4:203–204; Beauregard, "Drury's Bluff," 257–258; T. M. Logan to Beauregard, 2 January 1882, quoted in Roman, *Military Operations*, 2:559–560; Beauregard to Whiting, 4:15 P.M., 16 May 1864, Official Telegrams, 22 April–9 June 1864, Beauregard Papers, LC; Roman, *Military Operations*, 2:560–561.

25. O.R.A., 36, pt. 2, 198, 204; Beauregard, *Battles and Leaders*, 4:204; Beauregard, "Drury's Bluff," 258; Roman, *Military Operations*, 2:561; Owen, *Washington Artillery*, 319; Beauregard to Whiting, 6:45 P.M., 16 May 1864, Official Telegrams, 22 April–9 June 1864, Beauregard Papers, LC.

☆ 15 ☆

The Mystery of Chase Whiting
16 May 1864

Only forty years old when he received the call to join Beauregard in Virginia, William Henry Chase Whiting had long shown intellectual promise. At both Georgetown (D.C.) College and West Point he had compiled the best academic record of any student up to the time of his graduation. Serving conspicuously as Joseph E. Johnston's chief engineer in the First Manassas Campaign, he was rewarded by Jefferson Davis with an immediate promotion to brigadier general. This promotion in turn led to the command of an infantry division during the Peninsula Campaign. In November of 1862 Whiting was assigned to command the Military District of Wilmington. At Wilmington there was no glory to be gained leading a division in the field, only the prosaic work of the military engineer. Although he regretted his transfer, Whiting diligently planned and constructed the famous Fort Fisher and other coast defenses. For this service to his country, he was promoted to major general in early 1863.[1]

Although he was markedly successful in his engineering duties at Wilmington, Whiting never forgot his brief tenure as a field commander and longed for a more active role in the conflict. Once the major components of Wilmington's defenses were completed, there was little to challenge his intellectual capacities at the North Carolina post. Besides, the cosmopolitan society of wartime Wilmington contained some inherently demoralizing influences. Whether due to his own boredom or to the company he kept, Whiting soon began to imbibe larger quantities of liquor than was prudent, or at least he allowed such rumors to become common gossip. When Beauregard's summons gave him an opportunity to escape the ennui of garrison life temporarily, Whiting was eager to join his old friend.[2]

Arriving at Petersburg on 13 May, Whiting found himself placed in charge of the department while Beauregard marched to Drewry's Bluff. Handicapped by ignorance of the surrounding country and by the absence of his staff, harassed both by routine department business and by a stream of messages from his superiors, Whiting slowly began to lose control of the situation at Petersburg. Because he realized the significance of the city to the Confederacy, he became convinced that Petersburg was the primary objective of the powerful Army of the James.

Throughout 14 and 15 May, as Butler's army gingerly pushed northward toward Drewry's Bluff, Whiting expected to hear at any moment of a Federal advance upon the Swift Creek defenses. This constant anxiety and the resulting loss of sleep left Whiting unprepared for coping efficiently with the series of contradictory orders that arrived at Petersburg on 15 May. It was not until late in the evening that Whiting received Beauregard's final instructions to move northward toward the sound of the guns on the following morning.[3]

After another sleepless night marked by feverish preparations, Whiting rode out to the Swift Creek defenses. There he found the Virginia brigade of former governor Henry Wise, numbering some 2,300 men, and the North Carolina brigade of James Martin, 3,000 strong. Also present were several artillery batteries and some of James Dearing's cavalry. At Whiting's command, Wise's four regiments led the way across Swift Creek, followed by the artillery, while Martin's three regiments brought up the rear. Within a mile Federal pickets were encountered, which necessitated a slackening of the column's pace. At this point the Richmond turnpike continued due north, while the Old Stage Road diverged in a northeasterly direction, where it soon crossed the Richmond and Petersburg Railroad.[4]

At the junction Whiting decided to rearrange his units before proceeding farther. Concerned about his right flank, which would soon draw opposite the Federal camp at Bermuda Hundred, he assigned Wise's Brigade to advance along the turnpike, while Martin took the Old Stage Road to guard against a potential Federal turning movement. Because the terrain was rough and thickly wooded, Whiting asked D. H. Hill, who was still acting as an unofficial adviser, to supervise Wise's movements, while he remained with Martin. To ensure a further margin of safety, Dearing assigned the 62nd Georgia Cavalry to cover the infantry's right flank and the 7th Confederate Cavalry to operate on the left, so as eventually to link up with Beauregard's forces at Drewry's Bluff. As soon as the troops were deployed, Whiting's force resumed its northward march.[5]

Ahead of the Confederates the handful of Federal skirmishers retired slowly, fulfilling their role of harassment and delay all the way from Timsbury Creek to Port Walthall Junction. By this time Whiting's troops were only six miles south of the contending forces near Drewry's Bluff. Although the battle there had been raging since daylight, Whiting claimed he heard only three or four cannon shots, which did not signify the full-scale action he had been led to expect. To others, particularly Colonel Thomas Logan, who had brought Beauregard's attack order to Whiting the previous night, the firing signified that Beauregard's forces were engaged and that the plan was in motion. Uneasy, Logan waited for Whiting to increase the speed of the advance.[6]

Disregarding the distant sounds of conflict, Whiting pushed gingerly toward Port Walthall Junction, which was reached around 8:30 A.M. Arriving on the southern rim of the amphitheater created by the valley of Ashton Creek, the Confederates could see small numbers of Federals crossing the creek and ascending the ridge on the north side of the valley. Instead of impetuously following the retreating Federals into what might be a trap, Whiting halted his infantry and ordered his artillery to

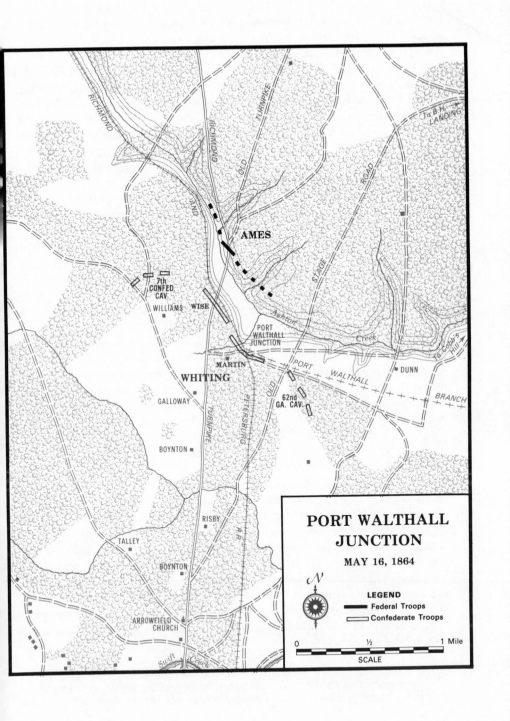

RICHMOND

RICHMOND

TURNPIKE

OLD

RICHMOND

To B.H.
LANDING

AMES

ROAD

7th
CONFED.
CAV.

STAGE

WILLIAMS   WISE

Ashton

PORT
WALTHALL
JUNCTION

Creek

To Cobb's
Hill

MARTIN

PORT   WALTHALL   DUNN

WHITING

OLD

62nd
GA. CAV.

BRANCH

GALLOWAY

PETERSBURG

TURNPIKE

BOYNTON

R.R.

RISBY

PORT WALTHALL
JUNCTION

MAY 16, 1864

TALLEY

$\mathcal{N}$

BOYNTON

LEGEND

Federal Troops

Confederate Troops

ARROWFIELD
CHURCH

0   ½   1 Mile

Swift   Creek

SCALE

bombard the opposite ridge. Following Whiting's orders, two Confederate artillery batteries unlimbered and began to rake the ridge with shells.[7]

Unknown to the Confederates, their elusive targets were only the 13th Indiana and 169th New York Infantry Regiments, Battery E, 3rd U.S. Artillery, and a detachment of the 1st U.S. Colored Cavalry, all under Brigadier General Adelbert Ames. Ames had had the disagreeable assignment of covering the rear of the Army of the James ever since the advance toward Drewry's Bluff had begun. Initially, his division had consisted of two brigades, but Confederate inaction and more pressing needs elsewhere had caused the early detachment of two of his regiments. Four of the remaining six regiments had been called north on the previous day to partici-pate in the planned Federal attack that never occurred. With three-fourths of his division already in action elsewhere, Ames found himself attempting to block the advance of two large Confederate brigades with two small regiments and a battery. Believing that the artillery bombardment was the prelude to an assault, he slowly began to withdraw his men northward. At 9:00 A.M. he was met by the 97th Pennsylvania Infantry, sent by Butler as a reinforcement. This unit had been stationed at Butler's field headquarters until it was ordered at 6:00 A.M. to move toward Port Walthall Junction.[8]

Both Ames's retreat and the arrival of the Pennsylvanians were noted by D. H. Hill from his vantage point with Wise's Brigade on the ridge south of Ashton Creek. Hill urged Whiting to order an advance across the creek and Whiting complied, but it was not until nearly 10:30 A.M. that the Confederate infantry reached the northern rim of the valley. By this time Ames's three regiments had retreated again, just out of the Confederates' reach. Once north of Ashton Creek, Whiting halted his men, although his officers desired to press the obviously weak Federals. Concerned about his right flank, which was only two miles distant from the Bermuda Hundred lines, Whiting dispatched scout Roger Pryor on a reconnais-sance. As he awaited Pryor's return, Whiting began to allow the uncertainties of his position to affect his judgment. Exhausted by three days of constant exertion, unacquainted with the tangled terrain, and out of touch with Beauregard, Whiting began to fear Federal moves against his left flank as well as his right. Repeatedly he ordered Henry Wise to guard his left and at last visited Wise in person with the same order, appearing so overwrought that Wise believed him to be intoxicated.[9]

By this time Wise had become thoroughly disgusted with Whiting and his erratic behavior, but Whiting appeared not to have noticed, returning instead to his nightmare world of massed Federals bearing down upon him. Even Ames's retreat was construed by Whiting as a ruse to cover a surprise dash against Petersburg. Whiting's confusion, both about Federal intentions and his own role in Beauregard's plan, is quite evident in a message dispatched to Beauregard about the time of his visit to Wise:

> I have been some time in advance of Walthall Junction, having drawn enemy, after sharp skirmish. He appears to be retiring to his line of fortifica-tion. I hear nothing of you. I cannot assault his left on Appomattox. I am

advancing my left, and have crossed Baker-house [Ashton] Creek. Enemy retiring in my front. If they cross the river Petersburg is gone. Can't you press down the river, provided you don't press him in my rear?[10]

While Whiting vacillated, D. H. Hill and Colonel Hilary Jones of the artillery rode forward to scout the Federal positions. By then Ames had put his own artillery in position and was making threatening demonstrations to further retard Whiting's progress. Hill was not fooled and returned to the Confederate lines with the intention of advising that the advance be resumed. Upon reaching Wise's headquarters, he was told that a heavy force of Federals was moving toward Wise's left. With a creek directly in their rear, Wise's infantrymen were in an awkward position to repel an attack, and, although he doubted the validity of the report, Hill advised a temporary withdrawal across the stream. According to his own testimony, Wise brushed aside Hill's recommendations until he received direct orders from Whiting, which he sourly obeyed. Yet Wise had only himself to blame, because it had been his erroneous report of Federal forces approaching the Confederate left that had triggered the retreat. Of course Whiting in his confused state had already concluded that such a Federal move was imminent, making Wise's report only the confirmation of a foregone conclusion. In his account of the day's events, Whiting spoke of much confusion during this period and it is obvious that he was passing beyond the ragged edge of self-control.[11]

The withdrawal was conducted during a heavy shower of rain. Riding up to the southern rim of the valley, Hill and Wise were horrified to find that the troops were not halting on the crest. Hurriedly seeking an explanation, Wise discovered that Whiting had ordered the retrograde movement to continue without informing the brigade commander. Learning what had happened, Hill rode to Whiting and persuaded the befuddled general to allow the troops to return to the ridge overlooking Ashton Creek, while Hill attempted to locate the Federals. Taking Colonel Logan along, Hill quickly ascertained that the only Federals in the vicinity were the handful of Ames's men that had been present all day. Sending Logan to inform Beauregard of affairs at Port Walthall Junction, Hill dashed off a note to Whiting advocating an immediate advance. This appeal was ignored by Whiting, who was content to rearrange his two brigades along the southern rim of the valley. There Whiting watched cautiously as Ames, emboldened by the inexplicable Confederate retreat, pushed his skirmishers forward to the crest so recently occupied by Wise's men. Fearing a Federal attack, Whiting ordered his artillery to shell the enemy skirmishers, and in that fashion the rest of the afternoon was spent.[12]

While Whiting dallied and his subordinates fretted, Colonel Logan made his way toward Drewry's Bluff. Guided by Dearing and a detachment of cavalry, Logan rode northward via Chester Station. There the mounted party encountered hundreds of fleeing Federal soldiers, the remnants of X Corps units that had been left behind during Gillmore's withdrawal. While his escort rounded up the demoralized Federals, Logan continued his journey, appalled at the opportunity Whiting had cast away by refusing to advance into the rear of the retreating Army of the James.

Finding Beauregard and President Davis in conversation near the captured Federal works, Logan reported that there was no need to rely further upon Whiting that day. Beauregard received the news calmly, giving Logan the impression that he had long since ceased to expect any contribution by Whiting to the battle at Drewry's Bluff.[13]

While Logan made his way to Beauregard, conditions at Port Walthall Junction were becoming even more chaotic. Some time after having advised Whiting to advance against Ames's pitifully small force, Hill rode to the headquarters of Brigadier General James Martin, a one-armed professional soldier from North Carolina who commanded the second of Whiting's two brigades. While Hill and Martin discussed the situation, Whiting appeared and ordered Martin to withdraw his skirmishers. Aghast, Hill remonstrated, "General Whiting, you cannot occupy this place if you withdraw your skirmishers." Whiting retorted, "You don't think that I intend to remain here?" Convinced that further conversation would be useless, Hill replied that he "did not know what his intentions were," and lapsed into silence. Whiting then directed Martin to withdraw his skirmishers, followed by his entire brigade. When Martin noted this was the exact opposite of customary procedure, Whiting remarked that "It makes no difference; there is no enemy in our front."[14]

Whiting explained his decision to retreat in a slightly different fashion in a later report to Beauregard. There he claimed that he based his decision on such factors as the lateness of the hour, the lack of news from the main army, and reports of Federal movements on his left, right, and rear. Unsure about whether Beauregard had engaged the Federals as planned, or about the location of the Army of the James, Whiting began to see his primary mission as the protection of Petersburg, seven miles in the rear. Reasoning that Port Walthall Junction was a poor place from which to cover Petersburg, Whiting decided to withdraw from what he felt to be a dangerously exposed position.[15]

As the afternoon passed, Wise's and Martin's infantry, the artillery, the supply wagons, and the ambulances all attempted to withdraw via the Old Stage Road. Half an hour after the colloquy with Martin and Whiting, D. H. Hill came upon the resulting traffic jam. Horrified that the retreating units were so inextricably jumbled in plain view of the enemy, Hill rode to tell Whiting of the situation. Whiting seemed genuinely puzzed as to what to do and asked Hill's counsel. Having seen his advice ignored all day, Hill was in no mood to be gentle. He pointedly reminded Whiting that two hours earlier he had suggested that the Federals be brushed aside at once. Whiting replied that he had not received Hill's note. For Hill this was the last straw. "Fearing that General Whiting might be embarrassed by the seeming divided responsibility of my presence, and feeling that I could accomplish nothing more, I retired to Dunlop's house."[16]

Soon after Hill departed for Swift Creek, a messenger brought Whiting news of Dearing's activities up to 1:30 P.M. The rider also brought a copy of Beauregard's 9:00 A.M. note to Whiting, by then hopelessly out of date. Nevertheless, Whiting was so stirred by this tangible sign of Beauregard's activity that he halted the retreat.

Dearing himself then arrived and confirmed the news already received, further strengthening Whiting's resolve to wait a bit longer before withdrawing to Petersburg. Since Ames had by that time been joined by two more regiments, the 11th Maine and the 115th New York, there was no thought in Whiting's mind of advancing, but at least he might tarry awhile in case Beauregard was on his way south.[17]

Some time after 7:00 P.M. Whiting received a copy of Beauregard's 4:15 P.M. message announcing the final drive against the fleeing Army of the James. As the sun had already set and the remaining light was failing fast, Whiting murmured "Too late for action on my part," and resumed his retreat to the Swift Creek defenses. In a 7:30 P.M. note to Beauregard, he explained that his inaction was due to the absence of sustained firing to the north and the slowness of messengers bringing Beauregard's orders. Promising to do better on the morrow, but still believing that his own situation was extremely precarious, Whiting begged Beauregard, "Don't let him press me to-night; position very bad." Across the creek, Ames called in his skirmishers as soon as darkness fell and withdrew to Bermuda Hundred, the last element of the Army of the James to return to camp.[18]

After nightfall Whiting personally sought out Henry Wise. Finding him in bivouac with his troops north of Swift Creek, Whiting groggily ordered him to allow the infantry to rest until 1:00 A.M., then fall back across Swift Creek. Wise, who had become increasingly suspicious of Whiting's curious behavior during the day, first begged to be allowed to maintain his position, then demanded a written order. After drafting the order, Whiting attempted to remount his horse, but was unable to do so without considerable effort and assistance. Watching this pitiful performance, Wise became convinced that Whiting was intoxicated, an opinion that he held strongly for the rest of his life. Drunk or sober, Whiting was still Wise's superior officer, so Wise reluctantly marched his brigade southward through the darkness. With the return of Wise's Brigade to Swift Creek the last combatants had left the field. The Battle of Drewry's Bluff was over.[19]

As his weary soldiers settled into the Swift Creek defenses, Henry Wise made his way to Dunlop's house for a few hours of rest. His casualties had amounted to a total of thirty men and he had taken ten prisoners, but Wise knew, as did Hill and Martin whom he found already at Dunlop's, that a great opportunity had slipped from the Confederate grasp.[20]

NOTES

1. Boatner, *Civil War Dictionary*, 916; Warner, *Generals in Gray*, 334–335, 398; James Ryder Randall, "A Plea for General W. H. C. Whiting," *Southern Historical Society Papers* 24 (1896):274. Whiting's academic record at West Point stood until 1903, when it was surpassed by Douglas MacArthur.

2. Randall, "Plea," 275–276.

3. O.R.A., 36, pt. 2, 259–260.

4. O.R.A., 36, pt. 2, 210, 256; B. H. Wise, *Life of H. A. Wise*, 339; Wise MS, Beauregard Papers, LC; T. M. Logan to Beauregard, 2 January 1882, quoted in Roman, *Military Operations*, 2:558;

Cutchins, *Richmond Light Infantry Blues*, 135; Field Return of Wise's Brigade, 16 May 1864, D. H. Hill Papers, VSL; *O.R.A.*, 33:1300.

5. *O.R.A.*, 36, pt. 2, 210, 256–257; Wise MS, Beauregard Papers, LC; Cutchins, *Richmond Light Infantry Blues*, 135.

6. *O.R.A.*, 36, pt. 2, 210, 257, pt. 3, 822; Cutchins, *Richmond Light Infantry Blues*, 135; T. M. Logan to Beauregard, 2 January 1882, quoted in Roman, *Military Operations*, 2:559. Charles Elliott of Martin's Brigade, who was temporarily serving on Whiting's staff, supported Whiting's contention that the distant firing was "not heavy." Charles G. Elliott, "Martin's Brigade, of Hoke's Division, 1863–64," *Southern Historical Society Papers* 23 (1895):190–191.

7. *O.R.A.*, 36, pt. 2, 210, 257, pt. 3, 822; B. H. Wise, *Life of H. A. Wise*, 339; Wise MS, Beauregard Papers, LC; Cutchins, *Richmond Light Infantry Blues*, 135. Ashton Creek is identified in some accounts as Bake-House Creek.

8. *O.R.A.*, 36, pt. 2, 257, 741, 806, 837, pt. 3, 822; Price, *Ninety-Seventh Pennsylvania*, 267, 413.

9. *O.R.A.*, 36, pt. 2, 210–211, 257, 258, 837; Price, *Ninety-Seventh Pennsylvania*, 267–268; Wise MS, Beauregard Papers, LC.

10. Quoted in Roman, *Military Operations*, 2:561.

11. *O.R.A.*, 36, pt. 2, 210–211, 257, 837; Clark, ed., *North Carolina Regiments*, 3:687; T. M. Logan to Beauregard, 2 January 1882, quoted in Roman, *Military Operations*, 2:559; Wise MS, Beauregard Papers, LC. According to Hill, Wise approved of the retrograde movement, yet Wise in later years vehemently denied that he had agreed to follow Hill's advice until peremptory orders came from Whiting. (Beauregard, who annotated Wise's manuscript, scrawled at this point in the margin "Carramba!—GTB.") On the other hand, Whiting in his report denied that he gave the order to retire, stating "that some one, I know not who, ordered the lines back, for I am satisfied these troops would never move back of their own accord."

12. *O.R.A.*, 36, pt. 2, 211, 257, 837–838; Wise MS, Beauregard Papers, LC; T. M. Logan to Beauregard, 2 January 1882, quoted in Roman, *Military Operations*, 2:559; Cutchins, *Richmond Light Infantry Blues*, 135; Price, *Ninety-Seventh Pennsylvania*, 268.

13. T. M. Logan to Beauregard, 2 January 1882, quoted in Roman, *Military Operations*, 2:559–560.

14. *O.R.A.*, 36, pt. 2, 211.

15. Ibid., 257–258.

16. Wise MS, Beauregard Papers, LC; *O.R.A.*, 36, pt. 2, 211.

17. *O.R.A.*, 36, pt. 2, 83–84, 258, pt. 3, 822; Beauregard to Whiting, 21 May 1864, Letter Book, April–May 1864, and Beauregard to Dearing, 7 June 1864, Letter Book, May–July 1864, both in Beauregard Papers, LC; Clark, *Iron Hearted Regiment*, 118–119; Brady, *Eleventh Maine*, 186.

18. *O.R.A.*, 36, pt. 2, 84, 258, pt. 3, 822; Roman, *Military Operations*, 2:210; Price, *Ninety-Seventh Pennsylvania*, 266, 269; Clark, *Iron-Hearted Regiment*, 119; Brady, *Eleventh Maine*, 186, 187. Ames's casualties were light. Of two regiments reporting, the 11th Maine lost only two wounded and the 97th Pennsylvania lost two wounded and five captured.

19. Wise MS, Beauregard Papers, LC. Wise's analysis of Whiting's condition can be found in the Wise MS, as well as in Roman, *Military Operations*, 2:209, and Hagood, *Memoirs*, 236. The testimony of D. H. Hill and other staff officers, however, as well as Whiting's own subsequent denials, casts considerable doubt upon Wise's conclusion. *O.R.A.*, 36, pt. 2, 211, pt. 3, 812, 845; Randall, "Plea," 276; Harrison, *Pickett's Men*, 127; Statement of W. C. Strong, 28 May 1864, W. H. C. Whiting Military Papers, National Archives, Washington, D.C. Uncorroborated elsewhere is Postmaster General Reagan's statement in his *Memoirs*, 191, that Whiting "frankly admitted" he was drunk "in a letter to the President." It is much more likely that Whiting had finally succumbed to both physical and mental exhaustion after three days and nights of unrelenting tension and activity. *O.R.A.*, 36, pt. 2, 259–260; Freeman, *Lee's Lieutenants*, 3:492–493. Whiting's claim that he was bereft of staff officers does appear to be false, since at least eight individuals were serving with him on 16 May. *O.R.A.*, 36, pt. 2, 259; Harrison, *Pickett's Men*, 126; Elliott, "Martin's Brigade," 190; Wistar, *Autobiography*, 457.

20. Wise MS, Beauregard Papers, LC; Reports of Casualties in and Prisoners Taken by Wise's Brigade, 16 May 1864, D. H. Hill Papers, VSL; *O.R.A.*, 36, pt. 2, 261.

☆ 16 ☆

The Return to Bermuda Hundred
17–22 May 1864

Protected by their fortifications, the men of the Army of the James at last gave vent to their emotions. The very sight of the camps so confidently vacated on 12 May brought tears to the eyes of many veterans when they thought of their comrades who would not be returning to their tents. Others were struck by the contrast between their own dirty, haggard appearance and the spit-and-polish sharpness of the newly arrived 1st Connecticut Heavy Artillery. Undaunted by the stories spread by the returning troops of thousands of pursuing Confederates, the Connecticut artillerymen and the camp guards turned out to welcome their comrades with rations, fresh water, and sympathy. Although some of the returnees collapsed into undisturbed sleep immediately, others took the time to bathe or to write letters home announcing their safe arrival.[1]

During the night some units conducted roll calls to determine losses and others completed that sad but necessary task on the following day. The final tabulations showed that slightly more than 3,000 Federal soldiers had been killed, wounded, or captured.[2] The Confederates had gathered up 1,388 prisoners, including many wounded. Most of the dead had been left on the field unburied, leaving only the returning wounded to be cared for. These had either been carried to regimental aid stations during the course of the battle or had stumbled to safety by themselves during the retreat. Upon reaching the fortifications, the wounded were taken first to the large hospital established near Butler's headquarters at Point of Rocks, where they were given such emergency treatment as their numbers would permit. Most were then transported in ambulances to the landings, where ships waited to carry them down the James River to the more elaborate medical facilities near Fort Monroe. In a few days, many were transferred from there to hospitals scattered throughout the North. For others, Fort Monroe was the last stop.[3]

Among Beauregard's forces, casualties had also been heavy, amounting to just under 3,000 killed, wounded, and missing.[4] Confederate wounded, however, had a much shorter distance to travel than did the Federals. From a collection point at Drewry's Bluff, they were conveyed by steamer or ambulance to Richmond and distributed among the city's military hospitals. Serving to mitigate the sense of loss among Beauregard's troops was the knowledge that, by almost any measurement, they had won the battle. Besides the nearly 1,400 Federal prisoners, the booty included five battle flags, five artillery pieces, 3,968 rifles, and more than 60,000 rounds of ammunition. Most important, the Federals had left the battlefield and retired behind their defenses, thereby vacating the transportation corridor between Richmond and Petersburg. Officers were proud of their men and the troops were proud of themselves. A Virginian expressed the sentiments of most when he told a relative that "we gave the Yankees the completest thrashing that they have ever had altho we fought them under great disadvantages for they certainly had five men to our one." Such optimistic assessments even gave rise to hope that the war would soon be successfully concluded; as a North Carolinian told his wife: "the yankeys say the war has to stop till the fourth of July I hope it will for the Yankeys are getting repulsed at all points."[5]

Following the battle, both sides indulged in recriminations. On the Federal side a soldier in the 23rd Massachusetts wrote his parents that "Old Baldy Smith is to blame I think for it was an ill managed consern." In a letter to his wife Colonel Joseph Hawley of the X Corps found fault at an even higher level: "Gen. Butler failed as a great general. Our position was weak & line thin. Most of the leading officers in our corps felt the defeat coming for two days." Others, however, were not so sure that the blame for the Federal defeat lay with Butler, claiming that Gillmore could have changed the outcome by attacking earlier on the left. Even among the victors, there was fault to be found, with Beauregard castigating both Ransom and Whiting for their dilatory movements. Nor was the government in Richmond totally satisfied, particularly since Jefferson Davis had argued strenuously against attempting to unite the Confederate forces on the field of battle.[6]

Friday, 17 May, was a day of rest and reflection for the Army of the James, after the haste and confusion of the previous twenty-four hours. Within their fortified base, Butler's men began to improve their defenses and camps in preparation for a long stay.[7] As the Army of the James recuperated from its ordeal, P. G. T. Beauregard's forces slowly pushed forward from their night bivouacs near the battlefield. The advance was conducted cautiously and it was not until the afternoon that Federal pickets were encountered screening Butler's front. As they marched, the Confederates remarked upon the large quantities of battle debris scattered about—broken drums, guns, and equipment of all kinds. Causing even more of a stir was the damage done to several fine homes that briefly had been behind the Federal lines.[8]

During the day several command changes occurred in Beauregard's army. When the brigades from Petersburg arrived, they were under the command of D. H. Hill, because Wise and Martin had refused to obey Chase Whiting's orders any longer. When Whiting, who had accompanied the column, asked to be officially relieved of field command, Beauregard readily consented. To replace Whiting, Beauregard provisionally appointed Hill as division commander and informed the War Department of his action. A highly competent officer, Hill had for some time been embroiled in a controversy over rank with Jefferson Davis, and therefore any permanent appointment would have to be approved at the highest level. Still another replacement was needed for Robert Ransom, who was recalled to the Department of Richmond. As Ransom's successor, Beauregard chose Brigadier General Bushrod Johnson, who had previously held divisional command in the Western Theater.[9]

The eighteenth of May was another day of consolidation for both sides, as Confederate skirmishers engaged the stoutly resisting Federal pickets. At times the action became heavy, particularly in the center of the Federal line, where the 97th Pennsylvania Infantry suffered fifty-seven casualties in losing and recapturing its picket line. As the skirmishing waxed and waned throughout the day, the majority of soldiers on both sides spent their time building or improving their defenses. Among the Confederates, particular effort was expended upon an earthwork located on a bluff overlooking the James River near the Howlett mansion. This work commanded a long sweep of the river known as Trent's Reach, in which lay the advance elements of Admiral Lee's fleet. Both Lee and the Confederates were well aware that, if completed, the Howlett battery would effectively close the James River to further naval penetration. As a result, the workmen from Terry's Brigade labored under constant bombardment from Federal warships.[10]

During the day an attitude began to materialize within the Confederate government that large numbers of Beauregard's troops could be used to better advantage elsewhere. Lee telegraphed Davis that Grant was being heavily reinforced, and he baldly stated: "The question is whether we shall fight the battle here or around Richmond. If the troops are obliged to be retained at Richmond I may be forced back."[11] Unaware of Lee's telegram, Beauregard drew up a memorandum calling for Lee's retreat behind the Chickahominy River, after which Beauregard would march north with 15,000 men to operate on Grant's flank. Following Grant's "certain and decisive" defeat, Beauregard would return southward with his own and some of Lee's troops and drive Butler into the James River. If his plan were rejected and Davis decided to reinforce Lee from his army, Beauregard estimated he could spare 3,000 men immediately and 2,000 more two days later, if his defensive line could be reduced in length. At the time he wrote, Beauregard's force at Bermuda Hundred comprised 19,000 infantry, 1,000 cavalry, and four artillery battalions, while Walker's South Carolina Brigade and two cavalry regiments garrisoned Petersburg.[12]

Within the Federal lines Benjamin Butler was convinced that he was outnumbered by his Confederate opponents. To Secretary of War Stanton he wrote: "We have opposite us a larger force than we have, after keeping open our communications on the river. . . . Can we not have re-enforcements? We can hold on as we are if they cannot be spared." Similarly, he informed his wife that "A part of Lee's army has been withdrawn and is here, Longstreet's Corps, I believe." This view was not credited elsewhere. Near Spotsylvania Court House, Grant received a telegram from Halleck informing him of Butler's withdrawal from Drewry's Bluff. Coupled with his own repulse by Lee's army and the news of Franz Sigel's defeat at New Market in the Valley of Virginia, word of Butler's troubles cast Grant into a depression. Believing that the Confederates would now reinforce Lee from Beauregard's army, Grant considered calling most of the Army of the James north at once. Upon reflection, however, he delayed the implementation of such a drastic step.[13]

Meanwhile, on their way to rejoin the Army of the Potomac, Philip Sheridan and James Wilson were conspiring to procure Butler's removal from field command. Convinced by what they had seen and heard at Bermuda Hundred that Butler was unfit for the task before him, Sheridan and Wilson decided to bring about a change via indirect channels. While still on the march, Sheridan drafted a letter to Colonel Cyrus Comstock, one of Grant's aides, and Wilson wrote a similar note to Brigadier General John Rawlins, Grant's chief of staff. According to Wilson, both letters called for replacing Butler with Baldy Smith and proposed that the Army of the James operate against Petersburg and its railroads. Secure in the knowledge that Rawlins and Comstock would know how to present their views to Grant in an unobjectionable manner, Sheridan and Wilson sent the letters ahead by courier so as to hasten the change.[14]

Thursday, 19 May, was a day of intermittent showers, which served only to deepen the yellow mud filling the roads and trenches. Perhaps because of the weather, activity on the skirmish lines was generally light, although artillerymen ashore and afloat did not slacken their fire. A few halfhearted probes showed that the opposing sides were yet in place, with no visible intention of retreating. Within the Confederate lines many soldiers who could get out of the rain wrote letters home. Behind the Federal fortifications similar letters were being composed, although the mood there was somewhat darker, because the defeat at Drewry's Bluff still rankled. According to a New Hampshire officer, "Our soldiers are so inexpressibly angry and disgusted, that they have ceased swearing about the defeat; and they would fight like mad furies if let loose upon the enemy now."[15]

During the morning Beauregard's memorandum calling for Lee's retreat and a junction with 15,000 of Beauregard's men was delivered to Jefferson Davis. Unwittingly, by admitting that he could detach 15,000 men from his front, if only for a brief time, Beauregard played into Davis's hands. Anxious to reinforce the Army of Northern Virginia, Davis seized upon Beauregard's figures with a vengeance and endorsed upon the memorandum: "If 15,000 men can be spared for the flank movement proposed, certainly 10,000 may be sent to re-enforce General Lee." Without even a nod to Beauregard's grand design, Davis instructed Bragg to order the detachment of Barton's, Terry's, Corse's, and Lewis's Brigades, along with Lightfoot's Artillery Battalion. In a separate decision, Colonel John Baker's 3rd North Carolina Cavalry was also put under orders to join the Army of Northern Virginia. At 3:15 P.M. the directive concerning the infantry reached Beauregard. Realizing that the loss of one-third of his infantry would greatly reduce his options even in the Bermuda Hundred-Petersburg area, Beauregard argued strenuously for a delay until he could shorten his lines. Yet it was all for naught. At 7:30 P.M. Bragg answered briskly: "The troops cannot be delayed. Transportation is now at Drewry's Bluff awaiting them. The emergency is most pressing."[16]

With no choice but to obey the original order, Beauregard withdrew the designated units from the front lines. At 9:15 P.M. part of Lewis's Brigade sailed from Drewry's Bluff. The remainder of Lewis's men departed by water shortly thereafter, followed by Barton's Brigade, while Corse's and Terry's troops marched overland. To partially replace the lost units, Beauregard called Walker's Brigade north from Petersburg. This in turn forced Whiting to cancel a plan to push forward some artillery to bombard the Federal camps from across the Appomattox River. With Walker's departure, Petersburg was guarded by only two infantry regiments, a few militia units, and part of Dearing's cavalry. This move represented a considerable risk, but Beauregard felt compelled to make an attack to reduce the length of his line, and Walker's Brigade would be needed to form part of the assaulting column. [17]

On the morning of 20 May, as Terry's Brigade paraded its captured battleflags through Richmond and the last dead were buried on the Drewry's Bluff battlefield, [18] Beauregard's troops advanced in an effort to secure more advantageous terrain. Because the front of the XVIII Corps on the Federal left was covered by a deep ravine, the Confederate assault was directed against Terry's and Ames's divisions of the X Corps, which occupied relatively level ground. Pressing forward under a heavy fire from the Federal pickets, the Confederates successfully gained the first line of rifle pits along most of Gillmore's front. The greatest penetration of the Federal defenses occurred in Ames's sector, where Wise's and Martin's Brigades, aided by Federal mistakes, advanced nearly three-fourths of a mile. To the north, Confederate units were not kept well in hand, and although they seized considerable ground, their hold on the position was tenuous. [19]

That afternoon Gillmore ordered a counterattack in the hope of regaining his lost picket line. On Ames's front the 97th Pennsylvania and 13th Indiana Regiments attempted valiantly, but unsuccessfully, to drive the Confederates from their new positions. There would be no return to Ames's old picket line, making it necessary to establish a new one nearer the Federal main line. By contrast, Terry's situation appeared much more favorable. Terry had lost only the southern portion of his picket line, which connected with that of Ames. Shortly after 2:00 P.M. Colonel Joshua Howell led two of his own regiments, supported by one of Joseph Hawley's, in an effort to recapture the lost ground. At the cost of numerous casualties, Howell eventually succeeded in driving the Confederates back toward their starting point, after which he reestablished the original Federal position. [20]

Just then Brigadier General William Walker's South Carolina Brigade arrived on the field and was ordered to drive Howell back before he had time to consolidate his gains. Unfortunately for the South Carolinians, Walker had not had time to familiarize himself either with the terrain or the situation. The resulting attack was a disaster. The individual regiments advanced disjointedly and were repeatedly flanked by the Federals. A survivor later admitted that "it was just such a place that this child never wants to be catched in again." Walker remained in the thick of action encouraging his men until it became obvious that the brigade would require aid to avoid destruction. Riding in search of help, he mistook his direction and headed directly toward the Federal lines. Realizing his error too late, Walker tried to flee, but was cut down by a volley from the 67th Ohio Infantry. While his men retreated in disorder, Walker lay on the field bleeding from three wounds until brought within the Federal lines. Near midnight, he was operated upon by Surgeon John Craven who, working by the light of a bonfire, amputated one of Walker's legs in order to save his life.[21]

Unaware of Walker's fate, Beauregard at 6:15 P.M. reported to Bragg that the terrain needed for the shortest possible defensive line had been acquired. At a cost of 800 Confederate casualties and 702 Federal, Beauregard's troops had established themselves in a continuous line across the Bermuda Hundred peninsula, and work began at once to fortify the position.[22] The new defensive line had been obtained none too soon, for during the day the War Department ordered Beauregard to transfer Gracie's Brigade to the Department of Richmond. Upon Gracie's departure, Beauregard had only 14,500 infantry, 2,500 cavalry, and 1,000 artillery with which to contain Butler's larger army and to defend Petersburg. Nevertheless, Beauregard continued to look for offensive openings. Because the possibility of further action south of the Appomattox required a more stable person in charge at Petersburg, Chase Whiting was relieved of command "at his own request."[23]

Although Beauregard reported to Richmond early in the evening that Butler had recently been reinforced, Jefferson Davis was contemplating even further reductions in the size of Beauregard's army. Writing to Lee, Davis promised that "If, as intended, Butler's force should be withdrawn to re-enforce Grant, we must endeavor, before he reaches there, to send the troops which now confront him, to join your army." Davis also informed Lee of Beauregard's proposal to concentrate both armies for a joint offensive against Grant. Noting drily that "My order for the movement of troops . . . is not in accordance with that plan," Davis nevertheless left the matter to Lee's discretion. In a letter of the same date to Beauregard, Davis explained that if rumors of Butler's impending departure proved true, Lee would welcome a large reinforcement under Beauregard's personal command. Although Davis's tone was soothing, there was no mistaking its import. Beauregard's plan for concentration would not be adopted unless the Federals withdrew from Bermuda Hundred.[24]

Within the Army of the James there was no talk of leaving the Bermuda Hundred peninsula. By 20 May, however, the frustration generated by the army's lack of success was beginning to emerge. When the Confederate attack showed that the defensive works did not join well at the boundaries of the X and XVIII Corps, Butler appointed his friend Godfrey Weitzel to supervise all engineering operations. This arrangement was fought bitterly by Gillmore and his engineer, Colonel Edward Serrell, with the result that Serrell was gently reprimanded by Butler.[25] During the afternoon a second incident occurred, when Butler ordered Smith to send Brooks's division to aid Gillmore in retaking his lost picket line. Smith was alleged to have replied, "Damn Gillmore! He has got himself into a scrape; let him get out of it the best way he can." Although Smith denied making the remark, it seems in character for him, and he definitely did not send the troops. Because Gillmore did not feel strong enough to recapture his line alone, he angrily gave up the attempt.[26] That night an altercation with the navy erupted when the *U.S.S. Commodore Perry* in the Appomattox River opened fire at the army's request, but without getting permission from Brigadier General Charles Graham, Butler's "admiral." Supported by Butler, Graham demanded an explanation from the *Perry's* captain, which was forbidden by Admiral Lee. Interservice cooperation declined accordingly.[27]

On 21 May the Confederate forces facing the Army of the James completed the occupation of their new line, roughly three miles long. At the same time, a further reorganization was necessitated by Jefferson Davis's refusal to allow D. H. Hill to hold divisional command. Hill had made known to Davis his willingness to serve on active duty, but he had refused to beg the president or Bragg in writing for a field command. Without such a letter, Davis was adamant in his stand against assigning Hill to such a position, and Beauregard had to relieve Hill at his own request. Hill returned to Beauregard's staff as a volunteer aide and his two brigades were distributed between Hoke's and Johnson's Divisions. Since Hoke was the only major general present, Beauregard requested that either Bushrod Johnson or Alfred Colquitt be promoted one grade.[28]

Now that the Army of the James was safely within the Bermuda Hundred peninsula, the tension that had gripped many Confederates began to ease. At the front some artillery batteries were relieved from duty and, in Richmond, diarist J. B. Jones recorded that "Nothing is feared from Butler." Similarly, a soldier in the trenches confided to his cousin: "if we still continue to be as successful during the summer as we have been so far I am almost satisfied that we will get our independence by next Christmas then wont we be a happy and free people." Yet J. W. Pursley, also stationed in the Bermuda trenches, had his doubts: "It is generally thought by all now that this year will end the war but I think it doubtful I have sit so many times for it to end and still it goes on I have all most give it up for a life time Buisness." In Petersburg Chase Whiting, preparing to return to North Carolina, suggested prophetically that Benjamin Butler might yet attempt to capture Petersburg.[29]

Throughout the day Federal fatigue details labored on the defenses, particularly on the more exposed X Corps sector. Since the Confederate attack of the previous day, it had been decreed that, until further notice, all troops would rise at 3:30 A.M. each morning and occupy the works until daylight. Although some units evaded the order by sleeping in the trenches, the long hours of watchfulness, the rigors of fatigue duty, and the harassing fire of the Confederates were sapping the troops' strength. In the XVIII Corps Smith tried to ameliorate the hardships by issuing to each man a morning ration of whiskey and quinine, or coffee, as long as the 3:30 A.M. alert remained in force. This measure was soon adopted in the X Corps also, although in one soldier's opinion the commissary whiskey tasted like "a 'wide awake' torch-light procession going down the throat." On the picket line another stimulant, tobacco, was obtained from the Confederate sentries in exchange for coffee or newspapers. Although frowned upon by officers, such illicit fraternization became a fixed custom as long as the lines remained static.[30]

While the Army of the James marked time, U. S. Grant was becoming impatient. Stifling for the moment his earlier impulse to withdraw most of the Army of the James from Bermuda Hundred, Grant wired Halleck to "send a competent officer there to inspect and report by telegraph what is being done, and what in his judgment it is advisable to do."[31] Seeing an opportunity to liquidate an operation to which he had long been opposed, Halleck acted with dispatch. Early in the afternoon he informed Grant that he had ordered Quartermaster General Montgomery Meigs and Chief Engineer John Barnard to go to Bermuda Hundred and evaluate the situation there. Before sailing from Washington at 4:00 P.M., Meigs and Barnard conferred with Halleck personally. The instructions that they received forecast possible trouble for Butler's future plans:

> General Grant wishes particularly to know what is being done there, and what, in your judgment, it is advisable to do. This of course involves an estimate of the enemy's force and defenses, the condition of our army, whether active operations on our part are advisable, or whether it should limit itself to its defensive position, and, if so, what troops can be spared from that department to re-enforce the Army of the Potomac.[32]

During the night a noisy skirmish erupted on the Bermuda Hundred picket line, but by dawn of Sunday, 22 May, the volume of fire had slackened. Hostilities generally continued at a reduced level throughout the day, except on the river where the Federal monitors vigorously pounded the Howlett battery.[33] In Beauregard's command it was a Sunday of leave-takings. Harvey Hill exchanged his field command for the job of superintendent of the defenses. The 3rd North Carolina Cavalry was finally replaced by some of James Dearing's men and left to join the Army of Northern Virginia, where the infantry brigades detached earlier were already arriving. At Petersburg, Chase Whiting also departed, returning to Wilmington and Fort Fisher. Before leaving, he wrote Beauregard, "When I shall have laid out all that is necessary to be done there, if you do not join in the censure to which I am now unfortunately subject here, I will be glad if you will call me to your side."[34]

The low ebb of activity at the front was not matched by a diminution of the internal troubles besetting the Army of the James. Although a visitor to headquarters informed Sarah Butler that her husband was "in very good spirits," there was much for Butler to be concerned about. The defensive works were still not complete, for which Butler blamed the disagreements between Smith and Gillmore. Tension between the army and the fleet was still high, and it was exacerbated further by the insubordination of an army tug commander carrying a message to Admiral Lee.[35] Although newspaper coverage of the campaign had previously been favorable or at least neutral, certain correspondents were beginning to take sides in the Gillmore-Butler feud, with nasty effects. This was particularly true among the staff of the New York Herald, as reporter William Stiner explained to his managing editor:

Sawyer [Oscar G. Sawyer, another *Herald* correspondent] gives great dissatisfaction. I should not be surprised if he was sent away. He is very unguarded in his language, and says to officers things which are uncalled for. Gilmore is deadly opposed to Butler & Sawyer seems to echo Gilmore's sentiments. S calls the campaign "Butler's blunders." Of course all this is reported at HdQrs & tends to demoralize the troops.[36]

Another potential problem for Butler, although he was not yet aware of its implications, was the arrival of Generals Meigs and Barnard. Passing City Point at dusk on 22 May, they continued upriver to Trent's Reach to meet Admiral Lee and remained there for the night. Ironically, at the very time of their arrival, Grant moved to make their mission superfluous. The general-in-chief had decided not to wait for Meigs's and Barnard's report after all, because there was evidence that reinforcements had reached Lee from Beauregard's army at Bermuda Hundred. Impatiently, Grant wired Halleck at 8:00 P.M.:

> The force under General Butler is not detaining 10,000 men in Richmond, and is not even keeping the roads south of the city cut. Under these circumstances I think it advisable to have all of it here except enough to keep a foothold at City Point. . . . Send Smith in command.[37]

If Grant's order were not rescinded, Butler's freedom of action would go the way of Beauregard's.

NOTES

1. Cunningham, *Adirondack Regiment*, 115–116; Derby, *Bearing Arms*, 278; Thompson, *Thirteenth New Hampshire*, 306–308, 319–320; Beecher, *First Connecticut Light Battery*, 1:451–453; Eldredge, *Third New Hampshire*, 481; Henry E. Taintor to his mother, 17 May 1864, Henry E. Taintor Papers, Duke University, Durham, N.C. The rumors of pursuing Confederates were generally uttered in jest.

2. Walter S. Clemence Memoranda, 16 May 1864, NCC; Drake, *Ninth New Jersey*, 211; Eldredge, *Third New Hampshire*, 481. The statement of Federal casualties found in O.R.A., 36, pt. 2, 13–19 covers the entire period from 5 May to 31 May 1864, and amounts to 5,778 men, if Kautz's and Hincks's commands are excluded. Federal casualties on 16 May 1864 have been computed as follows: From both official reports and regimental histories, casualties for the period 5–15 May, 1864 have been computed to be 1,698 in all categories. Subtracted from 5,778, this leaves 4,080 as the total casualties for the period 16–31 May 1864. According to William F. Fox, *Regimental Losses in the American Civil War, 1861–1865*, Reprint ed. (Dayton, Ohio: Press of Morningside Bookshop, 1974), 546, Federal losses during the period 18–20 May 1864 amounted to 948 (See also O.R.A., 36, pt. 2, 40.), and through the rest of May totaled 128. Subtraction of the total figure for 17–31 May 1864 (1,076) from the figure for 16–31 May 1864 therefore yields 3,004 as the total casualties for the Army of the James on 16 May 1864. At best, however, this figure should be taken as no more than a careful estimate, since the large number of variables necessary to its determination precludes a totally accurate accounting. Livermore, *Numbers and Losses*, 113, relies upon Fox to reach a total of 4,160 Federal casualties for the period 12–16 May 1864, which covers the entire period of the advance upon Drewry's Bluff. Livermore errs badly, however, in placing Federal losses for the period 7–31 May 1864 at only 4,260, thereby omitting entirely the 798 casualties suffered 6–10 May 1864 and underestimating Federal losses 17–31 May by 976. Humphreys, *Virginia Campaign*, 157–158, citing the calculations of Adam Badeau, places total Federal casualties on 16 May 1864 at 3,500.

3. O.R.A., 36, pt. 2, 31, 118–119, 206; Clark, *Thirty-Ninth Illinois*, 190, 322; Drake, *Ninth New*

Jersey, 357–358; William Coley to his father, 29 May 1864, Wiliam Henry Cooley [Coley] Letters, SHC. For a comparison of the Point of Rocks hospital both before and after 16 May, see Emmerton, *Twenty-Third Massachusetts,* 175–176, and Cunningham, *Adirondack Regiment,* 116–118.

4. Confederate casualties are listed by brigade in O.R.A., 36, pt. 2, 205–206, except for Terry's Brigade and Corse's Brigade, which filed no reports; the total was 2,506. According to Loehr, *First Virginia,* 48, Terry's Brigade lost 321 men up to 20 May, and 310 has therefore been estimated as the figure for that unit on 16 May. (However, Loehr, "Battle of Drewry's Bluff," 110, places Terry's total casualties at only 257.) At Corse's Brigade participated only briefly in the action, its losses have been arbitrarily placed at 150. (One of Corse's regiments, the 17th Virginia, lost 31 men killed and wounded. Wise, *Seventeenth Virginia,* 179–180.) Thus total Confederate losses have been placed at 2,966 in all categories for the units under Beauregard's direct personal command. There is, however, a discrepancy in the figures for Hagood's Brigade, Hagood's report giving a figure of 433 (O.R.A., 36, pt. 2, 254) and the consolidated statement for Beauregard's forces placing the total at 664. Thomas L. Livermore in *Numbers and Losses,* 114, estimates total Confederate casualties at 3,070. Losses in some individual Confederate units are listed in O.R.A., 36, pt. 2, 247, 249; O.R.A., 51, pt. 1, 225; Clark, ed., *North Carolina Regiments,* 3:211; Izlar, *Edisto Rifles,* 52–53; Jones, *Surry Light Artillery,* 190; Gregorie, ed., "Wescoat Diary," 86; List of Casualties and Memorandum of Movements (Co. F, 31st N.C.), Wilson G. Lamb Papers, NCDAH; Edward Phifer to George Phifer, 31 May 1864, Phifer Family Papers, SHC; John Lane Stuart to his mother, 23 May 1864, John Lane Stuart Papers, DU.

5. Emmerton, *Twenty-Third Massachusetts,* 192; Derby, *Bearing Arms,* 274, 277; Henry Machen Patrick to his wife, 19 May 1864, Henry Machen Patrick Letters, NCDAH; O.R.A., 36, pt. 2, 204, 206, 213, 254, 255; Hagood, *Memoirs,* 248–249; Thomas F. Kelley to "My Dear Cousin," 21 May 1864, Thomas F. Kelley Papers, Duke University, Durham, N.C.; N. A. Barrier to his wife, 19 May 1864, N.A. Barrier Papers, Duke University, Durham, N. C.

6. Alfred Otis Chamberlin to his parents, 18 May 1864, Alfred Otis Chamberlin Papers, DU; Joseph Hawley to his wife, 17 May 1864, Hawley Papers, LC; Copp, *Reminiscences,* 391–392; O.R.A., 36, pt. 2, 204; Williams, *Beauregard,* 221; Freeman, *Lee's Lieutenants,* 3:493.

7. Thompson, *Thirteenth New Hampshire,* 322–323, 333–334; Bartlett, *Twelfth New Hampshire,* 185, 187–188; Eldredge, *Third New Hampshire,* 481; Kreutzer, *Ninety-Eighth New York,* 195; Stowits, *One Hundredth New York,* 262; Cadwell, *Old Sixth,* 92–93; Valentine, *Story of Co. F,* 117; Clark, *My Experience,* 62; Putnam, *Story of Company A,* 283–284; Walter S. Clemence Diary and Memoranda, 17 May 1864, NCC; Trumbull, *Knightly Soldier,* 228; Derby, *Bearing Arms,* 291–292; *Twenty-First Connecticut,* 205; O.R.A., 36, pt. 2, 15; Emmerton, *Twenty-Third Massachusetts,* 194; Clark, *Thirty-Ninth Illinois,* 186; David F. Dobie to "Dear Friend Hattie," 17 May 1864, David F. Dobie Letters, VSL.

8. O.R.A., 36, pt. 2, 1017; Beauregard to Bragg, 17 May 1864, Official Telegrams, 22 April–9 June 1864, Beauregard Papers, LC; Hagood, *Memoirs,* 249–250; Edwin Baker Loving Diary, 17 May 1864, VSL; Henry Chambers Diary, 17 May 1864, NCDAH; William H. S. Burgwyn Diary, 17 May 1864, NCDAH; Cary Whitaker Diary, 17 May 1864, SHC; Wise, *Seventeenth Virginia,* 181; Henry Machen Patrick to his wife, 26 May 1864, Henry Machen Patrick Letters, NCDAH; Jones, *Surry Light Artillery,* 195. Some Federals admitted the truth of the accusations, but they were unrepentant. See Dickey, *Eighty-Fifth Pennsylvania,* 323, and Bowditch, "War Letters," 477.

9. O.R.A., 36, pt. 2, 198, 205, 258–260, 1016–1018; Cutchins, *Richmond Light Infantry Blues,* 136; Wise MS, Beauregard Papers, LC; O.R.A., 51, pt. 2, 939; Roman, *Military Operations,* 2:210–211, 221–222, 562; Beauregard, *Battles and Leaders,* 4:204; Beauregard, "Drury's Bluff," 259; Beauregard to Bragg, 9:00 P.M., 17 May 1864, Official Telegrams, 22 April–9 June 1864, Beauregard Papers, LC; Freeman, *Lee's Lieutenants,* 3:494–495; Boatner, *Civil War Dictionary,* 437; Bushrod R. Johnson Diary, 17 May 1864, Johnson Papers, NA. For a discussion of Hill's problems with the Davis administration, see Bridges, *Lee's Maverick General,* 239–270.

10. O.R.A., 36, pt. 2, 808, 898–900, 902, 905; O.R.A., 51, pt. 1, 224, 232; Owen, *Washington Artillery,* 322; Wise, *Seventeenth Virginia,* 182; Hagood, *Memoirs,* 251; DuBose, *History of Company B,* 64; Gregorie, ed., "Wescoat Diary," 86; Eldredge, *Third New Hampshire,* 482; Clark, *Iron Hearted Regiment,* 120; Price, *Ninety-Seventh Pennsylvania,* 270–272, 414; Clark, ed., *North Carolina Regiments,* 3:211, 355, 688; Henry Chambers Diary, 18 May 1864, NCDAH; William H. S. Burgwyn Diary, 18 May 1864, NCDAH; William Beavans Diary, 18 May 1864, SHC; Cary Whitaker Diary, 18 May 1864; SHC; Clark, *My Experience,* 62; Drake, *Ninth New Jersey,* 211; Cleveland, ed., "Campaign of Promise," 323; Brady, *Eleventh Maine,* 190; Cunningham, *Adirondack Regiment,* 124; Walter S. Clemence Diary and Memoranda, 18 May 1864, NCC; Johnston, *Four Years,* 321–322; Johnston, *Confederate Boy,* 257;

Loehr, *First Virginia*, 49; Edwin Baker Loving Diary, 18 May 1864, VSL; *O.R.N.*, 10:67–69; Bushrod R. Johnson Diary, 18 May 1864, Johnson Papers, NA.

11. Douglas Southall Freeman, ed., *Lee's Dispatches: Unpublished Letters of General Robert E. Lee, C. S. A. to Jefferson Davis and the War Department of the Confederate States of America, 1862–65*, new ed. (New York: G. P. Putnam's Sons, 1957), 186n, 186–187.

12. *O.R.A.*, 36, pt. 2, 1021–1022. A garbled version of Beauregard's proposal is presented in Davis, *Rise and Fall*, 2:514–515, which is rightly taken to task in Roman, *Military Operations*, 2:215. For Beauregard's strength, see Beauregard to Bragg, 10:40 P.M., 18 May 1864, Official Telegrams, 22 April–9 June 1864, Beauregard Papers, LC.

13. *O.R.A.*, 36, pt. 2, 898; Marshall, ed., *Butler's Correspondence*, 4:230; Grant, *Personal Memoirs*, 2:238–241; Porter, *Campaigning with Grant*, 124; Badeau, *Military History*, 2:200, 203.

14. Wilson, *Old Flag*, 1:417–418, 423.

15. Jones, *War Clerk*, 2:214; *O.R.A.*, 36, pt. 2, 171, 939; *O.R.A.*, 51, pt. 2, 230, 232; *O.R.N.*, 10:71; Gregorie, ed., "Wescoat Diary," 86; Wise, *Seventeenth Virginia*, 182; Henry Chambers Diary, 19 May 1864, NCDAH; William Beavans Diary, 19 May 1864, SHC; John Paris Diary, 19 May 1864, SHC; Cary Whitaker Diary, 19 May 1864, SHC; Drake, *Ninth New Jersey*, 211; Price, *Ninety-Seventh Pennsylvania*, 272; Eldredge, *Third New Hampshire*, 482; Thomas _____ to "Dear Friend Kittie," 19 May 1864, Kate Camenga Papers, Duke University, Durham, N.C.; N. A. Barrier to his wife, 19 May 1864, N. A. Barrier Papers, DU; J. H. McAlister to his mother, 19 May 1864, (written on the back of a captured Federal document), J. H. McAlister Paper, North Carolina Division of Archives and History, Raleigh, N.C.; Cleveland, ed., "Campaign of Promise," 323–324; Thompson, *Thirteenth New Hampshire*, 323–324.

16. *O.R.A.*, 36, pt. 2, 1021–1025, pt. 3, 808; *O.R.A.*, 51, pt. 2, 945, 947, 948, 950; Beauregard to Bragg, 6:00 A.M., 5:00 P.M., 5:30 P.M., and 6:00 P.M., 19 May 1864, all in Official Telegrams, 22 April–9 June 1864, Beauregard Papers, LC; Beauregard to Bragg, 19 May 1864, Letter Book, April–May 1864, Beauregard Papers, LC.

17. *O.R.A.*, 51, pt. 2, 948, 949; Beauregard to Bragg, 7:30 P.M., 19 May 1864, Official Telegrams, 22 April–9 June 1864, Beauregard Papers, LC; Johnston, *Confederate Boy*, 257; Wise, *Seventeenth Virginia*, 182; Warfield, *Memoirs*, 176; Loehr, *First Virginia*, 49; Clark, ed., *North Carolina Regiments*, 3:10; Kenan, *Forty-Third North Carolina*, 15; Edwin Baker Loving Diary, 19 May 1864, VSL; John Paris Diary, 19 May 1864, SHC; Cary Whitaker Diary, 19 May 1864, SHC; Beauregard to Whiting, 19 May 1864, and 9:30 A.M., 19 May 1864, also Beauregard to Johnson, 19 May 1864, all in Letter Book, April–May 1864, Beauregard Papers, LC; *O.R.A.*, 36, pt. 2, 1026, 1027; John M. Otey to D. H. Hill, 19 May 1864, D. H. Hill Papers, VSL.

18. Morgan, *Reminiscences*, 206; Loehr, *First Virginia*, 49–50; Loehr, "Battle of Drewry's Bluff," 107; Sumpter, "Fighting," 179, 182; Thomas F. Kelley to "My Dear Cousin," 21 May 1864, Thomas F. Kelley Papers, DU.

19. Confederate accounts of the morning's action are fragmentary. Scattered information can be found in *O.R.A.*, 36, pt. 2, 261, 264; B. H. Wise, *Life of H. A. Wise*, 339–340; Harrill, *Reminiscences*, 23; Gregorie, ed., "Wescoat Diary," 87; Elliott, "Martin's Brigade," 191–192; Clark, ed., *North Carolina Regiments*, 1:403, 2:4–5, 620, 797, 3:355–356; "Casualties in Wise's and Martin's Brigades," D. H. Hill Papers, VSL; Beauregard to Bragg, 2:20 P.M., 20 May 1864, Official Telegrams, 22 April–9 June 1864, Beauregard Papers, LC; Wise MS, Beauregard Papers, LC; Henry Chambers Diary, 20 May 1864, NCDAH; William H. S. Burgwyn Diary, 20 May 1864, NCDAH; John W. Calton to his father, 24 May 1864, John W. Calton Letters, NCDAH; Edward Phifer to his mother, 29 May 1864, Phifer Family Papers, SHC; Bushrod R. Johnson Diary, 20 May 1864, Johnson Papers, NA.

Federal accounts of the action, known as the Battle of Ware Bottom Church, are equally unsatisfactory, but the general outline of events can be learned from *O.R.A.*, 36, pt. 2, 40; *O.R.A.*, 51, pt. 1, 1235; Price, *Ninety-Seventh Pennsylvania*, 273–277; Stowits, *One Hundredth New York*, 263; Hyde, *One Hundred and Twelfth New York*, 79; Clark, *Iron Hearted Regiment*, 121; Cunningham, *Adirondack Regiment*, 125; Whitman and True, *Maine in the War*, 203; Beecher, *First Connecticut Light Battery*, 2:462; Joseph Hawley to his wife, 21 May and 26 May 1864, also Joseph Hawley to Gideon Welles, 19 June 1864, all in Hawley Papers, LC.

20. Price, *Ninety-Seventh Pennsylvania*, 273, 277–283, 414–415; Clark, *Iron Hearted Regiment*, 121–122; *O.R.A.*, 36, pt. 2, 40, 44, 48; *O.R.A.*, 51, pt. 1, 1235, 1237–1238; Clark, *Thirty-Ninth Illinois*, 192–197, 324–325; Dickey, *Eighty-Fifth Pennsylvania*, 317–320, 323–324; Cadwell, *Old Sixth*, 93; Croffut and Morris, *Connecticut During the War*, 553; Joseph Hawley to his wife, 21 May and 26 May 1864, also

Joseph Hawley to Gideon Welles, 19 June 1864, Hawley Papers, LC.

21. J. W. Pursley to his sister, late May 1864, and 9 June 1864, Mary Frances Jane Pursley Papers, Duke University, Durham, N.C.; Hagood, *Memoirs*, 252; Dickey, *Eighty-Fifth Pennsylvania*, 324; Clark, *Thirty-Ninth Illinois*, 196–197; Roe, *Twenty-Fourth Massachusetts*, 302–303, 303n; O.R.A., 51, pt. 1:1237; Clark, *Iron Hearted Regiment*, 122–123; Beecher, *First Connecticut Light Battery*, 2:462; John J. Craven, *Prison Life of Jefferson Davis* (New York: Carlton, Publisher, 1866), 11–17. Found on Walker were memoranda showing the strength of his unit, as well as a detailed map of the area between Petersburg and City Point. O.R.A., 36, pt. 2, 276, pt. 3, 140; Butler, *Butler's Book*, 664. The map is reprinted in Cowles, ed., *O.R. Atlas*, plate 56, 1.

22. O.R.A., 36, pt. 2, 40, pt. 3, 820; O.R.A., 51, pt. 1, 1238, pt. 2, 953. At this time the Confederate line was constructed only from the James River at Howlett's southward to Ashton Creek. The gap of one mile from Ashton Creek to Swift Creek was covered either by cavalry pickets or by infantry, depending upon Federal activity. Later the fortifications were made continuous. O.R.A., 36, pt. 3, 886. The line of works eventually came to be known as the Howlett Line. Roman, *Military Operations*, 2:223.

23. O.R.A., 36, pt. 3, 799, 808, 811, 824; O.R.A., 51, pt. 2, 951; Beauregard to Whiting, 20 May 1864, Letter Book, April–May 1864, and Beauregard to James Milligan, 20 May 1864, Official Telegrams, 22 April–9 June 1864, both in Beauregard Papers, LC.

24. O.R.A., 51, pt. 2, 951–953; Jones, *War Clerk*, 2:216.

25. Butler, *Butler's Book*, 664; O.R.A., 36, pt. 3, 31–39.

26. O.R.A., 36, pt. 3, 36, 37, 40; Butler, *Butler's Book*, 665–666; Smith, *From Chattanooga to Petersburg*, 141, 146–148.

27. O.R.A., 36, pt. 3, 29, 31; O.R.N., 10:72, 96–98. The army side of the controversy is documented in Charles K. Graham to J. W. Shaffer, letters of 23 May and 24 May 1864, General Correspondence, 1864, Butler Papers, LC.

28. Beauregard to Colquitt, and Beauregard to D. H. Hill, 21 May 1864, Letter Book, April–May 1864, and Beauregard to Bragg, 7:30, 21 May 1864, Official Telegrams, 22 April–9 June 1864, all in Beauregard Papers, LC; O.R.A., 36, pt. 3, 818, 821; O.R.A., 51, pt. 2, 954; "Special Orders No. 10, Department of North Carolina and Southern Virginia," 21 May 1864, D. H. Hill Papers, NCDAH; Bridges, *Lee's Maverick General*, 263–264. Johnson eventually was promoted to major general, to rank from 21 May. Warner, *Generals in Gray*, 158.

29. O.R.A., 51, pt. 1, 224, 230, 232; Owen, *Washington Artillery*, 323; Jones, *War Clerk*, 2:216; Thomas F. Kelley to "My Dear Cousin," 21 May 1864, Thomas F. Kelley Papers, DU; J. W. Pursley to his sister, late May 1864, Mary Frances Jane Pursley Papers, DU; O.R.A., 36, pt. 3, 822.

30. O.R.A., 36, pt. 3, 33, 69–71, 74; Dickey, *Eighty-Fifth Pennsylvania*, 324–325; Clark, *My Experience*, 62; Cleveland, ed., "Campaign of Promise," 325; Walter S. Clemence Diary and Memoranda, 21 May 1864, NCC; Eldredge, *Third New Hampshire*, 483; Bartlett, *Twelfth New Hampshire*, 185; Cadwell, *Old Sixth*, 93; Cunningham, *Adirondack Regiment*, 126; Walkley, *Seventh Connecticut*, 140; Kreutzer, *Ninety-Eighty New York*, 195; Stowits, *One Hundredth New York*, 263–264.

31. O.R.A., 36, pt. 3, 43. Grant may have been acting in response to the criticism of Butler embodied in the Sheridan-Wilson letters, which could have reached staff officers Comstock and Rawlins by that time.

32. O.R.A., 36, pt. 3, 44, 68–69; Montgomery C. Meigs Diary, 21 May 1864, Meigs Papers, Library of Congress, Washington, D.C.; Catton, *Grant Takes Command*, 250, 511.

33. O.R.A., 36, pt. 3, 70, 71; Price, *Ninety-Seventh Pennsylvania*, 284–285; Clark, *Iron Hearted Regiment*, 123; Brady, *Eleventh Maine*, 191; Roe, *Twenty-Fourth Massachusetts*, 304–305; Thompson, *Thirteenth New Hampshire*, 325–326; Trumbull, *Knightly Soldier*, 229; Cunningham, *Adirondack Regiment*, 125; Clark, *My Experience*, 62; Cleveland, ed., "Campaign of Promise," 325–326; Everts, *Comprehensive History*, 117; Walter S. Clemence Diary and Memoranda, 22 May 1864, NCC; Gregorie, ed., "Wescoat Diary," 87; William H. S. Burgwyn Diary, 22 May 1864, NCDAH; O.R.N., 10:36, 78. Bushrod R. Johnson Diary, 22 May 1864, Johnson Papers, NA.

34. D. H. Hill to his wife, 22 May 1864, D. H. Hill Papers, NCDAH; Bridges, *Lee's Maverick General*, 263; Beauregard to Samuel Cooper, 22 May 1864, Official Telegrams, 22 April–9 June 1864, Beauregard Papers, LC; Freeman, *Lee's Dispatches*, 190–191; O.R.A., 36, pt. 3, 824–825.

35. Edward E. Hale to Sarah Butler, 22 May 1864, General Correspondence, 1864, Butler Papers, LC; O.R.A., 36, pt. 3, 109–110; Butler, *Butler's Book*, 666–669; S. P. Lee to Butler, 22 May 1864, General Correspondence, 1864, Butler Papers, LC.

36. William Stiner to Frederic Hudson, 22 May 1864, James Gordon Bennett Papers, LC. For

examples of the favorable coverage, see *New York Times*, 22 May and 23 May 1864. Others besides reporters were choosing sides. Colonel G. V. Henry, commanding a regiment in the X Corps, pleaded strongly yet unofficially with Baldy Smith to arrange the transfer of Henry and his regiment to the XVIII Corps so that they could "serve under soldiers." *O.R.A.*, 36, pt. 3, 111.

37. Montgomery C. Meigs Diary, 22 May 1864, Meigs Papers, LC; *O.R.A.*, 36, pt. 3, 77. See also Grant, *Memoirs*, 2:568–569, and Porter, *Campaigning with Grant*, 146–147.

☆ 17 ☆

Stalemate
23 May–16 June 1864

By 23 May the military situation on the Bermuda Hundred peninsula gave every indication of having become a stalemate. Both armies occupied their time primarily by digging their trenches deeper and raising their parapets higher. To restrict the flow of information reaching the enemy, Beauregard warned Bushrod Johnson against casually accepting Federal flags-of-truce and he instructed D. H. Hill to enforce the order forbidding fraternization with the enemy's pickets. In an effort to breach this curtain, Butler offered $500 to those willing to penetrate the Confederate lines, and on 23 May several soldiers attempted to earn the reward. Although some were unable to pass through the lines, and others were captured, a few were successful enough to learn that the Confederates were still present in force and that the railroad had not yet been repaired.[1]

Both Lee and Grant were more than willing to accept a stalemate below Richmond in order to reinforce their own commands. Lee was now ready for cooperation with Beauregard, either above or below the Confederate capital, but he especially favored a concentration against Grant. As he explained to Davis:

> As far as I can understand, General Butler is in a position from which he can only be driven by assault, and which I have no doubt, has been made as strong as possible. Whether it would be proper or advantageous to attack it, General Beauregard can determine, but if not, no more troops are necessary there than to retain the enemy in his entrenchments.

At the same time Chief of Staff Halleck wrote to Grant that, as soon as Meigs and Barnard reported on the situation at Bermuda Hundred, he would transfer some of Butler's units to the Army of the Potomac.[2]

Unaware that Grant and Halleck had already decided to remove troops from the Army of the James, Meigs and Barnard landed at Bermuda Hundred early on the morning of 23 May. After meeting with Butler, they spent several hours touring the peninsula's defenses, then they crossed to City Point where they inspected Edward Hincks's garrison. At the end of the day the two officers returned to Bermuda Hundred and composed an interim report. Although Butler denied it, Meigs and

Barnard thought it possible "that very recently, and since our force has been entirely on the defensive, rebel troops have gone to Lee." Their preliminary investigation showed: first, that the defenses could be held by only 10,000 men, thereby freeing 20,000 for offensive operations; second, that personal relationships among the commanders were better than expected; third, that morale was good among the troops. As a result, Meigs and Barnard concluded: "We think that this force should not be diminished, and that a skillful use of it will aid General Grant more than the numbers which might be drawn from here."[3]

The twenty-fourth of May was a beautiful late spring day, fair and warm, with only an occasional thundershower. While their troops enjoyed the lull, Beauregard and Butler each reported to their superiors that the opposing forces were not being reduced. Beauregard's statement to the War Department that no units of the Army of the James had departed was quite accurate. Contrary to Butler's fervently expressed opinion, however, there had been a substantial reduction in Confederate strength at Bermuda Hundred. Nor were the detachments at an end, for that day the 6th North Carolina Infantry was ordered from Petersburg to rejoin Lewis's Brigade, serving with Lee. In addition, Robert Ransom suggested pointedly that he needed his brother Matt's old brigade north of the James River. The continuing demands for his troops notwithstanding, Beauregard had been able to disguise the dwindling size of his command from the Federals. Reporting to Stanton that he had 25,000 effectives at Bermuda Hundred, Butler claimed: "I know I am employing one-third more of the enemy's force than I have."[4]

As Beauregard and Butler attempted to stave off troop reductions at Bermuda Hundred, action flared downstream from City Point. In the early afternoon of 24 May the Federal garrison at Wilson's Wharf was approached by a large force of Confederate cavalry under Major General Fitzhugh Lee. After Brigadier General Edward Wild declined an invitation to surrender, the Confederates attempted to storm the position. Knowing their fate if the defense were unsuccessful, the garrison of 1,100 Negro troops resisted tenaciously. The beleaguered Federals were aided by the gunboat *U.S.S. Dawn,* as well as by passing transports that landed their cargoes of replacements and furloughed men under fire. Reinforcements were also dispatched from City Point, thereby denuding that post and necessitating the transfer of troops from Bermuda Hundred. Before the units arrived from upriver, however, the Confederates withdrew in defeat. Federal casualties totaled only twenty-three, while twenty dead Confederates were discovered and nineteen prisoners were taken.[5]

Although the affair at Wilson's Wharf revealed the tenuous nature of Butler's supply line, in Washington, Chief of Staff Halleck had already prepared orders detaching Baldy Smith and 20,000 men from the Army of the James. In a note to Grant, Halleck expressed regret that the number was not larger: "I wish everything was away from the south side of the James and with you." Yet, by that time Lee had retreated from the North Anna River and the Army of the Potomac was in pursuit. If the Confederates were falling back on Richmond, Grant told Halleck, he would want Butler's army to remain at Bermuda Hundred. Therefore, Halleck should tell

Butler to hold Smith's contingent in readiness, but to await further developments before sending it forward.[6]

Largely forgotten by Grant and Halleck were Generals Meigs and Barnard, finishing their investigation at Bermuda Hundred. After still another tour of the defenses and conferences with both Smith and Gillmore, the two officers drafted their final report before departing for Washington.[7] Sent by telegraph from Jamestown, the report represented a generally accurate analysis of the Army of the James's situation. Listed first were the achievements: occupation and fortification of a base, diversion of a significant number of Confederates, temporary disruption of the enemy's supply lines, and the collection of large stocks of forage, rations, and ammunition. As for the future, Meigs and Barnard proposed two options: take the offensive in an effort to cut railroads, seize Petersburg, and draw troops from Lee, or, alternatively, go entirely on the defensive, abandon the river garrisons, and send 20,000 men to Grant.

Meigs and Barnard had made their recommendations with the complex personal relationships among Butler, Smith, and Gillmore in mind:

> General Butler is a man of rare and great ability, but he has not experience and training to enable him to direct and control movements in battle. A corps gives its commander full occupation on the battle-field, and leaves him no time to make suggestions to the commander-in-chief as to the movements of two corps. General Butler is satisfied with the ability and aid of General William F. Smith. He does not appear to be satisfied with General Gillmore. General Butler evidently desires to retain command in the field. If his desires must be gratified, withdraw Gillmore, place Smith in command of both corps under the supreme command of General Butler. . . . You will thus have a command which will be a unit, and General Butler will probably be guided by Smith, and leave to him the suggestions and practical execution of army movements ordered. Success would be more certain were Smith in command untrammeled, and General Butler remanded to the administrative duties of the department in which he has shown such rare and great ability.[8]

Even though their advice was destined to be rejected, Meigs and Barnard had identified many of the problems besetting the Army of the James.

Daylight on 25 May found Meigs and Barnard far down the James River on their way back to Washington. Butler was pleased at their departure, telling his wife: "I have had Genls. Meigs and Barnard here—a sort of smelling committee, but I believe they have gone away satisfied."[9] Perhaps they had, but thirty miles north of Richmond Grant was once more becoming impatient. It now appeared that Lee's army was not retiring into Richmond's defenses as had first been hoped, so Grant wired Halleck to transfer Smith and 20,000 men to the Army of the Potomac. As for the remainder of Butler's troops: "The James River should be held to City Point, but leave nothing more than is absolutely necessary to hold it, acting purely on the defensive." Since the report submitted by Meigs and Barnard was not received at Washington until 10:30 A.M., it could not possibly have been transmitted to Grant before he made his decision at noon. Much more influential in that decision appears to have been the advice of Grant's staff. On the following day Colonel Cyrus Comstock, a recipient of one of the Sheridan-Wilson letters, confided to his diary: "We have at last got the general to order a large part of the force under Butler now doing nothing, to join us via West Point."[10]

At the front, 25 May was another quiet day. Fatigue details were still active, but a new spirit seemed to animate the combatants. On the picket line a soldier in the 56th North Carolina loaned his shovel to a Federal sentry who needed it to construct a new rifle pit. Other pickets leaned their guns against trees and read newspapers in full view of their opponents. Several flags-of-truce passed between the lines, in contravention of the spirit if not the letter of Beauregard's orders. Within the Federal works, spirits momentarily rose with the arrival of a War Department dispatch announcing that Grant had crossed the North Anna River and was in pursuit of Lee. Other Federals, hearing train whistles from the direction of the Richmond and Petersburg Railroad, doubted that the Union cause was so near triumph. Had they known that the railroad would officially be reopened to traffic on the following day, their doubts would have been even greater.[11]

Although there were no offensive operations on 25 May, both sides continued to seek opportunities to break the stalemate. Hindered on land by his lack of troops, Beauregard corresponded with Commander J. K. Mitchell in an effort to use the three ironclads of the James River Squadron, which had finally passed the obstructions at Drewry's Bluff. On the other side of the Bermuda Hundred peninsula the Federals were also probing for offensive openings. The southern half of Butler's defensive line ran along the eastern edge of a deep ravine that opened into the low ground of the Appomattox River flats. Because the terrain appeared unfavorable for assaults, the Confederate positions were located some distance to the west of the Federal line and were lightly manned. On 25 May, XVIII Corps units under Colonel Arthur Dutton penetrated that sector for nearly a mile without meeting any resistance. With Butler's blessing, Smith planned a more vigorous probe on the following day.[12]

The events of 26 May put a damper on the offensive hopes of both armies. Beauregard informed Commander Mitchell that the Howlett battery was not yet ready to assist a sortie by the ironclads and that further discussion between the two services would be necessary. Meanwhile, Smith's probe toward the Confederate right also came to nothing. Under the command of Brigadier General John Martindale, the Federals moved westward along both sides of Ashton Creek toward a mill owned by the Dunn family. Almost immediately the left column ran into Confederate fire and recoiled. Leading his brigade into a similar hail of bullets north of the creek, Colonel Dutton was mortally wounded before he could get his men under cover. While Martindale pondered whether to continue the probe or withdraw, a message arrived from Smith requiring his immediate return to camp.[13]

Martindale was recalled because Smith had just received the War Department's order for him to prepare to join the Army of the Potomac. Butler estimated that he could spare 17,000 troops if certain steps were taken to fill their place in line. These measures were outlined in General Order No. 70: Terry's division would take over the entire X Corps line; Kautz's cavalry division would occupy the line held by Brooks's division of the XVIII Corps; Cole's cavalry regiment and two infantry regiments would replace Martindale's XVIII Corps division (formerly Weitzel's); Hincks would form a provisional brigade to be stationed behind Kautz's right as a reserve; and finally, Gillmore would command the entire line of defenses. Such shuffling of units would free two divisions from each corps for duty in the mobile column.[14]

The necessity of appointing Gillmore to command the Bermuda Hundred defenses must have been galling to Butler, since he had a man in Washington lobbying heavily for rejection of Gillmore's promotion to major general. Meanwhile, Gillmore had given another apparent cause for complaint. On 24 May the *New York Evening Post* had published an article claiming that Gillmore had suggested that the Federals entrench at Drewry's Bluff on 15 May, but that Butler had curtly rejected the advice. Other papers then took up the story, culminating on 26 May with an editorial in the *New York Times* strongly criticizing Butler.[15] Surmising that Gillmore was involved, Butler launched an investigation that produced a complete denial from the corps commander. The trail led eventually to Colonel Edward Serrell of the 1st New York Engineers, who on 15 May had carried a verbal message from Gillmore to Butler

> about changing the enemy's lines we then occupied to defences for ourselves— to which Gen. Butler replied, "Say to Genl. Gillmore we are on the offensive not defensive, he need have no apprehension about his left."

Gillmore forwarded Serrell's explanation to Butler, who sought a retraction from the *Evening Post*. In a move that was probably not coincidental, Colonel Serrell was peremptorily transferred from X Corps headquarters to Edward Wild's command at Wilson's Wharf.[16]

From his vantage point, Butler saw dire portents in Grant's call for reinforcements from the Army of the James. He wrote his wife that "This is a sign of weakness I did not look for, and to my mind augurs worse for our cause than anything I have seen." Butler believed that Smith's contingent would arrive too late to be of any possible benefit to Grant, and he began to ponder ways to prevent its departure from Bermuda Hundred. Since Smith's force could not leave until sufficient shipping had been collected, there might be time to send part of it across the Appomattox to the Federal outpost at Spring Hill, from whence it could make a dash at lightly defended Petersburg. Seizing upon this scheme as a way to retain the XVIII Corps, Butler conferred at length with Smith and called Hincks across the river to add his expertise to the deliberations.[17]

Believing that the unusual Federal activity forecast an attack, Beauregard's soldiers braced for an assault at dawn, 27 May, but none came. By noon the evidence was overwhelming that the Federals were preparing for a movement. Generals Colquitt and Dearing, as well as signal officers on the Appomattox, reported that the Army of the James was striking tents. Increased wagon traffic was also visible. Yet from other signalmen on the lower James came reports that pontoons and transports bearing soldiers were moving upriver. Just after nightfall Gracie reported from the north bank of the James that there was unusual activity in the Federal fleet. At 9:00 P.M. Beauregard wired Bragg that a Federal move was imminent, but whether it was to be an attack or a retreat could not yet be ascertained. Meanwhile, in both the War Department at Richmond and the Bermuda Hundred defenses, rumors spread that Grant intended to transfer the Army of the Potomac to the south bank of the James River.[18]

While the Confederates unsuccessfully sought to determine his intentions, Butler continued to develop his scheme for the seizure of Petersburg. As finally agreed upon, the plan called for Smith secretly to move 11,000 men across the Appomattox River on a new pontoon bridge and concentrate behind a cavalry screen thrown up by Hincks from Spring Hill to City Point. Then at dawn of 29 May Hincks's men would surprise and capture the Confederate pickets, thereby allowing Smith's troops to dash into Petersburg unannounced. All of this was contingent upon the tardy arrival of the shipping needed to take Smith to join Grant. Smith received his written orders at 2:30 P.M. on 28 May but, only a few hours later, the operation was cancelled. Enough riverboats and barges had arrived to justify adherence to Grant's original order and Butler reluctantly abandoned his offensive.[19]

Before leaving to join the Army of the Potomac, Smith visited Butler's headquarters at Cobb's Hill for a farewell meal. The occasion was somber because all realized that a great opportunity to seize Petersburg had been lost, especially since new intelligence from Hincks indicated that the city's garrison was woefully weak. Butler doubted that transportation sufficient to carry Smith's entire contingent was at hand, but enough was present to make retention of the troops a disobedient act, so Smith had to go. By his own account Smith was taking with him 16,000 infantry, plus sixteen artillery pieces and a squadron of cavalry. In messages to both Grant and Secretary of War Stanton, Butler announced that Smith was embarking. To Stanton, Butler remarked plaintively, "I regret exceedingly the loss of this opportunity upon Petersburg."[20]

By the time the last transports pulled away from the docks on 29 May, the entire Bermuda Hundred peninsula had become strangely quiet. At the front there was hardly any firing at all and the opposing pickets calmly held bargaining sessions at which newspapers, coffee, sugar, and tobacco changed hands. The only sounds were those emanating from the Federal fatigue parties as they strung wire entanglements and raised their earthen parapets. Within the Federal lines Gillmore became involved in an altercation with Butler stemming from the absence of Colonel Serrell, thus proving that Smith's departure had not eliminated the conflicts within the Federal command structure. Across the trenches Beauregard spent the day attempting to arrange a conference with Lee in order to discuss possible cooperative actions. Notifying Davis of his intentions, Beauregard reported that few, if any, Federals had left Butler.[21]

Late in the afternoon Beauregard learned that Lee would meet him at Atlee's Station on the railroad north of Richmond. Before leaving by special train, he issued strict orders forbidding fraternization with the enemy and unofficially placed

D. H. Hill in charge of the Bermuda Hundred defenses. Arriving at Atlee's after dark, Beauregard conferred with Lee for several hours. He argued that his 12,000 infantry were hardly sufficient even for a defensive role and that none could be spared to reinforce the Army of Northern Virginia. For his own part, Lee saw no alternative to fighting Grant where he was, but he would not contest Beauregard's analysis of the situation at Bermuda Hundred. Since no cooperative arrangement could be devised, each general returned to his own command resolved to do his best alone.[22]

On the following day, 30 May, the arrival of fresh intelligence reports put the strategic situation in an entirely new light. Scouts on the lower James reported many transports coming down loaded with troops, while additional reports described Federal units crossing the Appomattox River on a pontoon bridge. Transmitting the reports to Bragg, Beauregard announced that a demonstration scheduled for 5:30 P.M. would tell more about Federal intentions, but that as a precaution he was preparing Hoke's Division for departure.[23] To the northeast, Lee also received reports indicating that Grant would soon be reinforced by a large contingent from Butler's army. If the Army of the Potomac were to gain a full corps, Lee would be facing disaster, and during the afternoon he wired Beauregard directly for support. Maddeningly, Beauregard replied that the "War Dept. must determine when & what troops to order from here." Because Beauregard refused to take the responsibility, Lee placed the question directly before President Davis at 7:15 P.M.: "The result of this delay will be disaster. Butler's troops (Smith's corps) will be with Grant to-morrow. Hoke's division, at least, should be with me by light to-morrow."[24]

While Davis pondered Lee's ultimatum, Beauregard sifted the meager information derived from his afternoon demonstration. Although the probe had furnished few clues to the enemy's intentions, by late evening Beauregard felt compelled to do something. Perhaps he acted to preempt the orders he suspected were forthcoming, or perhaps he believed that Lee's plight was desperate, because heavy firing could be heard in the distance. At any rate, by 10:00 P.M. Beauregard had decided to send Hoke's Division north.[25] Fifteen minutes later he informed Bragg of his decision. Coincidentally, Beauregard's message to Richmond passed in transit an order from Bragg requiring that Hoke's troops be sent to join Lee by rail. For once Beauregard could say that he had acted without prodding from Richmond, and he proudly reported to Bragg that Hoke's advance elements were already in motion. To replace them in the trenches, Johnson's Division was ordered to extend southward during the night.[26]

At Cobb's Hill Butler was still unwilling to accept the stalemate at Bermuda Hundred and was considering ways to circumvent it. In seeking avenues for offensive action his thoughts turned once more toward Petersburg. Although the neck of the Bermuda Hundred peninsula was sealed by Confederate fortifications, the pontoon bridge across the Appomattox from Point of Rocks to Spring Hill provided a convenient side door through which a Federal column could operate against Petersburg. It was just such a plan to outflank the formidable Confederate defenses that had been aborted when Smith's expeditionary force had been called away. Now Butler toyed with resurrecting the scheme by using Kautz's cavalry, supported by infantry drawn from City Point and the river defenses. When Hincks proposed a similar plan on 1 June, Butler called upon Kautz for further discussions. As Butler envisioned the operation, Hincks's infantry would divert the garrison's attention, while Kautz's cavalry dashed into Petersburg to burn the Appomattox bridges and public buildings. Kautz, however, was unenthusiastic: "I could not agree . . . about the feasibility of the plan, but expressed myself perfectly willing to undertake it and made my arrangements accordingly." The raid was scheduled for the next morning.[27]

Unaware that Petersburg was endangered more than usual, Beauregard, on 1 June, focused his attention to the north, where the daily rumble of artillery forecast the approach of Lee and Grant. Shortly after noon Lee wired Beauregard to suggest that the latter bring most of his troops north and take personal command of the right wing of the Army of Northern Virginia. Beauregard retorted at 7:00 P.M. that, as long as he was confronted by Gillmore's 8,000 troops, he could not leave Bermuda Hundred, unless the "Government shall have determined to abandon line of communication from Petersburg to Richmond." At 7:30 P.M. Beauregard ordered Bushrod Johnson to make a vigorous reconnaissance at dawn the next day. The information to be gained from the probe would be crucial, for Jefferson Davis had decided to detach Ransom's Brigade from Beauregard, unless a strong case could be made for its retention. If the Federals were still present in strength, Beauregard might not be forced to relinquish the North Carolinians.[28]

Just after 6:00 A.M., 2 June, Johnson's reconnaissance began. Heavy skirmish lines from Wise's, Ransom's, and Walker's Brigades leaped over their works and advanced purposefully toward the Federal pickets. Rough terrain in the southern part of the attack sector prevented most of Walker's Brigade from closing with the Federals, but Colonel O. M. Dantzler's 22nd South Carolina briefly pushed back part of the 7th Connecticut. Dantzler's death, however, and the timely arrival of Federal reinforcements, forced the Confederates to retire in disarray on that part of the field.[29] To the north, Ransom's troops struck the right of the 7th Connecticut and the left of the 39th Illinois. Exploiting a flaw in the Federal line, they surrounded two companies of the 7th Connecticut, which led to the retreat of both that regiment and the 39th Illinois. The withdrawal of the Illinois unit exposed the flank of the 11th Maine to assault by Wise's Brigade, attacking on Ransom's left. Resisting fiercely, the Maine soldiers fell back from their original position near Ware Bottom Church.[30]

Although the Confederates halted their advance after having captured the Federal picket line, the Federals believed it presaged an attack upon their main defensive positions. Therefore, Butler temporarily relinquished any thought of mounting a raid against Petersburg. Units that had arrived from Wilson's Wharf during the night for duty in the mobile column were held instead as a reserve for Terry. Their assistance proved unnecessary, and by early afternoon, Terry was able to report that the 3rd New Hampshire Infantry had regained the part of the picket line lost in the morning by the 7th Connecticut. Unfortunately, the rest of the line could not be recaptured and a new position had to be established several hundred yards nearer the Federal works. Terry's casualties for the entire day were 172 men.[31]

Beauregard's small force had been relatively successful on 2 June, but without Ransom's Brigade the effort could hardly be repeated. At 2:45 P.M. he wired Bragg that "it might be dangerous to send away Ransom's brigade, constituting over one-third available infantry force now here." In case Ransom was to be taken from him, Beauregard drafted a bleak contingency plan in which Bushrod Johnson would fall back with Wise's, Johnson's, and Walker's Brigades to Port Walthall Junction, while part of Dearing's cavalry covered the flanks. If Johnson's Division were ordered away, Wise' Brigade and two of Dearing's regiments would occupy the position at Port Walthall Junction. It was not likely that either action would long protect the Richmond and Petersburg Railroad, but Beauregard thought he would be blameless if the railroad were lost.[32]

The third of June was a dreary day with overcast skies and intermittent rain. Picket firing, which generally had been suspended prior to the action of the previous day, now resumed with a will. In the distance the sounds of the battle raging at Cold Harbor swelled in volume, as Grant hurled the Army of the Potomac, bolstered by Smith's corps, against Lee's heavily entrenched Army of Northern Virginia. Although the Federals were bloodily repulsed, Lee now had positive proof that a large portion of the Army of the James was in his front and he vigorously requested reinforcement. Lee's call was shunted to Beauregard by Bragg, but Beauregard, having seen his own force dwindle from twelve infantry brigades to four, was unwilling to voluntarily reduce his command further. Shortly after 9:00 P.M. the dreaded order came: Ransom's Brigade was ordered "temporarily" north of the James River. A flurry of activity on the picket line near midnight delayed the brigade's departure briefly, but with the morrow, it would have to go.[33]

Dawn of 4 June found Ransom's Brigade marching out of the Bermuda Hundred trenches, where it was replaced by the 4th North Carolina Cavalry of Dearing's Brigade. With the loss of Ransom, Beauregard's thin lines were stretched almost to the breaking point, but he informed Bragg that he would attempt to hold the fortifications as long as possible. To bolster Petersburg's defenses, Beauregard had already sent to Henry Wise, commander of the First Military District, his own 46th Virginia Infantry. This was a necessary move, but one that reduced the Bermuda Hundred garrison even further.[34] With Ransom gone and Gracie still north of the James, Beauregard estimated that he could deploy no more than 3,200 men at Bermuda Hundred and 2,200 around Petersburg, even if reserve and militia units of limited value were included.[35]

For the next several days relative quiet returned to the Bermuda Hundred front. The works were almost as strong as field engineering could make them and chopping parties had cleared away most of the intervening brush, leaving only sharpened branches as an impediment to assaults. Behind their defenses the men of both sides waited, passing the idle hours as best they could. Within the Federal lines, morale was improved by the distribution of soft bread and fresh beef, as well as by visits from Sanitary Commission representatives, who furnished delicacies such as pickles. The Confederates subsisted on scantier fare, but were equally adept at amusing themselves. Many passed the time writing letters, almost all of which reflected war weariness and a burning desire to see the end come quickly, with victory in its train. As the memory of 2 June faded, the pickets resumed their private truces and revived their bartering sessions, while only an occasional artillery bombardment broke the silence. Prayer meetings were held frequently and every night the Federal bands serenaded friend and foe alike.[36]

Gradually it became obvious that the armies of Lee and Grant would soon overlap the territory guarded by Beauregard and Butler, ending the limited independence cherished by the Bermuda Hundred forces. As early as 4 June, Grant had ordered the service troops in Butler's department to begin aiding the Army of the Potomac, a sure sign that the two armies would soon be united. On 6 June a pontoon train dispatched by Grant's engineers arrived off Bermuda Hundred Landing, giving another clue to Grant's plans. In a message drafted on the same day, Grant informed Butler that his army would soon be crossing to the south side of the James. At the same time he sent two staff officers to Bermuda Hundred to secure maps and select the best site for a pontoon bridge.[37]

Beauregard accurately surmised the Federal intentions. Noting on 7 June the arrival of the pontoon train, he wired Bragg:

> Should Grant have left Lee's front, he doubtless intends operations against Richmond along James River, probably on south side. Petersburg being nearly defenseless would be captured before it could be re-enforced. Ransom's brigade and Hoke's division should then be returned at once.

Such forecasts were hardly original, since the *Richmond Examiner* on the same day also predicted Grant's crossing of the James, and the common soldiers had guessed it even earlier. On 8 June the presence of heavily laden vessels and more pontoons was reported by Beauregard, who inferred from them that supplies were being collected in anticipation of Grant's arrival. Still, Bragg refused to rule upon Beauregard's request for the return of Ransom and Hoke, referring it instead to Lee.[38]

At Cobb's Hill Butler saw quite clearly that the arrival of the Army of the Potomac would eclipse whatever minor successes the truncated Army of the James might win thereafter. As a result, on 8 June he revived his dormant scheme for a dash into Petersburg. According to the plan, Hincks would use his reserve brigade from Bermuda Hundred, together with troops from City Point and the river forts, to distract the Confederates' attention while Kautz's cavalry entered the city. Learning of the proposal, Gillmore requested permission to lead the infantry force, a plea that could hardly be denied in view of Gillmore's rank and position. Although he had misgivings about Gillmore's competence and knew that Hincks personally detested the X Corps' commander, Butler authorized the change. Hawley's brigade was substituted for Hincks's troops at Bermuda Hundred and Hincks was reduced to leading several regiments from City Point under Gillmore's supervision. Kautz had his usual private reservations about the plan, while Hawley thought the attack "almost insane."[39]

Bold in conception although rather hazy in its ultimate goals, the operation was a fiasco from the beginning. Kautz's men had farther to go than expected and did not arrive at their attack position until afternoon. Meanwhile Gillmore and Hincks had reached Petersburg's defenses. Overawed by the terrain and a show of apparent strength by the defenders, Gillmore ordered Hawley to "simulate" an attack only, then he leisurely retired. Hincks, who was willing to do more, was forced by Gillmore's departure to retreat also. As the infantry withdrew, Kautz brushed aside a handful of elderly men and boys south of the city and headed toward the center of town. Just short of his goal he was met by some of Dearing's cavalry and artillery dispatched by Beauregard from Bermuda Hundred, as well as a motley collection of soldiers drawn from Petersburg's hospitals and the provost marshal's stockade. Hearing nothing from Gillmore, who by then was on his way back to camp, Kautz deemed it wise to withdraw also.[40]

Before he learned of the raid, Beauregard sent a long dispatch to Bragg requesting the return of Hoke's Division in order to prevent the loss of Petersburg. Yet Lee was unconvinced, and even Gillmore's attack left his conviction unshaken that the return of Ransom or Hoke to Beauregard was not yet wise. Similarly, once it was known that the Federals had retreated, Bragg suspended an order returning Gracie's Brigade to Bermuda Hundred from Chaffin's Bluff. On 10 June the War Department finally consented to transfer Gracie's Brigade south of the James, but it was not until 11 June that Gracie arrived. The Alabamians replaced Wise's Brigade, which moved south to Petersburg. Also on 11 June, D. H. Hill advised Beauregard plainly to tell the War Department that Bermuda Hundred and Petersburg could not be defended simultaneously, but Beauregard gently replied that his files were "all right." On 12 June Commander Mitchell, under pressure from his subordinates, repeated an earlier offer to place naval guns and crews in the unfinished Howlett battery, now named Battery Dantzler in honor of the South Carolina officer killed on 2 June. Although doubtful of his ability to defend the guns from a determined attack, Beauregard agreed on 13 June to activate the position with the navy's aid. Meanwhile, the conviction grew that Petersburg's remaining days of quiet were limited.[41]

For the Army of the James the days of mid-June were spent in familiar pastimes. At the front the men took turns serving on picket duty or resting in camp, where talk centered on Lincoln's renomination or the recent attack on Petersburg. At headquarters, relations among the generals sank to a new low. After conferring with Kautz and Hincks, Butler censured Gillmore for his conduct on 9 June and eventually relieved him of command. Yet Gillmore had his defenders, particularly Hawley, who firmly supported his actions.[42] On the other hand, Kautz believed a great opportunity had been lost on 9 June, and Hincks freely offered to take Petersburg with his own forces or resign his commission. On 11 June Grant advised Butler to seize the city, but "I do not want Petersburg visited, however, unless it is held, nor an attempt to take it unless you feel a reasonable degree of confidence of success." Grant's warning came too late, as the affair of 9 June had already served to bring Wise's Brigade to the city.[43]

As June's midpoint neared, signs of the impending arrival of the Army of the Potomac were on every hand. Grant had specified on 9 June that future reinforcements should be sent to Bermuda Hundred, and Butler soon was blessed with an abundance of fresh units. Eventually totaling seven regiments, the new arrivals were inexperienced "hundred days" men, so named because of their short term of enlistment. Even more welcome than the new recruits were the veterans of the XVIII Corps, who were returning by water from their sojourn with the Army of the Potomac. Fewer in number by the 3,000 casualties suffered at Cold Harbor, Smith's men were glad to be back among friends and none seemed more eager than their irascible commander. Pausing briefly at Fort Monroe on his way upriver, Smith visited Sarah Butler and poured out his disgust for George Meade and the tactics that had butchered so many of his best men. Smith seemed to believe he could have accomplished more by having remained with Butler and attacked Petersburg, as originally had been planned in late May. He was soon to get another chance, because Grant wanted Petersburg assaulted immediately, and Butler detailed Smith's troops, supported by Hincks and Kautz, to the task.[44]

At his headquarters south of Swift Creek, Beauregard was convinced that the day he had feared so long was at hand. At 7:15 A.M. on 14 June he wired Bragg: "Movement of Grant's across Chickahominy and increase of Butler's force render my position here critical. With my present forces I cannot answer for consequences." Hoping that Lee might be more amenable to his pleas, Beauregard sent an aide to the Army of Northern Virginia to explain the situation at Bermuda Hundred. Yet Lee was still unsure of Grant's intentions and he hesitated to act without further information. Not even an 8:10 P.M. telegram from Beauregard reporting the return of the XVIII Corps brought action. For a time at least, Beauregard would have to face the threat alone.[45]

Events moved quickly thereafter. On the morning of 15 June the XVIII Corps began assaulting Petersburg's outer defenses, while the Army of the Potomac marched to Smith's support. Only through a combination of Smith's native caution, heroic action by the handful of Confederate defenders, and sheer luck was Beauregard able to stave off defeat. At 11:30 A.M. Hoke's Division was finally transferred south of the James and started on a race for beleaguered Petersburg. Arriving on the evening of 15 June, Hoke's men were in time to save the city, but only with the aid of Johnson's Division, which Beauregard had been forced to withdraw from the Bermuda Hundred lines.[46]

Although Butler's pickets had heard considerable noise within the Confederate lines during the night, they were still surprised to find the works deserted when dawn broke on 16 June. During the day the Federals cautiously explored the Confederate trenches and camps, which they had viewed from afar for so long. Their visit was short-lived, however, as Pickett's Division of the Army of Northern Virginia drove them out again on its way to Petersburg. Lee's veterans thus slammed shut the open door to Richmond's lifeline that first Pickett and then Beauregard had labored so long to bar from Butler's Army of the James. Although few were aware of it at the time, the arrival of the Army of Northern Virginia signified that the Bermuda Hundred Campaign had ended, while the Petersburg Campaign had just begun.[47]

NOTES

1. Henry Chambers Diary, 23 May 1864, NCDAH; William H. S. Burgwyn Diary, 23 May 1864, NCDAH; Cleveland, ed., "Campaign of Promise," 326; Thompson, *Thirteenth New Hampshire*, 327; Beauregard to Johnson, 23 May 1864, Letter Book, April–May 1864, Beauregard Papers, LC; *O.R.A.*, 36, pt. 3, 144, 827; William F. Smith to Butler, 23 May 1864, General Correspondence, 1864, Butler Papers, LC; Drake, *Ninth New Jersey*, 212–215; Everts, *Comprehensive History*, 117–118; Foster, *New Jersey and the Rebellion*, 245–246.

2. Freeman, *Lee's Dispatches*, 195; *O.R.A.*, 36, pt. 3, 114, 115.

3. Montgomery C. Meigs Diary, 23 May 1864, Meigs Papers, LC; Edward E. Hale to Sarah Butler, 23 May 1864, General Correspondence, 1864, Butler Papers, LC; *O.R.A.*, 36, pt. 3, 140–141.

4. Jones, *War Clerk*, 2:218; Clark, *My Experience*, 63; *O.R.A.*, 36, pt. 3, 175–176; *O.R.A.*, 51, pt. 2, 957, 958; Beauregard to Colston, 24 May 1864, Letter Book, April–May 1864, Beauregard Papers, LC. Butler's estimate omitted Kautz's and Hincks's units.

5. *O.R.A.*, 36, pt. 2, 24, 31, 193, 269–272, pt. 3, 180–182; Butler, *Butler's Book*, 669–670; *O.R.N.*, 10:88, 90–91; Edward Simonton, "The Campaign Up the James River to Petersburg," *Glimpses of the Nation's Struggle*, 6 vols. (St. Paul, Minn.: Review Publishing Co., 1903), 5:482–486; Avery, "Gunboat Service on the James River," 16–24; Taylor, *First Connecticut Heavy Artillery*, 54; George T. Ulmer, *Adventures and Reminiscences of a Volunteer, or a Drummer Boy from Maine* (Chicago, 1892), 27–32; Livermore, *Days and Events*, 346; Merrill, *First District of Columbia*, 249.

6. *O.R.A.*, 36, pt. 3, 145, 176–177.

7. Montgomery C. Meigs Diary, 24 May 1864, Meigs Papers, LC; Marshall, ed., *Butler's Correspondence*, 4:246–247. Smith, in his book *From Chattanooga to Petersburg*, 19, emphatically denied that he met Meigs and/or Barnard at Bermuda Hundred: "I did not see them or either of them, or communicate with them directly or indirectly." Yet Meigs's diary is specific: "May 24. Visited Gen. Smith W. F. & Gillmore & after dinner rode out to the front."

8. *O.R.A.*, 36, pt. 3, 177–178.

9. Marshall, ed., *Butler's Correspondence*, 4:263.

10. *O.R.A.*, 36, pt. 3, 177, 183; West, *Lincoln's Scapegoat General*, 241; Cyrus B. Comstock Diary, 26 May 1864, LC. James Wilson believed that his and Sheridan's testimony had carried much weight in Grant's deliberations. Wilson, *Old Flag*, 1:423.

11. William H. S. Burgwyn Diary, 25 May 1864, NCDAH; Gregorie, ed., "Wescoat Diary," 87; Clark, *My Experience*, 63; Thompson, *Thirteenth New Hampshire*, 328, 329; Dickey, *Eighty-Fifth Pennsylvania*, 325; Roe, *Twenty-Fourth Massachusetts*, 306–307; Clark, ed., *North Carolina Regiments*, 3:357; Clark, *Iron Hearted Regiment*, 124; Henry Chambers Diary, 25 May 1864, NCDAH; Brady, *Eleventh Maine*, 192; Walter S. Clemence Diary and Memoranda, 25 May 1864, NCC; Drake, *Ninth New Jersey*, 215; Everts, *Comprehensive History*, 118; *O.R.A.*, 36, pt. 3, 315; Johnston, *Virginia Railroads*, 203–204.

12. *O.R.N.*, 10:649, 653, 656–657; *O.R.A.*, 36, pt. 2, 145, pt. 3, 204, 205, 828; *O.R.A.*, 51, pt. 2, 958–959; *Twenty-First Connecticut*, 205–206.

13. *O.R.N.*, 10:657–659; *O.R.A.*, 36, pt. 2, 145, pt. 3, 241, 242, 243; *O.R.A.*, 51, pt. 1, 1252; Bartlett, *Twelfth New Hampshire*, 195–197; Thompson, *Thirteenth New Hampshire*, 329; Waite, *New Hampshire in the Great Rebellion*, 437, 474; *Twenty-First Connecticut*, 200, 202, 206–207; *New York Times*, 29 May 1864; Walter S. Clemence Diary and Memoranda, 26 May 1864, NCC.

14. *O.R.A.*, 36, pt. 3, 234–236. Just before their departure, the four divisions were consolidated into three. The new organization can be found in *O.R.A.*, 36, pt. 1, 179–180.

15. Marshall, ed., *Butler's Correspondence*, 4:268–274, 315–317; Edward Serrell to Editor, *New York Evening Post*, 30 May 1864, General Correspondence, 1864, Butler Papers, LC; *O.R.A.*, 36, pt. 3, 238; *New York Times*, 26 May 1864; Andrews, *North Reports the Civil War*, 542.

16. John Clark to Butler, 27 May 1864, and Herman Biggs to J. W. Shaffer, 28 May 1864, both in General Correspondence, 1864, Butler Papers, LC; Marshall, ed., *Butler's Correspondence*, 4:271–274,

290; O.R.A., 36, pt. 3, 238, 282, 370–371; *New York Times*, 1 June 1864; Edward Serrell to Editor, *New York Evening Post*, 30 May 1864, General Correspondence, 1864, Butler Papers, LC.

17. Marshall, ed., *Butler's Correspondence*, 4:275, 276; Butler, *Butler's Book*, 671; Memorandum of 8 January 1879, Butler Papers, LC; O.R.A., 36, pt. 3, 266, 286.

18. Gregorie, ed., "Wescoat Diary," 87; John M. Otey to D. H. Hill, 7:30 A.M., 27 May 1864; D. H. Hill Papers, VSL; O.R.A., 36, pt. 3, 841–842; O.R.A., 51, pt. 2, 964–965; Beauregard to Major James Milligan, 27 May 1864, Beauregard to Bragg, 27 May 1864, and Beauregard to Bragg, 9:00 P.M., 27 May 1864, all in Official Telegrams, 22 April–9 June 1864, Beauregard Papers, LC; Jones, *War Clerk*, 2:220; Luther Rice Mills, "Letters of Luther Rice Mills, A Confederate Soldier," *North Carolina Historical Review* 4 (1927):299; Bushrod R. Johnson Diary, 27 May 1864, Johnson Papers, NA.

19. Marshall, ed., *Butler's Correspondence*, 4:283–284; Edward E. Hale to Sarah Butler, 29 May 1864, General Correspondence, 1864, Butler Papers, LC; Butler, *Butler's Book*, 671; Memorandum of 8 January 1879, Butler Papers, LC; Smith, *From Chattanooga to Petersburg*, 121; O.R.A., 36, pt. 3, 278–279, 285–288; Bowditch, "War Letters," 478; Solon A. Carter to his wife, 29 May 1864, Solon A. Carter Papers, USAMHI.

20. Edward E. Hale to Sarah Butler, 29 May 1864, General Correspondence, 1864, Butler Papers, LC; O.R.A., 36, pt. 3, 278, 280–281, 285, 288–289, 320; O.R.A., 51, pt. 1, 1252–1253; Smith, *From Chattanooga to Petersburg*, 21.

21. Gregorie, ed., "Wescoat Diary," 87; William H. S. Burgwyn Diary, 29 May 1864, NCDAH; John Lane Stuart to his mother, 29 May 1864, John Lane Stuart Papers, DU; *Eleventh Pennsylvania Cavalry*, 115; Dickey, *Eighty-Fifth Pennsylvania*, 326; Roe, *Twenty-Fourth Massachusetts*, 307; Eldredge, *Third New Hampshire*, 484; O.R.A., 36, pt. 3, 282–284, 317, 849; Beauregard to R. E. Lee, 6:30 A.M., 29 May 1864, and Beauregard to Bragg, 29 May 1864, both in Official Telegrams, 22 April–9 June 1864, Beauregard Papers, LC; Roman, *Military Operations*, 2:562.

22. Beauregard to A. R. Lawton, 4:00 P.M., 29 May 1864, Official Telegrams, 22 April–9 June 1864, Beauregard Papers, LC; "Special Orders, No. 15, Department of North Carolina and Southern Virginia," 29 May 1864, D. H. Hill Papers, VSL; O.R.A., 36, pt. 3, 849–850; Beauregard to Hill, 4:30 P.M., 29 May 1864, Letter Book, April–May 1864, Beauregard Papers, LC; Freeman, *Lee's Dispatches*, 204, 205, 205n, 208–209. See also Freeman, *Lee's Lieutenants*, 3:368–369.

23. Beauregard to Bragg, messages of 10:35 A.M., 11:25 A.M. and 5:00 P.M., 30 May 1864, and Beauregard to Lieutenant Cameron, 30 May 1864, all in Official Telegrams, 22 April–9 June 1864, also Beauregard to Colonel William Butler, 30 May 1864, Letter Book, May–July 1864, all in Beauregard Papers, LC; O.R.A., 51, pt. 2, 971–972; Bushrod R. Johnson Diary, 30 May 1864, Johnson Papers, NA.

24. Freeman, *Lee's Dispatches*, 207–209, 210n; Beauregard to Lee, 5:15 P.M., 30 May 1864, Official Telegrams, 22 April–9 June 1864, Beauregard Papers, LC; Roman, *Military Operations*, 2:563; O.R.A., 36, pt. 3, 850. Lee's telegram to Beauregard has not been located.

25. Henry Chambers Diary, 30 May 1864; NCDAH; O.R.A., 36, pt. 3, 370, 415; Eldredge, *Third New Hampshire*, 484; Roe, *Twenty-Fourth Massachusetts*, 307–308; Dickey, *Eighty-Fifth Pennsylvania*, 326; Joseph Hawley to his wife, 31 May 1864, Hawley Papers, LC; Roman, *Military Operations*, 2:563. Beauregard's possible motivations are briefly explored in Williams, *Beauregard*, 224, and Dowdey, *Lee's Last Campaign*, 282.

26. O.R.A., 36, pt. 3, 857; Roman, *Military Operations*, 2:563; O.R.A., 51, pt. 2, 966, 972; "Special Orders, No. 16, Department of North Carolina and Southern Virginia," 30 May 1864, and John M. Otey to D. H. Hill, 11:50 P.M., no date given, but 30 May 1864, both in D. H. Hill Papers, VSL.

27. Daily Journal, 1864, entries of 31 May, 1 June, and 2 June 1864, Kautz Papers, LC; O.R.A., 36, pt. 3, 420–421, 475; "Kautz in the Great Rebellion," Kautz Papers, LC.

28. O.R.A., 36, pt. 3, 864, 865, 866; Roman, *Military Operations*, 2:563; Beauregard to D. H. Hill, 7:30 P.M., 1 June 1864, D. H. Hill Papers, VSL; Beauregard to Johnson, 7:30 P.M., 1 June 1864, Letter Book, May–July 1864, Beauregard Papers, LC; O.R.A., 51, pt. 2, 978.

29. O.R.A., 36, pt. 2, 55–56, 63–64, 88, 193–195; 265–266, pt. 3, 514; O.R.A., 51, pt. 1, 1235, pt. 2, 980; Brady, *Eleventh Maine*, 193; Croffut and Morris, *Connecticut During the War*, 555–556; Hagood, *Memoirs*, 250–251; J. W. Pursley to his sister, 3 June 1864, Mary Frances Jane Pursley Papers, DU; Beauregard to Samuel Cooper, 8:45 P.M., 2 June 1864, Official Telegrams, 22 April–9 June 1864, Beauregard Papers, LC; Merrill, *First District of Columbia*, 254–256; Taylor, *First Connecticut Heavy Artillery*, 55; Bushrod R. Johnson Diary, 2 June 1864, Johnson Papers, NA.

30. O.R.A., 36, pt. 2, 55–56, 64–65, 88–89, 261–262; O.R.A., 51, pt. 1, 1235–1236; Henry Chambers Diary, 2 June 1864, NCDAH; O. D. Cooke to W. J. Clarke, 3 July 1864, W. J. Clarke Papers, Southern Historical Collection, University of North Carolina, Chapel Hill, N.C.; R. D.

Graham to W. A. Graham, 2 June 1864, William A. Graham Papers, Southern Historical Collection, University of North Carolina, Chapel Hill, N.C.; Edward Phifer to his mother, 3 June 1864, Phifer Family Papers, SHC; Mills, "Letters," 300; Cutchins, *Richmond Light Infantry Blues,* 137; Walkley, *Seventh Connecticut,* 140; Tourtellotte, *History of Company K,* 128–129, 210–212; Clark, *Thirty-Ninth Illinois,* 200–202, 368–548; Brady, *Eleventh Maine,* 194–203; Bushrod R. Johnson Diary, 2 June 1864, Johnson Papers, NA.

31. Marshall, ed., *Butler's Correspondence,* 4:299; Daily Journal, 1864, entry for 2 June 1864, Kautz Papers, LC; O.R.A., 36, pt. 2, 56–57, 65, 68–69, 89, pt. 3, 515–523, 566; O.R.A., 51, pt. 1, 1236; Eldredge, *Third New Hampshire,* 489–490; Waite, *New Hampshire in the Great Rebellion,* 206; Roe, *Twenty-Fourth Massachusetts,* 310; Croffut and Morris, *Connecticut During the War,* 556, 557; Joseph Hawley to his wife, 4 June 1864, Hawley Papers, LC.

32. O.R.A., 51, pt. 2, 979, 980; Beauregard to Bragg, 2:45 P.M., 2 June 1864, Official Telegrams, 22 April–9 June 1864, Beauregard Papers, LC; Roman, *Military Operations,* 2:564; O.R.A., 36, pt. 3, 518, 868.

33. Freeman, *Lee's Dispatches,* 214; Roman, *Military Operations,* 2:565; O.R.A., 36, pt. 3, 568, 870, 871; Clark, *Thirty-Ninth Illinois,* 203; Dickey, *Eighty-Fifth Pennsylvania,* 327; Eldredge, *Third New Hampshire,* 491; Roe, *Twenty-Fourth Massachusetts,* 310; J. W. Pursley to his sister, 3 June 1864, Mary Frances Jane Pursley Papers, DU; Henry Chambers Diary, 3 June 1864, NCDAH.

34. O.R.A. 36, pt. 3, 868, 874; Clark, ed., *North Carolina Regiments,* 3:139, 358; Henry Chambers Diary, 4 June 1864, NCDAH; O. D. Cooke to W. J. Clarke, 3 July 1864, W. J. Clarke Papers, SHC; J. W. Graham to W. A. Graham, 4 June 1864, William A. Graham Papers, SHC; Edward Phifer to his mother, 4 June 1864, Phifer Family Papers, SHC; Beauregard to Dearing, 2:00 A.M., 4 June 1864, Official Telegrams, 22 April–9 June 1864, and Beauregard to Dearing, 2:20 A.M., 4 June 1864, Letter Book, May–July 1864, both in Beauregard Papers, LC; Cutchins, *Richmond Light Infantry Blues,* 137.

35. The estimate given in the text is to be found in Roman, *Military Operations,* 2:229–230, 230n. Somewhat larger figures are in O.R.A., 36, pt. 3, 890–891, under date of 10 June 1864.

36. Beecher, *First Connecticut Light Battery,* 2:457, 473; Taylor, *First Connecticut Heavy Artillery,* 54; Kreutzer, *Ninety-Eighth New York,* 195; Foster, *New Jersey and the Rebellion,* 710, 715, 715n; Henry E. Taintor to his father, 6 June 1864, and 12 June 1864, Henry E. Taintor Papers, DU; Derby, *Bearing Arms,* 293; Cleveland, ed., "Campaign of Promise," 326; *New York Times,* 28 May 1864; Eldredge, *Third New Hampshire,* 491, 496; Dickey, *Eighty-Fifth Pennsylvania,* 328, 337; Mills, "Letters," 302; Abel H. Crawford to "Dear Dora," 5 June 1864, Abel H. Crawford Papers, Duke University, Durham, N.C.; Roe, *Twenty-Fourth Massachusetts,* 312–313; Joseph Hawley to his wife, 7 June 1864, Hawley Papers, LC; Clark, *Thirty-Ninth Illinois,* 203–204; Merrill, *First District of Columbia,* 256; O.R.N., 10:685.

37. Marshall, ed., *Butler's Correspondence,* 4:303; O.R.A., 36, pt. 3, 662; Porter, *Campaigning with Grant,* 187–188.

38. O.R.A., 36, pt. 3, 682, 878–879; Roman, *Military Operations,* 2:225, 566; Mills, "Letters," 299; Jones, *War Clerk,* 2:220; Beauregard to Bragg, 10:00 P.M., 8 June 1864, Official Telegrams, 22 April–9 June 1864, and Beauregard to Bragg, 8 June 1864, Endorsement Book, 1864, both in Beauregard Papers, LC; O.R.A., 51, pt. 2, 996.

39. The genesis of and planning for this operation are detailed in chapter 3 of William Glenn Robertson, "Cockades Under Fire: The Battle for Petersburg, June 9, 1864" (Master's thesis, Corcoran Department of History, University of Virginia, 1968). In addition to the sources cited therein, see also Livermore, *Days and Events,* 353; "Kautz in the Great Rebellion," Kautz Papers, LC; Gillmore to Terry, 8 June 1864, Terry to Hawley, 8 June 1864, and Hawley to Gideon Welles, 19 June 1864, all in Hawley Papers, LC.

40. Robertson, "Cockades Under Fire," chapters 4–11 and the sources cited therein. See also Livermore, *Days and Events,* 353; "Kautz in the Great Rebellion," Kautz Papers, LC; Joseph Hawley to Gideon Welles, 19 June 1864, Hawley Papers, LC; Cyrus B. Comstock Diary, 9 June 1864, LC; "Statement of Casualties," 10 June 1864, General Correspondence, 1864, Butler Papers, LC; Simonton, *Glimpses,* 5:489–490; Merrill, *First District of Columbia,* 256–258; Rowland Minturn Hall to his father, 10 June 1864, Julia Ward Stickley Collection, NCDAH; Wise MS, Beauregard Papers, LC.

41. Beauregard to Bragg, 7:00 A.M., 9 June 1864, and Beauregard to Johnson, 11 June 1864, both in Letter Book, May–July 1864, Beauregard Papers, LC; O.R.A., 36, pt. 3, 886, 887, 890, 896–898; O.R.A., 51, pt. 2, 1004, 1010; Roman, *Military Operations,* 2:225–226; Dowdey and Manarin, eds., *Wartime Papers of R. E. Lee,* 770–771; Mills, "Letters," 302; "Special Order No. 10, First Military District," 1:30 A.M., 11 June 1864, Raleigh E. Colston Papers, Southern Historical Collection, University of North Carolina, Chapel Hill, N.C.; O.R.N., 10:681, 688–689, 697–698; Abel H. Crawford to "Dear Dora," 12 June 1864, Abel H. Crawford Papers, DU.

42. Walkley, *Seventh Connecticut*, 148; Dickey, *Eighty-Fifth Pennsylvania*, 337; Stowits, *One Hundredth New York*, 267; Foster, *New Jersey and the Rebellion*, 714; Henry E. Taintor to his father, 12 June 1864, Henry E. Taintor Papers, DU; O.R.A., 36, pt. 2, 273–287; Joseph Hawley to Gideon Welles, 19 June 1864, and Joseph Hawley to his wife, 20 June 1864, both in Hawley Papers, LC.

43. "Kautz in the Great Rebellion," Kautz Papers, LC; Hincks to Butler, 13 June 1864, General Correspondence, 1864, Butler Papers, LC; Marshall, ed., *Butler's Correspondence*, 4:361; Livermore, *Days and Events*, 354–355; O.R.A., 36, pt. 3, 755.

44. O.R.A., 36, pt. 1, 178–180, pt. 3, 709, 745, 755–757, 770–771, 773–775; Beecher, *First Connecticut Light Battery*, 2:465; Dickey, *Eighty-Fifth Pennsylvania*, 337; Merrill, *First District of Columbia*, 258–259; Marshall, ed., *Butler's Correspondence*, 4:364, 365; Eldredge, *Third New Hampshire*, 496; Little, *Seventh New Hampshire*, 267; Thompson, *Thirteenth New Hampshire*, 380–381; Roe, *Twenty-Fourth Massachusetts*, 313; Porter, *Campaigning with Grant*, 197–198; O.R.A., 40, pt. 2, 18–19, 37, 40–41, 43–44; O.R.N., 10:147.

45. O.R.A., 40, pt. 2, 652, 653; Roman, *Military Operations*, 2:228, 567; O.R.A., 51, pt. 2, 1012.

46. O.R.A., 40, pt. 1, 705, pt. 2, 656–658, 676–678; P. G. T. Beauregard, "Four Days of Battle at Petersburg," *Battles and Leaders*, 4:540–541; Roman, *Military Operations*, 2:230.

47. Dickey, *Eighty-Fifth Pennsylvania*, 338; Eldredge, *Third New Hampshire*, 496; Trumbull, *Knightly Soldier*, 236–239; O.R.A., 40, pt. 2, 659–661.

☆ 18 ☆

Assessment

Although the Bermuda Hundred fortifications were occupied by the opposing armies from 16 June 1864 until the night of 2 April 1865, the time of fierce fighting on the peninsula had passed. Beyond occasional use of its road network to transfer Federal units across the James, the Bermuda Hundred sector served only as a quiet haven for battle-weary units of both sides during the remainder of the conflict.[1] Also, the arrival of the larger armies produced extensive command charges. After the Army of Northern Virginia reached Petersburg, P. G. T. Beauregard's troops were consolidated with it. Beauregard remained for a time, but he eventually departed for the Military Division of the West. In the Army of the James, Quincy Gillmore was relieved of command after the fiasco of 9 June and Baldy Smith soon followed, after his own failure against Petersburg a week later. Benjamin Butler remained as commander of the Army of the James until January 1865, when he was replaced after the repulse of his expedition against Fort Fisher. By the end of the war even the Federal corps' designations had been altered, the X and XVIII Corps passing out of existence on 3 December 1864 to be reorganized as the XXIV and XXV Corps.[2]

For one participant, the Bermuda Hundred Campaign never ended. As long as he lived, Benjamin Butler would be called "Bottled-up" Butler as a reminder of the seemingly ignominious position into which he had led the Army of the James. The phrase apparently originated with Brigadier General John Barnard, who had investigated the Bermuda Hundred situation for Grant and Halleck in late May. In a subsequent visit with Grant, Barnard compared Butler's position to being inside a tightly corked bottle. Grant then included the remark, without attributing it to Barnard, in his final report of 22 July 1865. Taking their cue from Grant, writers began immediately to employ the "bottle" image to describe Butler's campaign. Adam Badeau mentioned it in his history published in 1885, although Grant expressly asked that the reference be deleted, and the phrase has had a life of its own ever since. In interviews and in his own memoirs Grant apologized for his use of the "bottle" simile, but to no avail. Influential writers like Bruce Catton, Allan Nevins, and Clifford Dowdy perpetuated the sobriquet "Bottled-up" Butler, and even the most recent Civil War survey texts uncritically accept Barnard's inappropriate characterization of Butler's situation.[3]

In fact, the Army of the James was "bottled-up" physically in only one direction, due west. Although the Confederate fortifications facing Butler's army were probably impervious to assault if resolutely manned by veterans, several other options for offensive action were open to the Federals. On Bermuda Hundred neck itself there was approximately one mile of unfortified territory between Ashton and Swift Creeks. This sector was later fortified, but during May and early June it was lightly held by Confederate forces. Half-hearted Federal probes had been conducted on 25 and 26 May into the northern part of this sector, but the efforts had been abandoned due to Grant's order for Butler to relinquish the XVIII Corps. Nevertheless, with the completion of a pontoon bridge across the mouth of Ashton Creek to Port Walthall, a potential crack was opened in the very neck of the "bottle."[4]

After 16 May, the major opportunity for the Army of the James lay south of the Appomattox, where a Federal foothold at City Point and Spring Hill already existed. Butler was well aware of the opportunities presented by the southern bridgehead, and he proposed on three occasions to attack Petersburg via this route. The first attempt on 28 May was blocked by the arrival of the transports to take Smith's corps to join Grant; the second, on 2 June, was postponed because of Confederate offensive activities; and the third, on 9 June, came close to success before it succumbed to Quincy Gillmore's timidity. As further proof that this route remained a viable alternative to being "bottled-up," Baldy Smith's men followed the same path in their assault on Petersburg on 15 June. Although this option to move southward was known to perceptive observers at the time and was cited in several postwar regimental histories and reminiscences, the charge continues to be repeated that Butler's army was "bottled-up" after 16 May.[5]

Because neither Richmond nor Petersburg was captured by the Army of the James before Grant's arrival, most historians consider Benjamin Butler's Bermuda Hundred campaign to have been an abject failure, in Bruce Catton's opinion possibly the most "mishandled" campaign of the war.[6] By a liberal use of hindsight, particularly in regard to Petersburg, they have concluded that great blunders were made and that Benjamin Butler was primarily at fault. Mistakes there obviously were, and Butler was responsible for his share, but such a simplistic view of the campaign is not warranted by the facts. Contrary to the view generally prevailing, the Army of the James did achieve a considerable measure of success in its various missions, and when it failed, the blame did not always lie with Butler. Other Federal officers, both above and below Butler in the chain of command, also contributed to the difficulties experienced by the Army of the James. Nor did the Federal troops operate in a vacuum, since thousands of Confederates played an obvious role in limiting the success of Butler's army.

Butler's first objective, the seizure and protection of a base far up the James River, was attained easily. When the Army of the Potomac arrived on the south bank of the river, it found City Point to be an ideal site for its supply base; during the Siege of Petersburg, City Point became one of the busiest terminals in the United States. The second objective, the disruption of the Confederate transportation network south of Richmond, was also achieved, but for a limited time only. Kautz's two raids

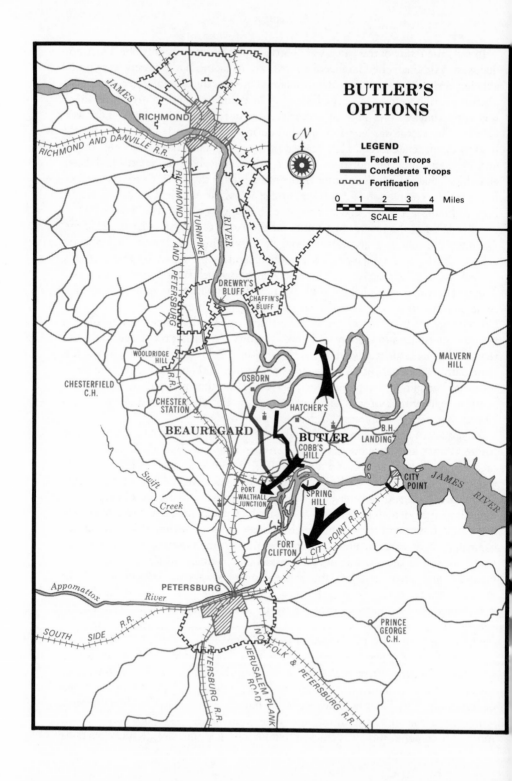

BUTLER'S
OPTIONS

LEGEND
Federal Troops
Confederate Troops
Fortification

0 1 2 3 4 Miles
SCALE

RICHMOND

JAMES

RICHMOND AND DANVILLE R.R.

RICHMOND AND PETERSBURG TURNPIKE

RIVER

DREWRY'S BLUFF

CHAFFIN'S BLUFF

WOOLDRIDGE HILL

MALVERN HILL

CHESTERFIELD C.H.

OSBORN

R.R.

CHESTER STATION

HATCHER'S

BEAUREGARD

BUTLER

COBB'S HILL

B.H. LANDING

Swift

PORT WALTHALL JUNCTION

SPRING HILL

CITY POINT

JAMES RIVER

Creek

CITY POINT R.R.

FORT CLIFTON

Appomattox

River

PETERSBURG

PRINCE GEORGE C.H.

SOUTH SIDE R.R.

PETERSBURG R.R.

JERUSALEM PLANK ROAD

NORFOLK & PETERSBURG R.R.

did delay the movement of supplies and troops northward, but his cavalrymen were not efficient railroad wreckers. More significant damage was done by the Federal infantry at various times to the Richmond and Petersburg Railroad. If ten days was the anticipated duration of the period during which the Army of the James had been expected to operate alone, this mission was accomplished relatively successfully. In general, success was also attained in Butler's third mission, the distraction of Confederate units that might otherwise have reinforced the Army of Northern Virginia. The Army of the James held the attention of over 20,000 Confederate troops until 18 May, and it continued to detain significant numbers of Confederates until the end of May.[7]

Only in its final mission, to threaten and possibly capture Richmond, did the Army of the James fall short of its goal, and even there the failure was only partial. Landing the troops and organizing them for offensive movement necessarily took time. In addition, the base of operations had to be established and protected. Richmond was at least sixteen miles away, and without adequate maps to show the way, the Federal advance would have been slow and cautious. Word of Butler's approach would obviously have preceded him and the James River bridges would surely have been defended or destroyed by the time Butler's men reached the river's south bank. Without a strong cavalry force to dash ahead and seize the spans, it is unlikely that the Federal infantry could have gotten into the city. Finally, if the Drewry's Bluff fortifications had not been neutralized, a pontoon bridge there could have provided Confederate access to Butler's rear. In sum, the seizure of Richmond by the Army of the James would have been extremely difficult, if not impossible. The only factor operating in the Federal favor was the initial lack of Confederate troops in the area between Richmond and Petersburg.[8]

Although he did not capture the Confederate capital, Butler did maneuver his army in front of Richmond's outer defenses within ten days of the beginning of the campaign. Unfortunately, he could not long remain there without the assistance of the Army of the Potomac. Had Grant's army arrived on schedule and merged with the Army of the James, the Bermuda Hundred Campaign would have contributed greatly to ending the Civil War in the East much sooner than April 1865. But Grant was delayed and the Confederacy was unwilling to allow Butler to loiter unmolested at Richmond's southern gateway. Lacking both the skill and the strength to remain at Drewry's Bluff indefinitely, Butler saw no choice but to withdraw to his base and wait for Grant's arrival. Much had already been gained, and to have attempted more might have jeopardized the solid accomplishments of an army that deserved much greater recognition than it has since received.[9]

Although the Federal army's inability to seize Richmond was regretted by postwar commentators, nothing so aroused their wrath as Butler's failure to capture Petersburg. In retrospect, after the Army of the Potomac had spent nine long months trying to batter its way into Petersburg at so great a cost, it appeared that the city should have been occupied at an earlier date. Yet this is reasoning by hindsight. In May of 1864 no one could have foreseen the bitter Siege of Petersburg that eventually resulted. To argue that Benjamin Butler should have prevented it is fatuous.[10] Grant's written instructions to Butler made Richmond the geographical objective of the Army of the James and those instructions did not mention Petersburg. The strategic importance of the latter city was explained verbally to Butler, but Grant admitted that Richmond was stressed as the focal point of the campaign.[11] Petersburg could have been captured as late as 9 May or possibly even 10 May, yet if Butler were to join Grant around Richmond by 15 May, the occupation and defense of the city had to be foregone. Butler's forces were already spread thin holding Bermuda Hundred, City Point, and the river forts. To garrison Petersburg against the Confederate brigades arriving by rail from the Carolinas would have required a major portion of Butler's remaining troops and precluded an advance in strength against Richmond as Grant's plan specified.

Obviously, the chief flaw in the Federal plan of operations was its fixation upon Richmond. Believing that he could drive Lee within the Richmond defenses by 15 May, Grant desired that the Army of the James arrange its timetable so as to join him there.[12] Grant underestimated both the tenacity of the Army of Northern Virginia and the Confederates' ability to move troops by rail from the Carolinas. Petersburg would have been a much more feasible objective for Butler's army, one that could have been gained quickly and was potentially defensible against counterattack, but the plan called for the Army of the James to move against Richmond, and this was incompatible with seizing and holding Petersburg. Perhaps a general combining great strategic vision with a willingness to disregard his superior's instructions would have seen that Richmond was out of reach and operated against Petersburg instead, but Benjamin Butler was not such a man. Nor, it can be said in his defense, were more than a handful of his contemporaries.[13]

The flawed plan of operations was not the only hindrance to a successful campaign by the Army of the James. The problems within the command structure of the army were also significant.[14] Simply stated, Benjamin Butler was a skilled and capable administrator, but as the commander of a field army engaged in an important campaign he was totally without practical training. Recognizing this, Grant had given Butler an experienced officer, Major General William F. Smith, in hopes that Smith could provide sound professional advice for Butler to follow. Although Smith was, in Grant's words, "likely to condemn whatever is not suggested by himself," he and Butler worked surprisingly well together initially. Unfortunately, Smith was bitterly opposed to the plan of campaign, and in addition he was afflicted with a painful deliberateness in his movements. For all his faults, however, Smith was apparently respected by Butler, who generally heeded his advice. In fact, Butler so depended upon Smith that when the latter temporarily lost his head on the morning of 16 May, Smith's behavior was allowed to determine the response of the entire army to the Confederate attack.[15]

Had Butler and Smith been allowed to conduct the campaign alone, as was later recommended by Generals Meigs and Barnard, more might have been accomplished, but they were joined at the last minute by another strongly opinionated officer, Major General Quincy Gillmore. Except for some limited, and catastrophic, offensive operations in the Department of the South, Gillmore was as inexperienced as Butler in commanding large units in a campaign of maneuver. Upon his arrival in Virginia, Gillmore found himself reduced in stature from the commander of a large department to a subordinate troop commander under a nonprofessional departmental superior.[16] Accustomed to doing things his own way, Gillmore did not work well in coordination with Smith, and in most instances Butler was entirely too tentative in his orders to compel the necessary cooperation. Since he had no authority over Gillmore and his troops, Smith could only suggest movements to Butler, who might or might not choose to order them executed. A strong-willed commander, confident in his own mind as to what he wanted done, might have forced the two balky officers to work together in harmony, but Butler was too unsure of himself to impose his will upon his subordinates, and generally he let them go their own way under an exceedingly loose rein.[17]

Tactically the Federals made a number of mistakes, as might have been expected from such a chaotic command system. The organizational phase of the operation was successfully handled by Butler, and the landings at Bermuda Hundred and City Point were models of their kind,[18] but once the troops began to maneuver, difficulties arose. Heckman's weak probe on 6 May could hardly have been expected to accomplish more than it did, but there could be no excuse for the limited results obtained by Brooks's five brigades on 7 May. Facing only two weak Confederate brigades, Brooks was able to destroy little more than one hundred yards of the Richmond and Petersburg Railroad. On 8 May the Army of the James rested, giving the Confederates additional time to concentrate a reaction force by rail. When Butler moved at last on 9 May, the equilibrium point for the opposing armies was fast approaching, because Robert Hoke's leading elements were nearing Petersburg. Once in motion, however, the Army of the James squandered most of the day chasing phantoms.[19]

On the evening of 9 May, acting upon erroneous information received from Washington, Butler turned his back on Petersburg and set his face toward Richmond. This was a mistake, but one that was justified by the plan of campaign and the messages sent from Stanton. Even Butler's severest critics are understanding, and properly so, of his reasons for turning the Army of the James northward, yet the manner in which he accomplished it does not merit approval. Instead of heading directly for the Confederate capital, Butler chose to return to the safety of the Bermuda Hundred defenses for a day of rest before advancing against Drewry's Bluff. The withdrawal of the Army of the James from the Richmond-Petersburg transportation corridor facilitated the passage of Hoke's seven brigades to create a force large enough to meet the Army of the James on relatively equal terms.[20]

Once the Federal advance against Richmond got underway on 12 May, it was again unconscionably slow. Without news from the Army of the Potomac, Butler chose to be cautious. Although understandable, this caution did allow Beauregard time to consolidate the various Confederate units into an offensive force of considerable power. Upon their arrival at Drewry's Bluff, the Federal commanders continued to make mistakes. On 15 May an assault was cancelled because of the misallocation of troops. Even worse, Smith's XVIII Corps was allowed to occupy a defensive position that left its right flank hanging in the air.[21]

The sixteenth of May brought the Federals' tactical mistakes to their zenith. Although the early morning fog was a significant factor in the battle, its blinding effects applied equally to both sides and cannot be used as an excuse for the Federal defeat.[22] Nor were the troops on the right flank of the Army of the James surprised; lacking inspired leadership at brigade, division, and corps levels, they were simply outmaneuvered. Influenced by the fog and an unfortunately timed, inaccurate report by Godfrey Weitzel, Baldy Smith lost his nerve and began to withdraw his corps before it became necessary, and indeed while most of his regiments were steadfastly holding their ground. As the army commander, Butler could have ordered Smith to stand firm, but he deferred to Smith's professional experience and let him have his way.[23]

Butler was only slightly more forceful with Quincy Gillmore. Early in the action he ordered Gillmore to counterattack, in hopes of either breaking the thin Confederate line or at least of relieving the pressure on the Federal right. Deceived by the apparent aggressiveness of the few Confederates facing him and inhibited by his own native caution, Gillmore delayed the counterattack so long that by the time he finally chose to act, Smith's withdrawal had totally altered the situation. Thus, instead of disrupting Confederate movements, Gillmore only maneuvered to maintain contact with the retreating XVIII Corps. Had Gillmore counterattacked promptly, the course of the Battle of Drewry's Bluff might have been decisively changed, but he did not do so and Butler did not press him to move after the initial order. Once again, an experienced, self-reliant army commander might have made a difference, but with a subordinate of Quincy Gillmore's temperament even such a man might not have been able to force the necessary action.[24]

The Federal retreat from Drewry's Bluff was conducted competently, and thereafter the defense of Bermuda Hundred was handled equally well, except for a few lapses on the picket line. Butler moved too slowly in organizing an attack upon Petersburg in late May, but this is overshadowed by Grant's unfortunate decision to remove the XVIII Corps from Bermuda Hundred just at the time when it might have struck an important blow. After Smith's departure, the Army of the James was so reduced in size that it was hard pressed to hold the territory already occupied. Yet Butler was still unwilling to consider Petersburg beyond his reach. Although the expedition of 9 June probably could not have held the city indefinitely, an enormous amount of damage could have been done to industrial and transportation facilities at a very critical time. Had Edward Hincks been in command of the infantry instead of Gillmore, a significant Federal success might have been achieved. However, Butler the nonprofessional soldier allowed Gillmore the West Pointer to assume command, and the opportunity was lost. With Gillmore's retreat, the final offensive thrust by the Army of the James during the Bermuda Hundred Campaign passed into history.[25]

As for the Confederates, almost all of their activities were in response to Federal initiatives. With help from D. H. Hill, Bushrod Johnson, and Johnson Hagood, George Pickett performed heroically in resisting Federal pressure for four days, until at length he cracked under the strain on 9 May. Although Pickett's efforts were relatively successful, the Confederate response might have been even more positive had the boundaries of the departmental system been drawn differently. The Federal landing site was located in the extreme northern sector of the Department of North Carolina and Southern Virginia, while the Drewry's Bluff fortifications just a few miles away and on the same side of the James River were controlled by Robert Ransom's Department of Richmond. Unknowingly, the Federals had landed directly in one of the interstices of the departmental system, a fact that tended to split what should have been a single Confederate reaction into two separate responses. Only because the Federals were slow to take advantage of their favorable situation and because Bushrod Johnson operated without reference to departmental boundaries on 6 and 7 May was this inherent Confederate disadvantage overcome.

Upon Beauregard's arrival in Virginia, the departmental problem eased for a time. Although out of favor with Bragg and Davis, Beauregard was an authentic Confederate hero. More important, although he was something of a posturer, Beauregard knew his business and his battle plan for 16 May was essentially sound. As an integral part, however, he envisioned that Chase Whiting's two brigades would strike Butler's rear for the *coup-de-grace*, a difficult maneuver under any circumstances. On the appointed day, Whiting failed to execute his part of the plan, due to massive physical and mental exhaustion. Although he was not the only Confederate general found wanting on 16 May, Whiting at least acknowledged his error and eventually atoned for any past mistakes by his last-ditch defense of Fort Fisher the following year, in which he sustained a mortal wound.[26]

Equally detrimental to Beauregard's expectations was the failure of his left wing under Robert Ransom to take advantage of its initial success early in the morning. After crushing Heckman's four regiments, Ransom's four brigades were so disorganized and short of ammunition that they were unable to continue offensive operations. Ransom's inability to extract further service from his division meant that Robert Hoke's brigades had to assault frontally against an unshaken Federal line, with predictable results. Only Baldy Smith's hasty decision to withdraw his corps and Quincy Gillmore's tardiness in counterattacking saved the day for the Confederates and allowed Beauregard to salvage the victory. Although Whiting's failure loomed as the largest negative factor in Confederate analyses, the inept performance of Ransom's Division was equally responsible for the escape of the Army of the James.[27]

Following Butler's retreat within the Bermuda Hundred defenses, Beauregard wisely seized the terrain needed to establish a strong defensive line that would protect the nearby transportation corridor. Thereafter, his chief concern was no longer the quiescent Army of the James, but the calls by his superiors for detachments to reinforce the Army of Northern Virginia. Typically, Beauregard responded by formulating grandiose plans by means of which the two Confederate armies could rapidly unite and defeat the Federals in detail. Perhaps one of these schemes might have worked, but it is much more likely they would have foundered on the time-distance factors involved. At any rate, the Davis administration rejected any spectacular attempts at concentration, preferring instead to shift units piecemeal between Lee and Beauregard.[28]

As it happened, Davis's conservative strategy succeeded in blunting the Federal thrusts north of the James River, but at a considerable risk to such poorly defended yet vital positions as Petersburg. If Edward Hincks had been sent against Petersburg on 9 June instead of Quincy Gillmore, the Confederate house of cards might have collapsed, but it was Gillmore who commanded, and the city gained a short reprieve. Beauregard was well aware of the danger facing Petersburg, and he even anticipated Grant's eventual crossing of the James River; yet he could do little without a larger force to deploy. Thus, as the Bermuda Hundred Campaign ebbed to a close, he awaited the impending blow with much foreboding. When at last it fell, the course of the war took a new turn and the Bermuda Hundred Campaign was largely forgotten. It remains so today, for history is not especially kind to might-have-beens, even those of such magnitude.

NOTES

1. For accounts of later activity at Bermuda Hundred, see Hyde, *One Hundred and Twelfth New York,* chapter 8; Mowris, *One Hundred and Seventeenth New York,* chapter 11.

2. Williams, *Beauregard,* 236–241; O.R.A., 40, pt. 3, 334; Catton, *Grant Takes Command,* 326–335, 401–403; O.R.A., 42, pt. 3, 791; O.R.A., 46, pt. 2, 60.

3. Raymond, "Ben Butler," 450; Trefousse, *Ben Butler,* 150; Grant, *Personal Memoirs,* 2:150–152, 568; John Russell Young, *Around the World with General Grant,* 2 vols. (New York: The American News Company, 1879), 2:247; Catton, *Never Call Retreat,* 351; Nevins, *Organized War to Victory,* 34; Dowdey, *Lee's Last Campaign,* 244; James M. McPherson, *Ordeal by Fire: The Civil War and Reconstruction* (New York: Alfred A. Knopf, 1982), 413; Herman Hattaway and Archer Jones, *How the North Won: A Military History of the Civil War* (Urbana: Univeristy of Illinois Press, 1983), 563; Allan R. Millett and Peter Maslowski, *For the Common Defense: A Military History of the United States of America* (New York: The Free Press, 1984), 222.

4. O.R.A., 36, pt. 3, 886. A map showing the geographical relationships is in Cowles, ed., *O.R. Atlas,* plate 65, 1.

5. Emmerton, *Twenty-Third Massachusetts,* 200; Kreutzer, *Ninety-Eighth New York,* 194–195. Two of Butler's biographers have argued strenuously against the "bottled-up" label, but to little avail. West, *Lincoln's Scapegoat General,* 244; Nash, *Stormy Petrel,* 197.

6. Bruce Catton, *A Stillness at Appomattox* (Garden City: Doubleday, 1953), 184.

7. Raymond, "Ben Butler," 453. According to Badeau, *Military History,* 257, Butler failed in all his objectives.

8. It is not surprising to find Butler being berated for not having seized Richmond in Charles A. Dana and James H. Wilson, *The Life of Ulysses S. Grant* (Springfield, Mass.: Gurdon Bill & Company, 1868), 184, since that volume was little more than a campaign biography. Yet Bruce Catton in *Grant Takes Command,* 246, also considers that an assault on Richmond "would have had a fine chance of success." Alfred Rockwell, a battery commander in the Army of the James, did not agree with this optimistic assessment. Rockwell, quoted in Beecher, *First Connecticut Light Battery,* 2:476; Rockwell, "Tenth Army Corps," 295.

9. Raymond, "Ben Butler," 452; Rockwell, "Tenth Army Corps," 292.

10. Critical of Butler's failure to seize Petersburg are Rockwell, quoted in Beecher, *First Connecticut Light Battery,* 2:337; Rockwell, "Tenth Army Corps," 292; Adams, *Studies Military and Diplomatic,* 273–274, 280; Dana and Wilson, *Life of Grant,* 220; John H. Anderson, *Grant's Campaign in Virginia, May 1—June 30, 1864* (London: Hugh Rees, Ltd., 1908), 97; Wolfson, "Butler's Relations," 387–388; Fuller,

Generalship of Grant, 260–261; Williams, *Beauregard,* 211; Catton, *Grant Takes Command,* 246; Trefousse, *Ben Butler,* 149–150.

11. Grant, *Personal Memoirs,* 2:148, 563.

12. See Footnote 27, Chapter 1 for citations. Nowhere did Grant mention in writing the ten-day time frame that Butler apparently considered himself bound by, yet something of the sort must have been discussed by the two officers. Bruce, "General Butler's Bermuda Campaign," 309–310. Grant seems not to have anticipated taking as long as he eventually did to reach the vicinity of Richmond. In a letter to Halleck dated 29 April 1864 (*O.R.A.,* 33:1017–1018), he even raised the possibility that Lee might retreat within Richmond's defenses without meeting the Army of the Potomac in battle. Bruce Catton comments: "In all of this there may have been too little concern about how Lee might respond when the Army of the Potomac advanced." Catton, *Grant Takes Command,* 170.

13. Humphreys, *Virginia Campaign,* 149; Smith, *From Chattanooga to Petersburg,* 116–117, 117n; Raymond, "Ben Butler," 451–452. Oddly, Grant himself remained vague on the subject of capturing Petersburg even in mid-June. See the chapter on "General Grant" by Colonel Theodore A. Dodge in Dwight, ed., *Critical Sketches,* 43.

14. Rockwell, "Tenth Army Corps," 295–296; Wilson, *Old Flag,* 1:361; Wall, "Raids," 194; Raymond, "Ben Butler," 452–453; Trefousse, *Ben Butler,* 149; Nevins, *Organized War to Victory,* 9.

15. Badeau, *Military History,* 2:43–44, 259; Porter, *Campaigning with Grant,* 246; *O.R.A.,* 36, pt. 3, 43; Smith, *From Chattanooga to Petersburg,* 17–18, 154–155; Catton, *Grant Takes Command,* 246–247. In regard to Smith's performance before Petersburg in mid-June, Catton wrote in *Never Call Retreat,* 367: "Smith served Grant now as he had served Butler a few weeks earlier; he saw risks rather than opportunity, went on the defensive, and made no further advance."

16. Badeau, *Military History,* 2:44; Rockwell, "Tenth Army Corps," 269; Kreutzer, *Ninety-Eighth New York,* 159, 177; Roe, *Twenty-Fourth Massachusetts,* 444; Gordon, *War Diary,* 188, 281, 284–285; Joseph Hawley to Mr. Faxon, 25 April 1864, Hawley Papers, LC. Both Sarah Butler and August Kautz recognized Gillmore's professional sensibilities to be part of the problem in his relations with Butler. Marshall, ed., *Butler's Correspondence,* 4:253; "Kautz in the Great Rebellion," Kautz Papers, LC.

17. Several participants placed the majority of the blame for the campaign's failures upon Smith and Gillmore. Copp, *Reminiscences,* 351–352, 391, 406–409; Heckman, quoted in Drake, *Ninth New Jersey,* 207; Bartlett, *Twelfth New Hampshire,* 188; Thompson, *Thirteenth New Hampshire,* 334. Even Grant, in later years, seemed to think that Smith and Gillmore had been poor choices: "Butler as a general was full of enterprise and resources and a brave man. If I had given him two corps commanders like Adelbert Ames, MacKenzie, Weitzel, or Terry, or a dozen I could mention, he would have made a fine campaign on the James, and helped materially in my plans. I have always been sorry I did not do so." Grant, quoted in Young, *Around the World with General Grant,* 2:304.

18. Bruce, "General Butler's Bermuda Campaign," 310; Rockwell, "Tenth Army Corps," 296.

19. Rockwell, "Tenth Army Corps," 295; Freeman, *Lee's Lieutenants,* 3:466.

20. Raymond, "Ben Butler," 452; Bruce, "General Butler's Bermuda Campaign," 325–326; Rockwell, "Tenth Army Corps," 282–284, 292; Wolfson, "Butler's Relations," 382–385.

21. Bruce, "General Butler's Bermuda Campaign," 326–328; Derby, *Bearing Arms,* 276–277, Smith, quoted in same, 288–289, and Weitzel, quoted in same, 289–290.

22. Bruce, "General Butler's Bermuda Campaign," 336; Rockwell, "Tenth Army Corps," 290–291; Emmerton, *Twenty-Third Massachusetts,* 185–186; Price, *Ninety-Seventh Pennsylvania,* 264. For a somewhat different view, see Derby, *Bearing Arms,* 271, and Clark, *Iron Hearted Regiment,* 116.

23. *O.R.A.,* 36, pt. 2, 129, 150; Derby, *Bearing Arms,* 291; Bruce, "General Butler's Bermuda Campaign," 335–344; Surgeon F. B. Gillette, quoted in Drake, *Ninth New Jersey,* 209.

24. Bruce, "General Butler's Bermuda Campaign," 344–345; Rockwell, "Tenth Army Corps," 291–292; Butler, *Butler's Book,* 664. In Dana and Wilson, *Life of Grant,* 220, and also in Badeau, *Military History,* 256, Butler is erroneously criticized for not having ordered Gillmore forward.

25. George Wolfson, one of Butler's severest critics, violently castigated Butler instead of Gillmore for the failure of this expedition. Wolfson, "Butler's Relations," 387. Yet Wolfson's facts are in error, as shown in Robertson, "Cockades Under Fire," Chapters 4–7.

26. Beauregard, *Battles and Leaders,* 4:200; Randall, "Plea," 276.

27. Humphreys, *Virginia Campaign,* 157; Hagood, *Memoirs,* 236, 244; Beauregard, *Battles and Leaders,* 4:204; Beauregard "Drury's Bluff," 258–259; Roman, *Military Operations,* 2:209; Harrison, *Pickett's Men,* 127; Izlar, *Edisto Rifles,* 58; Loehr, *First Virginia,* 48; Morgan, *Reminiscences,* 204; Sumpter, "Fighting," 180; Clark, ed., *North Carolina Regiments,* 3:137–138; Wise MS, Beauregard Papers, LC.

28. The interaction between Lee's army, Beauregard's dwindling force, and the Davis administration is detailed in Williams, *Beauregard,* 221–225, and Dowdey, *Lee's Last Campaign,* 239, 245–247.

Appendix 1:
Army of the James

5 MAY 1864

Major General Benjamin F. Butler

X Army Corps
Major General Quincy A. Gillmore

FIRST DIVISION
Brigadier General Alfred H. Terry

First Brigade

Colonel Joshua B. Howell
39th Illinois
62nd Ohio
67th Ohio
85th Pennsylvania

Second Brigade

Colonel Joseph R. Hawley
6th Connecticut
7th Connecticut
3rd New Hampshire
7th New Hampshire

Third Brigade

Colonel Harris M. Plaisted
10th Connecticut
11th Maine
24th Massachusetts
100th New York

Artillery

Connecticut Light, 1st Battery
New Jersey Light, 5th Battery
1st United States, Battery M

SECOND DIVISION
Brigadier General John W. Turner

First Brigade

Colonel Samuel M. Alford
40th Massachusetts
3rd New York
89th New York
117th New York
142nd New York

Second Brigade

Colonel William B. Barton
47th New York
48th New York
115th New York
76th Pennsylvania

Artillery

New Jersey Light, 4th Battery
1st United States, Battery B
1st United States, Battery D

THIRD DIVISION
Brigadier General Adelbert Ames

First Brigade

Colonel Richard White
8th Maine
4th New Hampshire
55th Pennsylvania
97th Pennsylvania

Second Brigade

Colonel Jeremiah C. Drake
13th Indiana
9th Maine
112th New York
169th New York

Artillery

New York Light, 33rd Battery
3rd Rhode Island Light, Battery C
3rd United States, Battery E

Unattached Troops

1st New York Engineers (eight companies)
4th Massachusetts Cavalry (1st Battalion)

XVIII Army Corps
Major General William F. Smith

FIRST DIVISION
Brigadier General William T. H. Brooks

First Brigade   *Second Brigade*

Brigadier General Gilman Marston   Brigadier General Hiram Burnham
81st New York   8th Connecticut
96th New York   10th New Hampshire
98th New York   13th New Hampshire
139th New York   118th New York

Third Brigade

Colonel Horace T. Sanders
92nd New York
58th Pennsylvania
188th Pennsylvania
19th Wisconsin

Artillery

Wisconsin Light, 4th Battery
4th United States, Battery L
5th United States, Battery A

SECOND DIVISION
Brigadier General Godfrey Weitzel

First Brigade   *Second Brigade*

Brigadier General Charles A.   Brigadier General Isaac J. Wistar
    Heckman
23rd Massachusetts   11th Connecticut
25th Massachusetts   2nd New Hampshire
27th Massachusetts   12th New Hampshire
9th New Jersey   148th New York

Artillery

New York Light, 7th Battery
3rd New York Light, Battery E
1st Rhode Island Light, Battery F
4th United States, Battery D

THIRD DIVISION
Brigadier General Edward W. Hincks

First Brigade	*Second Brigade*
Brigadier General Edward A. Wild	Colonel Samuel A. Duncan
1st U.S. Colored	4th U.S. Colored
10th U.S. Colored	5th U.S. Colored
22nd U.S. Colored	6th U.S. Colored
37th U.S. Colored	

Artillery

3rd New York Light, Battery K
3rd New York Light, Battery M
2nd U.S. Colored Light, Battery B

CAVALRY DIVISION
Brigadier General August V. Kautz

First Brigade	*Second Brigade*
Colonel Simon H. Mix	Colonel Samuel P. Spear
1st District of Columbia	5th Pennsylvania
3rd New York	11th Pennsylvania

Artillery

New York Light, 8th Battery (section)

Unattached Troops

1st New York Mounted Rifles
1st U.S. Colored Cavalry
2nd U.S. Colored Cavalry
13th Company Massachusetts Heavy Artillery

Appendix 2:
Beauregard's Field Command

16 MAY 1864

General P. G. T. Beauregard

RANSOM'S DIVISION
Major General Robert Ransom, Jr.

Gracie's Brigade

Brigadier General Archibald Gracie, Jr.
41st Alabama
43rd Alabama
59th Alabama
60th Alabama
23rd Alabama Battalion

Terry's Brigade

Colonel William R. Terry

1st Virginia
7th Virginia
11th Virginia
24th Virginia

Barton's Brigade

Colonel Birkett D. Fry
9th Virginia
14th Virginia
38th Virginia
53rd Virginia
57th Virginia

Hoke's Brigade

Colonel William G. Lewis
6th North Carolina
21st North Carolina
43rd North Carolina
54th North Carolina
57th North Carolina
1st North Carolina Battalion
21st Georgia

Artillery

Hankins's Battery
Rives's Battery
Thornton's Battery

Cavalry

5th South Carolina

HOKE'S DIVISION
Major General Robert F. Hoke

Corse's Brigade

Brigadier General Montgomery Corse
15th Virginia
17th Virginia
18th Virginia
29th Virginia
30th Virginia

Clingman's Brigade

Brigadier General Thomas Clingman
8th North Carolina
31st North Carolina
51st North Carolina
61st North Carolina

Johnson's Brigade

Brigadier General Bushrod Johnson
17th/23rd Tennessee
25th/44th Tennessee
63rd Tennessee

Hagood's Brigade

Brigadier General Johnson Hagood
11th South Carolina
21st South Carolina
25th South Carolina
27th South Carolina
7th South Carolina Battalion

Artillery

1st Company, Washington Artillery
2nd Company, Washington Artillery
3rd Company, Washington Artillery
4th Company, Washington Artillery

Cavalry

3rd North Carolina

COLQUITT'S DIVISION
Brigadier General Alfred H. Colquitt

Colquitt's Brigade

Colonel John T. Lofton
6th Georgia
19th Georgia
23rd Georgia
27th Georgia
28th Georgia

Ransom's Brigade

Colonel Leroy M. McAfee
24th North Carolina
25th North Carolina
35th North Carolina
49th North Carolina
56th North Carolina

Artillery

Macon's Battery
Martin's Battery
Payne's Battery (improvised)

Cavalry

7th South Carolina

WHITING'S DIVISION
Major General William H. C. Whiting

Wise's Brigade

Brigadier General Henry A. Wise
26th Virginia
34th Virginia
46th Virginia
59th Virginia

Martin's Brigade

Brigadier General James G. Martin
17th North Carolina
42nd North Carolina
66th North Carolina

Cavalry Brigade

Brigadier General James Dearing
7th Confederate
62nd Georgia
59th North Carolina
65th North Carolina
Barham's Virginia Battalion
Graham's Battery

Artillery

Blount's Battery
Bradford's Battery
Caskie's Battery
Cumming's Battery
Kelly's Battery
Marshall's Battery
Miller's Battery
Pegram's Battery
Slaten's Battery
Sturdivant's Battery
Wright's Battery
Young's Battery

Bibliography

MANUSCRIPTS

N. A. Barrier Papers, Duke University, Durham, North Carolina.

P. G. T. Beauregard Papers, Library of Congress, Washington, D. C.

P. G. T. Beauregard Papers, North Carolina Division of Archives and History, Raleigh, North Carolina.

William Beavans Diary, Southern Historical Collection, University of North Carolina, Chapel Hill, North Carolina.

R. M. Belo Reminiscences, Civil War Collection, Miscellaneous Records, North Carolina Division of Archives and History, Raleigh, North Carolina.

James Gordon Bennett Papers, Library of Congress, Washington, D.C.

Henry C. Brown Papers, North Carolina Division of Archives and History, Raleigh, North Carolina.

John H. C. Burch Reminiscences, Civil War Collection, Miscellaneous Records, North Carolina Division of Archives and History, Raleigh, North Carolina.

William H. S. Burgwyn Papers, North Carolina Division of Archives and History, Raleigh, North Carolina.

Benjamin F. Butler Papers, Library of Congress, Washington, D.C.

Bessie Callender Recollections, Petersburg National Military Park, Petersburg, Virginia.

John Washington Calton Letters, North Carolina Division of Archives and History, Raleigh, North Carolina.

Kate Camenga Papers, Duke University, Durham, North Carolina.

Mrs. M. C. Carmichael Letters, Virginia State Library, Richmond, Virginia.

Solon A. Carter Papers, United States Army Military History Institute, Carlisle Barracks, Pennsylvania.

Alfred Otis Chamberlin Papers, Duke University, Durham, North Carolina.

Henry A. Chambers Papers, North Carolina Division of Archives and History, Raleigh, North Carolina.

Civil War Times Illustrated, Collection of Civil War Papers, United States Army Military History Institute, Carlisle Barracks, Pennsylvania.

W. J. Clarke Papers, Southern Historical Collection, University of North Carolina, Chapel Hill, North Carolina.

Walter S. Clemence Diary and Manuscripts, North Carolina Collection, University of North Carolina, Chapel Hill, North Carolina.

Thomas L. Clingman Military Papers, Southern Historical Collection, University of North Carolina, Chapel Hill, North Carolina.

Cyrus B. Comstock Diary, Library of Congress, Washington, D.C.

William Henry Cooley [Coley] Letters, Southern Historical Collection, University of North Carolina, Chapel Hill, North Carolina.

Abel H. Crawford Papers, Duke University, Durham, North Carolina.

Charles A. Currier Recollections, United States Army Military History Institute, Carlisle Barracks, Pennsylvania.

David F. Dobie Letters, Virginia State Library, Richmond, Virginia.

R. D. Ferguson Papers, Southern Historical Collection, University of North Carolina, Chapel Hill, North Carolina.

John B. Foote Papers, Duke University, Durham, North Carolina.

William B. Franklin Papers, Library of Congress, Washington, D.C.

William A. Graham Papers, Southern Historical Collection, University of North Carolina, Chapel Hill, North Carolina.

George W. Grant Papers, Duke University, Durham, North Carolina.

Joseph R. Hawley Papers, Library of Congress, Washington, D.C.

Samuel P. Heintzelman Papers, Library of Congress, Washington, D.C.

D. H. Hill Papers, Virginia State Library, Richmond, Virginia.

D. H. Hill Papers, North Carolina Division of Archives and History, Raleigh, North Carolina.

Bushrod R. Johnson Papers, Record Group 109, National Archives, Washington, D.C.

August V. Kautz Papers, Library of Congress, Washington, D.C.

Thomas F. Kelley Papers, Duke University, Durham, North Carolina.

Charles Lafferty Letter, Fort Pulaski Papers, Southern Historical Collection, University of North Carolina, Chapel Hill, North Carolina.

Wilson G. Lamb Papers, North Carolina Division of Archives and History, Raleigh, North Carolina.

William Lancaster Letters, Virginia State Library, Richmond, Virginia.

William G. Lewis Papers, Southern Historical Collection, University of North Carolina, Chapel Hill, North Carolina.

Edwin Baker Loving Diary, Virginia State Library, Richmond, Virginia.

Richard L. Maury Papers, Duke University, Durham, North Carolina.

J. H. McAlister Paper, North Carolina Division of Archives and History, Raleigh, North Carolina.

Montgomery C. Meigs Papers, Library of Congress, Washington, D.C.

John Paris Papers, Southern Historical Collection, University of North Carolina, Chapel Hill, North Carolina.

Henry Machen Patrick Letters, North Carolina Division of Archives and History, Raleigh, North Carolina.

Christian T. Pfohl Papers, Southern Historical Collection, University of North Carolina, Chapel Hill, North Carolina.

Phifer Family Papers, Southern Historical Collection, University of North Carolina, Chapel Hill, North Carolina.

Isham Pitman Letter, Miscellaneous Confederate Papers, Southern Historical Collection, University of North Carolina, Chapel Hill, North Carolina.

Mary Frances Jane Pursley Papers, Duke University, Durham, North Carolina.

Regimental Record—Co. A, 25th Mass. Vols., Duke University, Durham, North Carolina.

Isaac C. Richardson Letters, Southern Historical Collection, University of North Carolina, Chapel Hill, North Carolina.

C. Eugene Southworth Papers, Duke University, Durham, North Carolina.

Julia Ward Stickley Collection, North Carolina Division of Archives and History, Raleigh, North Carolina.

John Lane Stuart Papers, Duke University, Durham, North Carolina.

John Swinton Papers, Southern Historical Collection, University of North Carolina, Chapel Hill, North Carolina.

Henry E. Taintor Papers, Duke University, Durham, North Carolina.

Cary Whitaker Papers, Southern Historical Collection, University of North Carolina, Chapel Hill, North Carolina.

W. H. C. Whiting Military Papers, Record Group 109, National Archives, Washington, D.C.

James Harrison Wilson Papers, Library of Congress, Washington, D.C.

Josiah Wood Papers, Duke University, Durham, North Carolina.

SIGNIFICANT GENERAL WORKS

Badeau, Adam. Military History of Ulysses S. Grant, from April, 1861, to April, 1865. 3 vols. New York: D. Appleton and Company, 1885.

Basler, Roy P., ed. The Collected Works of Abraham Lincoln. 9 vols. New Brunswick, N.J.: Rutgers University Press, 1953.

Brown, J. Willard. The Signal Corps, U.S.A. in the War of the Rebellion. Boston: B. Wilkins & Company, 1896.

Croffut, W. A., and John M. Morris. The Military and Civil History of Connecticut During the War of 1861–65. New York: Ledyard Bill, 1868.

Dowdey, Clifford, and Louis H. Manarin, eds. The Wartime Papers of R. E. Lee. Boston: Little, Brown and Company, 1961.

Dyer, Frederick H. *A Compendium of the War of the Rebellion.* 3 vols. Reprint ed. New York: Thomas Yoseloff, 1959.

Foster, John Y. *New Jersey and the Rebellion: A History of the Services of the Troops and People of New Jersey in Aid of the Union Cause.* Newark, N.J.: Martin R. Dennis & Company, 1868.

Fox, William F. *Regimental Losses in The American Civil War, 1861–1865.* Reprint ed. Dayton, Ohio: Press of Morningside Bookshop, 1974.

Freeman, Douglas Southall, ed. *Lee's Dispatches: Unpublished Letters of General Robert E. Lee, C.S.A. to Jefferson Davis and the War Department of the Confederate States of America, 1862–65.* New ed. New York: G. P. Putnam's Sons, 1957.

Humphreys, Andrew A. *The Virginia Campaign of '64 and '65: The Army of the Potomac and the Army of the James.* New York: Charles Scribner's Sons, 1883.

Livermore, Thomas L. *Numbers and Losses in the Civil War in America: 1861–65.* Reprint ed. Bloomington: Indiana University Press, 1957.

Marshall, Jessie Ames, ed. *Private and Official Correspondence of Gen. Benjamin F. Butler during the Period of the Civil War.* 5 vols. Norwood, Mass.: The Plimpton Press, 1917.

Official Records of the Union and Confederate Navies in the War of the Rebellion. 30 vols. Washington, D.C.: Government Printing Office, 1894–1922.

Rowland, Dunbar, ed. *Jefferson Davis, Constitutionalist: His Letters, Papers and Speeches.* 10 vols. Jackson: Mississippi Department of Archives and History, 1923.

Waite, Otis F. R. *New Hampshire in the Great Rebellion.* Norwich, Conn. and Concord, N.H.: J. H. Jewett & Company, 1873.

The War of the Rebellion: A Compilation of the Official Records of the Union and Confederate Armies. 70 vols. in 128. Washington, D.C.: Government Printing Office, 1880–1901.

Whitman, William E. S., and Charles H. True. *Maine in the War for the Union: A History of the Part Borne by Maine Troops in the Suppression of the American Rebellion.* Lewiston, Maine: Nelson Dingley Jr. & Company, Publishers, 1865.

PUBLISHED PERSONAL ACCOUNTS

Agassiz, George R., ed. *Meade's Headquarters, 1863–1865: Letters of Colonel Theodore Lyman from the Wilderness to Appomattox.* Boston: The Atlantic Monthly Press, 1922.

Archer, Fletcher H. "The Defense of Petersburg." In *War Talks of Confederate Veterans,* edited by George S. Bernard. Petersburg, Va.: Fenn & Owen, Publishers, 1892.

Avery, William B. "Gunboat Service on the James River." *Personal Narratives of Events in the War of the Rebellion, Being Papers Read before the Rhode Island Soldiers and Sailors Historical Society.* Third Series—no. 3. Providence, R.I.: The Society, 1884.

Beauregard, G. T. "The Defense of Drewry's Bluff." In *Battles and Leaders of the Civil War,* edited by Robert U. Johnson and Clarence C. Buel. New York: The Century Company, 1884, 1888.

———. "Four Days of Battle at Petersburg." In *Battles and Leaders of the Civil War*, edited by Robert U. Johnson and Clarence C. Buel. New York: The Century Company, 1884, 1888.

———. "Drury's Bluff and Petersburg." *North American Review* 144 (March 1887):244–260.

———. "Drewry's Bluff. A Letter from General Beauregard to General Wise Regarding the Battle, and the Difference between General Beauregard and General Bragg as to the War Policy at that Crisis." *Southern Historical Society Papers* 25 (January–December 1897):206–207.

Bowditch, Charles Pickering. "War Letters of Charles P. Bowditch." *Massachusetts Historical Society Proceedings* 57 (October 1923–June 1924):414–495.

Bruce, George A. "General Butler's Bermuda Campaign." In *Papers of the Military Historical Society of Massachusetts*. Vol. 9. Boston: Military Historical Society of Massachusetts, 1912.

Butler, Benjamin F. *Autobiography and Personal Reminiscences of Major-General Benj. F. Butler: Butler's Book.* Boston: A. M. Thayer & Company, 1892.

Cabell, George C. "Account of the Skirmish at Swift Creek." *Southern Historical Society Papers* 16 (January–December 1888):223–224.

Clark, Harvey. *My Experience with Burnside's Expedition and 18th Army Corps.* Gardner, Mass., 1914.

Cleveland, Edmund J., Jr., ed. "The Campaign of Promise and Disappointment— Diary of Private Edmund J. Cleveland." *Proceedings of the New Jersey Historical Society* 67 (1949):218–240, 308–328.

Compton, E. F. "About the Battle at Drury's Bluff." *Confederate Veteran* 12 (March 1904):123.

Copp, Elbridge J. *Reminiscences of the War of the Rebellion, 1861–1865.* Nashua, N.H.: The Telegraph Publishing Company, 1911.

Craven, John J. *Prison Life of Jefferson Davis.* New York: Carleton, Publisher, 1866.

Davis, Jefferson. *The Rise and Fall of the Confederate Government.* 2 vols. New York: D. Appleton and Company, 1881.

Day, D. L. *My Diary of Rambles with the 25th Mass. Volunteer Infantry, with Burnside's Coast Division; 18th Army Corps, and Army of the James.* Milford, Mass.: King & Billings, Printers, 1884.

De Forest, B. S. *Random Sketches and Wandering Thoughts.* Albany, N.Y.: Avery Herrick, Publisher, 1866.

Dibble, F. S. "South Carolina Command in Virginia." *Confederate Veteran* 23 (October 1915):458–459.

Gordon, George H. *A War Diary of Events in the War of the Great Rebellion. 1863–1865.* Boston: James R. Osgood and Company, 1882.

Grant, Ulysses S. *Personal Memoirs of U. S. Grant.* 2 vols. New York: Charles L. Webster & Company, 1886.

Gray, John Chipman. *War Lettes 1862–1865 of John Chipman Gray and John Codman Ropes.* Boston: Houghton Mifflin Company, 1927.

Gregorie, Anne King, ed. "Diary of Captain Joseph Julius Wescoat, 1863–1865." *South Carolina Historical Magazine* 59 (April 1958):84–95.

Griggs, George K. "Memoranda of Thirty-Eighth Virginia Infantry, From Diary of Colonel George K. Griggs." *Southern Historical Society Papers* 14 (January–December 1886):250–257.

Hagood, Johnson. *Memoirs of the War of Secession*. Columbia, S.C.: The State Company, 1910.

Harrill, Lawson. *Reminiscences, 1861–1865*. Statesville, N.C.: Brady, the Printer, 1910.

Harrison, Walter. *Pickett's Men: A Fragment of War History*. New York: D. Van Nostrand, Publisher, 1870.

Herbert, Arthur. "The Seventeenth Virginia Infantry at Flat Creek and Drewry's Bluff." *Southern Historical Society Papers* 12 (January–December 1884):289–294.

Hyde, Thomas W. *Following the Greek Cross or, Memories of the Sixth Army Corps*. Boston: Houghton, Mifflin and Company, 1897.

Johnston, David Emmons. *Four Years a Soldier*. Princeton, W. Va., 1887.

———. *The Story of a Confederate Boy in the Civil War*. Portland, Ore.: Glass and Prudhomme Company, 1914.

Jones, John Beauchamp. *A Rebel War Clerk's Diary at the Confederate States Capital*. 2 vols. Philadelphia: J. B. Lippincott and Company, 1866.

Kautz, August V. "First Attempts to Capture Petersburg." In *Battles and Leaders of the Civil War*, edited by Robert U. Johnson and Clarence C. Buel. New York: The Century Company, 1884, 1888.

Livermore, Thomas L. *Days and Events, 1860–1866*. Boston: Houghton Mifflin Company, 1920.

Loehr, Charles T. "Battle of Drewry's Bluff." *Southern Historical Society Papers* 19 (January–December 1891):100–111.

McGuire, Judith W. *Diary of a Southern Refugee, during the War*. 3rd ed. Richmond, Va.: J. W. Randolph & English, Publishers, 1889.

Mills, Luther Rice. "Letters of Luther Rice Mills, a Confederate Soldier." *North Carolina Historical Review* 4 (1927):285–310.

Morgan, William Henry. *Personal Reminiscences of the War of 1861–5*. Lynchburg, Va.: J. P. Bell Company, Inc., 1911.

Pickett, George E. *The Heart of a Soldier as Revealed in the Intimate Letters of Genl. George E. Pickett, C.S.A.* New York: Seth Moyle, Inc., 1913.

Pickett, LaSalle Corbell. *Pickett and His Men*. 2nd ed. Atlanta, Ga.: The Foote & Davies Company, 1900.

Porter, Horace. *Campaigning with Grant*. New York: The Century Company, 1906.

Pryor, Mrs. Roger A. *Reminiscences of Peace and War*. New York: The Macmillan Company, 1904.

Randall, James Ryder. "A Plea for General W. H. C. Whiting." *Southern Historical Society Papers* 24 (January–December 1896):274–277.

Reagan, John H. *Memoirs.* New York: The Neale Publishing Company, 1906.

Rockwell, Alfred P. "The Tenth Army Corps in Virginia, May, 1864." In *Papers of the Military Historical Society of Massachusetts.* Vol. 9. Boston: Military Historical Society of Massachusetts, 1912.

Roman, Alfred. *The Military Operations of General Beauregard in the War between the States, 1861 to 1865.* 2 vols. New York: Harper and Brothers, 1883.

Scott, John. "A Ruse of War." In *The Annals of the War Written by Leading Participants North and South.* Philadelphia: The Times Publishing Company, 1879.

Seay, W. M. "Vivid Story of Drury's Bluff Battle." *Confederate Veteran* 12 (May 1904):229.

Simonton, Edward. "The Campaign Up the James River to Petersburg." In *Glimpses of the Nation's Struggle.* 6 vols. St. Paul, Minn.: Review Publishing Company, 1903.

Smith, Daniel E. Huger, ed. *Mason Smith Family Letters, 1860–1868.* Columbia: University of South Carolina Press, 1950.

Smith, William Farrar. "Butler's Attack on Drewry's Bluff." In *Battles and Leaders of the Civil War,* edited by Robert U. Johnson and Clarence C. Buel. New York: The Century Company, 1884, 1888.

―――. *From Chattanooga to Petersburg under Generals Grant and Butler.* Boston: Houghton, Mifflin and Company, 1893.

Stansel, W. B. "Gracie's Brigade at Drury's Bluff." *Confederate Veteran* 12 (December 1904):592.

Sumpter, John U. "Fighting That Was Close by Us. One Who Was There Tells about the Battle of Drewry's Bluff—Many Errors Corrected." *Southern Historical Society Papers* 37 (January–December 1909):179–183.

Trumbull, Henry Clay. *The Knightly Soldier: A Biography of Major Henry Ward Camp, Tenth Conn. Vols.* Boston: Nichols and Noyes, 1865.

―――. *War Memories of an Army Chaplain.* New York: Charles Scribner's Sons, 1898.

Tucker James Marion. "Kautz Raiding around Petersburg." In *Glimpses of the Nation's Struggle.* 6 vols. St. Paul, Minn.: Review Publishing Company, 1903.

Ulmer, George T. *Adventures and Reminiscences of a Volunteer, or a Drummer Boy from Maine.* Chicago, 1892.

Wall, Edward. "Raids in Southeastern Virginia Fifty Years Ago." *Proceedings of the New Jersey Historical Society* 3 (1918):65–82, 147–161.

Warfield, Edgar. *A Confederate Soldier's Memoirs.* Richmond, Va.: Masonic Home Press, Inc., 1936.

Welles, Gideon. *Diary of Gideon Welles.* 3 vols. Boston: Houghton Mifflin Company, 1911.

Wilson, James Harrison. *Under the Old Flag.* 2 vols. New York: D. Appleton and Company, 1912.

Wistar, Isaac Jones. *Autobiography of Isaac Jones Wistar, 1827–1905: Half a Century in War and Peace.* Philadelphia: The Wistar Institute of Anatomy and Biology, 1937.

Young, John Russell. *Around the World with General Grant.* 2 vols. New York: The American News Company, 1879.

Younger, Edward, ed. *Inside the Confederate Government: The Diary of Robert Garlick Hill Kean, Head of the Bureau of War.* New York: Oxford University Press, 1957.

UNIT HISTORIES

Bartlett, A. W. *History of the Twelfth Regiment New Hampshire Volunteers in the War of the Rebellion.* Concord, N.H.: Ira C. Evans, Printer, 1897.

Beecher, Herbert W. *History of the First Light Battery Connecticut Volunteers, 1861–1865.* 2 vols. New York: A. T. de la Mare Printing and Publishing Company, Ltd., 1901.

Brady, Robert. *The Story of One Regiment: The Eleventh Maine Infantry Volunteers in the War of the Rebellion.* New York: J. J. Little & Company, 1896.

Cadwell, Charles K. *The Old Sixth Regiment, Its War Record, 1861–5.* New Haven, Conn.: Tuttle, Morehouse & Taylor, Printers, 1875.

Chase, Philip S. *Battery F, First Regiment Rhode Island Light Artillery, in the Civil War, 1861–1865.* Providence, R.I.: Snow & Farnham, Printers, 1892.

Clark, Charles M. *The History of the Thirty-Ninth Regiment Illinois Volunteer Veteran Infantry (Yates Phalanx) in the War of the Rebellion, 1861–1865.* Chicago, Ill., 1889.

Clark, James H. *The Iron Hearted Regiment: Being an Account of the Battles, Marches and Gallant Deeds Performed by the 115th Regiment N.Y. Vols.* Albany, N.Y.: J. Munsell, 1865.

Clark, Walter, ed. *Histories of the Several Regiments and Battalions from North Carolina in the Great War 1861–'65.* 5 vols. Goldsboro, N.C.: Nash Brothers, Book and Job Printers, 1901.

Cunningham, John L. *Three Years with the Adirondack Regiment: 118th New York Volunteers Infantry.* Norwood, Mass.: The Plimpton Press, 1920.

Cutchins, John A. *A Famous Command: The Richmond Light Infantry Blues.* Richmond, Va.: Garrett & Massie, Publishers, 1934.

Denny, J. Waldo. *Wearing the Blue in the Twenty-Fifth Mass. Volunteer Infantry, with Burnside's Coast Division, 18th Army Corps, and Army of the James.* Worcester, Mass.: Putnam & Davis, Publishers, 1879.

Derby, W. P. *Bearing Arms in the Twenty-Seventh Massachusetts Regiment of Volunteer Infantry During the Civil War, 1861–1865.* Boston: Wright & Potter Printing Company, 1883.

Dickey, Luther S. *History of the Eighty-Fifth Regiment Pennsylvania Volunteer Infantry, 1861–1865.* New York: J. C. & W. E. Powers, 1915.

Drake, James Madison. *The History of the Ninth New Jersey Veteran Vols.* Elizabeth, N.J.: Journal Printing House, 1889.

DuBose, Henry Kershaw. *The History of Company B, Twenty-First Regiment (Infantry), South Carolina Volunteers.* Columbia, S.C.: The R. L. Bryan Company, 1909.

Eldredge, Daniel. *The Third New Hampshire and All About It.* Boston: E. B. Stillings and Company, 1893.

Elliott, Charles G. "Martin's Brigade, of Hoke's Division, 1863–64." *Southern Historical Society Papers* 23 (January–December 1895): 189–198.

Emmerton, James A. *A Record of the Twenty-Third Regiment Mass. Vol. Infantry in the War of the Rebellion, 1861–1865.* Boston: William Ware & Company, 1886.

Everts, Hermann. *A Complete and Comprehensive History of the Ninth Regiment New Jersey Vols. Infantry.* Newark, N.J.: A. Stephen Holbrook, Printer, 1865.

Haynes, Martin A. *History of the Second Regiment New Hampshire Volunteers: Its Camps, Marches and Battles.* Manchester, N.H.: Charles F. Livingston, Printer, 1865.

———. *A History of the Second Regiment, New Hampshire Volunteer Infantry, in the War of the Rebellion.* Lakeport, N.H., 1896.

History of the Eleventh Pennsylvania Volunteer Cavalry, Together with a Complete Roster of the Regiment and Regimental Officers. Philadelphia: Franklin Printing Company, 1902.

Hyde, William L. *History of the One Hundred and Twelfth Regiment N.Y. Volunteers.* Fredonia, N.Y.: W. McKinstry & Company, Publishers, 1866.

Iobst, Richard W. *The Bloody Sixth; the Sixth North Carolina Regiment, Confederate States of America.* Durham, N.C.: Christian Printing Company, 1965.

Izlar, William Valmore. *A Sketch of the War Record of the Edisto Rifles, 1861–1865.* Columbia, S.C.: The State Company, 1914.

Jones, Benjamin Washington. *Under the Stars and Bars: A History of the Surry Light Artillery.* Richmond, Va.: Everett Waddey Company, 1909.

Kenan, Thomas S. *Sketch of the Forty-Third Regiment North Carolina Troops (Infantry).* Raleigh, N.C., 1895.

Kreutzer, William. *Notes and Observations Made during Four Years of Service with the Ninety-Eighth N.Y. Volunteers, in the War of 1861.* Philadelphia: Grant, Fairer & Rodgers, Printers, 1878.

Little, Henry F. W. *The Seventh Regiment New Hampshire Volunteers in the War of the Rebellion.* Concord, N.H.: Ira C. Evans, Printer, 1896.

Loehr, Charles T. *War History of the Old First Virginia Infantry Regiment, Army of Northern Virginia.* Richmond, Va.: William Ellis Jones, Book and Job Printer, 1884.

Merrill, Samuel H. *The Campaigns of the First Maine and First District of Columbia Cavalry.* Portland, Maine: Bailey & Noyes, 1866.

Mowris, J. A. *A History of the One Hundred and Seventeenth Regiment, N.Y. Volunteers.* Hartford, Conn.: Case, Lockwood and Company, Printers, 1866.

Nichols, James M. *Perry's Saints or the Fighting Parson's Regiment in the War of the Rebellion.* Boston: D. Lothrop and Company, 1886.

Owen, William Miller. *In Camp and Battle with the Washington Artillery of New Orleans.* Boston: Ticknor and Company, 1885.

Palmer, Abraham J. *The History of the Forty-Eighth Regiment New York State Volunteers, in the War for the Union, 1861–1865.* New York: Charles T. Dillingham, 1885.

Price, Isaiah. *History of the Ninety-Seventh Regiment, Pennsylvania Volunteer Infantry, during the War of the Rebellion, 1861–65.* Philadelphia: B. & P. Printers, 1875.

Putnam, Samuel H. *The Story of Company A, Twenty-Fifth Regiment, Mass. Vols., in the War of the Rebellion.* Worcester, Mass.: Putnam, Davis and Company, Publishers, 1886.

Roe, Alfred S. *The Twenty-Fourth Regiment Massachusetts Volunteers, 1861–1866.* Worcester, Mass.: The Blanchard Press, 1907.

Shaver, Lewellyn A. *A History of the Sixtieth Alabama Regiment, Gracie's Alabama Brigade.* Montgomery, Ala.: Barrett & Brown, Publishers, 1867.

The Story of the Twenty-First Regiment, Connecticut Volunteer Infantry, during the Civil War. Middletown, Conn.: Stewart Printing Company, 1900.

Stowits, George H. *History of the One Hundredth Regiment of New York State Volunteers.* Buffalo, N.Y.: Matthews & Warren, 1870.

Taylor, John C. *History of the First Connecticut Artillery and of the Siege Trains of the Armies Operating Against Richmond, 1862–1865.* Hartford, Conn.: Press of the Case, Lockwood & Brainard Company, 1893.

Thompson, S. Millett. *Thirteenth Regiment of New Hampshire Volunteer Infantry in the War of the Rebellion, 1861–1865.* Boston: Houghton, Mifflin and Company, 1888.

Tourtellotte, Jerome. *A History of Company K of the Seventh Connecticut Volunteer Infantry in the Civil War.* 1910.

Valentine, Herbert E. *Story of Co. F, 23d Massachusetts Volunteers in the War for the Union, 1861–1865.* Boston: W. B. Clarke & Company, 1896.

Walkley, Stephen. *History of the Seventh Connecticut Volunteer Infantry.* Southington, Conn., 1905.

Wise, George. *History of the Seventeenth Virginia Infantry, C.S.A.* Baltimore, Md.: Kelly, Piet & Company, 1870.

MAPS

Cowles, Calvin, D., ed. *Atlas to Accompany the Official Records of the Union and Confederate Armies.* Reprint ed. New York: Thomas Yoseloff, Inc., 1958.

Jeremy Francis Gilmer Papers, Southern Historical Collection, University of North Carolina, Chapel Hill, North Carolina.

Griffin, Tristram. "Sketch of the Battlefield of Drewry's Bluffs, Virginia, Morning of May 16, 1864." In *Papers of the Military Historical Society of Massachusetts.* Vol. 9. Boston: Military Historical Society of Massachusetts, 1912.

United States Geological Survey. Virginia 7.5 Minute Series. Drewry's Bluff, Dutch Gap, Hopewell, and Chester Quadrangles.

SECONDARY WORKS

Adams, Charles Francis. *Studies Military and Diplomatic, 1775–1865.* New York: The Macmillan Company, 1911.

Ambrose, Stephen E. *Halleck: Lincoln's Chief of Staff.* Baton Rouge: Louisiana State University Press, 1962.

Anderson, John H. *Grant's Campaign in Virginia, May 1–June 30, 1864.* London: Hugh Rees, Ltd., 1908.

Andrews, J. Cutler. *The North Reports the Civil War.* Pittsburgh: University of Pittsburgh Press, 1955.

Black, Robert C., III. *The Railroads of the Confederacy.* Chapel Hill: University of North Carolina Press, 1952.

Bland, T. A. *Life of Benjamin F. Butler.* Boston: Lee & Shepard, Publishers, 1879.

Boatner, Mark Mayo, III. *The Civil War Dictionary.* New York: David McKay Company, 1959.

Bridges, Hal. *Lee's Maverick General.* New York: McGraw-Hill, 1961.

Carroll, Daniel B. *Henri Mercier and the American Civil War.* Princeton: Princeton University Press, 1971.

Catton, Bruce. *A Stillness at Appomattox.* Garden City: Doubleday, 1953.

———. *Never Call Retreat.* Garden City: Doubleday, 1965.

———. *Grant Takes Command.* Boston: Little, Brown, 1969.

Cummings, Charles M. *Yankee Quaker Confederate General: The Curious Career of Bushrod Rust Johnson.* Rutherford, N.J.: Fairleigh Dickinson University Press, 1971.

Dana, Charles A., and James H. Wilson. *The Life of Ulysses S. Grant.* Springfield, Mass.: Gurdon Bill & Company, 1868.

Dowdey, Clifford. *Lee's Last Campaign.* Boston: Little, Brown, 1960.

Dwight, Theodore, F., ed. *Critical Sketches of Some of the Federal and Confederate Commanders.* Boston: Houghton, Mifflin and Company, 1895.

Freeman, Douglas Southall. *Lee's Lieutenants: A Study in Command.* 3 vols. New York: Charles Scribner's Sons, 1944.

Fuller, J. F. C. *The Generalship of Ulysses S. Grant.* New York: Dodd, Mead, 1929.

Hattaway, Herman, and Archer Jones. *How the North Won: A Military History of the Civil War.* Urbana: University of Illinois Press, 1983.

Holzman, Robert S. *Stormy Ben Butler.* New York: Macmillan, 1954.

Johnston, Angus James, II. *Virginia Railroads in the Civil War.* Chapel Hill, University of North Carolina Press, 1961.

McPherson, James M. *Ordeal by Fire: The Civil War and Reconstruction.* New York: Alfred A. Knopf, 1982.

McWhiney, Grady. *Braxton Bragg and Confederate Defeat. Vol. I: Field Command.* New York: Columbia University Press, 1969.

Millett, Allan R., and Peter Maslowski. *For the Common Defense: A Military History of the United States of America.* New York: The Free Press, 1984.

Nash, Howard P., Jr. *Stormy Petrel: The Life and Times of General Benjamin F. Butler, 1818–1893.* Rutherford, N.J.: Fairleigh Dickinson University Press, 1969.

Nevins, Allan. *The War for the Union: The Organized War to Victory, 1864–65.* New York: Charles Scribner's Sons, 1971.

Raymond, Harold B. "Ben Butler: A Reappraisal." *Colby Library Quarterly* series 6, no. 11 (September 1964):445–479.

Richardson, Albert D. *A Personal History of Ulysses S. Grant.* Hartford, Conn.: American Publishing Company, 1868.

Robertson, William G. "Cockades Under Fire: The Battle for Petersburg, June 9, 1864." Master's thesis, Corcoran Department of History, University of Virginia, 1968.

Trefousse, Hans L. *Ben Butler, the South Called Him Beast!* New York: Twayne Publishers, 1957.

Turner, George Edgar. *Victory Rode the Rails.* Indianapolis: Bobbs-Merrill, 1953.

Warner, Ezra J. *Generals in Gray: Lives of the Confederate Commanders.* Baton Rouge: Louisiana State University Press, 1959.

———. *Generals in Blue: Lives of the Union Commanders.* Baton Rouge: Louisiana State University Press, 1964.

Werlich, Robert. *"Beast" Butler.* Washington, 1962.

West, Richard S., Jr. *Lincoln's Scapegoat General: A Life of Benjamin F. Butler, 1818–1893.* Boston: Houghton Mifflin, 1965.

Williams, T. Harry. *Lincoln and his Generals.* New York: Alfred A. Knopf, 1952.

———. *P. G. T. Beauregard: Napoleon in Gray.* Baton Rouge: Louisiana State University Press, 1955.

Wilson, James Harrison. *Life and Services of William Farrar Smith, Major General, United States Volunteers in the Civil War.* Wilmington, Del: The John M. Rogers Press, 1904.

———. *The Life of John A. Rawlins.* New York: The Neale Publishing Company, 1916.

Wise, Barton H. *The Life of Henry A. Wise of Virginia, 1806–1876.* New York: The Macmillan Company, 1899.

Wolfson, George M. "Butler's Relations with Grant and the Army of the James in 1864." *The South Atlantic Quarterly* 10 (October 1911):377–393.

Index

Subentries are arranged chronologically by order of their appearance in the book, except for military units. These are arranged by size of unit, branch, and number.

275